Praise for

DEMOCRACY

"This heartfelt and at times very moving book shows why democracy proponents are so committed to their work...Both supporters and skeptics of democracy promotion will come away from this book wiser and better informed."

—Walter Russell Mead, *New York Times*

"Working daily alongside Condi at the White House and State Department, I witnessed firsthand her foundational belief in the power of human freedom and the crucial need for democratic institutions to protect it. This book, full of fascinating anecdotes and insights, is a sweeping view of the global struggle for democracy and a must-read for all who care about the future peace of the world and its people."

—Karen Hughes, former undersecretary of state
for public diplomacy and public affairs

"Condoleezza Rice serves as an able and insightful guide in this journey through democracy across the globe. Her knowledge and clear-eyed assessment of the challenges facing this system of government make this book an important contribution to a pressing debate on democracy today."

—Kofi Annan, former secretary general
of the United Nations

"At a time when democracy appears to be in retreat around the globe, Condoleezza Rice's DEMOCRACY offers a much-needed corrective. Weaving effortlessly between academic analysis and personal experiences—from Professor Rice to Secretary of State Rice and back again—Condi draws upon a series of case studies to offer a fresh perspective on how democracies emerge, how they sometimes endure but sometimes collapse, and especially why patience is required from us in observing and participating in the democracy-building process. A fantastic read!"

—Professor Michael McFaul, director, Freeman Spogli Institute for International Studies, Stanford University

"[A] ringing call for democracy promotion...Ms. Rice should be commended."   —Max Boot, *Wall Street Journal*

"[This book] could not have come at a better time. The most readable book on U.S. and Western democracy promotion since Natan Sharansky's *The Case for Democracy*."

—Daniel Runde, *Foreign Policy Magazine*

"A full-throated endorsement of overseas engagement and democracy building."   —NPR

"Authoritative...Readers interested in the history of political systems and governments will find her work informative and easy to understand."   —*Library Journal*

"[An] accessibly written study of that imperfect but ideal form of government...[One that] deserves a broad audience, especially in our current political climate."

—*Kirkus* Starred Review

DEMOCRACY

DEMOCRACY

Stories from the
Long Road to Freedom

CONDOLEEZZA
RICE

TWELVE

NEW YORK   BOSTON

Twelve
Hachette Book Group
1290 Avenue of the Americas, New York, NY 10104
twelvebooks.com
twitter.com/twelvebooks

Originally published in hardcover and ebook by Twelve in May 2017.
First Edition: July 2018

Twelve is an imprint of Grand Central Publishing. The Twelve name and logo are
trademarks of Hachette Book Group, Inc.

The publisher is not responsible for websites (or their content) that are not owned by
the publisher.

John Barnett | 4eyesdesign.com

Library of Congress Cataloging-in-Publication Data

Names: Rice, Condoleezza, 1954- author.
Title: Democracy : stories from the long road to freedom / Condoleezza Rice.
Description: First Edition. | New York : Twelve, 2017. | Includes
bibliographical references and index.
Identifiers: LCCN 2016056710| ISBN 9781455540181 (hardback) | ISBN
9781455571192 (large print) | ISBN 9781455540198 (ebook) | ISBN
9781478964575 (audio download) | ISBN 9781478964582 (audio book)
Subjects: LCSH: Democracy—History. | Democratization. |
Democratization—Government policy—United States. | World politics—1989- |
United States—Foreign relations—2001-2009. | Rice, Condoleezza, 1954- | Cabinet
officers—United States—Biography. |
BISAC: POLITICAL SCIENCE / Political Ideologies / Democracy. |
BIOGRAPHY & AUTOBIOGRAPHY / Personal Memoirs. | BIOGRAPHY &
AUTOBIOGRAPHY / Political. | BIOGRAPHY & AUTOBIOGRAPHY /
Women.
Classification: LCC JC421 .R49 2017 | DDC 321.8—dc23
LC record available at https://lccn.loc.gov/2016056710

ISBNs: 978-1-4555-4017-4 (trade pbk.), 978-1-4555-4019-8 (ebook)

Printed in the United States of America

LSC-C

10   9   8   7   6   5   4   3   2   1

To my parents

*To my ancestors, who against long odds continued to
believe in the promise of the Constitution*

*And to all those who still yearn for the dignity
that only liberty can afford*

CONTENTS

Prologue   1

Introduction: Is Democracy in Retreat?   5

Chapter 1: The American Experience   25

Chapter 2: Russia and the Weight of History   68

Chapter 3: Martial Law and the Origins of Polish
Democracy   126

Chapter 4: Ukraine: "A Made-Up Country"?   166

Chapter 5: Kenya: "Save Our Beloved Country"   202

Chapter 6: Colombia: The Era of Democratic
Security   236

Chapter 7: The Middle East: Can Democracy
Exist in a Cauldron?   267

Iraq: When Tyrants Fall   273

Egypt and Tunisia: When Old Men Fail   330

Arab Monarchies: Will They Reform?   355

Chapter 8: Are Authoritarians So Bad?   380

Chapter 9: What Democracy Must Deliver   402

Chapter 10: "Democracy Is the Worst...Except for
All the Others"   416

Epilogue: They Will Look to America 431

2016 439

Acknowledgments 445

Notes 449

Bibliography 465

Index 467

I have walked that long road to freedom. I have tried not to falter; I have made missteps along the way. But I have discovered the secret that after climbing a great hill, one only finds that there are many more hills to climb. I have taken a moment here to rest, to steal a view of the glorious vista that surrounds me, to look back on the distance I have come. But I can only rest for a moment, for with freedom comes responsibilities, and I dare not linger, for my long walk is not ended.

—Nelson Mandela, *The Long Walk to Freedom*, 1995

Prologue

Lisa, Christann, and I had been in Moscow for too long and we were happy to be headed home. Suddenly we were landing in Warsaw, an unscheduled stop. "Leave all your possessions and get off the plane," we were told over the PA system. We sat for hours in the airport, terrified that we were being detained for some unspecified crime. It was 1979 and we were three American girls in a communist country. After what seemed like a lifetime, we were told to get back on the plane. It took off, and when we landed in Paris—the site of our connecting flight to the United States and a city safely within the West—we cried.

Ten years later, in July 1989, I visited Poland again, this time with President George H. W. Bush. Mikhail Gorbachev was general secretary of the Soviet Communist Party and he was rewriting the rulebook for Eastern Europe, loosening the constraints that had sustained Moscow's power. Poland was a very different place now. The first night of the visit, we were in Warsaw, guests of a dying communist party. The lights went out during the state dinner—a perfect metaphor for the regime's coming demise.

The next day we went to Gdańsk, the home of Solidarity and its founder, Lech Wałęsa. This was the new Poland, experiencing dramatic and sudden change. We entered the town square where one hundred thousand Polish workers had gathered. They were waving American flags and shouting, "Bush, Bush, Bush...Freedom, Freedom, Freedom."

I turned to my colleague Robert Blackwill of the National Security Council staff and said, "This is not exactly what Karl Marx meant when he said, 'Workers of the world unite.'" But, indeed, they had "nothing to lose but their chains." Two months later, the Polish Communist Party gave way to a Solidarity-led government. It happened with dizzying speed.

The revolutions that began that summer in Poland and followed in most of Eastern Europe proceeded with minimal bloodshed and maximum support among the people. There were exceptions. In Romania, power had to be wrested by force from Nicolae Ceauşescu; he resisted and tried to flee but was ultimately executed at the hands of revolutionaries. In the Balkans the breakup of Yugoslavia unleashed ethnic tensions and violence, the legacy of which can still be felt today. Russia's own democratic transition at first appeared promising but ultimately failed entirely, replaced today by Vladimir Putin's autocratic rule and expansionist foreign policy. Yet, with these important exceptions, the end of the Cold War between the United States and the Soviet Union spawned several consolidated democracies and the region is largely peaceful.

The climb toward freedom in the broader Middle East and North Africa has been a far rockier story. Whether in still-unstable Afghanistan and Iraq, where the United States and our allies were midwives to the first freely elected governments; in Syria, which descended into civil war; or in Egypt, where the "awakening" of Tahrir Square turned into the thermidor of a military coup, there is turmoil, violence, and uncertainty. Turkey, perched between Europe and the Muslim world, has recently experienced a military coup attempt and subsequent crackdown. There and across the Middle East, citizens and their governments struggle to find the right marriage of religious conviction and personal freedom. The region is in a maelstrom.

I have been fortunate enough to be an eyewitness to these two great revolts against oppressive rule: the end of the Soviet Union at the close of the twentieth century and freedom's awakening in the Middle East at the beginning of the twenty-first. I have watched as people in Africa, Asia, and Latin America have insisted on freedom—perhaps with less drama than in the Middle East, but with no less passion. And in fact, as a child, I was a part of another great awakening: the second founding of America, as the civil rights movement unfolded in my hometown of Birmingham, Alabama, and finally expanded the meaning of "We the people" to encompass people like me.

These experiences have taught me that there is no more thrilling moment than when people finally seize their rights and their liberty. That moment is necessary, right, and inevitable. It is also terrifying and disruptive and chaotic. And what follows it is hard—really, really hard.

Introduction

IS DEMOCRACY IN RETREAT?

The Universal Declaration of Human Rights, adopted by the United Nations General Assembly in 1948, spells out a list of rights deemed to be non-negotiable: Everyone has the right to life, liberty, and security of person. Everyone has the right to freedom of thought, conscience, and religion. Everyone has the right to freedom of opinion and expression; to freedom of peaceful assembly and association; and to take part in their government, directly or through freely chosen representatives. The declaration does not use the term "democracy," but that is exactly what it describes.

Even leaders who are undeniably authoritarian make some claim to the mantle of democracy, either by holding sham elections or by trying to broaden the definition of "rights" to encompass goods they can deliver, like prosperity. Those who are not subject to popular will still crave legitimacy—or at least the appearance of legitimacy. Saddam Hussein held elections in Iraq in October 2002, just a few months before he was overthrown. (He was the only choice on the ballot and won 100 percent of the vote, with the official turnout also at 100 percent.) Few will say they simply rule by fiat, something that would have been wholly acceptable in times past. France's Sun King, Louis XIV, who declared, "I am the State," is one of many monarchs from history who claimed to rule by divine right.

If democracy is broadly understood to mean the right to speak your mind, to be free from the arbitrary power of the state, and to insist that those who would govern you must ask for your consent, then democracy—the only form of government that guarantees these freedoms—has never been more widely accepted as right.

Yet, while the voices supporting the idea of democracy have become louder, there is more skepticism today about the actual practice and feasibility of the enterprise. Scholarly and popular discourse is filled with declarations that democracy is in retreat or, at least, as Larry Diamond, my colleague at Stanford, has said, in "recession."[1]

The pessimism is understandable, particularly given events in the Middle East, where the promise of the "Arab Spring" seems to lie in tatters. If there is cause for optimism, it is in recognizing that people still want to govern themselves. Democracy activists in Hong Kong and mainland China risk persecution and arrest if they press their cause. Elections still attract long lines of first-time voters, even among the poorest and least-educated populations in Africa—and sometimes even under threat from terrorists in places like Afghanistan and Iraq. No matter their station in life, people are drawn to the idea that they should determine their own fate. Ironically, while those of us who live in liberty express

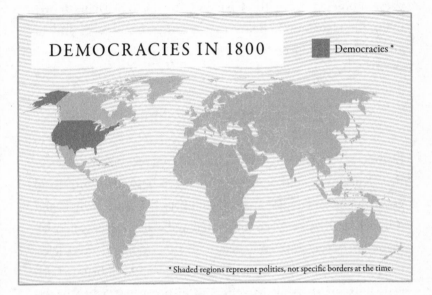

DEMOCRACIES IN 1800

Democracies *

* Shaded regions represent polities, not specific borders at the time.

skepticism about democracy's promise, people who do not yet enjoy its benefits seem determined to win it.

Freedom has not lost its appeal. But the task of establishing and sustaining the democratic institutions that will protect it is arduous and long. Progress is rarely a one-way road. Ending authoritarian rule can happen quickly; establishing democratic institutions cannot.

And there are plenty of malignant forces—some from the old order and some unleashed by an end to repression—ready to attack democratic institutions and destroy them in their infancy. Every new democracy has near-death experiences, crucible moments when the institutional framework is tested and strengthened or weakened by its response. Even the world's most successful democracies, including our own, can point to these moments, from the Civil War to the civil rights movement. No transition to democracy is immediately successful, or an immediate failure.

Democracy's Scaffolding

Democracy requires balance in many spheres: between executive, legislative, and judicial authority; between centralized government and regional responsibility; between civilian and military leaders; between individual and group rights; and ultimately between state and society. In functioning democracies, institutions are invested with protecting that equilibrium. Citizens must trust them as arbiters in disputes and, when necessary, as vehicles for change.

The importance of institutions in political and economic development has long been noted by social scientists in the field.[2] In 1990, the American political economist Douglass North provided a succinct definition of institutions. He called them the rules of the game in a society—or, in other words, "humanly devised constraints that shape human interaction."[3]

At the beginning, formal protections—such as constitutionally determined organizations, laws, procedures, or rules—may reflect bargains between various interests in the society. As such, they may be imperfect and sometimes contradictory. This will breed contention for years to come. Every democracy is flawed at its inception. And, indeed, no democracy ever becomes perfect. The question is not one of perfection but how an imperfect system can survive, move forward, and grow stronger.

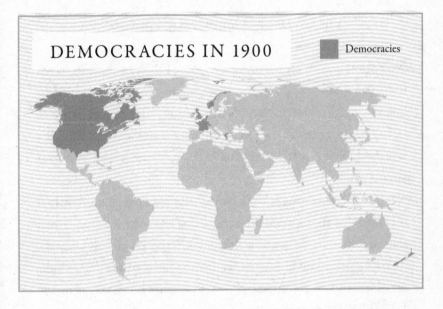

DEMOCRACIES IN 1900

Democracies

Moreover, these "humanly devised constraints" are, at the beginning, just words on paper. The puzzle is how they come to actually "shape human interaction." In other words, how do institutions become legitimate in the eyes of the citizen—legitimate enough to become the vehicle through which people seek protection and change?

We know the goal: Social and political disruption takes place within the institutions. While some fringe elements may operate outside of them, the great majority of people trust them to live up to their stated purpose. The paradox of democracy is that its stability is born of its openness to upheaval through elections, legislation, and social action. Disruption is built into the fabric of democracy.

The Myth of "Democratic Culture"

No nationality or ethnic group lacks the DNA to come to terms with this paradox. Over the years, many people have tried to invoke "cultural explanations" to assert that some societies lack what it takes to establish or sustain democracy. But this is a myth that has fallen to the reality of democracy's universal appeal.

It was once thought that Latin Americans were more suited for caudillos than presidents; that Africans were just too tribal; that Confucian values conflicted with the tenets of self-rule. Years before that, Germans were thought too martial or sub-servient, and—of course—the descendants of slaves were too "childlike" to care about the right to vote.

Those racist views are refuted by stable democracies in places as diverse as Chile, Ghana, South Korea, and across Europe. And, of course, America has now had a black presi-dent, as well as two secretaries of state and two attorneys general. Even if these "cultural" prejudices have simply not held up over time, the question hangs in the air: Why have some peoples been able to find the equilibrium between disruption and stabil-ity that is characteristic of a democracy? Is it a matter of historical circumstances? Or is it simply a matter of time?

Scholars have offered a number of answers to these ques-tions. Perhaps the most prevalent is that the poorer the country and the lower the levels of education, the less likely the chances for the establishment of a stable democracy.

Others have emphasized the type of interaction between

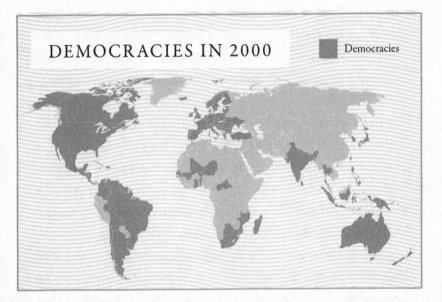

DEMOCRACIES IN 2000

Democracies

non-democratic regimes and their oppositions. If the end of the old order does not come through violence but rather through negotiation, the chances for success increase.

Finally, the state of the society itself is clearly a factor. A more ethnically homogeneous population is likely to find it easier to achieve stability. And if civil society—all the private, non-governmental groups, associations, and institutions in the country—is already well developed, the scaffolding for the new democracy is stronger.

Unfortunately, these idyllic conditions rarely exist in the real world. When people want to change their circumstances they are unlikely to wait until they have achieved an appropriate level of GDP. Sometimes the old regime has to be overthrown violently. Ethnically homogeneous populations are rare. More often, the history of revolution begins with oppression of one group by another. It is difficult for civil society to develop under repressive regimes. Checks and balances are most robust when they come from multiple sources—from outside governing bodies as well as within them. Authoritarians fully understand and depend on the absence of a well-developed institutional layer between the population as a whole and themselves. They trust that the mob will likely have incoherent views of its interests. The masses might even be easy to manipulate, producing fertile ground for the kind of populism associated with the Peronists in Argentina or the National Socialists in Germany.

But if the mob organizes independently and pursues its collective interest through new groups and associations, it can become an effective counterweight and a force for change. That is why from Moscow to Caracas, civil society is always in the crosshairs of repressive regimes.

In short, democracy, particularly in its first moments, will be messy, imperfect, mistake-prone, and fragile. The question isn't one of how to create perfect circumstances but how to move forward under difficult conditions.

It Depends on Where You Start

Democratic institutions are not born in a historical vacuum. A landscape is already in place when the opportunity for change—the democratic opening—comes. As important as larger factors like GDP and literacy may be, transitions to democracy are really stories about institutions and how quickly they can come to condition human behavior.

Below we identify four institutional landscapes. These categories are analytically discrete, but in reality there is likely some overlap. Yet grouping them in this way illuminates the institutional possibilities at the time of a democratic opening: The lay of the land matters. Leaders' choices matter too, but they are constrained by the institutional landscape within which they are expressed.

Type 1: Totalitarian Collapse: Institutional Vacuum

Totalitarians leave no aspect of life untouched—the space from science to sports to the arts is occupied by the regime. Benito Mussolini coined the term *totalitario*, describing it to mean "All within the state, none outside the state, none against the state." Existing institutions (the Ba'ath Party of Saddam, the National Socialists of Germany, Stalin's Communist Party) are little more than tools of the regime. In Nazi Germany, science was placed at the service of the "Aryan ideal," promoting eugenics and theories of racial superiority. The Soviet Union persecuted some of its finest artists, composers like Shostakovich and Prokofiev, for writing music that was not socialist enough. Saddam Hussein's henchmen brutalized members of the national soccer team for performances that did not glorify the regime.

Every aspect of life is penetrated in some way. The regimes are often "cults of personality"—the entire society bent to the whims of a single leader. North Korea is the most prominent example today.

When a regime of this kind is decapitated—often with the assistance of an external power—there is an institutional void and thus little that can channel the unleashed passions and prejudices of the population. These are revolutions. New institutions have to be built, and built quickly. And they have weak, if any, indigenous roots to support them. There is a wide gulf between the long time needed to build new institutions and the limited raw material to do so.

Because the experiences of Afghanistan, Iraq, and Libya are so recent and cataclysmic, these cases of totalitarian collapse have come to shadow discussions of the challenges facing democratic transitions. But these examples are the exception not the rule. Most are less chaotic and violent—though still exceedingly difficult.

Type 2: Gradual Decay of Totalitarian Regimes: Institutional Antecedents Remain

Communism died slowly. Soviet officials and the population alike referred to *zastoi*, or "stagnation." We know now that it was really decay. Repeated crises, usually because the governments could not deliver economic benefits, produced cycles of reform and repression. Each time, though, the distance between the party and the people grew.

Throughout the region, this situation elicited varying

responses. Romania staked its claim as a maverick within the Soviet bloc, playing a nationalist card and publicly insisting on independence from Moscow. Reformists within the Hungarian Communist Party turned away from repression and launched privatizing economic reforms. The trauma of 1968 caused the Czechoslovak Communist Party to toe the Soviet line. But within the country, survivors of that period created Charter 77—a movement of intellectuals devoted to human rights and freedom. Poland, as we will see, experienced multiple episodes of reform and repression. Only East Germany seemed solidly and irrevocably hard-line and uncompromising.

Gorbachev's arrival as general secretary of the Soviet Communist Party in 1985 boosted these liberalizing trends in East-Central Europe. The new Soviet leader made it very clear that change was needed. He encouraged reformers in Hungary and Poland and criticized laggards like Erich Honecker in East Germany. At first reform came mostly from within the communist parties but—owing to the growing sense of public openness—civil society and independent political forces also seized the opportunity before them.

In the Soviet Union itself, *perestroika* and *glasnost* gave life to opposition groups and created new institutional arrangements—particularly in Moscow and Leningrad. Similar developments also arose outside of Russia: in Ukraine, Georgia, and the Baltic states. Communist institutions remained, including youth organizations like the Komsomol. It was still the case until the end of the Soviet Union in 1991 that rectors of major universities could not serve without the party's approval.

Still, civil society groups began to organize around different issues, from the environment to disability rights. What began as societal, cultural, and economic space would soon become political.

Gorbachev did something else that changed the landscape: He delivered the population from the shadow of repression and fear. At every turn during this period, the Soviet Union failed to use sufficient force to change the course of events. And when it did use force, such as against anti-Soviet demonstrations in Tbilisi in April 1989 and in the Baltics in 1991, the regime eventually pulled up and backed down at crucial moments, in effect emboldening the opposition.

Meanwhile, another set of institutions emerged as Boris Yeltsin gained popularity—institutions of a separate Russian state within the Soviet Union. Like the other republics of the Soviet Union, Russia had long had a ceremonial presidency and a legislative council (called a soviet). But these paper organizations meant little until the reforms of the late 1980s. Up to that point, Russia and the Soviet Union had been virtually synonymous. Yet Yeltsin breathed life into these Russian institutions, noisily quitting the Soviet Communist Party in 1990 and then getting himself elected president of Russia in 1991. These unfolding events changed the landscape dramatically.

Years before, however, the Helsinki Accords of 1975, which gave the Soviets what they thought was a major political victory, in fact had created a safe haven for East-Central European and Soviet civil society, with reformers in the region joining European and American counterparts in seminars and annual conferences. There were three components to the accord—economic, security, and human rights. The Soviet Union wanted to emphasize the first two but—to the surprise of many—signed on to the human rights "basket" as well. Moscow erroneously believed that the West was legitimizing the post–World War II order, and Soviet power within it. But giving members of civil society a safe way to challenge their government turned out to be a Trojan horse.

These factors, stretching back for decades, explain in part why the institutional landscape was richer when the democratic opening of 1989–91 arrived. First came the sudden and nonviolent collapse of Soviet power in Eastern Europe, exemplified by the collapse of the Berlin Wall. Then came the end of the Soviet Union itself, with newly independent states carved out of its carcass. The events were in some sense rapid, unexpected, and challenging. But the institutional raw material was, to varying degrees, reasonably good.

Type 3: Authoritarian Regimes and the Struggle for Meaningful Political Space

Unlike totalitarians, authoritarian regimes leave space for groups that are independent of them. Non-governmental organizations, the business community, universities, and labor groups live in an uncomfortable cold peace with their rulers. They are often the lead element in pressing for change.

Up to a certain point, these organizations are useful to the regime. Well-regarded universities provide intellectual capital and their reputation is a source of national pride. Business elites are needed to provide jobs and economic growth. Civil society can be a canary in the coal mine—expressing views that leaders need to hear, a kind of barometer of public discontent. But there are limits to what the regime will tolerate. It is a matter of balance—act before independent groups are a threat but not so brutally as to provoke a backlash. Thus, while overt repression is always an option, it can be more effective to apply intermittent pressure, such as jailing key civil society figures and journalists, raiding their offices, or shutting down newspapers or blogs to reassert that consequential politics is off-limits.

And authoritarian regimes leave little doubt about who controls the actual political space. Political parties may exist, but they cannot function. Cuba is one of the few remaining single-party states. Most authoritarian regimes have some semblance of electoral competition. But it is largely a façade. In Putin's Russia, there is little doubt that the regime will win. Parliaments dare not challenge the president. The courts would never convict a member of the ruler's family or his political cronies. The military and the police stand by ready to make sure that no lines are crossed.

Type 4: Quasi-Democratic Regimes: Fragile and Vulnerable Institutions

Finally, some places have an open and active political sphere, but their institutions themselves are immature and often viewed as hollow and corrupt. In countries like Liberia, Tunisia, and

Iraq, the long struggle for democracy has just begun. Democratic institutions can be strengthened over time, but if they are viewed as ineffective, a vicious cycle can emerge as they fall into disuse, lose more credibility, and, consequently, are ignored. It is tempting to think that a good leader is all that is needed to make them work. But it is more likely that some seminal event or crisis will provide the crucible moment when the institutions can prove themselves—or not.

The analytic problem is that while democratic institutions are present in the landscape—parties, parliaments, courts, civil society groups—it is hard to know how strong or weak they are until they are tested.

Unlike in authoritarian regimes, elections in quasi-democracies are relatively free and fair, and people can change their leaders. So we can say that these states pass at least one important democratic milestone. In reality, though, elections can expose fissures in society. The results are often contested—there are many "50-50 countries" where the margins will be razor thin. Successfully navigating the aftermath is another milestone. Do candidates and their supporters go to the streets? Do they do so peacefully? In the best of circumstances, there are institutions that can respond—a court or electoral commission that can break the tie and make its ruling stick.

But the electoral story is only one element. Quasi-democratic states are in the midst of establishing the balance of forces needed to sustain democratic governance. In these places, civil society and a free press are critical checks on the power of government as events unfold. An independent judiciary is a bulwark against corruption and abuse. And the state has to be able to protect its people—that means it must maintain a monopoly on the use of force. Militias and armed insurgents can be the cause of state failure. Quasi-democratic governments may have passed the electoral test but the scaffolding of democracy may still be weak. The clay is not yet set. And an executive with too much power, ruling by decree and circumventing other institutions, is a sure path to authoritarian relapse. Such has been the case recently in Turkey and Russia and increasingly in Hungary.

Finally, when a country achieves a stable balance of democratic institutions, we can say it is a consolidated democracy. Some have described consolidated democracies as countries in which democracy becomes "the only game in town."⁴

What Can Outsiders Do to Help?

Now we come to another piece of the institutional landscape: the role of external actors. Let us stipulate that any democratic transition will be easier if indigenous forces are well organized and able to take power and lead effectively. The dictum that you cannot impose democracy from the outside is undeniably true. But it is rare that there is truly no indigenous appetite for change. Those advocating reform may be weak and scattered—this is unsurprising since authoritarians do everything possible to keep them that way. Yet they often find a way to make their voices heard, reminding us that given a choice, few would choose to be abused by their leaders. Today, when social media makes certain that what happens in the village won't stay in the village, people measure their circumstances against those of the larger world. So they will appeal to outsiders to help them. Their plight is hard to ignore.

The forces that have fed democratization have multiplied since the end of World War II. Civil society groups are well organized across borders. The machinery of the international community that supports democratic principles is highly developed. Organizations like Amnesty International train a spotlight on authoritarian regimes and pressure major powers not to back them. NGOs such as Freedom House, the National Endowment for Democracy, and the European Endowment for Democracy promote liberty and defend human rights. International election monitors now establish uniform standards for the peaceful transfer of power and call out regimes that don't respect them.

Countries that have recently gone through democratic transitions now offer their own expertise and experience to others. Both Poland and Hungary have established organizations, such as the Solidarity Fund PL and the International Center for Democratic Transitions, to support democratization in places like Burma. India, a remarkable consolidated democracy, was the first contributor to the United Nations Democracy Fund. Taiwan established a Foundation for Democracy fifteen years ago—the first such effort outside of Europe, North America, and Australia.

Moreover, foreign aid donors often insist on a say in matters ranging from corruption to human rights to electoral integrity. Sanctions against authoritarian regimes are powerful when they are dependent on external economic assistance. With every passing day, sovereignty is dying as a defense against oppression within one's borders.

And it is not as if the only active external forces are those promoting democracy. Cuba has long attempted to export its revolutionary ideology in Latin America. Venezuela's oil wealth in the early twenty-first century was used aggressively by the late Hugo Chávez to influence elections throughout the region. China's role in Africa is not an overtly political one, but economic assistance delivered without conditions emboldens those leaders who resist reform. Saudi Arabia supports hard-line Islamic elements in many countries. Obviously, the long reach of Putin's Russia into the politics of Ukraine and other parts of Europe is undeniable. In fact, the depth of Russia's interference in the political affairs of other countries—even those of the United States—is unfolding in shocking and disturbing ways.

In short, the question isn't "Will there be an international role in countries undergoing democratic change?" There will be. The issue is "What will that role be and who will play it?"

Among great powers, the United States has been the most committed to the proposition that sovereignty provides no immunity for repression. Though the principle has been applied unevenly, no American president to date has abandoned it. America's global reach has given it an outsized role in the promotion of democracy.

Perhaps this is why the template used by advocates for change bears a strong resemblance to America's own constitutional principles. The Founding Fathers were focused first and foremost on the question of balance—how to make the state strong enough to perform key tasks but not so strong as to threaten individual liberties. Madison, Hamilton, and others saw this balance as the key to democratic stability.

The Hard Road to Democracy

America has found a stable equilibrium, but the path to it was hard and often violent. The litigation and re-litigation of the meaning of the Constitution continues to this day. So this book begins with America's story as a primer on the institutions of consolidated democracy and as a reminder of the long road to get there and stay there.

We then examine several recent cases of democratic transitions. All involve choices by leaders, their people, and the international community as well, choices that were constrained by the institutional landscape they inherited.

We follow the struggles of Russia, Ukraine, Poland, Colombia, and Kenya to find a stable democratic equilibrium. We see institutions under fire and how they fared. Colombia is a tale of finding the sweet spot between chaos and authoritarianism that we call democracy. The jury is still out on Ukraine and Kenya. And Poland, once thought to be a fully consolidated democracy, is now experiencing new challenges.

Russia's failed attempt is a reminder that quasi-democratic states are also vulnerable to reversals. The term *thermidor* is associated with the French Revolution and the arrested democratization that followed the Reign of Terror and led to an emperor. Today's version in struggling democracies appears largely to be a story of executive authority that is outsized in comparison to other institutions. The landscape is not devoid of independent forces, but the scaffolding supporting them has collapsed. They are increasingly at the mercy of the president. Any country's institutional landscape will also include forces that are susceptible to populist appeals. Look closely at the constituencies that support Turkey's Erdoğan, Hungary's Orbán, and Russia's Putin and you will see substantial similarities: older people, rural inhabitants, religiously pious people, and committed nationalists.

There are no claims here of universal truths in these examples. They are cases that I know well from personal experience and that illuminate important lessons about the path to liberty. In looking at them in depth we can see common elements as people seek to find the balance that all democracies pursue.

It is in that spirit that we will then turn to the Middle East. We have learned that revolutionary change makes the road to democracy hard—that the institutional landscape is unfavorable and that external powers find it difficult to help. Yet the Middle East is complex and the institutional landscape far more variable than we sometimes acknowledge. Its governments cover a wide range of regime types.

The region is a cauldron, but steps toward the establishment of democratic institutions cannot be indefinitely delayed. The stories of other transitions in less chaotic circumstances chronicled below hold lessons even for the Middle East. Collectively they tell a tale of imperfect people in difficult circumstances creating institutions that can slowly come to govern human interaction—peacefully.

Data for the three maps that appear in this chapter are drawn from the following study, which classifies countries as democracies according to their levels of "contestation" and "participation," terms first coined in association with democracy by the scholar Robert Dahl: Carles Boix, Michael K. Miller, and Sebastian Rosato, "A Complete Data Set of Political Regimes, 1800–2007," *Comparative Political Studies*, December 2013, Vol. 46, No. 12: pp. 1523–1554.

Chapter 1

THE AMERICAN
EXPERIENCE

An hour before dinner one evening in May 2004, my fellow national security advisers from Europe and I took a boat ride through the canals of Berlin to view the rebuilding of the "new" German capital. The journey seemed endless as I tried to disguise my discomfort with being on the water and to make amends for a recent rather spirited defense of the prospects for democracy in Afghanistan and Iraq.

Earlier in the day, in response to one of my colleagues' comment that there was no "tradition" of democracy in either Iraq or Afghanistan, I asked pointedly, "What precisely was the German democratic tradition before 1945? Would that be the ill-fated experiment with the Kaiser? *Bismarck?* Hitler's election?" Germany had experienced the Enlightenment, but, obviously, democratic values didn't exactly take root. To be fair, my response had been provoked by a not too thinly veiled suggestion that Americans were naïve about the prospects for the spread of democracy. *I'd rather be naïve than cynical*, I had thought to myself.

That evening on the canal, I tried to soften what I had said, explaining that American democracy had taken a long time to mature. "The American Constitution was born of a compromise between slaveholding and non-slaveholding states that counted my ancestors as three-fifths of a man," I explained. "My father couldn't register to vote in Birmingham in 1952. And now Colin Powell is secretary of state and I am national security adviser. People can learn to overcome prejudices and govern themselves in democratic institutions." My colleagues seemed a bit taken aback by the personal nature of my policy comment. Perhaps they didn't think my race gave me a different perspective on democracy's challenges—and its opportunities.

Returning to my hotel, I felt *so* American—with a kind of optimism about the rightness of democracy for everyone, everywhere, at all times. And I realized that much of that conviction proceeded from my own understanding of and experience with American institutions.

"We Hold These Truths to Be Self-Evident"

Not long before my term as secretary of state ended, I accepted a long-standing invitation from the late Allen Weinstein of the National Archives for a visit and tour. I wanted first to see the Emancipation Proclamation, which freed my ancestors—or, more correctly, some of my ancestors. Like most black Americans, they were both slaves and slave owners. My great-great-grandmother Zina on my mother's side bore five children by different slave owners. She somehow managed to raise them all and keep them together as a family. My great-grandmother on my father's side, Julia Head, carried the name of the slave owner and was so favored by him that he taught her to read. Her precise relationship to the Head family remains something of a mystery, but you could look at her and see that her bloodlines, like mine, clearly bore slavery's mark: My DNA is 50 percent African and 40 percent European, and there is a mysterious 10 percent that is apparently Asian.

Reading the Proclamation, I could hear the footsteps of Rices, my father's ancestors, and Rays, my mother's. I marveled at their perseverance in the shackles of this most brutal of institutions. I said a little prayer of thanks to them, and moved on to the Constitution, and then all manner of treaties and executive agreements, signed by my predecessors as secretary of state. Preparing to leave, I realized that I had not seen the Declaration of Independence.

How long has it been since I read it? Have I ever read it in full—beginning to end? I didn't verbalize either question, perhaps a little embarrassed that the answer to the last question was probably yes, as a kid at Brunetta C. Hill Elementary School, but, just as plausibly, never.

So I stopped to read the Declaration in its entirety and contemplate what it says about the moment when people decide that they've had enough of tyranny and oppression. After the soaring and familiar rhetoric that enshrines the principles of equality for all ("We hold these truths to be self-evident, that all men are created equal"), the document recounts multiple grievances against the British crown and King George III himself. "He has plundered our seas, ravaged our Coasts, burnt our towns, and destroyed the lives of our people," it says. "He is at this time transporting large Armies of foreign Mercenaries to compleat the works of death, desolation and tyranny, already begun with circumstances of Cruelty & perfidy scarcely paralleled in the most barbarous ages, and totally unworthy the Head of a civilized nation." This fist-shaking litany is a reminder that the moment when people seize power is not the most propitious for rational discourse about how to secure newly won rights. A declaration throwing off the old order is most assuredly not the establishment of the new.

The Anglo-Americans were an ethnically homogeneous lot who left England and, having occupied the "New World" for more than a century, came to think of themselves as a people distinct from the British crown. The constant interference in their affairs had united a sizable portion of them in disgust and despair and provoked a strong impulse to separate.

"When in the Course of human events," the Declaration begins, "it becomes necessary for one people to dissolve the political bands which have connected them with another, and to assume among the powers of the earth, the separate and equal station to which the Laws of Nature and of Nature's God entitle them, a decent respect to the opinions of mankind requires that they should declare the causes which impel them to the separation."

America was a hardscrabble place where opportunity abounded, but only for those who would work for it, and so it attracted that kind of people. The old social classes and noble orders did not follow them to the New World because the rich and powerful of Europe were comfortable remaining where they were. Wide-open spaces and the possibility of acquiring land—at the expense of native populations—further encouraged social mobility. The country thus developed with a strong tradition of property rights. And without an aristocratic order to overthrow, America was born in as near to a state of tabula rasa as one can imagine.

Given the complexities of today's highly interconnected world, America's birth did indeed take place in simpler times. News traveled up and down the Atlantic coast at the pace of weeks, not hours. People and goods moved at the pace of months, not days. Colonial times were simpler, to be sure, but they were not wholly simple, and success in the American experiment was never preordained. Even with their manifold advantages, the Americans stumbled repeatedly along the path to a stable democracy. It is a point worth remembering as people in less favorable circumstances struggle too.

As we know, the revolutionaries came close to losing their war for independence. George Washington's ragtag forces were challenged not just by superior British military prowess, but also by weak institutions that almost failed to provide for the soldiers' needs. Rhode Island refused to pay its share of the costs for the army; the Continental Congress constantly interfered in matters of military strategy and tactics (leading Washington's aide-de-camp, Alexander Hamilton, to lose confidence in the structure of the government under the Articles of Confederation); and in matters of diplomacy to support the war effort, numerous states cut their own deals with European powers.

Indeed, the Articles of Confederation had created no executive at all. The system was just too weak to protect the interests of the new republic. The Founders learned from experience that the young country needed a central authority that worked.

Yet, born as the nation was out of a rejection of tyranny, they were suspicious too of a government that was too powerful. So the question was one of how to create institutions strong enough to protect the people's newly won rights, but not so strong as to threaten them. This essential balance lies at the heart of the rough-and-tumble story of the birth of America's Constitution. And it remains today the most important challenge in establishing a new order on the ruins of the old in countries across the world.

The narrative of those hot days in Philadelphia—hot both in temperature and in the intensity of debate—that gave rise to the American Constitution has been well chronicled elsewhere.[1] Suffice it to say that the great histories of those efforts show clearly that it was extremely hard to strike the balance that the Framers sought. And what they achieved is a remarkable compromise between competing visions and interests. The writing and ratification of the Constitution was an intensely political process, not a divine bolt from the blue that produced perfect institutions. As James Madison put it in *Federalist* No. 40, "The choice must always be made, if not one of the lesser evil, at least of the GREATER, not the PERFECT good." And in the last of the *Federalist Papers*, he said, "I never expect to see a perfect work from imperfect man." This rings true more than 220 years later when we are judging the efforts of those who are trying to establish a new order.

In the pages that follow, we discuss five key aspects of the Founders' institutional design. I have chosen these particular elements because they appear over and over in stories of democratic transitions of the past and in those that are still unfolding across the world.

First, the Founders tackled the challenge of creating institutional balance—between the states and the center through federalism—and among different parts of the federal government itself. Second, they were determined to limit the role of the armed forces—to maintain control so that they would protect the country but not threaten the political order. They understood that the state had to have a monopoly on the use of force. Third, these men were wary of a marriage between politics, religion, and the power of the state, and they sought to separate them. Fourth, they left space for the private sector and the emergence of civil society. These would be areas where government's role would be limited and individual initiative would flourish. Finally, they bequeathed a spirit of constitutionalism to their descendants. That has allowed generations of Americans to seek their rights through appeal to its principles. It has been a novel way to deal with the vexing problem of minority rights—even for those whose ancestors came to the country as slaves.

Constructing the Framework

The United States was fortunate to have Founders who both intellectually and emotionally understood the critical importance of institutions. It was, after all, the failure or absence of institutions that led them to rebel in the first place. British subjects had rights on paper and according to tradition, but those rights were being violated by the unchecked powers of other political actors—namely the King. The only way to make those rights meaningful, the Founders believed, was to build an institutional framework to protect them. They knew that if the nation were to be stable, individual rights had to be exercised according to rules that all people could understand and trust.

While tyrants were capricious with nothing to restrain them, democratic governments relied upon and were limited by the will of the people. But the people's wishes wouldn't be revealed every day, in every circumstance. Indeed, the Founders were concerned that the will of the people could easily become the preferences of the mob. Thus democratic institutions became a way not only to limit the government but to channel popular passions and interests. Citizens had to come to respect the institutions that would represent and protect their rights. They would be free to associate with others as they wished and there would be a watchful press that could not be abridged, censored, or otherwise checked by the government. The "Fourth Estate," a free press, would be the eyes and ears of the people, holding their leaders accountable.[2]

The debates were intense about every aspect of institutional design. The question of how to deal with executive power exposed splits among the Founders. Alexander Hamilton and James Wilson of Pennsylvania were advocates of strength. As Hamilton would say, "A feeble Executive implies a feeble execution of the government. A feeble execution is but another phrase for a bad execution; and a government ill executed, whatever it may be in theory, must be, in practice, a bad government."

Others worried that a strong presidency could evolve too easily into the very system they had fought to replace. As Patrick Henry warned supporters of the Constitution, "Your President may easily become King."

The delegates found a way to more or less satisfy both sides—settling on divided government. A scheme of checks and balances grants powers to two legislative houses and in turn three coequal branches. In its first incarnation, Hamilton notwithstanding, the balance clearly favored Congress. The legislative branch is commissioned in Article I, and the executive branch in Article II. And as my colleague at Stanford, American historian David Kennedy, has noted, there are fifty-one paragraphs addressing the role of the Congress and thirteen concerning the presidency—eight of which lay out mechanisms for election, and four of which detail presidential powers. By the way, one provides for impeachment.[3]

The debate about the executive was in some ways a proxy for the larger issue of the role of central authority in the new country. The Founders may have been chastened by their experiences with the Articles of Confederation, but they were not of the same mind about what to do.

Through a series of compromises they came to a conclusion: The United States would rely on a system of "enumerated powers." The new authorities that would be given to the central government would be explicitly spelled out in writing (they would be "enumerated"), and all powers not mentioned would be reserved for the states.

Still, federalism was not just a matter of constraining central authority. The Founders and many after them believed that government closer to the people was both more accountable and more effective. Federalism was a practical way to govern over a diverse and massive land.

The Founders established the capital of the new Union in the donated swampland between Maryland and Virginia in 1790, and many returned to their statehouses, thought to be of far greater importance. Early on the federal government was not intended to do very much.

Over time, buffeted by the requirements of continental conquest and defense, a Great Depression, the civil rights struggle, and ultimately the demands of modern governance, the role of the federal government would grow. In particular, the expectations of the president would multiply, and today we are closer to the strong executive that Hamilton favored. Nonetheless, the presidency is still encased in a web of institutional constraints—two houses of Congress made up of 535 people; and an independent judiciary comprising 108 federal courts, including the Supreme Court. And there are 50 governors and state legislatures with strong views about how their states should be run. The proper balance between central authority and the states is as hot a topic today as it was in 1787. Everything from voting requirements to K–12 educational standards to the adoption of environmental policies sooner or later becomes a test of where the writ of the center stops and that of the states begins.

"No Redcoats Here"

The Founders' concerns about balance reached even into the realm of military power. The proper use of the military has been a recurring theme throughout our history.

I will never forget President Bush's exasperation one day in a Situation Room meeting during the Katrina disaster, as survivors were pleading for help. "What in the world is posse comitatus?" he asked. He was frustrated with the constitutional lawyers around the table who were invoking this phrase when telling him why he could not send the American military into the streets to deal with the lawlessness of post-Katrina New Orleans.[4] Somebody needed to bring order to the situation— and assistance to the victims—and the military surely would have been capable. But there were other considerations— institutional considerations.

The Posse Comitatus Act of 1878 was passed as part of the compromise that withdrew American troops from the South and ended the period of Reconstruction. The meaning of the phrase is essentially "local law enforcement," and the 1878 act prevents the president from using federal troops "as a *posse comitatus* or otherwise to execute the laws" *within* the United States.

Militaries are necessary for the defense of the republic but are potentially a threat to its democratic governance—this is the paradox. A standing army could be used by the state to undermine the liberty of its citizens. In modern literature on civil-military relations, students of developing countries have frequently asked the question "Why does the military intervene?" The more relevant question is "Why doesn't the military intervene more often?"[5] Confronted with the failure of political institutions and ensuing circumstances, militaries—which are by definition armed and organized—are certainly in a position to take matters into their own hands.

Some of the most robust debates at America's founding emerged around this issue. Thomas Jefferson wanted simply to arm citizens in response to threats. The "Minute Man," one day a farmer and the next a fierce defender of the nation, was his ideal. He saw the British redcoats, professional and commanded by an autocrat, as the antithesis of democratic values. Washington, a military leader himself, recognized that standing armies could be "dangerous to a state." Another Founding Father from Virginia, Richard Henry Lee, said that standing armies "constantly terminated in the destruction of liberty." It's hardly surprising that men so preoccupied with the dangers of centralized power would find the idea of an army to protect that power absolutely terrifying. The Shays' Rebellion of 1786, led by a veteran of the Revolutionary War and drawing heavily on ex-military men, was the closest that America would ever get to a military coup—or at least that is the way it came to be portrayed—and it seared into memories the possibility of armed insurrection.[6]

On the other hand, Hamilton, Madison, and the Federalists were more concerned that the young republic be able to defend itself. And never one to worry much about contradictions (he was both a slaveholder and the author of the language of equality for all), Jefferson would become both the father of the American Navy and of West Point, the country's first military academy to train officers in the art of war—all the while glorifying the citizen solider, who was "in all manners a superior choice to defend the nation."

Interestingly, the Framers did not go to great lengths to address questions of civil-military relations or to ensure civilian control of the government in the Constitution. Rather, they tackled the problem by drawing upon the decentralized structure of the government and the ability of the three branches to check one another. The president would be commander in chief, but he could not declare war, nor could he fund the effort. The power to declare war would be vested with Congress. Other authorities would be divided between the House of Representatives (where all funding bills originate) and the Senate (which must ratify treaties and confirm all ambassadors and cabinet officials).

Moreover, the Framers used the federal structure to defend the country through recognizing state militias and constituting them into a National Guard. The states were not allowed to raise troops without explicit congressional authority. But the militias, made up of part-timers who lived at home and worked in civilian jobs until needed, were given the task "to execute the laws of the Union, suppress insurrections and repel invasion." The Congress was to assure a certain standardization of procedures and training, but for the first hundred years of the country's existence, the backbone of America's military force did not depend on professional soldiers. The Spanish-American War and then the successive world wars would shift us toward a professional military. The National Guard would remain the "citizen-soldiers" that Jefferson so admired.

The Guard (and a second component, the National Reserve, made up of soldiers recently retired from active duty) is to this day a critical part of America's fighting force in the country's wars. They also remain the first line of homeland defense against natural disasters and, sometimes, civil strife. That division of responsibility has permitted the United States to make war against external enemies but not bring the military into domestic conflicts and thus the country's politics.

Although the National Guard's role as a militia in each state leaves it under the command of that state's governor, the Guard can also be "federalized" under certain circumstances and called into the service of the president. When tensions or disagreements exist between a state governor and the president, the National Guard has sometimes been caught in between, leading to some of the most contentious moments in American history.

That includes the day in June 1963 when the Alabama National Guard was called upon by Governor George Wallace to prevent black students from entering the University of Alabama. Even though *Brown v. Board of Education* had declared segregation unconstitutional a decade earlier, university and state officials had gone to great lengths to prevent black students from enrolling. Now three admitted black students with impeccable credentials—Vivian Malone of Mobile, James Hood of Gadsden, and Dave McGlathery of Huntsville—approached the door to Foster Auditorium on campus, and the governor, backed by the Alabama National Guard, stood in their way.

My family and I watched the spectacle unfold on television. Standing in the doorway and flouting demands by federal marshals and the deputy U.S. attorney general that he step aside, the governor clearly did not intend to abandon his inaugural promise of "segregation now, segregation tomorrow, and segregation forever." A few hours later, the commander of the Alabama National Guard unit, General Henry V. Graham, approached Wallace. "Sir," he said, "it is my sad duty to ask you to step aside under orders of the president of the United States. As a member of the Alabama National Guard, I have been ordered into federal service this morning at approximately 10:30, and it is my duty to ask you to step aside in order that the orders of the court may be accomplished." Graham's Guard unit, the 31st Dixie Division, had been federalized and now reported to the president, not the governor. The general had been given conflicting orders and he had to choose which one to follow. Thankfully, he made the right choice. Wallace stepped aside from the doorway and the University of Alabama was integrated.

Americans have come to trust the arrangements that constrain the military's political role. Many questions that were raw at our founding have receded into history. President Bush's exasperation that he could not simply deploy the American military into the streets of New Orleans is testament to how distant concerns of a military takeover have become.

"Congress Shall Make No Law"

The marriage of religion, politics, and the power of the state has perhaps been the single greatest source of worldwide civil strife throughout history. Individual citizens hold multiple associations and loyalties and with varying intensity. Religion, though, makes a claim on the believer that is superior to any other. If that claim is confined to the individual and his right to practice matters of conscience freely, then there is not a problem. But if a group of citizens or the state itself transfers that superior call to the realm of politics, dissenters will by definition be disadvantaged. It is simply not possible to sustain freedom of religion for the individual if the state is committed to a particular set of religious beliefs.

The America about which we learned as schoolchildren was thus one in which freedom of religion and separation of church and state were foregone conclusions at the start. But as with everything in our history, practice has not always matched stated values. In the period before independence, some colonies had official churches, like the Anglican Church in Virginia, while other colonies, such as Rhode Island, imposed a stricter separation.

Many of the earliest settlers came to the new promised land fleeing religious oppression. Their experience imprinted the free exercise of their religion as a fundamental tenet of political life. The Puritans set themselves up in Massachusetts, endeavoring to build a pious society that would be a model for others. But although they were sure to protect their own rights to freely practice their faith, Puritan leaders were not as keen on respecting the rights of minority sects or nonconformists in their midst. Indeed, Roger Williams founded Rhode Island after being banished from Massachusetts for political agitation and not adhering to some aspects of the mainstream faith.

Religious difference was nevertheless tolerated to an almost unprecedented degree for the times. In part due to the bloody religious wars in Britain and Europe, the idea of religious tolerance in the colonies had a natural base of support—if only because the alternative would mean constant strife. Across the colonies there was great variation in both religious sects and religious freedom. Maryland, for example, under the stewardship of Lord Baltimore, a Catholic, passed a resolution that prohibited almost any negative action toward a fellow colonist based on his or her religion. In language that would serve as a model for the First Amendment more than a hundred years later, the Maryland Toleration Act of 1649 stated that "no person or persons whatsoever within this province…professing to believe in Jesus Christ shall from henceforth be in any ways troubled, molested, or discountenanced for or in respect of his or her religion, nor in the free exercise thereof." The limitation to Christian faiths notwithstanding, the Toleration Act was a groundbreaking document, not least because it came at a time of heightened religious tension back in England, where the Anglican monarch (Charles I) had just been overthrown and executed by Puritan leaders of Parliament, and where Catholics were increasingly being persecuted.

On the other hand, in Virginia, Baptists were hounded and imprisoned, and Presbyterians found it hard to establish churches and were subject to frequent property seizure. Madison was struck by the sight of a Baptist preacher who was convicted for his "insurrectionist" sermons and insisted on continuing to preach from his cell.

The Framers were appalled by such persecution, and when they set about the work of writing the Constitution, they sought to protect religious conscience and separate the church from politics.

Madison and others reserved their harshest criticism for state religions obsessed with earthly wealth and power. Their argument was two-pronged: State religion was bad for the individual citizen, interfering with his most basic and personal of choices, and it was bad for religion, condemning the church to worldliness and corruption.[7] Therefore, under the "establishment" and "free exercise" clauses of the First Amendment, the U.S. Congress can make no laws "respecting an establishment of religion or prohibiting the free exercise thereof." Freedom of religion for the individual thus became closely associated with the separation of church and state.

These high ideals have not prevented religious prejudice in American social life and politics. It was not too long ago that candidate John F. Kennedy had to assure Americans that he would not answer to the Pope when making decisions as president of the United States. Anti-Semitism has a long and dark history in America. And Muslim Americans find themselves constantly professing their loyalty to the United States in answer to those who too easily draw a link between them and the violent extremists in the Middle East. As long as human beings fear those who are "different," prejudice and suspicion will be a part of the human experience—and America is no exception.

Yet the Constitution gave "We the people" no religious identity. The state is to be blind to the question of the "true way." That is meant to be the ultimate guarantee that none will be persecuted by the state because of religious beliefs.

Many have made the point that Christians founded America. These men and women lived in a time when at least some expression of Christian belief was an absolute necessity for moral propriety. Like many religious people, I find great comfort in the stories of their personal struggles to find meaning and, in some cases, to find God. But in the final analysis it doesn't matter whether they were Christian believers, Deists, or atheists: Their intention was to create a system of governance that prohibited the privileging of one set of beliefs over another and allowed citizens the freedom to choose and practice religion without the interference of the state.

And through the constitutional process, Americans have been defining precisely what that means in practical terms. This flexibility has become more crucial as our own diversity has stretched to incorporate every known religious belief and the possibility of no religious faith at all. The questions that have arisen are wide-ranging. Some strike us as fundamental: Can the government compel obedience to a law that a citizen deems to be in contradiction to her religious beliefs? Others may seem more trivial: Do holiday decorations with a religious theme displayed on government property violate the separation of church and state? What is remarkable is that we have a Constitution that gives us a pathway to confront these questions. We do not, therefore, take up arms against one another to defend the claim that God is on our side.

Where Government Should Not Enter

The claim of America's founding documents that the government should undertake to protect the right of citizens to life, liberty, and the pursuit of happiness is so broad as to be almost absurd. It makes perfectly good sense that citizens should enjoy freedom of speech and of religion, protection from the arbitrary power of the state, and the right to select those who would govern them. But a right to pursue happiness? How in the world can government guarantee that?

The answer lies in the fact that the government's role was actually limited. There was no guarantee to happiness—only a promise to provide conditions of freedom and liberty that allowed citizens to pursue their goals. That has meant that happiness is pursued through individual initiative and free association with others.

The United States evolved in a way that made unprecedented room for private space and private activity. This is of course true for the economy, where in terms of "value added," private industries account for more than 87 percent of GDP.[8]

Then there is the role of civil society in our national life. Civil society strengthens democracy by encouraging citizen participation, fostering democratic values, advancing the general welfare, providing for public goods, and counterbalancing the government. The United States has more than one and a half million non-governmental organizations. Large numbers of them, like the Sierra Club and the Chamber of Commerce, press the government on matters of policy, while others, like

Common Cause and Judicial Watch, act avowedly as checks on the power of authorities. Still others allow citizens to organize and pursue good works on behalf of the less fortunate.

In America, civil society often delivers many of the services and societal goods that are wholly the purview of the government in other countries, even other democratic ones. Faith-based groups help resettle immigrants and refugees in their communities. Boys and Girls Clubs provide safe spaces for youth after school. National organizations like the Salvation Army and local soup kitchens and shelters feed, house, and clothe the poorest people. The Boy Scouts and Girl Scouts provide leadership training to young men and women, which the military recognizes with advanced enlistment ranks, and nonprofit blood banks provide lifesaving services to patients in hospitals, many of which are also private nonprofit organizations. All of these services depend on another "private" element that until recently was almost unique to the United States: philanthropy.

Rebuilding the nation after the Civil War, particularly in the area of education, was one of American philanthropists' first major projects. And the arts have long been sustained largely by private support.

Large-scale giving increased at the turn of the twentieth century, as the economy created a growing number of millionaires (there were one hundred in the 1870s, four thousand in 1892, and forty thousand in 1916).[9] And then in 1913, after the creation of the income tax, the government took an innovative step that entrenched philanthropy in American society: It made charitable giving tax-deductible. The philanthropic sector flourished in response. Foundations were established to take on a broader array of objectives and, no longer tied to specific projects, they increasingly had open-ended missions.

Neither was philanthropy the exclusive domain of the wealthy. Indeed, in the modern era, some research suggests that by some measures, less affluent Americans give just as much, if not more. In 2011, for example, Americans with earnings in the bottom 20 percent gave 3.2 percent of their incomes to charity, while those in the top 20 percent gave 1.2 percent.[10] And as Americans continue to lead the world in philanthropic giving as a percent of GDP, they continue to give more every year, at even a faster rate than the growing economy. Over the past fifty years, charitable giving per American has increased 190 percent, while GDP per capita has increased 150 percent.[11]

In sum, civil society plays a role in almost every area of social responsibility in the United States. Some will argue that this constitutes an abrogation of government responsibility. They will cite holes in the social safety net that only government can fill. But the relationship of the citizen to the government has become a dialogue about rights and very little about obligations. Yes, one pays taxes, serves on juries, and obeys laws, but everything else is voluntary—even voting and serving in the military. The truth is that the United States has a substantial welfare state, and it has grown immensely over the last five decades. Arguably, therefore, citizenship is finding its deepest expression in this private space where individual citizens or groups of citizens take responsibility for one another. This is one of the strongest pillars of a stable democracy.

A Spirit of Constitutionalism

The institutional landscape that the Founders built rested on essential principles: a limited executive, balanced by a separately elected legislature and an independent judiciary; federalism as a constraint on the power of the central government; a huge space for independent forces—civil society and a free press; and religious freedom unbound by the preferences of the state.

The system was built for what Alexis de Tocqueville called "ceaseless agitation." He noted that "Democratic liberty is far from accomplishing all the projects it undertakes with the skill of an adroit despotism...but in the end it produces more than any absolute government. [It] produces...an all-pervading and restless activity...a superabundant force, an energy which cannot be separated from it...and under favorable conditions... begets the most amazing benefits."[12]

The American government was designed to require constant engagement, not just by officials but by citizens at multiple levels—local, state, and national. Americans were thus given peaceful means to contest political questions. That battleground was and has always been to lay claims before an American Constitution that has by any standard enjoyed a remarkable run. The Founders presciently built in mechanisms for revision, litigation, and evolution. In a sense, the struggle to make America's democracy a bit better and inclusive—little by little—is the story at the core of its stability and success.

The experiment didn't, of course, work perfectly. The early history of America is a story of near misses that almost unraveled the compromises made on behalf of the young republic. The second president, the thin-skinned John Adams, signed into law the Alien and Sedition Acts, purportedly as wartime protection against foreign agents.[13] A clear challenge to the First Amendment, the acts' ban on criticizing the president or his administration was in practice used primarily to stifle attacks by political opponents and the press. Public opposition to the law was strong, however, and helped propel Thomas Jefferson to the presidency. Jefferson allowed the law to expire, but one can speculate that the United States of America would be a very different place had such a law remained in force. Early decisions can mark a country's institutions permanently. In this case, Adams's defeat in the 1800 election allowed the country to reverse course before the laws could do permanent damage. Today, America's protection of free speech and of the press is arguably broader and more far-reaching than that of any other government in the world.

The transition to democracy in America was almost cut short by other close calls. A few decades after the Constitution was written, the influential John C. Calhoun of South Carolina, who was then vice president, put forth the disruptive notion of nullification. In response to the passage of a tariff law, he claimed essentially that the states could cancel (or nullify) the laws of the Union with which they disagreed. By refusing to pay the tariff, South Carolina was challenging the authority of the U.S. government. In late 1832, President Andrew Jackson reinforced deployments of federal troops in the state's capital, Columbia, and positioned the navy off its shores. Jackson threatened to "hang" the members of the nullification movement (including Calhoun). The crisis was averted when Senator Henry Clay crafted a compromise to lower the tariff and undermine local support for the nullification movement, but not before South Carolina had already begun to raise its own army.

The first hundred years of America's history were marked too by corruption, patronage, and self-dealing that threatened both prosperity and faith in the institutions. Teddy Roosevelt was pivotal in cleaning up this part of the institutional landscape, especially in reforming the federal civil service, which had long been an epicenter of political patronage. It was a cause that Roosevelt had taken up early in his career, first as a state assemblyman and later as a vocal member of the Civil Service Commission. When he became president several years later, he used his powers to help ensure that federal jobs were assigned according to merit, not political connections. Still, Roosevelt's three-decade-long effort left many problems unresolved.[14]

Yes, America's transition to democracy was not so smooth after all. Even with all the country had going for it, the great experiment was threatened several times. And nothing would challenge the young republic like America's greatest birth defect—the original sin of slavery and its aftermath. Today, it is easy to forget that slavery was initially presented as a question of the proper balance between the power of the states and that of the federal government. The implications of that argument would stretch almost a hundred years beyond the end of the Civil War to the streets and lunch counters of Alabama.

America's Second Democratic Opening

Rarely do people think of the civil rights movement as a moment of democratic transition. But it was. Of all the amazing twists and turns of America's history, none is more remarkable than the degree to which the Constitution came to serve the cause of overcoming the legacy of slavery and legalized segregation. That the descendants of slaves would embrace the Fourteenth Amendment as a means to push for equal rights is testament to the document's extraordinary ability to channel and facilitate America's evolution.

In the view of many Founders, this was an improbable outcome. Thomas Jefferson was convinced that black slaves would not live in chains forever. "Nothing is more certainly written in the book of fate than that these people are to be free," he once wrote. But he was equally certain that whites and freed blacks "cannot live in the same government." Tocqueville, in viewing the fate of the "three races" that inhabited America in 1835 (the "whites," "negroes," and "Indians," as he put it), saw no way for them to live together in peace. Madison and other Founders so despaired about the future for freed slaves that they endeavored to return them to Africa, supporting the creation of what would become the country of Liberia. Even after the long and arduous struggle to end slavery, it took almost a hundred years, until the civil rights movement of the 1960s, to accomplish what many of the Founders thought impossible—the extension of "We the people" to black Americans.

The journey was a chaotic one. Certainly the Constitution

could not help slaves in the antebellum South. Yet a few had audaciously tried, with little success, to appeal to the courts for their freedom. Under the Slave Codes, slaves had no rights because they were considered property, not people. They could not testify in court against a white person, they could not enter into contracts, and they could not defend themselves against the violence of their masters. But in the North and the new states and territories of the West, legal challenges to slavery met with more success.

Although most cases took place at the state level, a few made it all the way to the U.S. Supreme Court. In one such case, none other than John Quincy Adams defended the kidnapped Africans who were being illegally transported from Africa to slavery on the ship *Amistad*. They had rebelled, killing members of the crew, and Adams won their acquittal in 1841.

A few years later, the Supreme Court heard perhaps its most infamous case. Dred Scott was a slave who had been brought to a free state by his owner and claimed he should therefore be free. Deciding the question of whether the descendants of Africa, free or enslaved, could be considered Americans, a majority of the court said no: "They are not included, and were not intended to be included, under the word 'citizens' in the Constitution, and can therefore claim none of the rights and privileges which that instrument provides for and secures to citizens of the United States."[15] Frederick Douglass, the leading abolitionist, who had escaped from slavery in his youth, denounced the 1857 ruling as the "most scandalous and devilish perversion of the Constitution" he had ever seen, calling it "a brazen misstatement of the facts of history."[16] And yet, he said, "My hopes were never brighter than now." The decision had been a clear setback in the legal battle for freedom, but in the political realm it had an unintended effect, energizing opponents of slavery and hastening the onset of the Civil War, which would settle the issue once and for all.

The immediate question at the end of the Civil War was broader than even how to treat the emancipated slaves; it was how to treat all citizens of the South—both white and black. It is testament to Abraham Lincoln's greatness that he immediately, even before the last shots were fired, found a formula for inclusion. The famous phrase "with malice toward none, with charity for all" was not just a line in the Second Inaugural Address. It was how Lincoln saw the task of bringing the country back together. And it stands as a remarkable example of one approach to the horrible question that so many emerging democracies face even today: How do you deal with rebels, insurrectionists, and those who are on the losing side of civil wars?

Lincoln, felled by an assassin just five days after the war ended, would not live to see how his vision for reconciliation would—or would not—play out. With the Union's victory, the federal government took steps to hold some rebel leaders accountable, but many of those actions were temporary or reversed soon thereafter. Only one military leader of the Confederate army was arrested; the others, including General Robert E. Lee, were allowed to go home. Civilian leaders of the Confederacy did not fare much worse. While several were arrested, not one was ever tried. Jefferson Davis, president of the Confederacy and a graduate of West Point, was imprisoned for a number of months but was eventually released without trial along with the others, and would live out his life as a symbol of pride to the most committed Confederates.

Meanwhile, freed slaves had been promised not only freedom but other forms of assistance as they tried to establish new lives. Part of the plan involved the redistribution of land from former slave owners to newly freed slaves, a policy that would have served both as a form of reparation and as a way to undermine the political power of slaveholding interests. But when Andrew Johnson took office after Lincoln's assassination, he reversed course. The properties that were to have gone to the freedmen never did, depriving the new black American citizens of their "forty acres and a mule."

It would nevertheless fall to Andrew Johnson, after considerable political debate in Congress, to grant the right to vote to freed slaves, making them under the Fourteenth and Fifteenth Amendments subject to "equal protection of the laws." The occupation of the South would usher in the era of Reconstruction, a set of policies intended to rebuild the region and reintegrate it into the Union. Reconstruction is considered by almost every historian to have been a failure. Still, there were some favorable elements: Military governors were sent to enforce the new laws; efforts were made to educate blacks; and freedmen were even seated in state legislatures.

Lincoln was spared the spectacle that would follow, as the South, which he had wanted to return to the fold, ultimately rejected the hand extended to it. Proponents of white supremacy began to regain their footing. The Ku Klux Klan was founded in 1865 by Confederate veterans in Tennessee and soon developed a presence throughout the region.[17] Violence and voter intimidation against blacks became commonplace. Republican-controlled state governments that were established during Reconstruction, and were supported by newly enfranchised black voters, were overturned in favor of the Democrats. State by state, the southerners who had fought on behalf of slavery became ascendant once again.

By the time of the presidential election of 1876, Washington was losing its appetite for occupying the South with federal troops. Their withdrawal was accelerated, however, as part of the deal that resolved an election dispute and made Rutherford B. Hayes president despite his losing the popular vote. After several recounts and contentious debate, Hayes secured enough Electoral College votes in the House of Representatives to win. He achieved the necessary margin only by promising to withdraw all Union troops from the South, which he did in the Compromise of 1877. With that, the effort at reconstruction and reconciliation collapsed, and the hated occupation of the South by the North was over.

Out of this dark moment in American history, institutional seeds were sown that would lead to advancement for the descendants of slaves. After the Civil War ended in 1865, the government established an agency called the Freedmen's Bureau to help former slaves adjust to postwar realities, and the bureau spearheaded the establishment of institutions, including Morehouse College and Howard University in 1868, to help educate the newly freed men (and women). These and other historically black colleges have since educated generation after generation of black Americans, among them some of the most celebrated figures in our national history, including W. E. B. Du Bois, Martin Luther King Jr., and Thurgood Marshall.[18]

But the Compromise of 1877 left southern lawmakers wide latitude to establish new rules for relations between the races. "Separate but equal" became an Orwellian phrase that defended racial segregation and gave it a legal foundation.

Jim Crow (named for a minstrel show in which white actors wore blackface to impersonate African descendants) would emerge as a violent and painful system of legalized segregation and oppression in the South of my birth. For those of us old enough to have lived through the horror of the Jim Crow period, its gruesome images are indelibly etched in our minds: lynchings and mob violence, burning crosses and hate speech. I never saw the Ku Klux Klan in action, but my parents did. I never saw anyone lynched, but I remember dreaming one night that my father didn't return home—he had been caught and hanged. That nightmare came shortly after my uncle told me about being pulled over by a Mississippi highway patrolman who told him and my father to have their "black [expletive] gone from this state when I return."

Sadly, my male relatives experienced many such incidents. My mother's father ran away from his family because he had beaten a white man who had assaulted his sister. He knew what his fate would be if he stayed around. There were so many martyrs to the cause of gaining equal rights, including my friend Denise McNair and three other little girls killed in a bombing at the Sixteenth Street Baptist Church in Birmingham in September 1963. They had been changing into choir robes in a basement restroom when terrorists detonated more than a dozen sticks of dynamite under the front steps of the church. This horrific attack devastated the community but helped galvanize support for passage of the Civil Rights Act the next year. I was born in 1954. America's hard times are not that far in the past.

My own personal experience in living under Jim Crow was of a kind of parallel political existence. My family participated in the democratic process as if it mattered, even when, in substance, it didn't. This inexplicable faith in the rights enshrined in American institutions, shared by countless black families, played a crucial role in finally gaining those rights, because it left open a pathway to change the course of America without resorting to violence.

Using the Constitution to Propel Democratic Change

Democratic transitions do not happen magically; they require people to have a view of a better future and the will to achieve it—and more than that, they require planning and determination. At the forefront of the battle for civil rights in the twentieth century was the NAACP, which used professed American values—hard work, ingenuity, and a belief in equality—to improve American institutions.

Throughout our history there were those black leaders, like Malcolm X of the Nation of Islam, who believed that the constitutional course would never succeed. They sought to overturn the political order by force and violence and equated

Martin Luther King Jr.'s doctrine of "nonviolence" with being "defenseless."

I heard one of those leaders, Stokely Carmichael, speak for the first time in March 1967, when my father, then dean of students at Stillman College in Tuscaloosa, Alabama, invited him to the campus, despite the misgivings of the college administrators and, indeed, the police. As leader of the Student Non-Violent Coordinating Committee (SNCC), Carmichael had made famous the phrase "black power," which was as stirring for some blacks as it was frightening for some whites. "Reverend, I don't want to rev up those country boys," the sheriff told Daddy when he heard about the event. "Nothing will happen," my father told him, hoping he was right.

When Carmichael came to Stillman, his speech was as fiery as expected. He criticized U.S. foreign policy and the war in Vietnam, recounted the double standards from American history, and called on the four hundred students before him to fight back against the system. "This country has law and order, but it doesn't know a damn thing about justice," he said. "If you want to be free, you've got to say, 'To hell with the laws of the United States.'" Carmichael's rhetoric was of liberation and resistance—not of constitutional change.

Carmichael later left SNCC and became associated with a much more militant group, the Black Panther Party, which acted well beyond rhetoric, with recourse to violence that rocked America even after the great civil rights legislation of the Johnson era. Established in 1966, after Malcolm X's assassination and the race-fueled Watts riots in Los Angeles, the Black

Panthers gained national notoriety when a few dozen armed supporters occupied the California legislature to protest a gun-control bill in 1967. Shortly thereafter the Panthers issued their ten-point platform, which sounded more like a call for revolution than reform. Identifying itself as a Marxist revolutionary group, the party advocated the arming of all black Americans, the release of all blacks from jail, and a blanket exemption from the draft and reparations for years of oppression. In ways both symbolic and real, the Black Panthers embraced militancy and engaged in violence, becoming involved in a number of bloody confrontations with police.

Frankly, they might have gained the upper hand were it not for Martin Luther King Jr. and others like him who used America's own laws and principles, rather than violence, to create a more equal nation. They summoned America to be what it said it was—using the very words of the Framers in the context of the Constitution that they authored.

The injustice confronted by black Americans in the pre–civil rights era was in many ways akin to the injustices faced by people living in non-democratic regimes around the world. What we have seen in so many of those cases, time and again, is that people will not accept the conditions of tyranny forever. Eventually, even if it takes generations, there comes a point at which they will revolt. Of course, unlike authoritarian regimes, the United States has representative institutions that provide the option of peaceful resistance—through the political process rather than around it. And leaders of the civil rights movement took full advantage of it.

The NAACP led this effort and engaged institutions

(chiefly the courts, but also the news media, religious groups, and others) to bring political change. Its success depended on a deliberate strategy, pursued by committed individuals who worked over the course of decades, constantly recalibrating in the face of many setbacks. The people at the NAACP persisted because they knew they were right, and they achieved success because they chose the right path.

There were four constitutional prerequisites for the NAACP's approach: the Thirteenth, Fourteenth, and Fifteenth Amendments; the independence of the judiciary; judicial supremacy; and the fact of individual rights. The first was the language to which they appealed. The next two meant that there was a chance that judges would act not in the interests of political forces but with a just reading of the Constitution.[19] The last made it possible to claim harm in the name of the individual citizen. Nathan Margold, a protégé of Felix Frankfurter, authored a kind of blueprint for the strategy. That effort would become known as the Margold Report, and it suggested using the courts to move the law forward. Secondarily, the activity in the legal system would "incite the passions of black Americans to fight for their rights."

Not every case was fought in the South, with landmark decisions, both pro and con, in Missouri and Oklahoma. But the old Confederacy was clearly the epicenter. Thurgood Marshall and the lawyers of the NAACP won some cases and lost some, but they kept refining the strategy, filing new cases, and ultimately moving the civil rights struggle into the consciousness of the country. As the late Jack Greenberg, a young lawyer in the cause, put it in his fascinating autobiographical chronicle of the times, *Crusaders in the Courts*, "Our job was to exploit favorable decisions and use them to overwhelm the unfavorable ones."

The legal strategy made incremental progress, but it was aided by the sacrifices of thousands of black Americans in World War II. That animated President Harry Truman's interest in civil rights. Truman is well known for having integrated the armed forces, recognizing the moral absurdity of returning these men to a country steeped in inequality. He is less well known for having created a Committee on Civil Rights, which issued a landmark report in 1947, *To Secure These Rights*, and set forth a program to overcome injustice and lay the groundwork for the great civil rights legislation passed almost two decades later.

Those fights—in the courts and in the streets, with demonstrations, marches, setbacks, and advances, and too many martyrs to the cause—finally gave meaning to the Fourteenth Amendment through landmark civil rights legislation. The passage of the Civil Rights Act of 1964 and the Voting Rights Act of 1965 can, I believe, be said to be America's second founding.

One may ask whether society has to change before laws or the other way around. The American experience would suggest that new laws do indeed lay the foundation for a changed society. It suggests too that democratic transitions—and that is the only way to think about the path from slavery to equal rights—require agency. Institutions are not worth the paper they are written on until people are willing to say that they must be what they claim to be and to sacrifice and even die to make the point.

The role of the Constitution in this painful history reminds us of the importance of founding documents—and of their place in evolving a society toward justice. Women have used the Constitution to gain suffrage and gay people have won the right to marry. But Tocqueville's third race, American Indians, were left outside of the Constitution's framework of protections until the Indian Citizenship Act of 1924. They have by and large suffered a much different fate and their condition remains an ugly stain on modern-day America.[20]

Even as the Constitution has been used to overcome the legacy of inequality, the arguments have gotten louder and more complicated about its proper purposes, none more so than those about affirmative action. It is a prime example of how the country has tried to balance competing principles in the pursuit of racial equality.

The idea was rather simple at its inception. Years of legal segregation and societal prejudice had led to an imbalance in the opportunities available to American minorities. When the policies first emerged in the 1960s, the Jim Crow era was coming to an end and the integration of the University of Alabama had just taken place. Not surprisingly, blacks were underrepresented in academia, government, and the corporate world. In theory, America was more equal than ever before, but the reality continued to tell a different story.

Lyndon Johnson argued that the country could not be satisfied with this paradox. As he put it, "You do not wipe away the scars of centuries by saying: Now you are free to go where you want, and do as you desire, and choose the leaders you please. You do not take a person who, for years, has been hobbled by chains and liberate him, bring him up to the starting line of a race and then say, 'you are free to compete with all the others,' and still justly believe that you have been completely fair."

A year after signing the Civil Rights Act, Johnson issued an executive order requiring federal contractors to take "affirmative action" to hire qualified minorities. In 1967, he expanded the order to include women. When Richard Nixon became president, he continued these efforts. In 1969, Nixon created the Office of Minority Business Enterprise to promote equal opportunity for minority-owned businesses. Labor Secretary George Shultz then approved the Philadelphia Plan, which required federal contractors to adopt "numerical goals and timetables" to desegregate their workforces. In 1970, the Labor Department issued an order applying the Philadelphia Plan to almost all government contractors, and a year later that order was also extended to include women.

It was not long, however, before tensions emerged between the principle of race-blind equality (the Fourteenth Amendment outlawed discrimination based on race, color, or national origin) and the desire to overcome a history of racial exclusion. From Ronald Reagan, who avowedly challenged affirmative action and sought to end it, to Bill Clinton, who promised to "mend it not end it," the tug and pull between the two principles continued.

Emotional cases before the courts pitted aggrieved individual white citizens against larger societal concerns. How was it possible that white teachers with many years in service could be laid off simply to assure racial balance in a school district? The white teachers won. Was it really right for black firefighters with lower examination scores to be promoted ahead of their white counterparts? No, not really. These questions frankly had no good answer when seen as a contest between two compelling principles.

Nowhere was the tension more pronounced than concerning the question of race in admissions in higher education. Access to quality education is at the core of fulfilling America's promise of upward mobility and personal progress. Choosing to advantage one student over another because of race, ethnicity, or gender seemed to some an assault on this promise.

As provost of Stanford in the 1990s, though, I knew we would enroll fewer minority students if we could not take race into consideration. The president of the university, Gerhard Casper, and I defended affirmative action in college admissions before alumni groups, a few skeptical faculty, and the board of trustees. For an elite university, I truly believed we were not making compromises of quality: Stanford, Harvard, and our peers are so selective and small that admissions officers can "handpick" minority students who can succeed, even if in some cases their test scores are slightly lower than their white counterparts.

At large state institutions, however, implementing affirmative action policies can be trickier. The University of Michigan had established a point system in admissions that awarded applicants a certain number of additional points if they represented a qualified minority group. A white student sued the school for discrimination in a case that ended up before the Supreme Court in 2003.[21] I was national security adviser to President Bush at the time, and he called me into the Oval Office one day. "I've got to make a decision in this Michigan case," he began. He was asking me to opine on an issue that was, of course, well outside of my job description: the language of the administration's amicus brief in support of the plaintiff in the landmark case.

The president explained that as governor of Texas, he had not supported quotas but had sought to pursue affirmative action through what he called "affirmative access." In the Texas program, the top 10 percent of every high school class was guaranteed a place in the Texas university system. In the Michigan case, on the other hand, the plaintiff alleged that the point system in undergraduate admissions amounted to a quota system. Quotas had been ruled unconstitutional by the Supreme Court in 1978, in a case called *Regents of the University of California v. Bakke*, but that decision also upheld the use of race as one of several factors in admissions decisions, given the compelling state interest in promoting diversity. The president had two options. One was simply to support the plaintiff's claims that the University of Michigan's point system was unconstitutional. The other was to go beyond that and ask the Court to overturn the last vestiges of affirmative action in college admissions and eliminate any use of race in admissions decisions, in effect overturning the *Bakke* precedent.

I felt a little odd weighing in on a matter of domestic policy, but knew that as a close adviser who was black and the former provost of Stanford, I should do so. I told the president that I personally would not have joined the amicus brief on behalf of the plaintiff, but he and his advisers had already decided to do that. But I also urged him not to support those who would overturn the *Bakke* decision. "Mr. President," I said, "this work isn't yet done. One day it will be, but not yet."

Later, I learned that Alberto Gonzales, the White House counsel at the time, who went on to become attorney general, had made the same case to him. Against the wishes of some in the administration, the president took the middle course we recommended. When the *Washington Post* published a story claiming that I had argued for overturning *Bakke*, I asked the president to allow me to do something that I had never done before: reveal the contents of our private conversation. He agreed, and I let everyone know that I was—and still am—a supporter of affirmative action. Sometimes when important principles clash, you have to choose: I believe that we still need to choose inclusion even if it collides with our desire to be race-blind.

The time is coming when we, as a country, may make a different choice. In her opinion on the Michigan case, Sandra Day O'Connor thought that the need for preferences would expire in twenty-five years. That would be 2028.

Affirmative action is also being challenged on a state-by-state basis. In 1996, for example, the people of California voted in a referendum to end affirmative action by state agencies in employment, education, and contracting.

But the underrepresentation of minorities in academia, the corporate environment, and the government persists. Affirmative action has caused people to stop and think and make good-faith efforts to diversify outside of traditional channels. I doubt that Stanford would have taken a second look at a young Soviet specialist from the University of Denver on a one-year fellowship without an eye toward diversification. But the university took a chance on me and I joined the faculty. It worked out well for both of us.

When I was secretary of state, I told my aides that it was appalling to me that I could go through an entire day of meetings and never see someone who looked like me. The president of the United States had selected two African Americans in a row, Colin Powell and me, to be the country's chief diplomats, and yet the Foreign Service was still just 6 percent black, a percentage virtually unchanged since the 1980s and half of what one would expect based on the population.

Obviously, it isn't easy to know what role choice plays in these and other circumstances of underrepresentation. I have argued to rooms full of minority students that they can't personally decide against studying a foreign language and expect the diplomatic corps to be diverse. I have told black undergraduates that they can't personally refuse to go on to PhD study and protest the lack of minority professors.

Moreover, as other groups have rightly claimed the need for relief from underrepresentation, further contradictions have appeared. Asian American representation in college admissions is arguably depressed by efforts to include other minorities. And I am very aware that every admitted minority student faces a kind of stigma due to affirmative action, no matter what universities argue to the contrary. I saw this so often that it ceased to come as a surprise.

One incident sticks in my mind. I asked a colleague at Stanford how his teaching was going. He told me that despite being very busy, he was holding an extra section to help his minority students come up to speed. The quarter had just started and I asked innocently if he had done an evaluation of the students to see if it was needed. He had never thought of doing so. I wanted to ask him, "Have you thought that your white students might need help too?" But I didn't. He meant well but had fallen into the worst kind of prejudice. In another context, President George W. Bush once called this "the soft bigotry of low expectations."

These are the tensions and contradictions that the admirable effort to overcome our nation's birth defect of slavery and prejudice has produced. That we are still struggling with these issues today, after more than two centuries as a nation, is yet another reminder that nothing is smooth on democracy's path.

As people around the world struggle to build democracies of their own, the effort to protect the rights of ethnic, religious, and other minorities is a daunting challenge. As the American experience shows, it will continue long after the democracy is stable. But it helps to have a "spirit of constitutionalism," and a belief that the institutions of the nation are in the end just—and that it is worth the trouble to use them.

The United States is a stable democracy today not because the Founders' institutional design answered every question for all time about how to balance the rights and interests of citizens and their state. They relied on necessary compromises to create a framework of principles and laws that could guide future generations as they met new challenges. The lesson for young democracies is that not everything can be settled at the start. But if the institutions are put in place and citizens use them, there is at least a way to channel the passions of free people and to resolve the hard questions of governing as they arise in future times.

Chapter 2

RUSSIA AND THE
WEIGHT OF HISTORY

The visit to Saint Petersburg had been surprising and even a little unnerving. Anatoly Sobchak, the reformist mayor of the city, had invited a group of professors from Stanford to help him think through the creation of a great new Russian university. It was 1992 and I was about a year removed from my stint in Washington as special assistant to the president for Soviet affairs. The Soviet Union had recently collapsed and I looked forward to my first visit to the Russian Federation. Once there, it was painfully clear to me that the Russians were struggling to find their footing in radically changed circumstances.

The artifacts in Sobchak's office were testimony to the temptation to situate the new squarely within the confines of the past. A map of the Russian Empire at its height and a portrait of Peter the Great adorned the walls. The symbol of the tsar, the double-headed eagle, sat on his desk. In one interpretation, the eagle looked both ways to remind his subjects that the tsar was at once human and divine.

Sobchak explained that the "European University" he envisioned would return Russia to its rightful place as an intellectual leader of the continent—a role that the Soviet "interlude," as he called the previous seventy-five years, had destroyed. Almost as an afterthought, Sobchak mentioned the recent decision to change the name of the great city of Leningrad back to Saint Petersburg. It had been controversial. World War II veterans were unhappy, he noted, but he said he would find some way to honor their sacrifice at the siege of Leningrad, which cost one million Russian lives. The change marked progress, he said, and now it was time to move on. I couldn't help but think that this kind of progress was decidedly backward-looking. The Russian nationalist restoration was well under way.

That evening, Sobchak held a reception for our group in one of the grand halls of the Winter Palace. The room was filled with Russian intellectuals, dressed in the all-black attire that was so popular at the end of the nineteenth century. Quite a few of them had also appropriated the names of the time. I met several Chekhovs, Tolstoys, and at least one Pushkin. These descendants, real and imagined, of Russia's great literary figures of the past were staking a claim to the country's future.

I broke away from the crowd and walked around, admiring, as I had on many occasions, the extraordinary beauty and artistry of Russia's greatest architectural treasure. A former home to the tsars, the palace is part of a complex of buildings on the Neva River. Its pastel rooms of blue and green are dotted with malachite columns and gold chandeliers. I eventually spotted a short, pale man with icy blue eyes standing alone in a corner. He seemed quite uncomfortable, dressed in a Soviet-era suit. I don't know what compelled me to seek him out and introduce myself; perhaps I felt a little bad for him because he seemed out of place. I walked over and stuck out my hand. The deputy mayor of Saint Petersburg and I said very little, or at least I remember very little of what was said.

Almost a decade later, President George W. Bush and I waited for the Russian president to arrive for their first summit in Slovenia in June 2001. The same pale man from the Winter Palace party walked briskly toward us. President Putin extended his hand and we exchanged greetings. I didn't say that we had met before. Neither did he.

Vladimir Putin personifies Russia's struggle to find its footing. As a KGB officer in East Germany he witnessed Gorbachev's reforms and the collapse of the Soviet Union. As Yeltsin's young prime minister he participated in the chaotic birth and failure of Russia's quasi-democratic institutions. In the end, he rode the wave of the population's frustration and fear, pulling the country back to its authoritarian past.

Winston Churchill once called Russia a "riddle wrapped in a mystery inside an enigma." When looking at Russia's journey, it is tempting to fall back on arguments about the country's uniqueness. I have heard more than a few exasperated people— experts, government officials, and commentators—revert to "It is just Russia" as an explanation.

It is tempting too to reference Russia's brutal and troubled history. The country began in the late fifteenth century as a collection of principalities that were systematically kludged together into the Russian state. A ruling dynasty arose in Moscow as the four tsars of the Rurik clan defeated and in some cases bribed landowning families (called boyars) to pledge allegiance to the central state and to build the core of what would become the Russian Empire. Loyalty was maintained by sheer force and fear. It was not unusual to see the severed heads of those who disobeyed displayed on stakes along the walls of the Kremlin fortress, which was made the headquarters of the new state by Ivan the Great.

What authority the tsar did not command by brute strength, he sought by fealty to the Orthodox Church. As head of the church, the ruler of Russia was believed to be both human and divine. The tsar protected and enriched the church, and the hierarchy of the church returned the favor. To celebrate a military victory, Ivan the Terrible commissioned a new cathedral near the Kremlin that was so beautiful it remains a symbol of Russia to this day. He in turn made sure that the masterpiece, St. Basil's Cathedral, would never be copied: The architects' eyes were reportedly put out so that they could never design anything again.

Then, in 1584, Ivan the Terrible died without a capable heir. His son Fyodor became tsar, but real power fell to a Russian boyar named Boris Godunov, and when Fyodor died in 1598, the Rurik dynasty died with him. Pretenders to the throne arose with alarming frequency, only to be murdered in their beds (quite literally) by other pretenders. Foreign rulers picked at the carcass of the vulnerable Russian state and sent their own candidates (in some cases their own children) to lay false claims to the Russian throne. When Boris Godunov died (he was driven to madness by the apparitions of those he had killed), Russia plunged into a long civil war. This period came to be known as the Smuta, the Time of Troubles.

Surely, one would think, an episode from five centuries in the past could not possibly have resonance today. Yet I will never forget going to the Bolshoi Theater in Moscow in the early 1980s to hear a performance of Mussorgsky's great opera based on this story. The spectacular coronation scene used the Kremlin bells, which can be heard clearly since the theater is only a few blocks away. Since they are the same bells that rang for Godunov's coronation, the experience was a bit chilling.

At the end of the opera, as the dead Godunov lies on the floor, the chorus implores the people to weep. And much to my surprise, the audience began to weep. Every Russian knows that the Time of Troubles is about to begin. Many years of civil war, in which the country is plunged into chaos at home and devoured by foreign powers, are upon them. And they take it personally.

They know that a young boyar will finally emerge in 1613 to establish the Romanov dynasty in the Kremlin. He and his heirs will expand the Russian Empire through wars abroad and brutal suppression of dissent at home. In doing so, the Russian identity and a sense of security will be built through conquest, religious orthodoxy, and authoritarian rule.

The vast landscape with no natural boundaries and certainly no oceans to protect it will eventually incorporate large parts of the Eurasian landmass. It will survive for three hundred years, until too many lost wars and internal revolt destroy tsarist rule and bring Lenin and the Bolsheviks to power. There will be more repression and more hardship. Yet the vast empire will be rebuilt, and within a few decades the Soviet Union will occupy essentially the same territory as the Russian Empire that it had destroyed.

Then twenty-five million Russians will die in World War II as another foreign power seeks to conquer. The Russian nation will rally and defeat the Nazis, extending Soviet power deep into Eastern Europe and establishing a "ring of socialist brother states" to protect its borders.[1] And it will stand astride Europe and Asia as a nuclear superpower, feared across the globe, until on one December night in 1991, the flag of the Soviet Union will come down from the Kremlin for the last time. Fifteen republics of the old Soviet Union will become independent states. And Russia's borders will be pushed back almost to those of Peter the Great.

The Russian language has a word, *vopros*, which means "question," "issue," or "problem." Those who study Russia know that the country's history has been characterized by a series of questions: Lenin's famous challenge to his Bolshevik comrades, "What is to be Done?" A constant obsession among the people with "Who is to Blame?" And terrible geography and a troubled history that cause Russians to ask, "Who are we?" and "What is Russia?" These questions have defied answers throughout the centuries and provoke another: Can democracy ever take hold in this rough and vast land?

Every country has some aspect of its history that could be used to explain why democracy can't succeed. Russia's modern story has a familiar theme in failed democratic transitions around the world: weak institutions that never took hold against a backdrop of economic decline and social instability. Russia is not Mars and the Russians are not endowed with some unique, antidemocratic DNA.

Yet there is a facet of this story that is unique to Russia. The collapse of the Soviet Union occurred contemporaneously with the birth of the new Russian state, which added a dimension of complexity and turmoil that was indeed different. The borders of the state, the identity of its people, and the system of economic and political governance were all in play at the same time. That is where the long, tortured history does matter and helps to explain why the transition to democracy was not a transition at all: It was the collapse of the Russian state within the collapse of the Soviet Empire. And in the end, it was too much to overcome.

The First Opening: "I Want the Soviet Union to Be a Normal Country"

Mikhail Gorbachev wanted to change the course of history by changing the Soviet Union. When he became general secretary of the Communist Party of the Soviet Union (CPSU) in March 1985, the political and economic systems were in deep crisis, and Moscow was mired in a costly war in Afghanistan, with America challenging Soviet power there and across the globe. President Ronald Reagan had launched huge defense budget increases and military-technological programs that Moscow could not match.[2]

And the country had seen three leadership changes in four years. The succession of aging Soviet leaders, Brezhnev,

Andropov, and Chernenko, dying one after another was a metaphor for the state of the Soviet Union itself.

The Russians used black humor to good effect to highlight the circumstances. A man tries to attend Brezhnev's funeral, an old joke went.

"You need a ticket," the guard tells him.

He returns for Andropov's.

"Where's your ticket?" the guard asks.

When the man comes for Chernenko's service, he tells the guard, "It's okay—I bought the season pass."

The people and even their leaders referred to *zastoi*, stagnation, to describe their circumstances.

Gorbachev was a breath of fresh air. And the next four years produced surprise after surprise as he endeavored to throw off the yoke of Soviet *zastoi*. The term that he chose, *perestroika*, encompassed a host of new ideas, all intended to shake up the central planning of the economy and introduce, carefully at first, competition, price reform, and market forces.

Though the reforms were cautious, they were in fact pretty radical when one remembers the tenets of central planning on which the Soviet economy had rested for sixty-five years. Inputs and outputs were determined not by supply and demand but by a series of plans, adopted every five years by the government. Remarkably, the plan was intended to lay out every transaction within an economy serving nearly three hundred million people over eleven different time zones.

One year the plans for forks and towel racks got mixed up. Workers produced, nonetheless, according to the plans. No one stopped to notice that the towel racks were incredibly light and the forks unbelievably heavy. They were shipped to the stores, where Soviet consumers presumably made do with what they got. This was the nature of central planning, and it governed everything from the production of shoes, refrigerators, and automobiles to the provision of machine tools for heavy industry and armaments for the military.

One of the first reforms allowed for small, privately owned restaurants, which were called "cooperatives" to give them socialist cover. Sitting in one of them during a visit to Moscow in 1988, I was struck by how good the food was and the care with which it had been prepared. I had never seen pasta in the USSR or vegetables so fresh. When I was a graduate student there in 1979, it was common to enter a state-owned restaurant (they were all state-owned) and be told that there were no tables, this despite the fact that the place was absolutely empty.

If you were seated, the food was barely edible stale bread, chicken that was mostly skin, and whatever vegetables happened to be around—usually cucumbers and the occasional tomato. The staff mostly didn't bother to try since there was no reward for good service or good food.

Gorbachev's new entrepreneurs could not have been more different. They wanted customers, they needed customers, and they treated them well. I asked one of the owners about the freshness of the food. He drove every morning, he said, to a farm on the outskirts of the city, paid the farmer twice what the state would offer, and therefore got the very best produce available. Then he drove back to Moscow and he and his wife prepared the evening meal. They had to charge a little more, he explained, but customers kept coming.

There were other signs that a rudimentary form of capitalism was starting to take hold. In the past, every Soviet grocery store looked like every other grocery store: dingy, poorly lit, and with few products on the shelves. But when under *perestroika* the managers could "lease" the store and were allowed to keep some of what they made (though it wasn't called profit), they began to work to gain customers. Window displays competed with one another to draw buyers in.

The reforms of *perestroika* were accompanied by *glasnost*, a series of political changes that were intended to reduce resistance to the economic overhaul. Gorbachev seemed to believe that he could safely remove the key constraints of the political system—propaganda and fear. He wanted, he told many people, including me, to make the Soviet Union a "normal country."

Like the economic reforms, *glasnost* (roughly meaning "transparency") started modestly. The Communist Party took the lead, publishing revisions of the whitewashed history of the country. For example, there had long been a debate about how many people perished in the purges of the 1930s under Josef Stalin. The British-American historian Robert Conquest was excoriated by academics for claiming in 1968 that twenty million had been killed. As late as the mid-1980s, some scholars described the number of victims as only "many thousands."[3] Yet when the official story was told, we learned that Conquest's numbers were gruesomely accurate. Approximately one in three party members (and many ordinary citizens) were branded as traitors and purged during Stalin's reign. Many were executed outright, while others were sent to Siberia and similar detention camps, where they died under the harsh labor conditions and a few, very few, lived to tell the story when *glasnost* made it safe to do so. Under *glasnost*, great dissident writers like Alexander Solzhenitsyn who had chronicled the brutality of the Stalinist years (and beyond) were welcomed back into the good graces of their country.

The Soviets' intention, though, had been to control the narrative—careful and selective in what was to be criticized and thrown aside and what was not. But that strategy would prove unsustainable, and criticism began to reach beyond history's confines to the modern leadership.

During a monthlong visit to Moscow in 1988, I walked along the Old Arbat, a street not too far from the American ambassador's residence. The cobblestoned pathway was filled as it had always been with people selling artifacts. I picked up a matryoshka (the little nesting dolls that contain ever smaller versions of themselves). This one was in Gorbachev's likeness, and he held inside him each of his predecessors until one arrived finally at a tiny little Lenin. *That's odd*, I thought. It seemed, well, disrespectful.

I continued down the pathway to a place where a street theater performance had drawn a large crowd. Struggling at first with the colloquial Russian, I soon realized that the comic was making fun of Gorbachev, his anti-alcohol campaign, and the Kremlin's general incompetence.

Yet Russia had almost always (Stalin would have been an exception) allowed a little mild satirical criticism of the government. During tsarist times, writers like Nikolai Gogol made fun of stupid bureaucrats in satires like *The Inspector General*.[4]

This was different, though. Underneath, something more

fundamental was taking place. The people of the Soviet Union were losing their fear of their rulers. Gorbachev believed that stripped of fear and the lies about history, the population would rally to the goodness of the country and embrace a new and vibrant future.

Instead, the political landscape kept shifting. What many assumed would simply be a loosening of constraints *within* the existing system soon became an attack on the system itself. Intellectual debate (and even television commentary) started to turn to forbidden subjects like whether the party could and should maintain a monopoly on power.

Gorbachev himself had an interesting view that I had a chance to discuss with him when he visited the United States in 1990. The Soviet Union, he thought, was not ready for a multi-party system. That wasn't surprising. But then he noted that "factionalism" was already growing within the Soviet Communist Party and that would eventually be the basis for new parties. Well informed about the political histories of other countries, he reminded me that some of America's greatest leaders (like George Washington) never belonged to a party. Japan had been ruled by one party (the LDP), but factions had provided turnover in the political leadership through elections, he said.

Moreover, Gorbachev said that eventually he saw a day when the Soviet Union's political system would be the far-left part of a European spectrum of parties—communist, social democrat, conservative. This, he said, should have been the outcome of the Russian Revolution. The problem was that the political system had been hijacked by Josef Stalin and separated from Europe. I thought his was an interesting if flawed take on Soviet history. Yet it revealed that Gorbachev's faith in a reformed Soviet Union was real.

Already in 1987, just two years after becoming party secretary, he had proposed plans for democratization of local government and the CPSU. That year, for the first time, local elections would feature more than one candidate in some constituencies. And though only about 4 percent of the elected deputies were from contested elections, some well-known people actually lost in their election bids. This carefully orchestrated change nonetheless began to stimulate others to push the envelope of reform. In May of the next year, a group of pro-democracy activists formed the Democratic Union. They "declared their organization to be a political party, the first opposition party to the CPSU in seventy years."[5]

The pace of change accelerated throughout 1988 with the Gorbachev reforms targeting the role of the party itself in governance. There had always been parallel structures in the Soviet Union—the party and the government. For instance, *Pravda* (Truth) was the party's newspaper and *Izvestiya* (the News) belonged to the government. Still, any high-ranking member of the government was also a member of the party, and there was little doubt that real authority rested in the Politburo of the CPSU and its general secretary.

Gorbachev proposed a presidential system for the USSR, changing the institutional basis for leading the country. Power would now rest in the president, not in the general secretary. The 1977 constitution was amended as well, creating a bicameral legislature with the Congress of People's Deputies as the lower house and the Supreme Soviet as the upper house. This was an early attempt to create a legislature, theoretically independent of the party. ("Soviet" is the Russian word for "council," so the name of this organization did not mean that it was a part of the Communist Party.)

The new rules also set "a freer and fairer process for elections." As scholars have noted, "They were only partially free and competitive."[6] Yet in the elections the next year, dozens of independent and reform-minded candidates defeated party regulars. Then, in 1989, the Supreme Soviet banned censorship of the press.

Gorbachev took the subordination of the party to the government seriously—though in never standing for election to the newly empowered Soviet presidency, he forfeited a chance to create a popular mandate for the position and for himself. Nonetheless, he valued the trappings of the office. In planning the U.S.-Soviet summit for the summer of 1990, we were told that Gorbachev should no longer be referred to as "General Secretary of the Communist Party" but as "President Gorbachev." And to prove the point, he arrived in Washington in 1990 in an Aeroflot plane proudly carrying the flag of the Soviet Union and the letters CCCP (the Russian abbreviation for the USSR).

He wanted to act like a president too. Standing in the office of George H. W. Bush at Camp David, Gorbachev expressed interest in the calendar that the president pulled out of his pocket. "That's a smaller version of my schedule," the president said. Apparently, Gorbachev asked who produced the schedule. "Well," President Bush replied, "my scheduler who works with my chief of staff." "I don't have one of those," Gorbachev said, not making clear whether he meant a scheduler or a chief of staff.

Those of us on the White House staff had always wondered, because scheduling a call with Gorbachev was a nightmare. No one ever seemed to know where he was or what he was doing. He didn't use the Communist Party apparatus, apparently not trusting it, and he didn't yet have a presidential one.

President Bush dutifully asked if he should send some people to show the Soviet president how to run an office. Gorbachev readily accepted. And in the fall of 1990, Chief of Staff John Sununu led a delegation of American staffers to Moscow to help set up the Gorbachev presidency.

These changes were not intended to destroy the CPSU's hold on power. Gorbachev intended to democratize and modernize the Communist Party, giving it greater legitimacy among the Soviet people. He seemed to believe that it could gain the trust of the people, no longer needing coercion and repression to command their loyalty. Yet by creating and allowing new institutional arrangements, he provided space for other forces that he could not control. And in short order these seemingly breathtaking changes were revealed to be too little too late. Pressures from the left (conservatives in Russian political parlance) and from the right (liberals) left little room for Gorbachev's middle ground.

On the left, powerful figures like Politburo member Yegor Ligachev feared (correctly, it turns out) that the CPSU was committing suicide. Ligachev was stripped of responsibility for ideological matters as a result of his views and put in charge of agriculture. Everyone understood the significance of that, since the portfolio had often been a sign of political exile. Still, open criticism in the Soviet press and the appearance of reactionary factions within the Party itself grew more urgent and more common. But Gorbachev pushed ahead, declaring at the 28th Party Congress in July 1990 that the Politburo of the Party would have no role in governing the country. Earlier that year, Gorbachev engineered an amendment to Article 6 of the Soviet Constitution that eliminated the CPSU's monopoly on power and allowed the creation of multiple parties.

While these decisions terrified conservatives, they were not radical enough for the liberals, led by Boris Yeltsin. He had been expelled from the Politburo three years earlier and in July 1990 abruptly resigned his membership in the CPSU.

From that time on, he would lead the pro-democratic forces and he would do so in a way that created another, ultimately fatal fissure in the political landscape. Yeltsin would begin to advocate for loosening the ties of the republics within the Soviet Union itself, insisting on something closer to confederation than a unitary state. Ironically, Yeltsin used a provision of the Soviet constitution that gave the republics the right to secede. No one had ever thought it important, but it shows that sometimes a law on the books can suddenly have new resonance in changed circumstances.

Gorbachev tried to preempt Yeltsin, proposing change after change that would give more power to the republics. But again he was too late: Yeltsin created parallel structures in the Russian republic that effectively ripped the heart out of the Soviet Union. After all, what was the Soviet Union without Russia at its core?

Desperate to hang on to a coherent Soviet state, Gorbachev sponsored a referendum in March 1991 on the question of unity.

And though large majorities voted to preserve the Soviet Union, six republics (Armenia, Georgia, Moldavia, Lithuania, Latvia, and Estonia) boycotted. And more critically, Russian voters backed an empowered Russian presidency. When Yeltsin was elected president of Russia in June 1991 he had an institutional base from which to demand independence for the republics. Soon there was nothing left of Soviet power.

Lifting the Iron Curtain

Internal reforms for a great power do not take place in isolation. Foreign policy had to be altered too. And the change in the Soviet Union was a dramatic one.

The Soviet state emerged in 1922 from the remains of the Russian Empire, fueled by the fiery ideology and rhetoric of class conflict and the epic struggle between communism and capitalism. The belief that both could not survive was perhaps best captured in Nikita Khrushchev's threat to "bury" the West, and his ill-advised timeline of a couple of decades until the triumph of socialism.

Though the passion about and belief in socialism's triumph waned over the years, giving way to peaceful coexistence and ultimately détente with the West, the notion of two systems in competition with one another remained a defining characteristic of the international system throughout the Cold War. In everything from the space race to Olympic hockey, a victory for the Soviet Union was taken as a victory for socialism. As a child I remember our shock and dismay when the Soviet Union launched the first man into space in 1961. On the other hand, Americans were heartened when U.S. chess prodigy Bobby Fischer defeated Boris Spassky to become the world grandmaster, and when Van Cliburn became the first non-Russian to win the international Tchaikovsky piano competition in 1958. This little girl studying piano wanted to be Van Cliburn. In 1980 the defeat of the Big Red Machine (as the Soviet hockey team was nicknamed in the West) by a collection of young American amateurs at the Olympics in Lake Placid was seen as a stinging loss for communism and a victory for capitalism and democracy. That was the zero-sum nature of the relationship between East and West.

Gorbachev rejected that view. He went in search of a foreign policy that was sustainable—no longer requiring the overreach of wars like Afghanistan and a defense budget that consumed more than 25 percent of the GDP—and he abandoned "class struggle" as an organizing principle.[7] Within a coterie of the Soviet establishment, led by intellectuals such as Alexander Yakovlev, a future adviser of Gorbachev, the argument emerged that the modern world required cooperation, not conflict. The international equivalent of the "normal" domestic politics of the new Soviet Union became the "Common European Home." In this context, Gorbachev's view that the Soviet Union would simply take its place on the continuum of European political forces made perfect sense.

Though we were skeptical in the White House at first, it became clear that Gorbachev meant what he said. The Soviet Union ended its war in Afghanistan and its forces went home. Eastern Europe was freed to go its own way and Soviet troop strength was cut back dramatically on the continent.

On the economic side, Gorbachev sought to be welcomed into the international capitalist system. Soviet economists were regular visitors to Washington, London, and Paris to learn about how those economies worked. As these inquiries increased, it was easy to forget that central planning and communism had once been hailed as a viable, even preferable alternative to capitalism in Asia, Latin America, Africa, and, of course, Eastern Europe. Now its failure was obvious and the Soviets were fully prepared to admit it, though their understanding of capitalism was flawed at best.

At one of the sessions with his counterparts, my colleague Mike Boskin, chairman of the Council of Economic Advisers for President George H. W. Bush, gave a little lecture on markets. At the end of his talk, the Soviet finance minister raised his hand. "Thank you, Dr. Boskin," he began. "But there is one thing I don't understand. Who sets the prices?"

The desire of the Soviet reformers to be accepted into the fold was incredibly strong—a pull that would fade as time went on. In one sad episode, Gorbachev sent a letter to the meeting of the G-7 taking place in Paris in 1990. He essentially asked to be invited. The startled leaders didn't welcome him that year, but, fearful that his reforms were losing ground, they did invite him to the G-7 in July 1991, one month before the coup attempt against him and five months before the Soviet Union collapsed altogether. That is how the G-7 became the G-8.

Gorbachev had managed to secure a place for the Soviet Union in his "Common European Home." But it had come at a cost. As one exasperated East German intellectual put it, "If there is not class conflict, what is the argument for two Germanys?" Pretty soon that would be answered too and Germany would unify completely and fully on Western terms.

On a visit to Moscow in February 1990 as Soviet influence in Germany was waning, I met with Gorbachev's adviser on the United States. It was already dark at half past four in the afternoon and snowing outside as I waited in the Kremlin anteroom. Finally, Vadim Zagladin appeared. He was an hour late. "I am sorry," he said. "But every day we come to work to see what disaster has befallen us now."

I delivered my points about how the unification of Germany would benefit everyone. There would be no losers in ending the Cold War. "Stop," Zagladin said. "There used to be two Germanys—one was yours and one was ours. Now there will be one and it will be yours. That, Professor Rice, is a strategic defeat." I couldn't say much, because he was right.

Gorbachev insisted on signing away the Soviet Union's "Four Power Rights and Responsibilities" and returning Germany to full and complete sovereignty, not in the Kremlin but in a Moscow hotel.[8] That is how forty-five years of Soviet dominance in Eastern Europe ended—in the lobby of a hotel. The Soviet Union's military alliance, the Warsaw Pact, dissolved a few months later, and NATO did not. Gorbachev had gone too far, and as Soviet power collapsed across Europe, the Cold War ended and Moscow suffered a humiliating "strategic defeat."

Hard-liners finally rallied and launched a coup against Gorbachev in August 1991. But it was too late. The army was split, some supporting Yeltsin and the reformers and others holding views even more conservative than those of Gorbachev. The

KGB was split and no one could fully count on its loyalty. Boris Yeltsin and Russian institutions had emerged as an alternative to Gorbachev and the Soviet Union—a challenge from the radical side. Gorbachev reportedly asked his defense minister whether the army would stand by him if he tried to resist Yeltsin's demands. The defense minister said he was not sure.

In short order Yeltsin engineered the creation of the Commonwealth of Independent States to replace the Soviet Union. Gorbachev did not resist. And on December 25, 1991, the Hammer and Sickle, the flag of a superpower with thirty thousand nuclear weapons and four million men under arms, was lowered from above the Kremlin for the last time. More than seventy years of communism ended quietly and was buried with few mourners and little fanfare. But the demise of the Soviet Union left a mark on the emerging new Russian state and tainted the critical and chaotic first years of its attempted transition to democracy. Perhaps it also sealed its failure.

The Second Opening: The New Russian State Is Born

Political choices do not take place on a blank canvas: What has gone before matters. Gorbachev's effort to make the Soviet Union a "normal" nation introduced important democratizing reforms, essentially for the first time in the country's history. The only other episode had been tragically brief. Alexander Kerensky established an independent parliament, a freer press, and rule of law when he took power after the abdication of the tsar in March 1917. The victory of the Bolsheviks eight months later put an end to that experiment. And thanks to the telling of history in Soviet times, few Russians knew that story.

The Gorbachev reforms were thus pathbreaking: the creation of a quasi-independent parliament; a presidency divorced from the Communist Party structure; careful but palpable freeing of the press; and the first civil society institutions that advocated on behalf of non-political causes.[9] Unfortunately, these fledgling institutions would soon be overrun by the chaos engulfing the country.

In the wild days immediately after the end of the Soviet Union there was unbridled joy and optimism in the West that capitalism and democracy would take hold in Russia and in the Baltic states. Observers were less sanguine about the newly independent Ukraine, Belarus, Central Asia, and the Caucasus. Most of their new leaders did little to encourage hope, falling almost immediately into corruption and infighting or simply transferring power to authoritarian communists who now called themselves nationalist democrats.

But Russia seemed different. The country enjoyed a high level of economic development, a population that was almost 100 percent literate, and relative ethnic homogeneity.

Obviously, Russia's totalitarian history would be a concern. Yet Gorbachev had in seven years loosened the constraints without mass violence and handed the reins peacefully to Boris Yeltsin. Yeltsin, in turn, proved a popular leader, made even more legitimate by his valiant defense of the people and the nation in front of the Russian White House in the summer of 1991. The image of Yeltsin facing down the coup plotters from the top of a tank and turning the army against them gave the country a rallying point. The Russian people had reason to believe that they were finally about to erase hundreds of years of revolution, oppression, and political turmoil. Now, with the collapse of the Soviet Union, Russia could become a normal country.

And the West wanted desperately to help. It is true that Russia was not offered a Marshall Plan, comparable to what had been done to support European reconstruction after World War II. But the circumstances were different. Russia was not without resources given its vast oil wealth, a well-educated population, and high levels of industrialization. The question seemed to be how best to unleash the forces that had been held back by Soviet communism. The raw clay for a successful democratic transition was present and abundant.

This explains in large part the path adopted by the United States and Europe to assist the Russian democratic transition. Large numbers of experts, both governmental and private, deployed to Moscow to help establish capitalism and provide advice on how to develop democracy. While a few voices suggested that too much was being expected too soon, proponents of radical surgery prevailed.

The Soviet economy needed to be transformed. That much was clear. But in retrospect, those who advised the Russians, not to mention the Russians themselves, had no earthly idea how to break up and reconstitute the deeply dysfunctional economy. The recent successes in transforming the Polish economy gave a false sense of certitude to the effort. But Poland was, as we will explore, very different, with nascent institutions of democracy and capitalism that proved essential in its success.

In Russia, the speed of change clearly outpaced the development of rules of the game and institutions to contain the new forces. Events quickly overwhelmed what was left of Gorbachev's reforms and raced ahead of what Yeltsin's government could achieve.

We have seen that America's Founding Fathers worried about creating a state that would be too strong and thus a threat to democratic values. But they understood that the state had to be strong enough to carry out certain functions: protecting the country from foreign enemies; the establishment of a national currency; the maintenance of civil order; the ability to tax its citizens fairly; and the confidence that the states would carry out federal laws. Somewhere between chaos and authoritarianism lay democracy.

Russia did not find that sweet spot. Rather, the period was characterized by wild schemes to privatize the economy rapidly, creating massively rich new elites while real income plummeted and poverty levels soared for the general population. Organized crime emerged as a potent force, offering protection to companies and individuals (for a fee) that the state could not provide. Regional and local authorities simply ignored the policies of the central government. The Russian citizen experienced daily life as one of humiliation, deprivation, and chaos.

The economic collapse of the country was at the core of the despair. "Shock therapy," a term given to rapid reform of an economy, didn't capture the earthquake that Russia experienced. In 1988, 96 percent of the Russian labor force was dependent on the state for employment and almost all of the population's income came either from this source or from direct transfers from the state (pensions, child benefits, and so on).[10] By 1994, the non-state sector accounted for more than half (55.3 percent) of total employment, and 70 percent of all state assets had been privatized.[11] Over the same time frame the number of people living in poverty went from 2 percent of the population to 50 percent.[12] That meant that nearly seventy-four million people saw their income and earning power plunge in that period as they joined the ranks of the officially poor. From 1991 to 1998, Russia's GDP contracted by roughly 30 percent, wiping out many Russians' savings and precipitating a capital flight from the country of nearly $150 billion from 1992 to 1999.[13]

The numbers are staggering, but, if anything, they understate the impact that one could see on the streets. On a visit to Moscow in 1993, I again walked along the Old Arbat. But where in 1988 the atmosphere crackled with the energy and excitement of *perestroika*, this time the scene was very sad indeed. Old ladies were trying to sell broken teacups and pottery for whatever they could; men begged passersby for bread; and recently discharged soldiers—withdrawn from Eastern Europe with no place to live at home—exchanged Red Army greatcoats for a few dollars.

Who Is to Blame?

Russia's first privatization program was passed by the Supreme Soviet and signed into law by Yeltsin in 1992. It allowed managers and employees of enterprises to acquire shares in newly private companies through vouchers. Shares were also set aside for private citizens, who could buy them through banks.

To be fair, Russia faced the daunting task of privatizing 225,000 enterprises and doing so rapidly. Two well-regarded economists, Yegor Gaidar and Anatoly Chubais, with the help of foreign advisers devised a voucher scheme. It was based on a successful but much smaller effort in the Czech Republic.

The terms were extremely favorable for the insiders, who could buy up to 51 percent of the company at a discount and use the enterprise's money rather than their own. Eighty percent of firms adopted this program, which resulted in the privatization of roughly half of the companies, including three hundred of the nation's largest. The effect was immediate. When one visited these enterprises, as I did on several occasions, it was not surprising to be handed a business card. "Plant Manager" had been crossed out and the holder of the card was now the "CEO."

A particular subset of these privatizations tried to convert the Russian defense industry to civilian use. The Soviet Union's military had commanded the best resources and technology, employed the best workers and scientists, and produced the country's only globally competitive goods—military equipment. Why not use these industries as a leading edge to rebuild the economy?

Together with my Stanford colleagues, former secretary of defense William Perry and David Holloway, one of the West's leading experts on the Soviet military, I visited two of these conversion projects in 1992. The first CEO that day was explaining that his plant was adept at making really hard materials. He kept emphasizing *really hard*. It wasn't long before we understood exactly what he was saying. These workers had perfected the materials that were used to harden Soviet nuclear missile silos. Now they were trying to figure out what commercial value this could possibly have. Later that afternoon, we visited another plant where the CEO proudly displayed baby carriages and a giant food processor—made of the titanium that had been used to produce military equipment. It was surreal.

The second privatization program, though, would ultimately shift the landscape more dramatically. This program was initiated by presidential decree and not by legislation. By 1995, there were still many state-owned enterprises that needed to be privatized. Moreover, the Russian government was running out of money due to capital flight and a rapidly devaluing currency. Moscow needed a way to fund its budget. A number of individuals who had become quite wealthy in the first privatizations of banks provided loans to the government with the proviso that they would receive a stake in various companies if the money was not repaid. It was a good bet. The corrupt and secretive bidding process handed some of the country's biggest assets to these men. Boris Berezovsky and Roman Abramovich acquired oil giant Sibneft in a sweetheart deal; Vladimir Potanin bought Norilsk Nickel for $170 million, though its annual profits were $400 million, and he was named deputy prime minister; and Mikhail Khodorkovsky would acquire a controlling share of Yukos, the large oil company, for $309 million. Within a few years his personal fortune would reach as high as $15 billion.

This is how these oligarchs and many like them came to be.

Arguably, the state received the loans it needed and many of the companies were reorganized, given new management, and brought to profitability by those who acquired them. But the fire sale of Russian state assets lives on today in the consciousness of ordinary citizens and Russia's rulers, who use it to intimidate, cow, and extort loyalty from the very rich.

It is said that Vladimir Putin (a wealthy man in his own right) told the oligarchs that he had a deal for them. He would not challenge their ill-gotten gains if they stayed out of politics. Most followed the script, and when Mikhail Khodorkovsky did not, the Kremlin made an example of him, breaking up his company and jailing him for ten years. Popular jealousy of the oligarchs has been one of Putin's most potent weapons against those who are wealthy and influential enough to challenge him. In other words, it was easy to find an answer to the question "Who is to blame?"

The Russian State Is Overwhelmed

Clearly, the abrupt shift to capitalism outpaced the establishment of rule of law and institutions that could regulate against its excesses. The Russian state couldn't contain the economic effects that it had unleashed. Before long, it could no longer provide security to the population either. Organized crime became a daily fixture of life in Moscow, providing protection to small shopkeepers and oligarchs alike. And with that came a spike in violence that made the capital city feel unsafe for both citizens and visitors.

In May 1994, I got out of the car at my favorite Moscow restaurant, the Café Pushkina located on Tverskaya Street, just a few blocks from the Kremlin. All of a sudden there was a big commotion behind us. The driver said, "Oh, there is a man with a machine gun." I looked back to see two burly bodyguards, bracketing an equally burly "businessman." They were toting Czech Samovals. My escort pushed me into the restaurant, where my host suggested that we sit "away from the window." Apparently this was a common occurrence in the summer of 1994. I remember thinking that my friend Andrei seemed relatively calm.

The police could no longer control the streets, caught between the Russian mafia and rampant corruption within their own ranks. Homicides tripled from 1988 to 1994. Brazil had about the same number of people as Russia at that time, and in 1988 it had nine thousand more homicides than Russia; yet by 1994, Russia had fifteen thousand more homicides than Brazil.[14] The absolute numbers are not very high, but the spectacular nature of the crimes in Russia gave a great sense of insecurity to a population unaccustomed to random violence.

Bombings and assassinations of businessmen, journalists, and bankers added to the chaotic atmosphere. Just weeks after I stayed at the Radisson Hotel in central Moscow, the lobby nearly became a shooting gallery as special forces troops stormed in without warning to raid a suspected meeting of mafia chiefs.

The erosion of state capacity and authority didn't stop with the inability to control criminal elements. Regional and local officials took full advantage of Moscow's weakness. Anxious to reap the benefits of privatization, some of them tailored their political programs for maximum personal gain. Federalism can be a means to greater efficiency. Political and economic decentralization can be healthy. The United States is not the only country with strong regional powers: Germany, Brazil, and India all lodge considerable authority in their states.

But in Russia federalism had simply become an excuse for local leaders to do whatever they wished. This was true not only of governors but of mayors as well. The mayor of Moscow, Yuri Luzhkov, improved the city in many ways, including raising money to restore beautiful old treasures like the Cathedral of Christ the Savior. But his wife owned the real estate around many of the restoration projects and benefited greatly. These personal deals were the rule, not the exception.

Boris Yeltsin, who had once exhorted the regions to "grab as much authority as they could," would soon see the disasters that were unfolding as taxes went unpaid, decrees were ignored, and the regions prospered as the national government faltered. Beginning in 1994, he signed a series of "treaties" with different regions to try to bring order to governance. But the Russian state had been seriously wounded. The centrifugal forces that had collapsed the empire and freed Ukraine, Belarus, and the other republics of the Soviet Union seemed to be rolling back toward Moscow itself.

The country was in chaos and the Russian people could see and feel it all around them. Pensioners who were forced now to live with their children were humiliated. Soldiers sleeping in Gorky Park, having returned from Eastern Europe with nowhere to go, were humiliated. Industrial workers with no job to do were humiliated.

The Soviet Union was gone and Russia was failing. Even the symbols of the nation seemed to be trapped in purgatory. Standing on the White House lawn at the arrival ceremony for Boris Yeltsin in 1994, I listened to an unfamiliar song. I turned to a Russian diplomat and asked him if it was the new national anthem. "No," he replied, "it's just some song by Glinka." At the Olympics in 1992, the athletes of the former Soviet Union marched under the Olympic flag and stood on the podium to hear the Olympic hymn. One of the skaters said poignantly that he had trained all of his life for the moment of the gold medal ceremony. "And now I stand on the podium to hear a song I have never heard under a flag that I do not recognize," he said. In 2000, at the urging of Vladimir Putin, the Russian parliament would vote for a new national anthem: the tune from the anthem of the Soviet Union—with new words. Confusion and fear had engulfed the Russian people. They were exhausted and ready for order.

Still, with all the chaos surrounding and devouring Russia, things might have turned out differently. Democratic transitions do not succeed suddenly, and, conversely, they do not fail in one moment either. There are, in retrospect, important inflection points that might have taken a different turn.

The Third Opening: The Elections of 1993

Despite the troubles, the political system was developing in favorable ways. New political parties and coalitions dotted the landscape in 1992–93, hundreds of independent newspapers sprang up across the country, and small numbers of civil society groups began to flourish. The worsening economic situation formed the backdrop for disaffection with the government's policies. Demonstrations were commonplace and for the most part tolerated by the government. Some of democracy's scaffolding was emerging.

But at the top of the political system, constant conflict between the parliament and the president seemed to throw the new Russian state into crisis on what seemed like a daily basis. Boris Yeltsin was a mercurial figure, often bristling at challenges to his power and ideas. There were repeated fights over economic policy. At one point, in December 1992, the Congress of People's Deputies stripped Yeltsin of the extraordinary powers that they had only recently granted him and forced him to fire his prime minister.

The parliament challenged the president on political matters too, including the growing power of the republics and the nature of constitutional reform. When Yeltsin outlawed a coalition of reactionary political parties, the National Salvation Front, the Supreme Court ruled his action unconstitutional.

Yeltsin was increasingly frustrated with what he saw as interference with his efforts to overthrow old economic and political structures. In a speech to the Civic Alliance in February 1993, he said that he could no longer "tolerate the parliament's parallel government."

In a temporary truce, the president and the parliament were able to agree on a political referendum that for the moment forestalled a complete breakdown of civil order. In that vote, Yeltsin won the backing of 59 percent of the population, but 49 percent wanted new elections for parliament and the presidency.

Many Russians came to think that constitutional reform was the only answer to the clear dysfunction of the new institutions. Not surprisingly, the presidential administration and the parliamentary committee produced radically different versions of a proposed new constitution. Yeltsin wanted a strong presidency. The opposition, including his own vice president, Alexander Rutskoi, accused him of wanting a dictatorship. Yeltsin suspended Rutskoi, who took his case to the Constitutional Court.

One could imagine this tug-of-war between the president and the parliament and their invocation of the courts as a hopeful sign for democracy. It was not. While Russian citizens suffered economic ruin and the streets of Moscow grew more dangerous by the day, the politicians in Moscow, struggling over constitutional questions, seemed out of touch with the concerns of the people. Governance ground to a halt.

Yeltsin suspended the parliament. The Constitutional Court declared his decree unconstitutional. The Congress of People's Deputies voted to impeach him. And in short order, violent demonstrations rocked Moscow. After a day of rioting, Yeltsin moved to crush the rebellion with military force. Army units stormed the parliament, and Rutskoi, who had tried to surrender, was arrested for plotting a coup. The Constitutional Court was suspended. One hundred and forty people were killed in the confrontation.

It was against this backdrop of violence and confrontation that Russian voters went to the polls to elect a new parliament and vote on the constitutional referendum in December 1993. The final results were not released for two months. When they were, liberal parties had won only 34.2 percent of the vote. The parties that were a loose confederation of oppositionists to Yeltsin won 43.3 percent.

In fact, liberal parties had been unable to organize effective campaigns, instead criticizing and undermining each other. An eleventh-hour effort to present a unified bloc fell apart when the leaders of the main parties refused to cooperate. After their crushing defeat in 1993, these same leaders became dispirited and even less capable. Several parties became closely identified with single personalities, like Grigory Yavlinsky's Yabloko (which means "apple"), rather than with political platforms. The parties had no reach into the population and no real program for governing. Outside of Moscow and Saint Petersburg, these liberal forces ceased to matter at all.

The rough birth of Russia's first constitution in 1993 and the lingering animosity toward the president by parliamentarians doomed the chances for the legislative and executive branches to govern effectively. In fact, Yeltsin ruled more and more by decree, particularly on economic matters, ignoring the parliament whenever possible. For all that he had done to free the Russian people, he did little to transfer his personal standing and authority into the institution of the presidency. His rule became self-centered and erratic.

The first president of a country sets the tone for how future presidents will behave. Just imagine if George Washington had given in to the desire of many to make him king. Instead he understood that the presidency had to be something more than the person who inhabits it at any one time. Nelson Mandela refused to serve a second term to show others that the office is not meant to be a personal fiefdom. Yeltsin did not see this, acting arbitrarily with increasing frequency. This prevented the young institutions of the new Russian government from gaining strength and legitimacy as they were simply cast aside.

By the election of 1996, Yeltsin's message had become undeniably populist—a direct appeal to the street, not to democratic institutions. He criticized his own prime minister for "forgetting about people living on wages and pensions." Facing a runoff after receiving only 36 percent of the vote, Yeltsin ordered a sweeping shake-up of his government. It was as if he divorced himself from responsibility for all that was happening to his country.

The democratic opening was overshadowed too by Chechnya and the rise of terrorism in Russian cities. By 1994, the restive Muslim-majority republic in the country's unstable south had slipped into civil war. Following the collapse of peace negotiations in the fall, Yeltsin ordered the invasion of Chechnya by forty thousand federal ground forces. For twenty months the war raged, with more than five thousand Russian troops and tens of thousands of Chechens dead. The war was unpopular but tolerated. When in 1995 the militant Chechen leader Shamil Basayev took a thousand people hostage in Russia proper, the government agreed to restart peace talks. Still, from that time on, Russia could add to its list of woes terrorism at home, stemming from the suppression of the majority Muslim populations of the south. In time, Basayev would fall into bad company, training with al-Qaeda, radicalizing further, and producing calls from the Russian population for tougher measures against those hated minorities suspected of endangering the homeland.

And finally there was the matter of Boris Yeltsin's health. The president was repeatedly hospitalized, disappearing from the public eye with frightening frequency. As Russia slipped deeper and deeper into trouble, particularly during the Asian financial crisis of 1997–98, Boris Yeltsin failed to inspire confidence in his people or among leaders abroad.

In 1999, an exhausted Yeltsin named a former KGB officer, Vladimir Putin, to become his fourth prime minister in a year and a half. Then, on December 31, 1999, Yeltsin resigned, leaving Putin as Russia's president in an acting capacity. Putin was elected three months later in March 2000. Many believe that he was chosen because he alone—the former KGB colonel—was prepared to protect Yeltsin's family and its ill-gotten gains. This single act would have a dramatic effect on Russia's future. One only needs to remember that one of the other candidates to succeed Yeltsin was the late liberal hero Boris Nemtsov.

The Democratic Opening Closes

Knowing now that Vladimir Putin would become an autocrat at home and an aggressor abroad, it is hard to go back and look dispassionately at the circumstances in which he came to power. By the end of the decade of the 1990s, the Russian state needed to be rebuilt, confidence had to be restored in its leadership, and the chaos had to be ended.

The Russian people were frightened. Throughout the country's history, times of trouble had been associated with a weak state, weak leaders, and enemies that picked at the bones of its vulnerable territory. The strong state and a strong man were associated with order and safety. That would become the rallying cry of Vladimir Putin, chosen by a frail and spent Boris Yeltsin to succeed him as president.

By the time Putin took power, Yeltsin's efforts to contain unrest in Chechnya were failing. Russian cities increasingly experienced terrorist attacks from the troubled region. The origin of some of these incidents was suspicious—leading many to believe that Russian security services might have been involved. Whether it was on the basis of a pretext or indeed in response to actual terrorism, Putin's forceful actions in Chechnya were welcomed by frightened Russians and enhanced his reputation as a tough guy who would defend the country.

Putin was systematic in centralizing power after his ascendance to the presidency. On the surface, some of his reforms seem aimed simply at reversing the corrosion of state power. In 2001, the laws were amended to establish a mechanism for "federal intervention" if regional lawmakers persistently violated the Russian constitution or federal laws.[15]

Putin changed the way that members of the Federation Council were chosen, replacing governors with "senators" selected by the central government to represent the governors. Putin established the State Council as a forum for the governors, but it was now purely advisory. And in 2004, new legislation created seven federal jurisdictional districts and placed those under super governors, all appointed by the Kremlin.

These moves taken together might have been seen as a way to rein in out-of-control regional leaders and put Moscow back in the game. But five of the seven new regional governors had, like

Putin, made their careers in the KGB or armed services. This began the ascendancy of the *siloviki* ("powerful")—men who had largely come from the same institutions: the security services.

Meanwhile, the raging war in Chechnya, which had resumed in 1999, continued to produce violence in Russian cities. The calls for a crackdown reached a crescendo in September 2004 after an attack on a kindergarten at Beslan. More than 150 children were slaughtered and the population demanded an answer. Putin drew upon the anger and the not too thinly disguised racism against those from the Caucasus in order to solidify the Kremlin's assault on the independence of the regions.

As Moscow's grip tightened, tax reforms after 2005 sealed the fate of healthy federalism, making the regions dependent on a revenue-sharing formula devised annually in the capital. Putin would then take a final step in recentralizing power over the regions, abolishing the election of governors and appointing them in Moscow. But this decision appeared to be a bridge too far and was so unpopular that then-president Dmitry Medvedev reversed course in 2012 and reinstated direct elections of governors. That lasted one year. In 2013, Putin returned to the presidency and reversed Medvedev, cynically citing concerns for the well-being of minorities in the regions.

The genius of these steps was that they were rooted in a certain reality: The regions had taken advantage of Moscow's weakness, and the imbalance between the center and the periphery had to be addressed. The Kremlin, though, blasted through an equilibrium that might have created sustainable federalism and concentrated power again in the center—indeed, in the hands of the president himself.

All other nascent institutions of Russian democracy were crushed in their cribs one by one. The parliament was transformed from a raucous and admittedly ineffective legislature to the president's rubber stamp. The 2003 election reforms banned parties from forming election blocs to receive seats in the State Duma (the lower house), reduced the minimum number of parties to be represented in that chamber from four to two, and increased the financial requirements for the formation of parties. Independent liberal parties that had enjoyed some popularity in the 1990s found themselves under attack after 2000 and by the middle of the decade unable even to register.

By the time Putin became president in 2000, the "right forces," meaning liberals, were already disorganized, fighting among themselves and ill-suited to challenge the emerging authoritarianism at the center. Political parties continued to exist, but in time, only those that were loyal to the president gained access to the government-controlled media, particularly television.

And Putin made certain that the media would help to doom political opposition. During the 1990s there were hundreds of independent newspapers, ranging from responsible ones, like *Vremya* (the Times), to simple scandal sheets. The press was most assuredly free with criticism of the government, reporting on official corruption and open debate about Russia's political future. The print media was largely untouched well into the first decade of Putin's presidency. That is because he concentrated first on the electronic media, perhaps realizing its greater reach and impact.

Immediately after the collapse of the Soviet Union, independent television stations, funded by the newly rich, sprang up across the airwaves. Three outlets had national reach—RTR, which was always state-controlled; and ORT and NTV, owned, respectively, by oligarchs Boris Berezovsky and Vladimir Aleksandrovich Gusinsky. In a period spanning about five years, Putin hounded both men with trumped-up criminal charges until Berezovsky fled and Gusinsky was convicted of tax evasion and forced to sell his station and his two independent newspapers as well, *Itogi* (Issues) and *Sevodnya* (Today).

The Kremlin's policies toward the independent press were becoming more and more repressive. And journalists were increasingly targeted for harassment and, in some sad and celebrated cases, death.

Anna Politkovskaya, for example, had refused to be intimidated in her efforts to bring the truth about the Chechen wars to the Russian people. She bravely traveled to the war-torn region repeatedly to chronicle the abuses of the Russian military there. Even after she was poisoned in 2004 while reporting on events in Beslan, she refused to quit. "We are hurtling back into a Soviet abyss, into an information vacuum that spells death from our own ignorance," she declared after that attack on her life.

On October 7, 2006, she was murdered in her Moscow apartment. Two weeks later, I was in Moscow for diplomatic meetings. I started the day, though, in a hotel conference room where Politkovskaya's son, Ilya, and several of her colleagues from *Novaya Gazeta* were gathered. No words seem adequate at times like that. The sense of deep grief and anguish was overwhelming. I promised the support of the U.S. government in pressing the Russian government to find her killer. But of course

I knew—as did her colleagues—that the Kremlin had no interest in doing so.

That moment felt to me like a watershed in Russia's democratic transition. The killing of a celebrated journalist was only part of the story. There was something even more dispiriting—the looks of resignation and desperation on the faces of the mostly young journalists in that room. They had lost faith in a democratic future for Russia. You could feel it.

Still, for a brief time another medium—the Internet—seemed poised to escape the Kremlin's control. On a subsequent trip to Moscow, I asked our ambassador to arrange a meeting with some of Russia's young entrepreneurs and businesspeople. Before leaving for Spasso House (the U.S. residence), I was watching television in my hotel room, something that I always did immediately upon touching down in order to activate my "Russian ear." I knew that the electronic media had been under siege, but I was not prepared for what I saw. The news was mostly a celebration of the exploits of Vladimir Putin, with some favorable economic news thrown in for good measure. Frankly, it looked a great deal like Soviet TV programming when I was a graduate student in 1979. There were, to be sure, popular Western-style programs that would not have been possible in the Soviet era: American shows like *The Sopranos* and *Friends*; *Klub Vesyólykh i Nakhódchivykh* (Club of the Funny and Inventive), a competitive comedy show that had been banned by Soviet censors; singing contests and documentaries about expensive automobiles. But the news was pretty close to pure propaganda.

At the session with the young Russians later that day, I

brought up the state of television. One young man stopped me. "Let me tell you what you saw on the news," he said. "The first story was about the great man [Putin]. The second about whatever successor to the great man is in favor today." I understood the reference. The presidential "elections" were about a year away and everyone knew that Putin would choose either Dmitry Medvedev or Defense Minister Sergei Ivanov. "The third story," he continued, "was about whatever innocent people you Americans killed today. And the fourth—the amazingly good state of agriculture."

"That's about it. Doesn't that trouble you?" I asked.

"No," he replied.

"Who watches television?"

"My friends and I all get our news from the Internet." Everyone nodded in agreement.

To the degree that the Internet was a safe haven for open expression in 2007, it didn't last. When Vladimir Putin returned to the presidency in 2012, he completed the extermination of media outlets that might challenge him. Bloggers like Alexei Navalny who used the Web to organize politically were arrested. Other reformist websites first experienced outages and then were shut down altogether. In July 2012 the Duma passed a law allowing the government to create a list of websites that were to be blocked without any mechanism of appeal. While the measure was portrayed as intended to block pornography and extremist content, it silenced legitimate websites. In 2014, Vkontakte (VK), known as the Facebook of Russia, came under the control of Putin's allies. The sin of VK had been its use as a vehicle to organize anti-Putin rallies during the elections. Its young founder, Pavel Durov, was forced to step down, and in 2015 he left the country.

Step by step, young institutions that might have sustained Russian democracy disappeared—independent regional leaders, the free press, and what was left of a working legislature after Yeltsin's assault on it. The remnants of an independent judiciary disappeared in the political prosecutions of oligarchs that Putin targeted and laws that brought appointments to the courts, all the way up to the Supreme Court, under the Kremlin's control. The last vestige of an incipient democracy was a civil society that fought the swing toward authoritarianism more valiantly than liberal politicians were ever able to do.

Many of the NGOs were well funded by outside private sources and Western governments, including the United States through USAID. The National Endowment for Democracy is a private organization with a board made up of esteemed citizens but it does receive U.S. government funding. Together with its European counterparts, it helped to sustain these young Russian institutions. The leaders traveled abroad for conferences and their names were well known in the international community that advocated publicly for them.

At home, these organizations were popular and noted for doing good works. For instance, on one of my trips I met an extraordinary woman, Svetlana Kotova, whose own limited sight led her to appeal to the conscience of the country on behalf of people with disabilities. Everyone knew that in Soviet times, when society idolized the perfect Soviet man, the disabled were treated like trash—literally swept off the streets by the police. Kotova's compassionate outcry to overcome this history was so popular that even Putin tried to ride her coattails, inviting her to hold a summit on the disabled at the Kremlin in 2005.

But eventually the Duma passed laws requiring NGOs to register and to disclose foreign funding. Soon the law made it illegal to receive resources from abroad under the guise of protecting the national security of the country. Hundreds of the organizations dried up, and the few that remained endured prosecutors' charges and police raids. Like every authoritarian, Putin knew that allowing citizens to organize in private space had political ramifications no matter how compelling the social good. With the demise of civil society, the destruction of the nascent institutions of democracy was complete.

The events that followed the ascendance of Vladimir Putin and transpired over roughly fifteen years raise a disturbing question: Is it really possible that one man could dismantle the institutional basis for democracy in his country in so short a time span? We have seen how the conditions of the Soviet Union's collapse and the chaos that unfolded laid the groundwork for the rise of authoritarian government in Russia. But unlike Saddam Hussein or the Kim dynasty in North Korea, Putin does not rule as an absolute tyrant. Rather, he skillfully constructed and nurtured an alternative institutional basis from which to undermine liberal change.

In today's interconnected world, the creeping and subtle authoritarianism of illiberal elected leaders is a greater threat to democracy than if they were to crush it with tanks in the city square. Vladimir Putin uses just enough repression to cow the population but not too much so that blood runs in the streets. And he enjoys a significant hold on the loyalty of enough of his citizens to sustain his power.

While it is hard in Putin's Russia to know how reliable polls are that show him to be popular at the level of 70 percent or better, there is no doubt that he has a loyal base of support. When Putin came to power in 2000, his support was remarkably broad, reflecting roughly the demographics of the country. His supporters spanned all age groups, income brackets, and levels of education. Today, his most ardent support comes from rural voters, older people, the military, and those middle-class citizens who are dependent on the state for their income. And Putin has taken care of them with largesse ranging from enhanced pensions to spending on infrastructure projects outside of the cities in his most reliable districts.

Indeed, he is regarded as the leader who fixed a broken pension system. More than 35 percent of the country's electorate is composed of pensioners (Russia is an aging country with low birth rates and high morbidity and mortality). In the 1990s, pension income dropped by as much as 40 percent, and simply receiving a check had become an unreliable waiting game. In 2002, Putin set repairing the system as one of his chief goals, and despite economic arguments to the contrary, he refused to raise the generously low retirement age: fifty-five for women and sixty for men. Not surprisingly, this has endeared him to the old.

Additionally, Putin's opposition is largely based in Moscow. In fact, in the election of 2012, the one district that he did not win was the capital. But rural voters love him, and it is in those districts that his image, burnished by favorable stories on state television, is most heroic. Putin maintains contact with these voters through his selection of presidential envoys to each federal region.

The story of Igor Kholmanskikh illustrates the point. In the span of just a few months, Kholmanskikh went from being an unknown tank factory worker in the Ural Mountains to Putin's presidential envoy to the region. He first appeared on the national scene during one of Putin's televised call-in shows in the run-up to the 2012 presidential election, ridiculing anti-Putin protesters in Moscow and offering to bring his crew of factory workers to help the police "defend stability." Putin later featured him at campaign rallies as the epitome of the Russian worker, and Kholmanskikh's efforts on Putin's behalf were duly rewarded. After Putin's return to the presidency, Kholmanskikh was appointed his personal envoy to the Ural Mountain region, becoming the first such envoy to serve without any prior government or political experience.

This story bears a strong resemblance to the folklore of an era long past. Heroic laborers who through hard work and grit industrialized the country and farmed the land have long been admired, whether in Russia or in the Soviet Union. Their towns have changed little in decades—they are rough and polluted rust belts. Their isolated villages and farms would look at home in the late nineteenth century. When the president needs support, his presidential envoys find it easy to arrange it for him far from the glittering streets of the country's cosmopolitan cities.

While there is a popular base for Putin, his more important political allies are those oligarchs whom he has courted and sometimes coerced into loyalty, and the men of the security services—the *siloviki*—who share his KGB upbringing and disdain for Russia's weakness after the Soviet Union's collapse. Fueled by oil wealth, personal fortunes, and the power of the state, this syndicate really runs Russia. It is hard to tell whether Putin is just first among equals or something more. But slowly, the men who were once members of the prestigious First Directorate of the KGB in Soviet times and served together in espionage across the world have become the dominant personalities in modern-day Russia.

They share too a suspicious, almost xenophobic view of the outside world. And it is this that has served to unify Russia's authoritarian turn at home with an aggressive foreign policy abroad, aimed at redressing the "tragedy," as Putin called it, of the Soviet Union's demise.

"Ukraine Is a Made-Up Country"

It had been a difficult NATO summit in Bucharest. In President Bush's last year in office, we hoped to solidify the commitment of the alliance to Eastern Europe. The expansion of NATO to Poland, Hungary, the Czech Republic, and then all the way to the Baltic states had been relatively seamless—a joint project of the Clinton and Bush administrations. The new members were energetic, devoted to the principles on which the alliance had been founded—the defense of democracy and liberty in Europe and beyond. For most of Europe and even the United States, the other purpose of NATO—keeping the Soviet Union or now Russia at bay—had long since lost salience. We had really come to believe that the Cold War was over, Europe was whole, free, and at peace, and even if they didn't like the outcome, the men in the Kremlin were resigned to it. It turns out they were not.

With every round of NATO enlargement, Moscow felt the pain of lost influence. NATO tried to extend a hand of friendship to Russia. The creation of a NATO-Russia Council in 2002 was intended to show the Kremlin that the alliance was no longer trapped in Cold War thinking.

Russia's first ambassador to the council spoke neither English nor French. He was apparently not unpleasant, but he was worthless as a diplomatic link between East and West. A few years later the Russians sent one of their most disagreeable officials, the head of a nationalist political party, to be ambassador to NATO. Dmitry Rogozin made it clear that he had no desire to be in Brussels nor any plans to cooperate on just about anything. One had to conclude that Moscow had no intention of making the council work.

To be fair, the personal dynamics in the meetings of the council were complicated and often hard. After years of resentment of their treatment at the hands of Moscow, the new Central European members didn't hesitate to remind the Russians that they had lost the Cold War. "Welcome to NATO, Sergei," the Polish foreign minister said to the Russian foreign minister. "Yes, you are always welcome to visit the alliance," the Czech or Romanian would say, in a tone dripping with sarcasm. I always found myself a little embarrassed by the whole thing, but forty-five years of pent-up resentment is hard to wash away.

Russia's tolerance for NATO expansion—and, it turns out, Germany's—finally reached its limit at the NATO summit in Bucharest in 2008. The elected and pro-Western governments of Ukraine and Georgia wanted to be admitted to the Membership Action Plan (MAP). MAP was not membership but a kind of incubator status for countries that needed to make major political and military reforms in order to fulfill the requirements of NATO membership. There was nothing automatic about acceptance in the alliance, and it took a long time. Albania had waited ten years after being accepted into MAP to join the alliance.

Still, for several members of NATO, particularly Germany, launching Ukraine and Georgia on this path was unacceptable. They argued that the alliance should not take on the defense of corrupt, unstable new governments whose territory was riddled with ethnic conflicts and border disputes. The United States and the new East European members argued that the purpose of MAP was to overcome these difficulties. Nothing was guaranteed for membership.

After difficult negotiations—at one point among Chancellor Angela Merkel, the East Europeans, and me—we came up with a communiqué that affirmed NATO's open door and said that Ukraine and Georgia would become members someday. They were denied MAP for the moment, but it kept their hopes alive. The East Europeans were unhappy but resigned to the decision. A key fissure was exposed nonetheless. Poland, the Czech Republic, the Balts, and others reasoned that Moscow still needed to be deterred. A day would come, they believed, when the alliance would again have to resist Russian aggression. That was not the view of Germany.

Though President Bush wanted Ukraine and Georgia to be granted MAP, we were all aware that it would have created an awkward situation. Vladimir Putin had been invited to a meeting of the NATO-Russia Council on the last day of the summit.

He had been outspoken in his opposition to any further "expansion" of NATO by any means, including MAP. The Russians had begun to talk in the language of the past about encirclement and threats to their security. The communiqué allowed Putin to come to the meeting (he would likely not have come had MAP been granted). It also allowed President Bush to go ahead with the visit to Sochi for his last meeting with Putin, who was stepping down as president as well. It was one of those moments when you breathed a sigh of relief, even if the outcome didn't feel quite right.

Putin walked into the room, greeted everyone, and sat down. At the beginning, his speech sounded almost perfunctory and a bit valedictory. I was listening in Russian because I always found that interpreters didn't quite get Putin's harsh and combative tone. All of a sudden, I thought that my Russian was failing, and so I started going back and forth between the English translation and the Russian. *Did he really just say that Ukraine was a made-up country?* Yes, he did. There it was, a declaration that was so Soviet, or actually tsarist, that I couldn't believe my ears.

We know now that from the time of the Soviet Union's breakup, Vladimir Putin mourned the collapse of empire and looked for an opportunity to return the Russian people to greatness. When he said that the collapse of the Soviet Union was the greatest geopolitical tragedy of the twentieth century (quite a statement for a country that lost twenty-five million people in World War II) he added a rationale: because twenty-five million Russians had been "orphaned" in other newly independent countries. There were ethnic Russians in the Baltic states, Poland, Kazakhstan, Ukraine, and Georgia. Putin has taken it as his historic duty to unite them and "protect" them.

This historical messianism is dangerous. Already in 2008 when Russia invaded Georgia, one of the justifications was protection of the Russian populations in Abkhazia and South Ossetia. Of course the real cause was Putin's disdain for the pro-Western democratically elected government of Mikheil Saakashvili. This was followed by the annexation of Crimea in 2014, and the creeping occupation of eastern Ukraine, setting Putin's Russia against Europe and the United States.[16] But these acts of aggression have solidified his popularity at home. In 2013, Putin's standing was at a low point—still well above 60 percent, but headed downward. His expensive Sochi Olympic adventure had turned out to be not very popular.

The annexation of Crimea propelled Putin to new highs. What most of the world saw as an outright violation of international law—countries don't annex the territory of their neighbors in the twenty-first century—Russians saw as returning the territory to its rightful home. In their version of events, Catherine the Great conquered Crimea in 1783; the idiot Nikita Khrushchev gave it to Ukraine as a gift for three hundred years of Russian-Ukrainian friendship in 1954; when Ukraine became independent in 1991, Kiev didn't give it back. Vladimir Putin set all of that right. Crimea was once Russian, and it was Russian again.

Putin has played the politics of Russian identity brilliantly. The problem is that Russia has rarely been a defined geographic entity; it is more like a tide that has gone deep into Europe when it is powerful and receded to the outskirts of Moscow when it is weak. Putin has relied on this sense of vulnerability to build a narrative of a West that takes advantage of Russia, does not accord it respect, and encircles it. He has employed raw nationalism to remind the Russian people that they are great and deserving of the respect that, in his narrative, they have been denied. Popular culture, television, and movies have been harnessed to build images of great (mostly blond) Slavs—soldiers, farmers, workers who are the Russian ideal type. And he has clothed them in the garments of religious orthodoxy and conservatism—singling out gay people, ethnic minorities (who are often branded as extremists), and female rock stars whose profane language offends many.

Sergei Ivanov, Putin's former chief of staff and once a candidate to succeed him as president, was charged with writing a kind of manifesto to guide Russia's development. The document emphasizes Russia's uniqueness—neither European nor Asian—and warns that the Russian soul is weakened by Western ideas of tolerance and multiculturalism. It is a dark and insecure take on who the Russians are and what is needed to sustain them. One has to wonder if this is really where Russia is going. If it is, there are tough times ahead for a creative and brilliant people whose political choices have always managed to retard the country's progress and driven so many of its best and brightest to simply give up and leave.

Does It Really Have to Be This Way?

Russia's failed experiment with democracy is an undeniably sad story for a people whose culture and intellectual life rivals the world's great civilizations. It begs the question of whether there might have been an alternative path, or perhaps whether there is still a different road ahead for Russia. Will there be another democratic opening?

Putin's authoritarianism at home and aggressiveness abroad remind us that a great deal is at stake not just for the Russians but for the entire world in the answer to that question. Theoretically, the talented and creative Russian people, long known for their prowess in mathematics and science, should be leading the knowledge-based revolution. There is no reason that the economy has to be dependent on commodities—oil, gas, and minerals—for more than 70 percent of its exports. Consider this: When was the last time you bought a consumer product made in Russia?

For a brief moment in the interregnum when Putin stepped down as president and Dmitry Medvedev succeeded him, it looked as if Russia might try to take a different course. Medvedev came to power saying bluntly that Russia should not be a nineteenth-century extractive industries economy. He visited the great technology centers of the world in search of ideas to build a Russian Silicon Valley.

In June 2010, he visited the actual Silicon Valley. I received a call from President Obama informing me that Medvedev wanted to come to Stanford. The president asked me to make certain it was a good visit. Medvedev turned up in blue jeans and an Armani jacket and read his speech from an iPad. He completely looked the part of a young, hip entrepreneur.

After several hours in Silicon Valley visiting companies like Google and Facebook, Medvedev and I sat down with a few others to talk. Listening to venture capitalists, engineers, and business leaders clearly had an effect on him. "I get it," he said. "It is an ecosystem." One sensed some sadness in the realization that what he had seen in Palo Alto could not easily be transported to Russia. But he tried, supporting the building of Skolkovo, touted as Russia's high-tech hub.

I visited Skolkovo the next year. Palo Alto it was not. The huge, several-stories-high modern-style campus outside Moscow was a kind of metaphor for Russia's notions of innovation. It was big, centralized, and already incredibly bureaucratic. The Kremlin told the scientists and engineers that they should innovate but almost immediately started dictating what that would mean. Not surprisingly, Skolkovo has produced little and is now under constant criticism from conservatives who never liked the effort. The question is whether the prosecutors will soon follow.

Some efforts have fared better, like the state-owned venture fund Rosnano. Founded to invest in nanotechnology and its applications, the fund is headed by Anatoly Chubais, a wily veteran of Soviet and Russian politics and perhaps a little more attuned at how to maintain support. And there are private equity funds (that are mostly private), such as DST and software companies like Yandex, that are well respected internationally for their competence and talent. But it is not clear that this young Russian technology sector can survive the exigencies of the security state and the country's isolation from the international economy due to Ukraine-related sanctions.

The best hope for a different Russia probably rests with those who are engaged in the tech sector. They would seem to be a natural constituency for a more liberal political direction. And they are not alone. In the two decades since the collapse of the

Soviet Union, Russians have studied abroad in American and European universities, business schools, and law schools. They have worked in Western firms and still do. These mostly young people should be the vanguard of a movement to give Russia another chance at democracy.

Moreover, they should be able to garner support from a middle class that has become accustomed to travel, imported goods, and personal freedoms unmatched in Russia's history. These people hold thirty-year mortgages on their apartments, buy their furniture at IKEA, and spoil their children at McDonald's.

On the other hand, Putin counts on the *siloviki* and the erosion of democratic institutions to prevent the rise of opposition that might rally these constituencies that are not dependent on him. He probably counted too on the high price of oil to fund the largesse that he doles out so that Russians have a sense of well-being.

In this regard, there is a prevailing myth in the country about the Putin years that bears watching. He undeniably brought stability and order to a people who were hungry for it. But the prosperity that Russians have enjoyed was almost totally the result of the bonanza of oil and commodities prices and a sensible decision to put money away in reserves for turbulent economic weather.

Now, with the price of oil at half of the $103 a barrel needed to sustain the Russian budget, the strategy has fallen on hard times. There are reports of strikes and riots among workers in the rural Russian heartland on which Putin relies for support. Inflation is once again eating away at the salaries and pensions of ordinary Russians. Putin's claim to have made Russians not just more secure but also more prosperous is beginning to ring hollow.

Yet it is hard to imagine internal opposition to Putin that is significant enough to unseat him. For a brief moment in December 2011 and the winter of 2012, people again took to the streets to protest the creeping authoritarianism in their country. It didn't last. Putin brutally crushed the dissent, jailed his opponents, and was elected once again to the presidency in a process widely criticized as fraudulent. With the closing of that window for democracy in Russia, Putin cemented his rule. If he fulfills all of the terms available to him, he could be president of Russia until 2024.

Some hope that those around him, the *siloviki*, will start to see Putin's policies as antagonistic to their interests. The theory is that in a den of thieves, there is no trust and no friendship, only self-interest. In part, the sanctions against those in his inner circle are aimed at provoking splits among the hard men of the Kremlin. Perhaps. But if you are going to challenge the king, you had better kill him. It is more likely that the fates of these men are so inextricably woven together that no one will risk breaking ranks.

Recently, Putin has begun replacing some high-profile members of the *siloviki*. Sergei Ivanov, the man long thought to be closest to him, was fired as chief of staff. Younger men more beholden to the president are being promoted to important security and political posts.

If he cannot be challenged by the *siloviki*, can Putin himself experience a Gorbachev-like epiphany and reverse course? That is hard to imagine. He is too personally identified with the

Russian nationalist, conservative course on which he launched his country. And he believes in it.

One of my last meetings with him at the Kremlin was not long before the invasion of Georgia in the summer of 2008. It was "one on one," meaning just the two of us and an interpreter. "You know us, Condi," he began. (Somehow, Putin rather liked me, I think. When I became secretary of state he told me that it was good to have a Russian specialist in that role. "Now the relationship will get the attention it deserves," he said.)

Yet whenever he began, "You know us, Condi," I could sense that something was coming that would be difficult to swallow. This particular time, I was right. "Russians have always been at their best when they have been ruled by great men. Peter the Great, Alexander II. Russia needs a strong hand," he said. I resisted the temptation to ask if Vladimir the Great was in that succession. But I suspect that is exactly what he had in mind.

And now he is acting it out. He presents himself as a strong, conservative ruler who has the backing of the Orthodox Church. He has the support of the salt-of-the-earth people—soldiers, workers, and farmers. Intellectuals do not love him but they are fearful of crossing him. He has a security apparatus that enforces his arbitrary application of the law. And the motherland (or *Rodina*, as Russians call it) is once again secure.

There thus isn't much room for the controlled chaos that is democracy in this version of Great Russia. But authoritarian systems are brittle, and the good news for Russia is that there is an educated and sophisticated population in waiting should an opportunity for democracy come.

Russians are different than they were before Gorbachev.

They are accustomed to travel, study abroad, and enjoy the better things in life. Surely a return to the fearful and isolated lives of their parents and grandparents holds no allure for them.

The problem is that the interests of these elements of the Russian population have found no institutionalized way to express their views, mobilize around particular reforms, and seek political change. Even before Putin's assault on civil society, the sector was small—aimed at a few social issues, but lacking political direction. Political parties have failed to excite the passions of the citizenry and to penetrate their political consciousness or command their active participation. Russia is a classic case of new political institutions being created but divorced entirely from the life of the people and the society. The Russian people never came to own their institutions, trust them, use them, or give them legitimacy. And their leaders gave them little reason to do so. The rule of law, an independent judiciary, and political parties that connect to the people have all been ephemeral in post-Soviet Russia.

Nor is there certainty that a challenge to Putin's rule would come from these "enlightened" forces. There is an undercurrent of nativism and conservatism in the Russian population that can be tapped by the right leader. The Orthodox Church remains a bulwark of reactionary views and political influence.

If Russia gets another chance to move toward democracy, it will need institutions that can connect the population to politics and channel the violent energy of radical change. The failure to do that until now is the essence of the story of Russia's failed democratic experiment.

Chapter 3

MARTIAL LAW AND THE ORIGINS OF POLISH DEMOCRACY

I admit to having always had a soft spot in my heart for Poland. Most students of Eastern Europe of my generation do. Throughout the Cold War, the Poles more than any other nation maintained their fiery nationalism and hatred of communism. Moscow was never able to crush their spirit.

They were rewarded for their steadfastness in 1989 when Solidarity led them to freedom. Now, standing in the courtyard of the Presidential Palace in 2001, I felt a tremendous surge of emotion as I witnessed what Poland had become.

We were in Warsaw for President Bush's state visit. During the arrival ceremony we listened, as was customary, to the playing of the American and Polish national anthems. Then the flags were raised—the Stars and Stripes and the red and white horizontal bars of Poland. The NATO banner stood alongside them. I was overwhelmed and tears flowed freely down my face.

Poland was now an American ally in a Europe that was finally whole, free, and at peace.

A few minutes later, we watched as Polish troops paraded in front of the president to honor him. They were goose-stepping in the tradition of the armies of the Warsaw Pact. As each row passed, heads tilted to the side—also a feature of Soviet bloc armies—the president saluted the troops of the NATO alliance, who looked more at home in their past than in the present. I chuckled to myself and pointed it out to a couple of others standing nearby. No one else seemed to get the irony. And, of course, it didn't matter. Poland was now a reliable ally and a stable democracy, even if some of its military traditions needed reform.

The Long Road to a Free Poland

Poland, perhaps more than any other country, exemplified the tragedy of Europe's division after World War II. It had always been the most restive member of the Soviet bloc. Passionate nationalism, deep Catholicism, and fierce if sometimes passive resistance to Moscow's dominance always made the Poles, well, difficult.

The hostility between the Russian and the Polish peoples was long-standing, driven by wars and political settlements that continually altered the borders between them over centuries. Poland sometimes had the upper hand, even installing a Polish prince as tsar during times of Russian weakness in the early

1600s. When Russia eventually emerged stronger under the Romanov dynasty, it retaliated by taking Polish territory and forcibly integrating large chunks of it into the Russian Empire. Back and forth it went, sealing a historical narrative of distrust and animosity.

The modern version of this instability grew out of the events leading to the start of World War II. In 1932, Poland signed a nonaggression pact with Josef Stalin's Soviet Union, and two years later did the same with Nazi Germany. But the pacts were not honored, and in 1939, Poland was invaded from the west by Germany and from the east by the Soviet Union. Years of brutality against the population ensued, mostly at the hands of the Germans. But the Soviet Union did its part. In one of the most infamous incidents, twenty-two thousand Polish army officers and civil servants were massacred near the Katyn Forest region in Russia. The Soviets attributed the crime to the Nazis. But every Pole knew what Mikhail Gorbachev would finally admit in 1990, that the Katyn massacre had been perpetrated by the Soviet secret police.

Despite the brutality and the long odds, the Polish resistance fought gamely against the Nazis, even taking control of Warsaw in August 1944. The Nazis retook the capital in October and burned the city to the ground, rounding up and executing ordinary citizens and resistance fighters alike. Soviet forces were marching rapidly westward at the time but did not reach the city in time to prevent the German massacre. Or, many believe, the Red Army *chose* to wait, condemning the population to Nazi atrocities and making easier the pacification of the population upon "liberation." The Soviets took Warsaw in January 1945 and the rest of Poland by March.

When the final peace settlement was sealed at Potsdam between the victorious Allies a few months later, the facts on the ground in Poland favored Stalin. The Western Allies tried to insist on free elections, but the fate of Poland was sealed. In 1947, Soviet-sponsored "elections" were won by Bolesław Bierut, who quickly declared that Poland had become the Communist People's Republic of Poland. In 1955, Poland became a founding member of the Soviet military alliance, the Warsaw Pact. Its integration into the Soviet bloc was now complete.

Yet, for the next three decades, Poland remained a thorn in the Kremlin's side, constantly producing crises between the Polish people and the communist rulers. The only tool that the party could use was to bring relative prosperity to the population. It did so, but largely by borrowing money from Western Europe and the United States. By 1970, that strategy began to unravel as loans came due and the real economy began to shrink. Strikes and food riots broke out in Gdańsk in December, leading to many deaths when the authorities used force to restore order.

Fearing for stability, the West continued to ply Poland with loans, forgiving some, rescheduling others, and allowing the country to continue to build up debt. But by 1980 the country owed more than $18 billion, almost as much as its entire GDP. Foreign sources of funding were slowly drying up and the largesse that had kept wages high was unsustainable. Depressed wages and soaring prices for basic goods—up 60 percent or more on certain items—fueled protests across the country.

Now the party was out of money and face-to-face with a restive and angry population.

Throughout the summer of 1980, strikes and work stoppages multiplied. The government reacted with wage increases that it could not afford, but even that did not contain the "rolling" labor actions that were paralyzing the country. When eighty thousand workers joined a strike in Lublin, the army had to be called in to maintain basic services.

Then the regime made a fatal mistake in Gdańsk, long the hotbed of worker activism at the ironically named Lenin Shipyard. Anna Walentynowicz, a popular crane operator, was fired five months before her retirement. Led by Bogdan Borusewicz and an electrician named Lech Wałęsa, the Gdańsk shipyard workers began striking. Within days, two hundred factories had joined the strike committee, setting out demands and insisting on the right to have independent trade unions and to strike. As the labor actions spread, the government tried intimidation first, arresting leaders of the dissident organizations and declaring that the strikes were political, not just economic. But the chaos continued, and on August 24 the communist government agreed to negotiate.

The Gdańsk Agreement of August 31 contained breathtaking concessions. In addition to allowing independent trade unions, it pledged new legislation allowing the right to strike without reprisals. It also called for greater safeguards for press freedoms, increases in pay, and improved working conditions. Employees would be allowed to take Saturdays off, and Sunday mass would be broadcast into workplaces over loudspeakers. The agreement was meant to give the communist government breathing room. The hard-line but incompetent premier, Edward Gierek, was dismissed. His successor, Stanisław Kania, promised to honor the agreements, noting ominously, however, that "antisocialist elements" were turning the country's problems to their own purpose. We know now that at the same time these agreements were struck, the National Defense Committee was developing an action plan for the implementation of martial law.

Still, the government had shown weakness and the newly empowered labor unions were not about to relieve the pressure. A single national labor organization was formed at a meeting in Gdańsk on September 17, and just to drive home the point, a one-hour work stoppage, a "warning strike," paralyzed the country again.

The history of what transpired after that is murky and there are competing versions of Poland's road to martial law. Did Polish communist leaders declare the state of emergency to preempt a Soviet invasion? Or did the Poles themselves simply decide to put an end to domestic unrest?

Clearly, the rise of an independent trade union, a key element of a potentially independent civil society, got the dreaded attention of Moscow. Andrei Gromyko, the Soviet foreign minister, reportedly said that "we simply cannot and must not lose Poland." The implication was, of course, that if the Polish government was too weak or too stupid to act, Moscow might have to do so in its stead.

And it was easy to see that the Communist Party of Poland was in chaos at every level. The Party's first secretaries in eighteen of forty-nine provinces were ousted on November 22. A few days later, the governments across Eastern Europe began issuing denunciations of the developments in Poland. This was reminiscent of the rhetoric employed by Warsaw Pact states against the regime of Alexander Dubček in Prague in 1968 that was seen as too compliant and insufficiently tough to defend party control.

The United States was sensing too that a repeat of the invasion of Czechoslovakia might be in the offing. President Carter sent a hotline message to Brezhnev saying that the United States would not exploit the issue but warning against Soviet action. When the Warsaw Pact convened an extraordinary meeting in Moscow on how to deal with the crisis, the ground was clearly being laid for intervention. Reportedly, the Polish leaders told Soviet leaders at that meeting that they would prevent a change to the constitutional order by whatever means necessary. They were trying to buy time to solve the crisis themselves.

But the troubles did not abate. Indeed, before the ink could dry on one agreement between the government and the unions, it would break down, only to be followed by another pact, and another. Perhaps to bring order, but more likely to prepare for the army's intervention, General Wojciech Jaruzelski was appointed prime minister. Ross Johnson of the Rand Corporation and one of America's best experts on Poland noted that there was a kind of creeping coup. "Every day another ministry falls under the control of a general," he told me.

The government, though, seemed to be torn between a desire to end the crisis by accommodation and increasing pressure to end the insurgency by force. The plans for a state of emergency continued to mature and harassment of Solidarity leaders accelerated. And yet on March 30, 1981, the Polish government reached an agreement with Solidarity and secured a promise from Lech Wałęsa to postpone the general strike scheduled for the next day. The political events and efforts at compromise were unfolding against a backdrop of increasing chaos.

The same indecision that characterized the party leadership was evident within Solidarity as well. Some members of the union argued for cooperation with what they saw as an increasingly compliant government. Others, though, believed that the communists could not be trusted and pressed for doubling down on confrontation.

The West too seemed uncertain of what to do. Hoping to avoid the complete breakdown of order in Poland, Western governments agreed to allow more time for the repayment of billions of dollars in Polish debts.

The Communist Party continued to waver as the crises worsened, sending contradictory signals and indeed experiencing internal radicalization not unlike that challenging the leadership of Solidarity. At the end of an Extraordinary Plenum of the party in July 1981, only four of the previously selected eleven members of the Politburo remained. Jaruzelski was among those selected to remain.

By the fall, it was clear that neither the economic nor the political crises were abating. Solidarity had moved well beyond the agenda of workers' economic rights to an avowedly political agenda, calling in September for free elections at the local and national levels. Everyone in the country seemed to know that martial law was being prepared and becoming more likely. But Solidarity was now unwilling to pull back. And the leadership could likely not have done so in any case. Even more radical elements were emerging. A group calling itself the "Self-Governing Republic Clubs—Freedom, Justice, and Independence" announced on November 30 that it would no longer agree to "one more attempt to preserve the monopoly of a narrow elite for party power."[1] That attack on the monopoly of power of the Communist Party was likely the last straw for Warsaw and certainly for Moscow.

The sense that the country was reaching a point of no return came to a crescendo in the first half of December. Comments by Lech Wałęsa were leaked and broadcast nationwide. In them, he advocated for confrontation with the regime. He would say that the remarks were taken out of context, but now the hardest-line elements had what they needed: "evidence" that Solidarity was interested in the revolutionary overthrow of the communist regime.

The middle ground had collapsed on both sides. Moscow was very much present too—anxious and hovering and insisting on action of some kind to stop the erosion of communist authority. And so Jaruzelski took the step that most had come to expect: Martial law was declared late on December 12, 1981. Before the public announcement the next morning, Wałęsa, Solidarity activists, and other opposition figures, including reformist communists, were rounded up—several thousand in all—and imprisoned. The military took over and basic rights were suspended. Meetings were banned, curfews were imposed, and the only available news came from one government channel. The Kremlin orchestrated a statement of support for Poland's leaders from socialist countries across the Warsaw Pact.

Protests spread across hundreds of enterprises, but the army was now in control. Six thousand soldiers in tanks and armored vehicles backed up "citizens' militias," the party's paramilitary force, known as ZOMO, and they took over striking factories in cities across the country. In Silesia, nine miners were killed and scores were injured there and in other places. It did not take long for resistance to collapse, with the last of the strikes called off at the Piast coal mine on December 28. Trade unions, including Solidarity, were banned on October 8, 1982, by an act of parliament.

The comprehensive siege did not last long. Pope John Paul II visited the country in June 1982, obtaining the release of thousands of prisoners and amnesty for them. And the world recognized Lech Wałęsa, who had been released from prison in November 1982, with the Nobel Peace Prize. Martial law formally ended in July 1983.

The Polish Communist Party, or, more accurately, the Polish military, had asserted control and the "uprising" was over. Poland's leaders were anxious to return to something resembling normalcy. They needed help from the West and knew it. The leadership in Warsaw and, more important, in Moscow, could afford to be generous. The "constitutional order" in Poland had been preserved.

In one of history's great ironies, though, this dark moment for freedom in Poland laid the groundwork for communism's undoing when a democratic opening—Mikhail Gorbachev's reforms—came. The opposition's organizational capacity survived underground between 1981 and 1989, gaining strength and nurtured by an unlikely international troika: Lane Kirkland mobilized the AFL-CIO using a network of American and European NGOs, Ronald Reagan turned to the CIA to help covertly, and the Polish Pope's "divisions" of local Catholic priests became foot soldiers for change.

How Many Divisions Does the Pope Have?

When Harry Truman mentioned the Catholic Church in Poland, Josef Stalin famously and sarcastically asked that question. History would show that the answer was, "A lot."

Some have called it a miracle that Pope John Paul II emerged as leader of the Catholic faith in the late 1970s. The Polish cardinal Karol Józef Wojtyła was the first non-Italian Pope in more than four hundred years. And he ascended at a time of growing Polish nationalism and anti-Soviet resentment. His first visit to his homeland as Pope, in June 1979, was a sensation. The economy was worsening, discontent was rising, and the crowds were immense. He provided spiritual inspiration to Poland's drive for freedom, and to the institutional power of village priests who rallied the faithful against communist rule.

Workers were the second element of Poland's rich institutional landscape. We have seen that strikes and work stoppages were for decades a potent weapon against the regime. In the late 1970s, the AFL-CIO began providing financial support to a Polish organization called the Committee for Workers' Defense, a forerunner of Solidarity. Ironically, workers were central to the communist mythology. They were in Marxist lore the "vanguard of the revolution." But in the end their true champion would turn out to be the independent trade unions of the free world. The AFL-CIO's head, Lane Kirkland, was a staunch anticommunist who became enthralled with Solidarity's cause and went on to serve as one of its greatest advocates in the West.

After the summer of strikes in 1980, the Carter administration became concerned that the AFL-CIO's growing support for Solidarity would provoke a backlash from Soviet hard-liners, who would use the excuse of American meddling to intervene on behalf of their beleaguered comrades. U.S. officials urged Kirkland to keep a low profile, and he did, but he never wavered in his support.

Kirkland believed Solidarity embodied the kind of popular outpouring that had brought down many authoritarian regimes in the past. "History moves when civil society reaches a critical point," he later said. "It is not decided in the foreign ministries or in the palaces of power but on the streets and in the workplaces. And when a critical mass has been reached, then there is nothing you can do unless you are willing to kill and slaughter and put the whole country in chains."

The imposition of martial law in December 1981 was an attempt to do exactly that—to put the genie of Solidarity back into the bottle and to restore communist authority once and for all. But instead, the events convinced Solidarity's international supporters of the need to do more.

The third element of the troika, the CIA, began providing significant sums of money—hundreds of thousands of dollars— to several Polish groups, mainly run by Poles in exile. They in turn supported organizations that were trying to subvert the communist regime from within the country. Instead of lethal aid, the CIA provided the means for Solidarity to tell its story and rally its supporters. The assistance included printing materials to publish leaflets and journals, communication equipment to circumvent the ban on meetings, and financial support to the families of political prisoners. The National Endowment for Democracy (NED) also provided support openly to a range of groups associated with the Polish opposition—even during the period of martial law. As a result of these efforts, Poland had a strong indigenous movement at the ready when Gorbachev began to encourage change in Eastern Europe.

The Pope returned to Poland for his third visit in June 1987. He held prayers alongside one and a half million worshippers in Gdańsk. On the very same day, and only a few hundred miles away, President Reagan was standing at the Brandenburg Gate in Berlin, challenging Mr. Gorbachev to "tear down this wall." The Polish people were about to dismantle their communist regime—peacefully.

∽

When Brent Scowcroft called after the 1988 election to offer me the job as the White House Soviet specialist, he made a firm but understated pitch. "A lot is happening with Gorbachev," he said. "This could be an interesting time and the president needs someone to help him sort it out."

A month or so later when George H. W. Bush assumed office in January 1989, it was pretty clear that the times would be not just interesting, but historic. Still, when I took up my role as director for Soviet and East European affairs, we were feeling our way. How much would Mikhail Gorbachev tolerate? It was one thing to pronounce, as the Soviet leaders had done in December 1988, that the countries of the socialist brotherhood could go their own way. It was quite another to see that "their own way" might mean the end of communist rule in the Soviet bloc.

I followed events hour by hour. But even as one of the closest observers in the American government, I was shocked at how quickly Soviet and communist power collapsed in the summer and fall of 1989.

The year before the Bush administration arrived in Washington had been an extraordinary one in Eastern Europe. Throughout 1988, Solidarity had sparred with the government, calling and suspending strikes as it positioned itself for the upcoming Round Table talks, during which the authorities had agreed to sit down with the opposition. Protests throughout 1988 weakened the hand of a government that seemed powerless to do anything about the deteriorating economy. Once again, price hikes—40 percent on food, 50 percent on rents, and 60 percent on fuel—helped to mobilize the population. Intellectuals within universities, workers within shipyards and mines, and churchgoers in villages repeatedly took to the streets to demand change.

Though the government kept insisting that it would not negotiate fundamental changes like the legalization of independent trade unions, it was clearly running out of options. The Polish Communist Party needed Lech Wałęsa more than he needed them. Finally, the members of the Party Plenum said the magic words: They were prepared to accept pluralism in the trade union movement. The shocked reaction of the official trade union leader, who complained of feeling "bitterness and dissatisfaction," said it all. Solidarity had won the right to negotiate with the government on an equal, if not better, footing.

The talks began on February 6, 1989, just two weeks after George H. W. Bush took office. The president welcomed the negotiations, noting the importance of national reconciliation. I followed every twist and turn of the talks, frankly surprised at how rapidly they were moving to conclusion. When on April 5 the parties announced agreement, we were ready with a response from the White House. Actually, we were a little too ready.

Marlin Fitzwater, the White House spokesman, was about to hold his noon briefing. We gave him a prepared statement applauding the outcome of the Round Table negotiations. Unfortunately, the actual participants had broken for dinner and had not yet concluded the agreement. No one seemed to notice, though, and a few hours later the talks were indeed finished.

Solidarity was legalized under the agreement and new elections were set for June. The Round Table accords stipulated that 65 percent of the seats in the Sejm (the parliament) were reserved for the United Workers' Party (the communists) and their affiliated groups. The upper house, the Senate, had no such limitation.

In assessing the situation, we expected a slow and relatively orderly transition based on the blueprint laid out that April day. There might, we thought, be a slight non-communist majority in the Senate, but the communists would lead the government. Eventually, perhaps in the next election, the democratic forces would triumph once and for all. It was to be what political scientists call a "pacted transition," with the old regime essentially negotiating itself out of power.

The Polish people had other ideas. In the actual election, Solidarity won virtually every available seat in the lower house. In the newly created Senate, it won ninety-nine out of one hundred seats. The communists, on the other hand, could not even fill their uncontested seats, because none received more than 50 percent of the vote.

In the second round, Solidarity agreed to modify the election rule and urged their followers to vote for reform-minded communists, but with only minimal success. More astonishingly, Jaruzelski ran unopposed for the new post of president and still managed only a one-vote margin. He, in turn, asked another communist general, Czesław Kiszczak, to form a government. Protests erupted, and with Solidarity voicing its opposition to him, he could not do so. Though Solidarity wanted to observe the Round Table formula, the inevitability of a coalition led by the labor union was growing.

When President Bush arrived in Poland a month after the election, the political situation was still chaotic. Wałęsa asked the president to talk to Jaruzelski and urge him to accept the presidency. The general was a proud man, Wałęsa explained, and, stung by the election results, was reluctant to serve. The Round Table accords provided certainty—the communists, Solidarity, and Moscow were all on board. Wałęsa said publicly that he did not want Poland to have the "Chinese experience" (meaning Tiananmen Square), a point that he reiterated to President Bush.

But the accords were being overtaken by events and the sentiments of the Polish people, who were fed up with the communists and Moscow's yoke. Everyone hoped that the communists might hold on with just enough votes, counting, of course, their coalition partners, to fulfill the terms of the agreement. That too was not to be.

On the second day of the president's trip, the American ambassador held a lovely lunch in his spectacular garden to honor George Bush and members of the Polish government. Lech Wałęsa was not present, having overseen the dramatic events of the president's visit to Gdańsk the day before. But there was significant representation from Solidarity as well as from the Polish government. The only observably odd note came during the toasts. President Bush toasted the Polish and American people: nothing strange there. But Jaruzelski toasted "the ladies." *What was that?* I thought. The Polish legislator sitting next to me explained that President Jaruzelski did not want to risk being rebuffed by his countrymen if he dared raise a glass to "the Polish people."

But the real drama was unfolding in hushed conversations on the sidelines of the lunch. The American delegation, including the president, did not know that a deal was being struck that would nail shut communism's coffin.

The Polish Communist Party had, since the rigged elections of 1947, had non-communist coalition partners. The actions of the Peasant Party and another small party (the so-called Democratic Party) didn't really matter, since the communists were in complete control. They were in no sense independent, voting compliantly with the party for forty years. It was a coalition in name only.

In the new circumstances, though, these "minor" parties suddenly found a new role. A month after their consultations at the American ambassador's residence that day, they defected to Solidarity's side and agreed to take part in a non-communist coalition proposed by Wałęsa. It was, in fact, a kind of constitutional coup d'état. That is what the Poles were doing while most of us dined on a scrumptious meal on a warm Warsaw summer day.

The communists would have to accept the inevitable: They could no longer govern Poland alone. On August 19, one of the founders of Solidarity, Tadeusz Mazowiecki, was asked to form a government. Jaruzelski agreed to become president but was effectively without power.

The world held its breath to see what Moscow would do. Mazowiecki had been careful to reaffirm Poland's obligations to the Warsaw Pact and to leave the communists in charge of both the Defense Ministry and the Interior Ministry. In several interviews, he made clear that he wanted good relations with Moscow.

He did not have cause for worry. Mikhail Gorbachev, not Leonid Brezhnev, was in charge in the Kremlin. In his UN speech in 1988, Gorbachev had disavowed the Brezhnev Doctrine that defended the right of the Soviet Union to intervene in the internal affairs of countries of the socialist bloc—by force if necessary.

When *Izvestiya* published a statement on August 20 saying that Moscow would "wait and see" in relations with the new

Polish government, it was clear that Gorbachev would keep his promise. For good measure, the Soviet government newspaper added that the communist party of Poland was now associated with crisis and failure and would have to rebuild itself.

Two days later, Mieczysław Rakowski, the outgoing communist prime minister, reportedly called Gorbachev for advice and was told to allow the Solidarity-led coalition to go forward. Poland was free.

Democracy Prevails

There was palpable excitement that September in Washington as we anticipated the visit of Leszek Balcerowicz, Poland's deputy prime minister. Balcerowicz was highly respected in the West and serving simultaneously as the finance minister. The new government was coming to terms with the challenges it faced. The communists were gone, and the economic woes, accumulated over decades, now belonged to the new democratic government.

Several weeks before the meetings were to begin, Jan Nowak, an iconic Polish American leader who had headed Radio Free Europe for Eastern Europe, came to see me. He had just returned from Warsaw, where he had met the Mazowiecki government.

Jan was one of my favorite interlocutors. He was small in stature and more than eighty years old. But he was a giant to me, one of those extraordinary men, like my mentor and professor, Josef Korbel, who had survived both the Nazis and the communists by fleeing to the United States. Yet, like Korbel, he had never really left his country or his countrymen behind. Jan was a fierce fighter for their liberty and dignity.

That August afternoon on the third floor of the Old Executive Office Building, Jan pleaded for resources for the Solidarity-led government. He used a hard sell. The United States had stood by Poland during all those years of captivity: Now we had to stand by his native land in freedom. Those words were so powerful and resonated with me. The Poles had powerful friends in the U.S. Congress too. Senators George Mitchell and Bob Dole were just two who represented the bipartisan support that Poland enjoyed.

Both American politics and faithfulness to American values were on Poland's side. But I knew that we had budget limitations and worried that we could never live up to the Marshall Plan–like expectations that East Europeans would have. It was with some trepidation, therefore, that I prepared for the National Security Council meeting that would take place to finalize the offer that President Bush would make to the new Polish government.

I held a meeting of the assistant secretaries from around the government to review the bidding. The State Department proposed a series of visits and perhaps a donor conference for Poland; Agriculture proposed more food aid; Treasury took a hard line, insisting that, at most, Poland might receive several hundred million dollars from the IMF after a long series of negotiations; and the Commerce Department proposed to take a trade mission to Warsaw. That's right: at this moment of historic change, a trade mission made up of CEOs.

My colleague and the head of my directorate, Bob Blackwill, a strong proponent of robust aid, was out of town. I knew that Bob would have been furious at the pittance that we were about to propose, and frankly I was just embarrassed. So I broke ranks and went to see Bob Gates, the deputy national security adviser. "Bob," I said, "the Cold War is ending and we are proposing to hold a trade show in Warsaw." I knew I had Bob's support when he chuckled. He too was a Soviet specialist and didn't want to let the historic moment pass. He encouraged me to come up with something bigger—outside of the "interagency" process.

One of the ideas floating around Washington was to have the IMF grant Poland a "standby" loan of $1 billion. The number needed to be very large because the Poles would use the confidence that it implied to go ahead and "float" the złoty (in other words, let the currency find its true market value) as a crucial first step to market reform. But if Polish people panicked and made a run on the banks in an effort to protect their savings, there would be widespread chaos.

Jeffrey Sachs at Harvard had been a strong advocate for standby loans and had used our academic connections to get in touch with me. We talked through the mechanism and the likely resistance from the Treasury Department, which would, at the very least, argue that this could not be done quickly. The U.S. Treasury would say it could not support the loan before the IMF concluded negotiations. That would take months. We had a few days.

I knew well that I didn't have the credibility to put an economic proposal before the president that Treasury would oppose. But I knew someone who did, my colleagues from Stanford: Michael Boskin, the chairman of the Council of Economic Advisers, and John Taylor, a senior member of the council.

Armed with Bob Gates's permission to circumvent the process, I went to see Mike and John. "Is there any evidence that these standby facilities work?" They agreed that they could in some cases. Israel had been one such example. I explained that I needed a paper for the president to that effect. Thanks to Mike and John, President Bush had the argument before him prior to the NSC meeting.

I thought, though, that I had better inform the secretaries that the president would want to raise the idea of a standby loan. Secretary James Baker at State was delighted. I tried to reach Secretary Nicholas Brady, but his staff failed to connect us. When the meeting took place, the treasury secretary was not prepared for the argument. He said that he was not in principle opposed, citing the fact that he himself had mentioned the possibility of a standby loan. But it just couldn't be done quickly. If we broke process here, he argued, "we would have to do it for everyone, including Argentina!"

Secretary Baker spoke next, and he was prepared. "The Cold War didn't begin in Argentina and it won't end there," he countered. That was the winning argument and the United States settled on a kind of compromise. We would make the announcement before Poland's negotiations were complete, but disbursement would await final agreement between the IMF and Warsaw. The U.S. portion was to be $200 million in an internationally supported package. (The money, by the way, was never needed because the currency float was orderly and successful.)

Poland would receive further aid too. Congress seemed to try to outdo the president by offering an aid package several times larger than his original proposal. Given the nation's budget difficulties, this set off a confrontation between the White House and Capitol Hill. Jim Baker accused the Congress of politically motivated efforts to embarrass the president. To say that the response of the United States to this great historical moment was messy is an understatement. As Brent Scowcroft, then the national security adviser, has noted, most of us agreed more with the Congress than with our own administration. But we did what we could, and the Poles received significant help. And the aid provided a strong signal of support from Europe and the United States. It was not exactly the Marshall Plan, but it did help the new government pursue economic reform in a timely fashion.

In fact, one of the most successful endeavors was actually quite small in absolute dollar terms. The idea, which took root just as the changes in Poland were beginning to unfold, was for an enterprise fund to provide seed grants to small businesses across the country. It was intended as a kind of venture capital investment to bypass the communist government and help loosen the reins of the centrally controlled economy. In essence, the U.S. government would provide capital to private bakeries, auto shops, hair salons, and other entrepreneurial activities for a small stake in the enterprises. An independent international board of Poles and distinguished Americans would oversee the program.

President Bush first mentioned the idea in a speech in April 1989, and he reiterated it during his address to the Polish parliament in July 1989. But in a sign of how quickly events were changing on the ground, by the time the proposal was approved by Congress, Solidarity had already taken control of the government. The Polish American Enterprise Fund was nevertheless granted $240 million to begin making investments, and it continued to operate throughout the 1990s.

Years later when I was back at Stanford, I received a call from an NSC staff member in the Clinton administration. The United States, it seemed, had a dilemma. The Enterprise Fund had not only not lost money, it had made money: The original $240 million investment was worth nearly $300 million. Should the Poles repay it?

I asked President Bush and Brent Scowcroft. They said that we hadn't really expected to be repaid. (Brent said, "Who makes money on foreign assistance?") We should probably just consider the "profits" to be a grant. The bulk of the principal should be repaid to the U.S. Treasury, and the rest should go to the Poles. President Clinton agreed. Warsaw graciously used the funds to continue its work and venture enterprises in other, less fortunate East European countries.

U.S. assistance and that of the European Union (EU) certainly played a role in stabilizing the Polish economy and ultimately its political system. Poland's story reminds us that targeted international assistance can ease transition. But without committed and competent indigenous leaders and a favorable institutional landscape, success can be elusive.

In this, Poland was blessed with both. Poland's agriculture was never collectivized, giving farmers an early stake in feeding the country as economic freedom took hold. Small political parties that had meant nothing under communism switched sides at a crucial moment in 1989. Due to the depth of religious conviction among the population, the Catholic Church remained powerful even in Stalinist times. At the moment of the opening this provided John Paul II with the metaphorical "divisions" of village priests that he mobilized on the ground. And Solidarity emerged from events after martial law intact and ready to take up a political mantle when the time came.

The country also had formidable leaders, many of whom had cut their political teeth as members of Solidarity. As such they enjoyed the admiration of the population, reinforcing their willingness to move quickly and decisively on reform. It is no exaggeration to say that Poland's founding fathers were an extraordinary collection of people whose values and patriotism created the country's democracy.

Lech Wałęsa will deservedly go down in history as the inspiration for Solidarity and in many ways the father of democratic Poland. A simple man who started out as an advocate for bread-and-butter issues as a labor leader, Wałęsa would become the symbol of freedom for Poles. What he lacked in political sophistication, he made up for in sincerity and authenticity. When I first met him in Gdańsk, I wondered if he could corral all that he had unleashed. It was easy to underestimate him, and early on the communists clearly did. In one of the memorable events in a decade of memorable moments, the party arranged a televised debate between Alfred Miodowicz, the head of the official trade union and an accomplished speaker, and Wałęsa. The ratings were through the roof: A poll in Warsaw found that 78 percent of the population watched as Wałęsa kept

Miodowicz on the defensive throughout. That night, Solidarity emerged as a legitimate contender for power—not at all what the party had intended.

And Solidarity would produce other key leaders who did not enjoy Wałęsa's deep moral authority but nonetheless simply knew how to get the work of the transition done:

Leszek Balcerowicz, the author of the economic reform plan, had been an economics professor and member of the communist party. He joined Solidarity soon after its founding in 1980 as an adviser. His commitment to rapid market reform and tight monetary policies is widely regarded as having smoothed Poland's economic transition.

If Balcerowicz was the father of Poland's market economy, Tadeusz Mazowiecki, a journalist, was a fierce defender of individual liberties and a multiparty state, leading to a constitution that protected these basic democratic rights.

Adam Michnik founded *Gazeta Wyborcza*, which had become Poland's largest newspaper and a voice for Solidarity, even under martial law. He was a powerful advocate for a free press.

Bronisław Geremek founded in 1987 the Commission for Political Reforms of the Civic Committee, which drafted a plan for Poland's democratic transition, taking advantage of the breathing space accorded by Mikhail Gorbachev. A quiet and scholarly professor of medieval Polish history, Geremek was in many ways an unlikely father of social and political reform.

These and others like them were deep believers in liberty. They had suffered what seemed to be an irrevocable defeat with the imposition of martial law. But they took advantage of that

time to deepen their understanding of democracy's requirements and to develop uniquely Polish responses to them. As
such, Poland was ready to make the transition in 1989 in ways
that few countries have been.

A New "Special Relationship"

When President Bush took his first trip to Europe in 2001, one
stop was an absolute must—Warsaw. Everyone knew of the
"special relationship" with Britain. Poland seemed poised to be
a special ally in its own right. America had remained devoted
to the country in the darkest days, and now celebrated a bright
future with its friend. Poland's story was quite simply a story of
freedom's triumph.

We seemed to see eye-to-eye with Poland on everything.
Sitting in a meeting between President Bush and his Polish
counterpart was stress-free and productive. In NATO, Poland
brought new energy to the aging alliance, reminding its members to support those still living in tyranny in Iraq, Afghanistan, and the Middle East. Poland's special forces, along with
those of Australia and Britain, joined Americans in the initial
phase of the invasion of Iraq. The Poles agreed to host missile
defense deployments despite Moscow's resistance. In any meeting with the European Union, whether on climate change or
trade, Poland was a friendly voice. The Poles took on hard tasks
like trying to help the Ukrainians solve their multiple governance crises. I told President Kwasniewski on one occasion that

Poland had become one of America's most important allies and a real power in European politics.

That assessment of Poland's foreign policy was accurate. But at home, the democratic political system was struggling to govern. In a sense, the problems were to be expected and were ones that bedevil almost every new democracy. Poland was experiencing political fragmentation, electoral volatility, and fissures in society.

How Many Parties Does a Country Need?

A year after the extraordinary events of 1989, Solidarity, a movement, gave way to the creation of political parties. Fissures emerged within the labor movement as the threat from a common foe, the communists, receded. The splits followed predictable lines: social and religious orthodoxy versus more liberal views; intellectual elites against workers and "common people"; rural interests against those of urban dwellers. Parties were founded representing all of those interests and many more. Former communists who had sufficiently reformist and nationalist credentials found their place in Polish politics, repackaging themselves in center-left parties.

There was even a Polish Beer Lovers' Party, founded in 1990 by a television star. It had ten thousand members devoted to a philosophy of "live and let live." The party would eventually attract people with an economic agenda for consumerism. Not surprisingly, this was resented by the original membership that just wanted to enjoy life, and a split ensued, with twelve deputies leaving to form a new parliamentary association.[2]

The multiplying parties and intense political activity were signs of healthy engagement of the population and elites alike, at least in those early days. But the complexity of the institutional landscape would make governing difficult. In 1991, a hundred organizations fielded candidates, and twenty-nine parties won seats. In the first eighteen months after the first free election there were four prime ministers. The average tenure of a government in the first five years was ten months. The electoral laws were revised in 1993, raising the threshold for party participation to 8 percent. Since then, there have been five or so major parties.

Still, from 1991 to 2015, no party had won a majority and all governments ruled in coalition. And the country's political landscape has experienced considerable electoral volatility, alternating between center-right and center-left governments. That has made it difficult to sustain a consistent policy course.

Early on, Poland was also rocked by crises related to the treatment of former communists and their role in future governments. Wałęsa himself was accused of "defending the post-communist system" in his appointment of government ministers.

And the former communists did fare well in the years that followed democratization. Their main party won a plurality in the Sejm in 1993. Its leader, Aleksander Kwasniewski, was a longtime communist and had taken part in the Round Table negotiations on the side of the government. He was later elected as president, replacing Wałęsa.

Tensions remained, though, as the new Poland tried to resolve questions of the past. There were numerous resignations due to charges of corruption and even one charge of conspiring for a military coup. But the hardest cases involved well-regarded figures whose names appeared in archives suggesting that they had maintained steady contact with the secret police during communist rule.

Sometimes the sin had been simply to agree to talk to the secret police or to answer questions when asked, but in the charged atmosphere of the early 1990s, that was enough to brand someone as a collaborator. And sometimes the charges were more substantial and troubling.

In the most notorious episode, in 1992, the interior minister handed over a list of the names of deputies, senators, and civil servants who, according to his ministry, had been "agents" of the security services. The "Portfolio Affair" implicated dozens of people, including some who had been members of anticommunist opposition groups. In the confusion that followed, Wałęsa said that the lists were doctored and called for the resignation of the government of Jan Olszewski. The members of that government, in turn, formed a new party.

These accusations and counteraccusations would dog Polish politics for years to come. In 2007, the Archbishop of Warsaw resigned over revelations that he had cooperated with the secret police during communist rule. A second prominent Catholic clergyman did the same the next day. And several months later, a former minister committed suicide in the face of similar charges.

Poland, like every other country in transition, found it

difficult and divisive to find justice for the past and reconcile it with the need to move forward. Poland's democratic transition was thus not smooth, but it was smoother than most. It is fair to say most Polish leaders in these crucible years were not just committed to democracy; most wanted to anchor the country in a democratic Europe by seeking membership in the European Union. And the high regard and affection that Poles felt for the United States drew them to integration in NATO too, an association that would carry protection from Moscow—just in case.

One of the underestimated factors in the mostly successful transitions in Central and Eastern Europe was the role that the European Union and NATO played as north stars for democratic change. In order to gain membership, those countries had to follow a careful and specific map for institutional reform. Many democratic transitions are heavily influenced by single, overwhelming personalities like Boris Yeltsin in Russia. They never take the next step toward the development of institutions that can withstand the vagaries of particular leaders. In the Russian case, the highly personalized and powerful presidency meant one thing with Boris Yeltsin as its occupant. Vladimir Putin would mean quite another.

In Poland, the lure to be included in NATO and the EU put the emphasis for reform in the right place—on institutional change. The effort to gain membership provided a careful and specific set of requirements for institutional reform.

Poland's association with the European Union had begun just a few months after Solidarity's electoral victory with a trade and cooperation pact. Together with Hungary and Czechoslovakia (soon to be two countries, Slovakia and the Czech

Republic), Poland formed the Visegrad Group, which sought full integration into European institutions. The same group would simultaneously seek membership in NATO.

The EU accession process forced countries desiring membership to conform domestic legislation to European standards in thirty-one issue areas, or "chapters." These included economic issues like the freedom of movement of capital and goods, taxation, and agricultural reform. On the political side, everything from consumer and health protection to justice and home affairs to cultural policy had to be reformed and judged consistent with EU requirements. Political institutions were also under scrutiny, and there have been cases of direct intervention from the EU to warn an aspirant that antidemocratic practices can derail the path to membership.[3]

NATO added yet another set of institutional requirements related to defense but touching on domestic reform. Such was the insistence on "democratic and civilian control" of the military as one foundation of stable democracy.

In 1997, Poland was invited to join NATO. It became a full member of the European Union seven years later, in 2004. After World War II, Poland had been where it first became clear that the Soviet Union would accept only communist governments in Eastern Europe. It took roughly fifty years, but the country was now fully integrated into a democratic continent.

In the twenty or so years since, there has been a good deal of debate about the decision to offer membership in the formerly "Western" institutions to Moscow's former client states. NATO in particular has drawn fire for moving the battle lines of the Cold War eastward toward Russia's borders.

But it should be remembered that NATO at the time of its creation had two purposes. One was to stop Stalin's military forces from threatening the part of Europe that was free of Soviet influence. That was accomplished by a huge conventional force presence and the extended deterrence that American nuclear weapons provided.

That was not, however, NATO's only purpose. Those who created it believed that it would provide a security umbrella for the reconciliation of old enemies in a democratic peace—in short, to provide a new environment in which France and Germany would never have cause to fight again. Believing deeply in what political scientists now call the "democratic peace," they thought that an association of free peoples would prevent war.[4] This emphasis on liberty as an antidote to conflict was at the heart of a postwar strategy that relied on democratizing Germany and integrating Europe politically *and* militarily. And it succeeded brilliantly.

The completion of the European project could not be achieved, however, until Central and Eastern Europe could be a part of it. That is why a Europe "whole and free," as George H. W. Bush put it, required an open door to the new democracies of Europe. That path provided an impetus for domestic reform, and it provided, as the framers of the European institutions had expected, an institutional home for old enemies to become allies. Just as few would have taken the odds on a permanent peace between Germany and France in 1945, many expected open conflict between Hungary and Romania or Turkey and Bulgaria over ethnic and territorial differences that had been submerged under communist rule.

Thanks to its relatively rich institutional profile at the time of the democratic opening—and its integration into Europe—Poland is both fully democratic and fully European. At least as of this writing.

Is Polish Democracy in Danger?

The work of building a stable democracy is never really done. The institutions are constantly challenged, sometimes in small ways, and often in more fundamental tests. The United States has been through Watergate and a contested presidential election in just the last forty years. The institutions were strong enough to withstand the turbulence.

Poland is now going through one of those periods of testing, and its young democratic institutions are most certainly at risk. In part, this is to be expected as a phase in democratic consolidation. Yet that does not fully explain the situation that the Poles face.

Every democracy rests upon a foundation of societal attitudes and values. The genius of democratic institutions is that they can absorb the contest between competing views. The political system permits the expression of all of them in debate, elections, and judicial decisions.

In Poland today, the resurgence of deeply conservative social attitudes, including religious piety, is clashing with evolving and more liberal European values and beliefs. As discontent with the European Union has grown on the continent—even leading Great Britain to exit—Poland too has found its Euroskeptics.

Some Poles feel that Europe is too socially liberal and disrespectful of its national traditions. There are those who now want a divorce. Too many Poles feel that wages are not rising fast enough and that inequality is growing. Polish workers who have crossed borders to find work in Germany or Ireland or the UK say that they experience discrimination and prejudice. Disaffected Poles blame their own leaders and they blame Europe.

These circumstances have fostered the emergence of rightwing parties that are strongly nationalistic and religiously fundamentalist. While this is a broader trend across Europe, relatively young democracies like Poland are particularly vulnerable to the rise of populists who can give voice to such grievances. Those leaders have then tended to challenge the fragile institutional order—amassing greater power in the presidency and seeking to weaken other forces.

In October 2015, the populist Law and Justice Party scored a stunning victory in parliamentary elections. For the first time since liberation, a single party holds a majority in the parliament *and* the presidency under Jarosław Kacyziński. Since taking power, Law and Justice has carried out several popular changes, such as reversing the decision that increased the retirement age. It has raised the child benefit for families with two or more children and increased the minimum wage. These populist policies reflect underlying demographic trends. Poland's population is declining and aging, and older people are demanding security. And the Catholic Church has long urged the government to encourage couples to have more children.

But other steps are more worrying and could threaten Poland's democratic constitutional order. The most serious of these has provoked a crisis between the government and the Constitutional Tribunal—one of four judicial institutions. While Poland has a Supreme Court, it does not engage in judicial review as in the United States. That is the role of the Constitutional Tribunal, which judges "the constitutionality of laws." This means that it is the most important of the judicial institutions in constraining executive power.

The Law and Justice Party first raised eyebrows just after taking power in 2015 when it refused to seat justices legally appointed by the outgoing Civic Platform government. The new leaders compounded their actions by appointing replacements for two additional judges before their terms expired. The Constitutional Tribunal refused to swear them in. This led the president of the tribunal—an ally of the government—to do so over the objection of other members of the court. Poland essentially had two sets of judges.

Law and Justice then moved to modify the tribunal's operations, eventually passing legislation through the parliament that it dominates. Again, the tribunal reacted, declaring the new laws unconstitutional. There has been a standoff between the government and the tribunal ever since—and this part of the judiciary is essentially not functioning.

In response, the European Union has adopted a resolution calling the actions a "systematic threat to the rule of law in Poland." Poland is subject to action under Article 7 of the EU treaty, which could sanction the country and suspend its voting rights. Hungary has a veto, however, and its prime minister, Viktor Orbán—a burgeoning political strongman in his own right—has threatened to block any such steps.

There is also a tremendous tug-of-war over the control of state media. The government has created the National Media Council with the right to hire and fire personnel for state television and radio. Saying that private media is too responsive to ratings, officials have argued that state media should instead foster patriotism. There are, they complain, too many shows like *Dancing with the Stars*.

Many suspect, of course, that this rationale is really a subterfuge. The real purpose is to make the media a mouthpiece for the regime—something that it does clumsily at times.

When visiting Poland in 2015, President Obama reminded the government that it must live up to its democratic principles—a gentle rebuke to the actions of Law and Justice. The state media altered his comments. It appeared as if the president only complimented the Poles on their democracy. Of course, the American press reported the outrage, and so did the free Polish press, much to the embarrassment of the government.

And while private media has been immune so far, many worry that it is only a matter of time until the government encroaches on that space too. A law that would limit foreign ownership (Poland's three largest private media companies are owned by Germans) is of particular concern. And the government is reducing advertising dollars to these outlets. This goes to the heart of one of the private media's weaknesses in Poland—indirect dependence on the government for resources. If foreigners cannot own the outlets and the government will not spend on them, the private media could simply wither away.

Still, there are clearly limits to what Law and Justice can do. An effort to outlaw abortion has thus far failed. Poland already has the most restrictive laws in the European Union, but an out-right ban drew large protests. Eighty-five thousand Facebook users flooded a page named "Women for Women," and several hundred people walked out of mass when priests pressed congregations to support the measure.

One scholar of Poland argues that the fight over abortion is not really about abortion but about the role of the church in politics.[5] Poles, she argues, are extremely religious, but that does not mean they want the church to dictate policy. If accurate, this would be a watershed development in such a deeply Catholic country.

Poland's democracy is not likely to be destroyed by the current challenges. Still, the careful balance between state authority and political freedom is once again in play. The country has achieved all of the milestones that we associate with democratic consolidation: repeated peaceful elections; a relatively independent judiciary; civil-military stability; a free press; a vibrant civil society; and respect for human rights.

Yet the current circumstances in Poland remind us that democracy's development is never a straight line. Rather, it is a step-wise process that will often include steps backward along the way. Some have argued that Poland's democratic forces became complacent—believing that their democratic consolidation was irreversible. The Civic Platform, it is said, failed to see that the rapidly rising expectations of the population were not being met. And pro-Western leaders failed to see the growing distance between some of the cultural values of Brussels and those of the Polish heartland.

That said, Poland's democracy is far from lost. I was in

Warsaw in June 2016 and participated in a forum with the former foreign minister, Radek Sikorski. The conversation was mostly about geopolitical affairs—but no one seemed reluctant to talk about Poland's challenges either.

One could see that the independent Polish press and civil society are fighting back, publicly and vigorously. Articles appear daily in the press and on the Internet challenging the policies of the government and calling attention to those that seek to expand its authority. The atmosphere remains open and free for now.

Poland's history suggests that it can handle the turbulence that it is now experiencing and emerge strongly democratic on the other side. But there is no guarantee, and that is always the case. The defense of democracy is never finished.

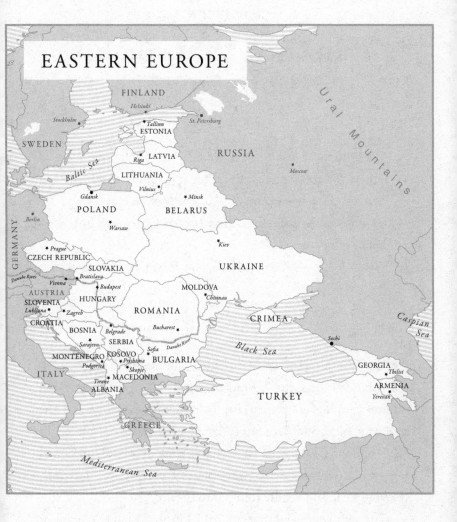

EASTERN EUROPE

FINLAND
Helsinki

Stockholm

SWEDEN

Tallinn
ESTONIA

St. Petersburg

RUSSIA

Moscow

Ural Mountains

Baltic Sea

Riga LATVIA

LITHUANIA

Vilnius

Gdansk

POLAND

Minsk

BELARUS

Berlin

Warsaw

Prague

CZECH REPUBLIC

Kiev

SLOVAKIA

UKRAINE

Danube River

Bratislava

Vienna

Budapest

AUSTRIA

HUNGARY

MOLDOVA

Chisinau

SLOVENIA

Ljubljana

Zagreb

ROMANIA

CROATIA

CRIMEA

Caspian Sea

BOSNIA

Belgrade

Bucharest

Sarajevo

SERBIA

Danube River

Black Sea

Sochi

MONTENEGRO KOSOVO

Prishtina

Sofia

Podgorica

Skopje

BULGARIA

GEORGIA

Tbilisi

ITALY

Tirane

MACEDONIA

ARMENIA

ALBANIA

TURKEY

Yerevan

GREECE

Mediterranean Sea

Chapter 4

UKRAINE: "A MADE-UP COUNTRY"?

We didn't just lose a town, we lost our whole lives. We left on the third day. The reactor was on fire. I remember one of my friends saying, "It smells of reactor." It was an indescribable smell.... They turned Chernobyl into a house of horrors.

—NIKOLAI KALUGIN, PRIPYAT, UKRAINE[1]

The Chernobyl tragedy unfolded one hundred miles north of Kiev near the Ukrainian city of Pripyat. Some ten million people were put at risk for radiation exposure and the environmental and economic damage has been estimated at $235 billion. Ukrainians were the victims of a badly designed Soviet reactor that lost containment of radioactive materials, spewing toxic and deadly fumes into the air.

The awful events of that time in 1986 are a kind of metaphor for the fate of Ukrainians: For much of their history, decisions of epic proportion—and their sometimes disastrous results—

were made in Moscow, not in Kiev. The Ukrainian people have thus been anxious to control their future.

The Russians and the Ukrainians are ethnically the same— they are Slavs—and they speak similar but not identical languages. Russians tend to overstate the links between the cultures and ignore the distinctiveness of Ukrainian national identity. Ukrainians resent this and sometimes overstate their uniqueness. These questions of identity have led, not surprisingly, to uncertainty and conflict about what actually constitutes Ukraine. Russians and Ukrainians have had very different answers to that question.

When Vladimir Putin declared at the 2008 NATO summit in Bucharest that "Ukraine is a made-up country," he was stating what many Russians believe to be historical fact. Vladimir Zhirinovsky, the ultra-nationalist leader of Russia's falsely named Liberal Democratic Party, put it a bit more bluntly in 2014: "Why don't we take eastern Ukraine and give Poland the west? Then it can be back to the way it's always been."

Ukrainians would not, of course, agree. The country has a rich history, albeit one that has always unfolded in Russia's shadow.

Slavic culture began in Kiev in the ninth century, when two priests, Cyril and Methodius, settled the territory, bringing with them the Orthodox Church and an entirely new language. Cyrillic, the alphabet of both Russian and Ukrainian (with some small differences), takes its name from Saint Cyril. In the fourteenth century, Ukraine was a center of Slavic civilization, evidenced today by some of the most extraordinary onion-domed churches in all of Eastern Europe. From the sixteenth century on, however, Ukraine's unfortunate geography—no natural barriers but very desirable access to the Black Sea—would leave it vulnerable to more powerful states. The Ottoman Empire, the Austro-Hungarian Empire, the Russian Empire, Poland, the Soviet Union, and Germany at one time or another incorporated parts—or sometimes all—of Ukraine within their territory.

Ukraine's brief periods of independence came at those moments when empires collapsed or big states were defeated. In 1918, the death of the Russian Empire allowed the creation of a new Ukrainian state. That would last three years until the Russian Red Army conquered two-thirds of the country. The western third was incorporated into Poland. Josef Stalin's brutal campaign of "Russification" quickly wiped out vestiges of Ukrainian identity. Russian became obligatory in all schools and was designated the official language of the Ukrainian government.

Then, in 1939, taking advantage of a temporary alliance with Hitler, Stalin's forces seized most of the land of western Ukraine. Of course, the Molotov-Ribbentrop Pact was ephemeral—broken in June 1941 by the Nazi invasion of the Soviet Union. As the Wehrmacht pushed east, Ukraine was devastated by the Nazis' occupation and extermination policies, which resulted in the deaths of five million Ukrainians (about one-eighth of the total population) and a majority of its one and a half million Jews.

But the collapse of Soviet power led some within Ukraine to make a fatal choice. Hitler encouraged the establishment of an independent Republic of Ukraine, a satrapy that muddied the story of Ukrainian resistance to the Nazis. Faced with two historical enemies—Russia and Germany—some fought the former and others the latter. Those in the East overwhelmingly fought with Russia. This handed Stalin an exaggerated charge of western Ukrainian collaboration with the Third Reich. He used that indictment to justify the brutal repression of any vestige of resistance to Moscow. The false narrative of a collaborationist western Ukraine exists to this day, fueling hatred on both sides. At war's end, Ukraine returned to its prewar status as a republic of the Soviet Union. There, politics languished, dependent in large part on the few openings Moscow provided.

One such opportunity came after the death of Josef Stalin in 1953. Nikita Khrushchev's reforms now seem modest in comparison to what Gorbachev would launch thirty years later. At the time, though, they were dramatic. Like Gorbachev, he sought to put the Soviet Union on a firmer, more legitimate footing, denouncing Stalin's brutality in a secret speech to the 1956 Party Congress. The remarks were leaked (probably by Khrushchev's enemies) and were an immediate sensation. This gave rise to a brief period of reform and outspokenness in the Soviet Union and in Eastern Europe.

The Hungarian Revolution later that year ended the Kremlin's tolerance for dissent in the bloc, though. And when Khrushchev was ousted, any remaining vestiges of the thaw went with him. In Ukraine, human rights activists were put on trial, dissidents were arrested, and tough new measures were adopted against Crimean Tatars. The latter, a restive, majority-Muslim population, had suffered large-scale deportation under Stalin and had long sought a return to their homeland. The new constitution of the Ukrainian Soviet Socialist Republic made clear that that would not happen. The Brezhnev period was a sterile one for politics anywhere in the bloc and the republics were made to toe a very narrow line.

Then the arrival of Mikhail Gorbachev loosened Moscow's grip throughout the region. Ironically, it might have been the horror of the meltdown of the nuclear reactor at Chernobyl that was at least in part responsible for *glasnost* associated with Gorbachev. Despite the danger to surrounding populations, nearly three full days passed before the Soviet media acknowledged the incident, and even then it was said only that an "accident" had occurred and that authorities had taken measures to "eliminate the consequences." Meanwhile, the scope of the catastrophe was becoming increasingly clear on the other side of the Iron Curtain, as countries such as Sweden began to report dangerous levels of radioactivity. Eighteen days passed before Gorbachev addressed the incident himself, and he gave very few details. He later told President George H. W. Bush that he had learned a lesson from this experience. "You have to tell people the truth," he said. "It is worse when you hide it and they find out anyway."

Ukraine's Democratic Opening

The Gorbachev reforms gave Kiev its first opening to build nascent democratic institutions. As in Moscow, civic groups protesting everything from efforts—or the lack thereof—to deal with the aftermath of the reactor disaster, to language issues, to political freedoms dotted the landscape. By 1988, a burgeoning nationalist movement had taken root. Known as the Ukrainian

People's Movement for Restructuring (Rukh), it was led by some of the country's most famous writers and intellectuals. Gorbachev gave a further push to these activities when he replaced one of his opponents, Volodymyr Shcherbytskyi, as head of the Ukrainian Communist Party in September 1989. On the heels of that, the Rukh held its first national congress and began to prepare for elections to the Ukrainian Supreme Soviet.

Ukraine was alive with political activity. And much of the action was in the parliament with its new chairman, Leonid Kravchuk. He was a communist but facile and able to seize upon and appropriate the nationalist mood of the country. Under his leadership, Ukraine's Soviet parliament annulled Article 6 of the constitution, eliminating the Communist Party's principal role in politics. Within parliament, the communists were split between reformers and conservatives—the former making common cause with the fledgling democratic opposition.[2]

Yet Ukrainian domestic politics was intertwined with the question of independence. This complicated relations between Gorbachev's reformers and Boris Yeltsin's separatists in Moscow and those advocating for change in Kiev. In 1990, a newly elected parliament declared Ukraine sovereign but stopped short of calling for an independent state. The difference was something akin to a nullification movement, serving notice that Ukraine's laws were superior to those of the Soviet Union. John C. Calhoun would have recognized this stand.

It was a delicate balance. Gorbachev had been Ukraine's benefactor, but Yeltsin was pushing harder toward the breakup of the Soviet Union. Thus when Gorbachev, desperate to save the USSR, proposed reforms to the relationship between the republics and the center in the summer of 1991, the Ukrainian parliament was reluctant to go along.

Then, later that summer, hard-liners finally acted to change the course of events in Moscow. They launched a coup against Gorbachev, imprisoning him in Crimea and declaring themselves the new leaders of the Soviet Union. The events served only to quicken the impulse toward independence in Ukraine and other republics. The coup failed and Gorbachev returned to the Kremlin late on August 21, 1991.

But the landscape had changed dramatically in his absence. Trying to find a formula to save the USSR, Gorbachev undertook a series of desperate steps. He resigned as general secretary of the Soviet Communist Party, removed political commissars from the security services, and moved to disband the Central Committee. He was seeking to accelerate the political reforms, still trying to make the Soviet Union a "normal country." But it was too late. Four months later, Belarus, Russia, and Ukraine established the Commonwealth of Independent States and the Soviet Union came to an end. Ukraine was finally independent.

Independent but Still Divided

The country remained very much a three-part entity, though— western Ukraine (Ukrainian-speaking), eastern Ukraine (largely Russian-speaking), and Crimea. Ninety-two percent of the inhabitants voted for independence in the western part of the country and 80 percent in the east. In Crimea, 54 percent voted to separate from the Soviet Union.

Until Vladimir Putin annexed Crimea in 2014, many had forgotten its strange history. Crimea is a beautiful area along the Black Sea that was conquered by Catherine the Great in 1784. This allowed the landlocked Russian Empire to finally have access to a warm-water port. For almost three hundred years, Crimea was an important military asset and a playground for well-to-do Russians who vacationed on its shore, which enjoys an extraordinary Mediterranean climate.

In 1954, Nikita Khrushchev had a bizarre and, in retrospect, foolish idea. Why not give Crimea back to Ukraine to celebrate three hundred years of friendship between the peoples? It didn't matter, of course, since Ukraine was an integral part of the Soviet Union, ruled by Moscow and serving its interests.

That is until December 25, 1991. The Soviet Union's collapse created fifteen newly independent states, including Ukraine. A Russian friend likened the loss of Ukraine to having an arm amputated, and the loss of Crimea as tearing out a piece of your heart.

Still, in the early years, the separation proceeded relatively smoothly. The Ukrainians, after some prodding by the United States and Europe, stepped aside so that Russia would be the "successor" state to the Soviet Union. In diplomatic terms this meant that Moscow would retain its status as a Permanent Five member of the UN Security Council. After initially declaring that it would destroy the nuclear weapons on its territory, Kiev agreed to have them transferred to Russian soil. About one-fifth of the Soviet Union's arsenal was on Ukraine's territory, so this was no small concession. Early on, Kiev claimed that the Black Sea Fleet (which had existed since Catherine the Great) was an "integral part of the Ukrainian armed forces." This led the parliament in Moscow to declare that Sevastopol in Crimea was a Russian city. Eventually, the Ukrainians backed down, granting Moscow control of roughly 90 percent of the base there. The new security relationship was codified in two agreements. In 1994, in exchange for a non-nuclear Ukraine, Russia promised to respect the territorial integrity of its neighbor. A broader ten-year treaty was signed in 1997, including arrangements for Sevastopol. Again Moscow declared Ukraine's borders inviolable. The two seemed to settle into a relatively amicable relationship between democratizing countries.

"Vote for Us and You'll Never Have to Vote Again"

But Ukraine began to stumble almost immediately as it tried to carve out an identity divorced from its neighbor. Think back to the comment that losing Ukraine was like an amputation. Essentially all of the Soviet Union was hacked into parts. The infrastructure of a single country was divided at the borders of several—whether the division made sense or not. Gas pipelines, the electrical grid, industrial sites, even military bases were affected. In one peculiar incident, Soviet cosmonauts had to orbit in space while Russia and Kazakhstan negotiated the right for them to touch down. They had taken off from the Soviet Union. The landing strip now belonged to Kazakhstan.

Ukraine was most affected by the sudden dissolution and the divorce from Russia. Yes, independence felt good. But the two countries were inextricably tied together. Intermarriage between Russians and Ukrainians was commonplace. Russians had dachas in Ukraine and Ukrainians had dachas in Russia.

And of the two, Ukraine was clearly poorer and less developed. This was particularly true in terms of human capital. In Soviet times, upward mobility usually meant getting out of Kiev. The great universities and the best scientific institutes were in Russia. The most accomplished artists performed at the Bolshoi in Moscow and the Kirov in Leningrad. The political up-and-comers and the best technocrats headed for the Soviet capital. Even the most vibrant dissident movements and human rights advocates were in Russia, not Ukraine.

Leonid Kravchuk, Ukraine's first president, was a clever communist who skillfully led the country to independence. But he turned out to be less effective at governing. Not surprisingly, Ukraine experienced immediate economic chaos because divorced from Russia it had a far inferior base for its economy. In Russia, rapid privatization was the culprit. Ukraine did the same, privatizing a large industrial base, but one that did not rival Moscow's for sophistication and talent. Still, a class of oligarchs found plenty to buy, and, as in Russia, these rich beneficiaries dotted the landscape in Kiev and across the country.

Ukraine's first steps after independence were faulty at best. Its first prime minister, Leonid Kuchma, was appointed in October 1992 and resigned just one year later. He went into opposition, blaming the president for blocking his reform efforts and promising to run against him in the upcoming elections. He did so and defeated Kravchuk decisively, winning 52 percent of the vote.

I was traveling in Kiev in 1994, a couple of months before those elections took place. I was joined by my colleague from Stanford, Chip Blacker. We had just been in Moscow, where new restaurants, hotels, and shopping malls masked much of the economic turmoil that ordinary Russians were experiencing. There was no such Potemkin village in Kiev. The buildings were as run-down and the hotels as grim as in Soviet times. As we walked along, a campaign poster caught my eye. Russian speakers can read Ukrainian relatively easily. I turned to Chip. "Does that really say what I think it does?" I asked him. "Yep. Vote for us and you'll never have to vote again." We chuckled, knowing that the party in question probably meant it as a promise to govern wisely. The poster didn't quite capture the essence of electoral democracy. And neither did Ukraine's first leaders.

The first post-Soviet constitution was based on a promising institutional balance. Adopted in 1996, two years after Kuchma became president, the document established a mixed system with the president as head of state and the prime minister as head of government. The parliament was accorded considerable de jure authority to check the power of the president.

But because the communists were the largest faction, though not a majority, they engaged in blocking maneuvers constantly. Liberal forces fought among themselves, somehow more threatened by each other than by the communists. Kuchma was frustrated with both and threatened to launch a sweeping constitutional referendum. The challenge worked and the liberals united momentarily to oust the pro-communist speaker. The new leader of the parliament pledged cooperation with the president, who was clearly strengthened by the events that had transpired.

President Kuchma did not waste the moment and sponsored and won a more limited referendum. He would now have the right, under certain circumstances, to disband the legislature. Though the constitution was not amended to reflect the change (it would have taken a two-thirds vote of the parliament), Kuchma governed as if it were. The presidency had become by far the strongest post-Soviet institution in Ukraine.

The other means of balance, the relationship between the president and the prime minister, didn't hold either. The unenviable job of fixing the economy always fell to the latter, providing successive presidents with someone to blame when reform failed. And there were plenty of failures. Ukraine's early history was therefore one of a tug-of-war between the two offices and a series of short-term prime ministers.

In 1998, Kuchma turned to Viktor Yushchenko, who had been chairman of the National Bank of Ukraine. The president desperately needed a competent prime minister. Yushchenko had the right credentials. He was best known for having successfully introduced the country's currency, the hryvnia, and skillfully moderating the effects on Ukraine of the Russian financial crisis of 1998. He did his job well, achieving growth rates above 5 percent after nine years of contraction and earning the respect and approval of the IMF and the World Bank.

Despite his sterling record, the Yushchenko government was dismissed following a no-confidence vote in the parliament after only one year. It seems the prime minister had angered powerful business interests with his aggressive anticorruption campaign. Yushchenko also ran afoul of the president, who became jealous of his successful and popular colleague. The ousted prime minister decided to form a coalition called Our Ukraine. In the parliamentary elections the next year, the new party won 112 seats. Yulia Tymoshenko, a wealthy oligarch allied with Yushchenko, did well too. Together they lacked a majority, but their bloc was influential and vibrant.

Now Kuchma had real opposition—and he did not react in a democratic spirit. Rather, the president turned to old authoritarian methods. Journalists were increasingly intimidated. The government issued a secret order forcing the media to print stories sponsored by the government (*temnyky*). Kuchma appointed a corrupt and hard-line former communist apparatchik to carry out his orders. He sacked yet another prime minister, bringing an ally, Viktor Yanukovych, the governor of the Donetsk region in the east, to Kiev.

But by March 2003, Kuchma was losing his grip on the country. He had clearly underestimated the degree to which freedom of association and a still relatively independent press would complicate his efforts to crack down on dissent. Tens of thousands demonstrated, demanding his resignation and constitutional changes to limit the power of the president. Media outlets began to report instances of corruption within the Kuchma clique. The use of *temnyky* was openly reported, and protested too. And a few brave journalists began to publish stories questioning the president's role in the disappearance of opposition figures.

Then a small city election in a remote region gave the opposition a rallying point. Ernest Nuser, Kuchma's candidate, defeated Our Ukraine's candidate, Viktor Baloha, in a contest widely regarded as fraudulent. Observers reported incidents of violence and ballot tampering. The reaction was intense, many worrying that the events portended similar ones in the upcoming presidential elections. Nuser had to resign as mayor one month later.

Kuchma was now under intense pressure. He pledged to undertake constitutional reform but also pledged not to seek reelection. Yanukovych took up the president's mantle and would a few months later become the candidate of the Party of Regions. On the other side, representing Our Ukraine, would be Viktor Yushchenko. The presidential election that followed was the stuff of Hollywood—intrigue, drama, and a poisoning.

"Meet Viktor Yanukovych"

Vladimir Putin was justifiably proud of his new office in the president's dacha some twenty kilometers outside Moscow. On that day in May 2004, he had invited me to chat before our formal meeting with others. Now we stood looking through the French doors at an extraordinary expansive, sunlit garden. *Reminds me a bit of the Rose Garden. But bigger,* I thought.

Before I could reflect on that much further, a side door suddenly flew open. Out walked a tall, graying man who grasped my hand in a firm handshake. "Meet Viktor Yanukovych," the Russian president said to me. "He is running for the presidency of Ukraine." It was one of those odd moments that often happened with Putin. He was never subtle. He might as well have said, *Meet Viktor Yanukovych. My man in Kiev.*

Yanukovych undoubtedly appreciated Moscow's support.

But his real advantages came through Kuchma, who used the state apparatus to tip the scales in his favor. International observers reported threats against students, workers, and government employees who dared support Yushchenko. The increasingly cowed media was heavily biased toward the president's handpicked successor. European, U.S., and Canadian officials all expressed concern about the course of the electoral campaign, but to no avail. The playing field was by no means level.

Then events took a melodramatic turn. Viktor Yushchenko woke up violently ill the morning after a dinner with the chief of the Ukrainian security services. The doctors could not immediately determine what was wrong with him, but he believed that he had been poisoned. One of Kuchma's representatives suggested that Yushchenko use a food taster "as they did in the Middle Ages." The signal wasn't in the least bit subtle: Challenging the president could cost one his life. A team of Western doctors would later determine that Yushchenko had indeed been poisoned with dioxin.

Despite his deteriorating condition, he pressed on in the campaign. The battle lines were becoming clear—this was a contest between a conservative, pro-Russian camp and one that looked west toward Europe. On the campaign trail, Yanukovych promised to hold a referendum that would not only grant Ukrainians new pathways to dual citizenship with Russia but also codify Russian as the country's second official language. This was popular among some constituencies in the east of the country, but terrifying to the pro-Western liberals in Kiev.

As the election proceeded, the corruption of the process

by Kuchma's forces intensified, so that when the balloting was finally held on October 31, 2004, it came as no surprise that, in the understated assessment of an international monitor, the voting "did not meet... the standards for democratic elections."[3] The Central Election Commission actually stopped counting ballots as Yushchenko started to gather momentum, fueling theories that it intended to block his victory no matter what. In any case, neither man received the 50 percent of the vote required to avoid a runoff.

Less than a month later, Ukrainians voted in record numbers in the second phase. It would take three days to certify the vote. In the interim, large crowds turned out in major cities to support Yushchenko. Several city councils, including that in Kiev, recognized him as president. Meanwhile, the Russian president congratulated his man, Yanukovych, based on the initial but incomplete findings of the commission. When the final vote was certified on November 24, Yanukovych was declared the winner—49.46 percent to 46.61 percent.

International monitors did not believe the results. The United States, Europe, and Canada did not believe the results. Most important, the supporters of Viktor Yushchenko did not believe the results. Protesters blocked government offices, cheering as their standard-bearer symbolically took the oath of office in the parliament building. Huge crowds, some estimated at two hundred thousand people, occupied the square every day. The Ukrainian parliament, responding to the people in the streets, passed a nonbinding resolution calling the elections invalid.

The country's allegiances were split, however. It was a very different story in the east, where several regions threatened to secede if the election results were not upheld. Counterdemonstrations dotted the landscape in that third of the country. Ukraine was in crisis.

In these chaotic circumstances, Ukrainian institutions had what may have been their finest hour. The Ukrainian Supreme Court stepped in and agreed to take Yushchenko's case, delaying certification of the results until a hearing set for November 29. The evidence presented to the court personally implicated Yanukovych in election fraud. Now on the defensive, Kuchma called for new elections. Four days later, the Supreme Court invalidated the November 21 ballot. Yushchenko won the revote, 51.99 percent to 44.19 percent. Yanukovych stepped down as prime minister and leader of his party. On January 23, Viktor Yushchenko became Ukraine's president. Luminaries from across the West attended, including Secretary of State Colin Powell. The Russian ambassador represented Moscow.

President Bush and I finally had a chance to meet Ukraine's new democratic leader at the NATO summit in February 2005. We were a bit early for the meeting, as was often the president's habit. We all looked forward to meeting the brave and somewhat legendary Yushchenko. But now there was a bit of apprehension settling on our delegation. "Don't be surprised," John Herbst, our ambassador to Ukraine, warned. "His appearance is shocking." John was emphatic, but nothing prepared us for what we were about to see.

Yushchenko was tall, and it was easy to imagine that he had once been very handsome. Now, due to the poisoning, his face was a pockmarked mess of purple and green splotches and his ears had ballooned in size. His beautiful, elegant wife accompanied him, holding on to his arm. No one said anything about his appearance, of course, though the president did ask if he was feeling okay now. "Yes, I'm recovering," Yushchenko said.

President Bush soldiered on through the conversation, looking him in the eye but trying not to stare. They talked about Yushchenko's election pledge to remove Ukrainian troops from Iraq. The president reassured him that he understood. They discussed the state of the economy. Yushchenko pledged to fight corruption and secure private investment. Everyone tried to stay on point. But it was hard to concentrate on what the Ukrainian said. The whole situation was just so sad. It must have been awful to look in the mirror every morning and see how much his commitment to his country had cost him.

Still, the personal sacrifice had to be put into perspective: Ukrainian democracy had held and this man was the freely elected president of the fledgling independent country. Yushchenko told President Bush right then and there that he wanted to join NATO. "It will guarantee our democracy," he said. The president of the United States demurred—not wanting to promise something he might not be able to deliver. But he never forgot that moment when the president of Ukraine—disfigured by a clumsy assassination attempt—asked for America's protection.

The Orange Revolution Turns Sour

The leitmotifs of Ukrainian politics—corruption, personal animosity between key figures, shifting alliances, and Moscow's interference in the affairs of the country—emerged soon after independence and have complicated its road ahead ever since. This has led to the repeated breakdown of politics in Ukraine, leaving the population with no recourse but to take to the streets. And each time, the institutions have become less trusted and less legitimate.

The afterglow of the Orange Revolution, as the events of late 2004 came to be called, lasted less than a year. Yushchenko nominated Yulia Tymoshenko to be his prime minister. The two had apparently signed an agreement before the election promising her support in exchange for the post if he won. The parliament enthusiastically approved her appointment in February 2005. By September 2005, she was gone. The frustrated Ukrainian people watched during that time as personal animus between these two veterans of the Orange Revolution stalled the process of governing.

Tymoshenko was a force of nature in her own right—beautiful, rich, popular, and fiercely competitive. She wore fashionable clothes, her blond hair arrayed in a crown of braids that made her look like a cross between Princess Leia and that Swiss Miss character of hot cocoa fame.

When we first met, she took care to remind me that we were both women in a tough world. But I was stunned to hear her continuously refer to herself in the third person. "Yulia is really concerned. Yulia is determined to do it." It was just bizarre. But it revealed a kind of aggressive self-confidence and a significant ego. Well, one did need both as a woman in East European politics, so I was inclined to ignore the implications of her personality. Still, it left me with the sense that I never quite knew where she stood, though I found her easy to like.

Knowing the two protagonists, it wasn't hard to see why they clashed. Both were strong-willed and stubborn—and jealous of each other. Still, the disagreements between the president and the prime minister were not wholly personal. Real policy differences emerged almost immediately. Tymoshenko undertook populist measures that undermined the economic reforms that Yushchenko—a banker by trade—championed. She tried to impose price controls, eroding market forces. She raised stipends for students, pensions for older people, and salaries for workers, ignoring the budget implications of her decisions. The president feared that she was running for office, not governing the country.

But rather than work through his differences with his prime minister, Yushchenko became one of her most vocal and public critics. They simply couldn't work together and their hatred for each other grew, becoming legendary among Ukrainians and the rest of the world.

This fracturing of the Orange coalition allowed Viktor Yanukovych to reemerge in the parliamentary elections of 2006. Though Tymoshenko and Yushchenko garnered larger shares of the vote, they were unable to form a government. The smaller Socialist Party that had been part of their coalition switched sides and, together with Yanukovych and the Party of Regions, took control. The new coalition demanded the post of prime minister. Left with no options, Yushchenko agreed and ceded the role to his old rival. Not surprisingly, the two were an even more combustible duo.

Over the next months, the government lost good and sound people, hounded by one or the other leader and ultimately just fed up with the daily intrigue. Among them was the highly regarded foreign minister, Borys Tarasyuk. I had come to admire this former Soviet diplomat, an understated and intelligent man, who served Ukraine's interests well in international affairs. When he resigned I called him to thank him for what he had done. He didn't mince words. "It just isn't possible to work—to do anything—to accomplish anything," he said. That was the perfect description of Ukrainian politics. Less than a year after forming the new government, Yushchenko dissolved the parliament and called for elections yet again.

Ukrainian politics began to resemble a game of musical chairs. Each time the music stopped, either Yushchenko or Tymoshenko or Yanukovych was left with nowhere to sit. In 2007, Tymoshenko's Fatherland Party received 30.7 percent of the vote, Yanukovych's Party of Regions 34.5 percent, and the once popular Yushchenko's Our Ukraine only 14.1 percent. This left the latter with only one option—go back into coalition with Yulia. He did. They fought again. Both lost popularity among the people, who were weary of their personal jousting while the country's problems festered. Yushchenko became an even more outspoken critic of Yulia. But it was *his* credibility that was severely damaged. In the presidential election of 2010 he was odd man out, not really a factor in the balloting. In two electoral rounds, Yanukovych defeated Tymoshenko by a margin of three points. She refused to concede and insisted on remaining prime minister. This time the last chair would belong to the new president. The parliament ousted Yulia in a vote of no confidence on March 3, 2010.

Yanukovych moved swiftly to wipe out opposition. He brought in a prime minister from his own eastern region. Just to make sure that he was secure, he turned to Constitutional Court—now made up of his loyalists—to weaken the position. The Orange Revolution reforms that had divided power between the two were overturned in favor of the presidency.

Then, in December, Tymoshenko and the former interior minister, Yuriy Lutsenko, were indicted on allegations of mishandling state finances. Several months later, the former prime minister was hauled off to jail, accused of harming Ukraine's interests in carrying out negotiations with Russia over the price of natural gas. She was to be excluded from politics for ten years and fined $190 million.

The sentence provoked an outcry internationally. While no one was willing to vouch for the deal that Tymoshenko struck with the Russians, the charges clearly carried a taint of political retribution. Yanukovych gratuitously noted that the decision was not final and there was always the possibility of appeal. Tymoshenko was jailed for four more years—out of the political process but not out of the limelight. She remained a popular figure as her supporters proclaimed her innocence at home and abroad.

Tymoshenko's imprisonment complicated Yanukovych's efforts to carve out a reputation as a man who could do business with both Europe and Russia. On the one hand, he desperately wanted to complete an association agreement with the

European Union. On the other, the president was clear that Ukraine should not seek to join NATO. This was a very big departure from the views of his predecessors.

From that first meeting with President Bush when Yushchenko mentioned NATO membership, Ukraine had sought closer association with the alliance. Everyone knew that membership would be far into the future, if at all. Ukraine simply didn't meet the criteria. Still, it got closer to its goal at the NATO summit in Bucharest in July 2008.

As we saw earlier, the question of Georgia's and Ukraine's desire to join MAP—effectively an interim step toward NATO membership—had been contentious in the alliance. It was a hard decision for the Bush administration too—trying to balance relations with Russia and our commitment to democracy in the former Soviet states.

When the president asked for my recommendation during our deliberations, I told him that I was torn. I didn't think that I could deliver the allies, particularly Germany. There was even some uncertainty about whether support for MAP was really solid in Ukraine, particularly in the east. Yet the Ukrainians and the Georgians deserved their chance to earn NATO membership. I told my NSC colleagues that I had been very much affected by Yushchenko's personal appeal a few months earlier.

The Ukrainian had asked to see me on the margins of the Davos Conference in Switzerland in January 2008. It had been difficult to get to him, with my driver trying to navigate the traffic and the treacherous, narrow roads. We were sitting in the car and going nowhere. I was checking my watch. Finally, I said, "We'll walk."

"You're kidding," Marty Kraus, the head of my security detail, said.

"We'll never get there by car," I replied.

So we got out and trudged up the hill toward the president's hotel, the Belvedere. I was thankful that I'd spent a lot of my early years as an ice skater—it was pretty slick. But we made it, breathing a little hard but on time.

Yushchenko didn't waste a moment. "We must have MAP," he said. I started to explain the difficulties and suggest that maybe it was best to put off the decision until the alliance was more united. He interrupted, "It will be the end of our democracy if we don't get in. We don't know who will come after President Bush, and we trust him." I looked at his disfigured face and noticed that his eyes were welling up with tears. I had to fight hard not to cry too.

To President Bush's credit, he didn't try to split the difference between Moscow and Germany on the one hand, and the Ukrainians and the Georgians on the other. We went to the NATO summit intent on trying to secure MAP for Kiev and Tbilisi. The East European members of NATO delivered impassioned pleas in favor of MAP. At one point, the Polish foreign minister, Radek Sikorski, called out his German counterpart in an unforgettable exchange. Frank-Walter Steinmeier said that NATO should not import frozen conflicts. Georgia had disputed territory—Abkhazia and South Ossetia, which was essentially occupied by the Russians. Sikorski retorted, "You were a frozen conflict for forty-five years," referring to the postwar division of Germany. "NATO saved you from Stalin. How dare you leave others unprotected from Moscow." *Well*, I thought. *That was rough*. But in the end, we couldn't unite the alliance to deliver MAP for Ukraine and Georgia. The Bucharest communiqué was a compromise, and a good one. It stated unequivocally that Ukraine and Georgia would one day be members of NATO.

The Ukrainian parliament closed off that pathway in 2010, with President Yanukovych pushing through a vote to end Ukraine's aspirations to join the military alliance of Europe's democracies.

Ukraine's Third Revolution

The parliamentary elections of October 2012 again pitted Yanukovych against Tymoshenko. Yulia organized the challenge to the president from her jail cell. The Front for Change, several smaller groups, and her own Fatherland Party united in opposition to the Party of Regions. Tymoshenko's coalition, not surprisingly, was particularly strong in the west. But Yanukovych won decisively. This time, the balloting was largely free of outright fraud. Yet international observers noted that the playing field had not been level, given the president's control of the media and the fact that the key opposition leaders were in jail. This led the head of the Organization for Security and Co-operation in Europe (OSCE) observer mission to say that the "democratic process appears to have reversed in Ukraine."

His hand strengthened by the elections, Yanukovych resumed negotiations to complete the agreement with the European Union. In April 2013, the president expressed confidence that the remaining issues—concerning justice and electoral reform—would be resolved rapidly. He pardoned Yuriy Lutsenko but not Tymoshenko in response to calls for the release of political prisoners. Everything seemed to be on track for the conclusion of the trade and political agreement between Ukraine and the EU.

But apparently Yanukovych had not quite read Moscow correctly in his desire to walk a middle course. In July, Russia suddenly halted imports of chocolate from Ukraine's main confectioner, saying the products didn't meet safety standards. Then, in August, toying with Kiev, Russia started to subject all Ukrainian imports to more thorough customs inspections. The restrictions were lifted temporarily about a week later. An aide to Putin didn't mince words, though, saying that the problems could become permanent if Ukraine signed the agreement with the EU.

It isn't really clear if Yanukovych just misread Moscow or hoped to present the Kremlin with a fait accompli when the accord was signed. Some Ukrainians believe that the president was double-dealing all along—knowing that Russia would bring pressure on Kiev to halt the process of integration. Whatever his motivation, it is true that Yanukovych faced the threat of crippling sanctions from his largest trading partner.

On November 21, 2013, Ukraine announced that it would no longer seek an accord with the European Union. Instead, it would turn to the east and pursue partnerships with Russia and a trade bloc of former Soviet states called the Eurasian Economic Union. The Kremlin said it welcomed "the desire of our close partner Ukraine to optimize and develop trade and economic cooperation."

Shock, dismay, and outrage spread through the streets of

Kiev almost immediately. Within twenty-four hours, tens of thousands of protesters rushed into the Maidan, the central square of Kiev, as well as into cities across the country. The United States and Europe expressed concern. Ukrainians accused the president of bowing to the Russians in a treasonous act.

For the next three months, Ukraine was again in chaos, ungovernable and at the edge of civil war. The police used tear gas and truncheons to break up the demonstrations. That just brought more people into the streets. Security forces could not hold the protesters back and they eventually occupied several buildings. Opposition politicians quickly jumped on the bandwagon of the enraged population. Vitali Klitschko, a former heavyweight champ turned liberal legislator, emerged as the voice of dissent: "If this government does not want to fulfill the will of the people, then there will be no such government, there will be no such president. There will be a new government and a new president."

At first, Yanukovych sought to remain above the fray, leaving the prime minister, Mykola Azarov, to be the voice of the government. The president said only that people should observe the law. The prime minister accused the protesters of trying to launch a coup. The president carried through on a state visit to China on December 4. The visuals were awful. While people rioted in the streets of Kiev, Yanukovych toured a museum of ancient artifacts and a factory.

The president's casual approach to the unfolding chaos only enraged the protesters further. On December 8, hundreds of thousands of people descended on the square, smashing a statue of Lenin. The crowd roamed the city, blockading buildings and forming a tent city. The police stood aside, refusing to repeat the violent crackdown of the week before. Soon, antigovernment demonstrators had unwelcome company—large crowds supporting Yanukovych.

The president could no longer ignore the peril that he and the country faced. In a sense, he had to make a choice—and not surprisingly he turned eastward, securing a $15 billion loan from the Russians on December 16. Putin tried to give the embattled Ukrainian leader space. He announced that the two leaders had not discussed membership for Ukraine in the customs union of Russia, Belarus, and Kazakhstan.

But for the opposition, the loan was further evidence that Yanukovych was now doing Moscow's bidding. The demonstrations continued and got larger. In response, the Party of Regions sponsored legislation restricting protests and promising harsh penalties for those who participated in them. On January 16, 2014, the parliament passed a bill prohibiting people from installing tents or sound systems in public and exposing the organizers of unauthorized meetings to criminal penalties. Opposition leaders cried foul, with Klitschko saying, "What happened in the parliament is a violation of all rules and laws, it carries no legal weight."

The threats had little effect. Tensions worsened, and in February several protesters died in clashes with police. International mediators stepped in, hoping to force a stand-down by both sides. For a brief time it seemed as if they had succeeded. Demonstrators ceded some buildings to OSCE monitors in exchange for amnesty for those who had "violated public order" between December 27 and February 2. The president withdrew riot police from the front lines of the confrontation.

The uneasy calm broke suddenly and violently on February 18. In a two-day period, nearly ninety people were killed and hundreds were wounded as police and protesters battled for the streets around parliament and Independence Square. The apparent spark for the unrest was a rumor that the Rada (as the parliament is called) would not restore the Orange Revolution–inspired constitution of 2004.

International leaders watched with alarm as Kiev began to resemble a war zone. Russia, France, Germany, and Poland sponsored talks between Yanukovych and the opposition leaders. They reached an agreement, with the president promising to return to the constitution of 2004. Ukrainian legislators passed an amnesty for all antigovernment protesters, and called for assistance to the relatives of those and for the release of Yulia Tymoshenko.

A moment comes in every revolution when people are no longer fearful of their government. When I visited Bucharest with President Bush in 2005, the Romanians described such a time. In 1989, with revolutions toppling communist governments throughout Eastern Europe, Nicolae Ceauşescu went into the public square to tell the people all he had done for them. Suddenly, one old lady yelled, "Liar!" And then ten people, one hundred, one thousand, and soon the entire square was yelling, "Liar!" Ceauşescu, seeing the rising tide against him, fled. But he was caught by the military, handed over to the opposition, and he and his wife, Yelena, were executed.

Perhaps Yanukovych had in mind the "Ceauşescu moment" when he decided to flee Kiev. His own party condemned his "cowardly flight." Despite claiming that he would not resign and he would remain in office—he obviously had not. Ukraine appointed an interim president and prime minister and prepared for new elections. Yanukovych would eventually show up in Moscow, where Putin was willing to protect *his man* from his own people.

The world breathed a sigh of relief. President Obama and Chancellor Merkel both talked to the Russian president by phone. There were promises to work for a peaceful and stable Ukraine—together.

Vladimir Putin, it turns out, had a different definition of a stable Ukraine—one without a part of its territory. In late February 2014, Russian forces seized Crimea. Pro-Moscow separatists held a referendum that supposedly affirmed the citizens' desire to be incorporated within Russia. The Russian parliament claimed that it could not, of course, deny the Crimeans that privilege, and it voted to annex the territory on March 23, 2014.

A month later, pro-Russian separatists moved against mainland Ukraine, taking over in parts of eastern Donetsk and the Luhansk region along the Russian border. Moscow denied the involvement of its own forces. But European and American satellite imagery suggested otherwise. Nevertheless, Putin gave a clear rationale for why he might want to invade, even while denying he had done so. He explained that ethnic Russians living in eastern Ukraine had to be protected from Kiev. They had suffered discrimination and their rights had been abridged since independence. That argument had been used before: Adolf Hitler claimed to be protecting ethnic Germans in 1938 when he annexed Austria and the Sudetenland, territory located within the borders of Czechoslovakia.

But there was little that the international community could do. Since the climactic events in the early days of 2014, two agreements, negotiated in Minsk in September 2014 and February 2015, have been violated again and again. Cease-fires have been negotiated, broken, and renegotiated. The Russians have stopped short of supporting independence for eastern Ukraine, but Kiev doesn't really govern it either. Ukraine is a partitioned state: Crimea gone; eastern Ukraine occupied and unstable; and the west trying to build a functioning democratic government under trying circumstances.

The man whom the Ukrainians elected in 2014, businessman Petro Poroshenko, has that unenviable task. He has sought closer cooperation with the European Union, establishing a free trade zone committed to removing tariffs and other barriers over time. The Ukrainians have received significant aid from the United States, the EU, and other countries. Some reforms have been carried out, including changes to the tax code backed by the IMF and passing budgets with a deficit that falls within internationally acceptable standards.

Poroshenko has tried to bring decent and talented people into his government. Ukraine is blessed to have a large and educated diaspora. People of Ukrainian descent have come back from Canada, the United States, and other parts of Europe to try to help since the events of the Maidan. Natalie Jaresko, an American citizen who once worked for me at the State Department, is emblematic of this trend. Widely regarded as competent and honest, she was able to accomplish a great deal as finance minister.

But it is still, as former foreign minister Tarasyuk said several years ago, hard to get anything done in Kiev. In February 2016, the economics minister, Aivarus Abromavičius, a Ukrainian of Lithuanian descent, resigned, saying that powerful figures were derailing reforms through pressure and intimidation.

The difficulty is most evident in the on-again/off-again efforts to root out corruption. Still, to be fair, Poroshenko has achieved more in his term of three years than his predecessors did in their combined years.

Before he took office, anticorruption efforts in Ukraine effectively amounted to sound and fury. The Yushchenko administration had spent years trying to pass a package of anticorruption laws through parliament, and it finally succeeded in 2009. But a year later, Yanukovych was elected and had them overturned.

Yanukovych would go on to oversee the deepening of corruption, including the takeover of strategic industries by his cronies. His family benefited too as his son Oleksander quickly became the second-richest man in Donetsk. Ukraine plummeted to 144th place on the international Transparency Index, a scale that measures and compares corrupt practices across the globe.

After Yanukovych was ousted, Poroshenko moved quickly to pass legislation and to create new institutions devoted to fighting corruption. The National Anti-Corruption Bureau, which reviews complaints from citizens, is paired with the National Agency for the Prevention of Corruption, which is a watchdog over the activities of government officials. There is a new Law on the Judiciary and the Status of Judges to try to force greater judicial independence. And there have been a few prosecutions of high-ranking officials—principally from the Yanukovych period. Efforts have been made to boost government accountability and transparency through the introduction of innovative electronic platforms for public procurement and financial disclosure by public officials. Steps have also been taken to limit bribes and fraud in the customs system.

These are very helpful and welcome steps. But there is also a troubling tendency in Ukraine to use corruption as an epithet against those with whom you disagree. Charges of complicity or outright participation in shady dealings fly around almost every major politician.

This has not improved the atmosphere for governing. And the country has pressing problems. While it has experienced periods of significant growth since independence, the economy has contracted in recent years—7 percent in 2014 and 10 percent in 2015. The chaos in the eastern part of the country has caused stagnation in some of the most important industrial regions, like Donetsk. Pension reform needs to be completed to relieve the pressures of entitlements to an aging population. The eastern third of Ukraine remains poor, polluted, and undereducated, providing fertile ground for Putin's appeals to the Russian-speaking population there. There is so much to do.

Facing these challenges, Ukraine continues to experience repeated political crises within the leadership that hinder progress. The latest occurred in the winter of 2016 when the president tried to sack his prime minister, Arseniy Yatsenyuk: a familiar pattern since independence.

The unpopular Yatsenyuk fought back, though, threatening to take the whole government down with him if he was removed. He won a vote of no confidence but not the support of the president. This locked the two in a battle that once again set governing aside while they engaged in political theater, which Yatsenyuk eventually lost.

"You Don't Need Another Revolution"

"How can you cooperate with corrupt people?" I was in Kiev in 2016 and engaged in a roundtable discussion with some young parliamentarians. My host, Victor Pinchuk, warned me that these twenty-somethings were not much interested in the art of compromise. "They are young and determined—patriotic but not sure how to move the political process forward," he said. The parliamentarians represented mostly liberal political parties, including the president's, identifying themselves as members of the Poroshenko faction.

The young man's question came in response to my admonition to work together and forge legislation across party lines. "That's what governing is," I said. But it was clear that most of them were in no mood to hear about compromise. They considered themselves to be challengers to the system, to the status quo—to the very parliament that they represented. The legislature was not a place to govern; it was a place to demand outright victory. It was easy to see why very little was getting done.

Yet these young parliamentarians were a compelling group. They wanted the best for their country and they wanted to help build democracy in Ukraine. They were passionate and sincere. *Now if they could just overcome their stubbornness,* I thought.

Later that day, I spoke to a group of some two hundred students from local universities. I expressed my outrage at what Vladimir Putin had done in partitioning the country. I said that I understood how hard it was to govern under Ukraine's "international circumstances."

But I went on to say that the country could not let its grievances with Russia retard the effort to build a stable democracy. "Suppose West Germany had taken that course and waited until it was unified to build a strong and vibrant state. The Federal Republic of Germany would not have been able to take advantage of the collapse of the Soviet Union and integrate East Germany, completely on Western terms," I said. I wanted to be careful not to offend my audience, but I felt strongly about what I said next. "You have had three revolutions in twenty-five years: independence, the Orange Revolution, and the Maidan," I began. "It is time to stop having revolutions and to start governing." The students burst into applause and onto their feet. *The Ukrainians are tired of the drama,* I thought. *Can't their leaders see?*

That night my host gave a lovely dinner in his spectacular downtown apartment. The living room was adorned with extraordinary works of European art and a grand piano that I was dying to play, but chose not to. Several key political figures were there, including Yulia and the soon-to-be-ousted prime minister, Yatsenyuk. They all talked in apocalyptic terms about the battles going on inside the parliament. The conversation was surreal—no names were attached to the accusations and no actual examples of corruption were given. They talked instead in circles—about self-dealing and conflicts of interest. Still, one got the impression that everyone thought the person sitting next to them was likely corrupt. They were self-absorbed and focused on the political intrigue that seemed to consume them.

As the plane took off that night, I looked out over the vast territory of Ukraine. The country wasn't dealt a very good hand. It is dogged by questions about its identity as a nation; shadowed by a neighbor that poses an omnipresent threat; and subjected to leaders who constantly seem to confuse the personal with the political.

Institutions are supposed to help contain and overcome human imperfections. I reflected on Madison, who said that the American Constitution was not perfect—it was the hard work of imperfect men. Ukraine has thus far survived multiple crises and lived to fight another day. That means its leaders still have a chance to deliver stable democracy to Ukraine—no matter their imperfections.

Chapter 5

KENYA: "SAVE OUR BELOVED COUNTRY"

The old man shuffled into the Oval Office holding on to a beautifully handcrafted ivory walking cane to keep him upright. It was June 27, 2001, and Kenya was to hold elections the following year. Daniel arap Moi had led the country for more than two decades. Now he wanted to be president again.

Colin Powell had met with Moi a month earlier and urged him to honor the constitutional provision barring him from seeking reelection. Moi had made no such commitment. Now it was President Bush's turn to deliver the message. Just before the Kenyans arrived, Jendayi Frazer, the NSC Africa specialist, briefed the president. "Mr. President, you have to let him know in no uncertain terms that we will not support him if he tries to hold on to power," she said.

Jendayi knew Kenya. A highly regarded Africanist, she had been my PhD student at Stanford. My mind flashed back to 1991 during my first stint at the White House. Jendayi was on the phone asking to speak with me urgently. She was doing field research in Nairobi. "Things are a little tense here and there is a lot of violence," she said. "Could you ask someone in the government if I should leave?" I walked down the hall and put the question to the special assistant for African affairs, David D. Miller. He didn't hesitate. "Tell her to get the hell out of there." I did, arranging for Stanford to get money to her so that she could come home.

As Moi began his pitch, he seemed to be leaning the wrong way. His eyes darted back and forth, staring at each of us as he recited the old slogans about ethnic tensions in his country and how the next election might exacerbate them. The implication was clear, though he didn't actually say it: Moi wanted to run again because he was the best man to unify Kenyans. His country needed him.

The president told him flatly to step down. "Everyone's time comes to leave office. When the American people are done with me, I'll go back to Texas, proud to have served but glad to be an ordinary citizen again. You need to go home to your children and grandchildren," he said.

Moi was clearly unhappy with the message, but he seemed to understand that time was up. When the two men met again three months later on the sidelines of the United Nations General Assembly in New York, the Kenyan was ready to do the right thing. It was, after all, not just the president of the United States who thought it was time for him to go. His people were ready for a change too.

Moi stepped aside, and on December 29 of that year, Mwai Kibaki, only seven years the president's junior, was elected. Uhuru Kenyatta, the son of the country's founder and Moi's handpicked successor, conceded the next day. The transition was relatively smooth.

Kenya's Hard Road to Democracy

That day had been a long time coming for Kenya. For forty years—from independence in 1963 to the watershed election of 2002—the Kenyan people struggled against authoritarian rule.

The struggle actually went back even further. The British East Africa Protectorate was formed in 1895, with white settlers arriving shortly thereafter. The British government appointed a Legislative Council to represent the settler community in 1906, and the first elected representatives were selected by six thousand settlers in 1919.[1] A British governor was appointed in 1920 and the protectorate was turned into a colony, now known as Kenya.

The system stayed in place until the upheaval of World War II stirred Africans across the continent to seek independence. Jomo Kenyatta, widely viewed as the father of modern Kenya, became the head of the Kenya African Union in 1944 and the voice of the people's political push for sovereignty. He, together with Patrice Lumumba of Congo, Kwame Nkrumah of Ghana, Julius Nyerere of Tanzania, Félix Houphouët-Boigny of Côte d'Ivoire, and others, was a powerful advocate for an end to colonialism. These leaders mobilized public opinion across the world to support their cause.

This political movement was essential, but in Kenya the British were also pressed by some of the most violent resistance activities on the continent. A secret group of fighters from the Kikuyu tribe, known as the Mau Mau, carried out a campaign against white settlers for four years, from 1952 to 1956. The Mau Mau rebellion cost fourteen thousand Africans and a hundred or so Europeans their lives.[2] The British eventually declared a state of emergency and crushed the guerrillas by force. Kenyatta, despite no direct connection to the rebellion, was tried, arrested, and imprisoned for nine years.

But London's appetite for maintaining its colonial possessions across Africa and Asia was waning. The United Kingdom had been flattened economically by World War II and was yielding global leadership to the United States. The sun was indeed setting on the British Empire.

Kenya's First Democratic Opening

In March 1960, the British laid down a framework for a transition to Kenyan independence under majority rule. The Legislative Council, which had been created to allow white settlers to govern themselves, was to be given over to a narrow African majority, though there were seats reserved for Asians and Europeans.[3] The Kenya African National Union (KANU) and the Kenyan African Democratic Union (KADU) were formed as political parties on the eve of independence. Kenya held multiparty elections for the first time in February 1961, and then again in May 1963. KANU won both decisively. Kenyatta became prime minister, leading the transition to independence six months later.

The institutional landscape of Kenya at the birth of the new nation looked promising. The country carried out multiparty elections to the legislature and Kenyatta was a revered civilian leader and a strong figure to unify Kenya's many ethnic groups. Unlike nearly all other newly independent African states, Kenya would never experience a successful military coup d'état.[4]

But the external trappings were deceiving. Kenya was and is a country with deep tribal fissures. Its tribes are not tightly knit clans in isolated areas. They are more like ethnic groups that share distinctive cultural, linguistic, and historical roots. Some groups are predominant in certain towns and neighborhoods, but they are generally dispersed throughout the country and the population is mixed. Kenyatta, who became Kenya's first president, was a Kikuyu. Moi, his vice president and successor, was a Kalenjin. Although they accounted for only a third of Kenya's population, these two tribes have always wielded outsized political influence.

Ethnic Group	Percent	Key Figures
Kikuyu	22%	Jomo Kenyatta, Mwai Kibaki, Uhuru Kenyatta
Luhya	14%	Michael Kijana Wamalwa
Luo	13%	Oginga Odinga, Raila Odinga
Kalenjin	12%	Daniel arap Moi
Kamba	11%	
Other African	27%	
Non-African	1%	

Source: "Kenya," *CIA World Factbook*, https://www.cia.gov/library/publications/the-world-factbook/geos/ke.html.

The country's demographics drove two institutional debates that conditioned Kenya's road ahead for years to come. One was the question of federalism—how much devolution of power to the regions was appropriate. The centralized state was seen by some as a safeguard against tribalism and the epitome of Kenyan unity. But others saw the strong state as a stand-in for tribal dominance by the Kikuyu, the largest group. The second related question, over the power of the presidency, reflected deep suspicions that any institution was just a cover for tribal and personal loyalties. And, indeed, leaders repeatedly appealed to the streets—speaking of one Kenya but falling back easily on tribal politics in the hardest of times.

The End of Multiparty Rule

Kenyatta did not tolerate dissent for very long. Five months after independence, the government banned public meetings. KADU, the rival political party, was effectively absorbed into KANU, as member after member saw no other choice but to defect.[5] The new government was left without formal opposition. In December 1964, the position of prime minister was abolished and Kenyatta became president. His longtime ally, Oginga Odinga, was named vice president, only to resign that position two years later and create the Kenyan People's Union (KPU). The expressed purpose of the KPU was to oppose the Western orientation of the country and move leftward toward class struggle and state ownership of the economy.

Political parties were losing relevance, however, sidelined by an increasingly centralized state under an increasingly authoritarian president. The Senate was abolished, and the unicameral National Assembly was dominated by Kenyatta's allies. When Kenyatta died in office in 1978, Moi, his vice president, succeeded him. The next year, Moi ran unopposed. In June 1982, he declared Kenya a one-party state, formalizing the reality of politics in the country for more than a decade.

For the next ten years, Kenya experienced outbreaks of ethnic conflict, economic stagnation, and unsustainable debt to well-meaning foreign donors. The dependence on foreign assistance, however, gave the international community leverage to push for change in support of a Kenyan populace fed up with the state of affairs. By the late 1980s, the economy had stalled. Then it began to contract. GDP per capita was only $382 in 1988, but it declined further, to $366 in 1990, and $328 in 1992.[6] Meanwhile, inflation continued to rise. Facing economic crisis, the Kenyan regime sought to reach agreement with the IMF and the World Bank for continued economic support. The "Washington consensus," as it was known at the time, required countries seeking assistance to take painful steps, including cutting budget deficits, privatizing industries, devaluing currencies, and tackling corruption.[7]

In Kenya's case, the United States agreed to forgive $44.7 million in loans immediately and another $130 million over two years if the government abided by the requirements of the IMF/World Bank program.[8] This was part of a larger plan to forgive $735 million owed by twelve sub-Saharan African countries. Unfortunately, the rulers of these nations were in many cases more concerned with personal glory than with performing for their people. In Kenya, for example, the government was insistently pursuing plans for a $200 million, sixty-story skyscraper that would have been Africa's tallest commercial building. The leaders relented and downsized the project only after coming under criticism from the World Bank and donor countries.

The pressure to reform economically would slowly bleed into concerns about the political system. As much as the two are theoretically separable, economic and political institutions do affect one another. But precisely how they interact is a matter of debate. Some have argued that economic reform should be the priority. Democracy is messy, with veto-wielding groups and noisy constituencies that make tough choices untenable: better to liberalize the political system after a country can deliver basic goods and comforts to the people. Support for this view could be found in the stories of the Asian Tigers from Taiwan to South Korea, which built a sound economic foundation and have since become stable democracies.

The alternative view is that many of the ills that limit economic progress can be addressed only through political reform. Law is arbitrary in authoritarian regimes because power rests in too few hands. Corruption is hard to deal with when it is practiced by the leaders and their cronies. And until there is some modicum of free thought and expression, the most capable and creative citizens will seek to live where those liberties exist. In this narrative, some of the Asian Tigers are the exception to the rule, not the other way around.

Those who were faced with this question in confronting the Kenyan regime were largely of the latter view. The degree to which international players insisted on political and not just economic reform is remarkable and a successful example of "democracy promotion." But importantly, the international pressure was supporting powerful domestic forces that were determined to be heard.

Moi's stranglehold on power was slowly eroded as political and economic conditions fostered the emergence of counterbalancing forces in Kenya's institutional landscape. Aided by the regime's abysmal economic performance, opponents were able to highlight Moi's failed policies and brutal repression of opposition. They championed a multiparty system as an antidote to Kenya's ills.

At first the president stood fast, opening a session of the parliament in February 1990 with a resounding rejection of political change. "Kenyans are not opposed to the multiparty system because of ideological reason or designs by those in leadership to impose their will on the people. What we have said is that until our society has become cohesive enough so that tribalism is of no significance... the strategy of a mass-based democratic and accountable one-party system is best," he said.[9]

Of course, the party was neither democratic nor accountable. And though ethnic cleavages were most certainly present in Kenya, they were widely viewed as a convenient excuse to ward off change. Former members of the president's own cabinet, Charles Rubia and Kenneth Matiba, fired the first salvo with calls for a transition to multiparty politics. They were quickly arrested but could not be silenced. Thousands of supporters gathered to demand their release, leading to mass rioting. Scores of people died. And despite Moi's personal order to muzzle the press, the events were fully covered.

Gibson Kamau Kuria, an opposition lawyer representing Rubia and Matiba, sought asylum at the U.S. embassy, causing an outcry from the government against "unwarranted interference in Kenya's affairs."[10] Arrests of opposition leaders escalated, but the crisis didn't abate. Events then followed a familiar cycle in challenges to autocratic regimes: Repression led to further protests, which led to further repression and more protests. With each successive round the regime became more isolated and illegitimate.

A central question in democratic transitions is whether the opposition can organize effectively to take advantage of an opening. In Kenya, the key institutional elements were rapidly emerging to do just that: the press that refused to be silenced; civil society groups, particularly human rights lawyers defending prisoners; a business community that championed change; and charismatic leaders, who spoke out from jail cells and the underground. Prominent Luo leader Oginga Odinga summed up the situation in a widely publicized letter to the president: "The message that Kenyans are sending you is they are tired and dissatisfied with your leadership."[11]

The opponents of the regime adopted a strategy for the next eighteen months calibrated to stay technically within the law. Initially, in February 1991, Oginga Odinga formed an opposition party (the National Democratic Party) dedicated to ending the constitutional requirement of a one-party state. He was, of course, unable to register NDP. But within months, he and his allies announced the formation of a different organization, the

Forum for the Restoration of Democracy (FORD), calling it a lobby group instead of a political party. Historians have noted that the name was designed to echo the Civic Forum movement in Czechoslovakia and East Germany.[12] That effort had incubated the opposition that eventually helped to bring down communist regimes in Eastern Europe.

Nonetheless, the designation that skirted the legal issue didn't provide protection from the regime. When FORD attempted a rally in November, armed riot police officers fired tear gas and used batons to disperse the demonstrators. Five leaders of the opposition were arrested as they drove to the meeting place. A total of twelve opposition leaders were jailed.

Kenyans—thanks to domestic press coverage—and the international community angrily watched events unfold. The regime's brutal behavior drew rebukes from across the globe, most importantly from donor nations. At a November meeting, twelve governments, including the United States, Britain, Japan, and others, threatened major aid cuts within six months if Kenya did not improve its performance on human rights and make economic and political reforms. Shortly before the announcement, the Kenyan foreign minister called the U.S. ambassador a racist in a news conference, saying, "I have told the U.S. ambassador that the Kenyan government is very unhappy with his personal behavior, that he is an arrogant man with contempt for Africans, his attitude is that of a slave owner, and he has no respect even for the head of state."[13] The attempt to play the race card made the regime seem even more desperate. It was, after all, Kenyans who had lost respect for the head of state.

Under intense pressure, in December 1991, Moi finally

announced that he intended to revise the constitution to allow political opposition to operate legally. An amendment was introduced a few days later and came into effect. But Moi left no doubt about the reasons for his change of heart. "It is because of the Western media set against us, because of the economic setting today. The trend of the world economies is being controlled by developed countries, and I didn't want my people to be hammered and bothered for a long time.... Don't you ever believe that multipartyism will produce stability in Africa. It will never."[14]

For a while it appeared that he was right. The country was hit with wave after wave of ethnic violence. And, indeed, much of it stemmed from the tribal underpinnings of the political forces. Members of the opposition belonged largely to the Luo, the second-largest tribe in the country. The Kikuyu, the most populous group, made clear that it would vote along ethnic lines. And the president's own tribe, the Kalenjin, used the moment to settle grievances and seize fertile farmland in the Rift Valley. Non-Kalenjin farmers abandoned their land, leading to cuts in food production. In a matter of months, ethnic conclaves were hardening, with the tribes determined to defend themselves and exact revenge on others.

By the spring of 1992, the *New York Times* reported, "for the first time since independence from Britain nearly 30 years ago, fierce ethnic violence has raised the specter of civil war in Kenya.... Bodies were still being found today in bushes... and in houses after a wave of killings, burnings and terror by Kalenjin warriors.... Some who ventured back to retrieve their belongings... escaped death only by following orders... to chant an oath in support of the Kalenjin-dominated Government."[15]

The political system fractured further when FORD split along ethnic lines. Odinga, a Luo from western Kenya, led one faction and Matiba, a Kikuyu, headed the other. Mwai Kibaki, also Kikuyu, took the reins of the Democratic Party. Despite their mutual opposition to Moi, the two largest tribes remained wary of one another, always concerned that the other would gain the upper hand in the battle for political power.

In this chaotic environment, it is not surprising that the country's first multiparty elections in December 1992 failed. Moi took advantage of the opposition's disarray and won the contest, which was widely regarded as tainted by cheating and vote rigging. The opposition refused to accept the outcome. Moi ignored them, governing with an iron fist over a decaying economy and a badly fractured country.

But the calls for democracy did not end. Over the next five years, student protests, outcry from the Roman Catholic Church, and international condemnation pressured the regime. Events reached a crescendo on July 7, 1997, when riot policemen crushed pro-democracy rallies across the country. Two days later, the regime closed five university campuses in the Nairobi area, hoping to quell student activism.

The Moi regime was facing a more organized effort this time. While political parties remained weak and given to infighting, civil society was beginning to coalesce. Seeking to update the constitution before the elections, the non-governmental organization Citizens Coalition for Constitutional Change organized a National Convention Assembly to press for reforms. Funded by the Ford Foundation, the group demanded changes to the constitution and threatened civil disobedience if the demands were not met. A number of key political figures, including Kibaki, attended the meeting.

Once again domestic unrest and international pressure were closing in on the government. The regime promised to consider reforms but did virtually nothing. Fearful that civil war was indeed approaching, moderates within the president's own party sought compromise with moderates from the Citizens Coalition.

Against the backdrop of worsening chaos, in the fall of 1997, Moi endorsed the moderates' package of reforms, wrong-footing civil rights advocates, clergy, and politicians who were pushing for more dramatic moves. There were important changes nonetheless, reducing state authority, ending preventive detention, and creating a new election commission with wide powers. Finally, the reforms called for a review of the constitution.

Realizing that he had split the opposition, Moi called for elections to be held on December 29. There was, of course, no time for reforms to take hold, though the Electoral Commission of Kenya (ECK) was constituted to oversee them. The chaotic elections produced confusion, and for a time it appeared as if neither Moi nor the opposition would reach the 25 percent threshold in several provinces needed to avoid a runoff. When the smoke cleared, however, the president was declared the winner. Despite all the benefits of incumbency and considerable fraud on his behalf, the president won only about 40 percent of the vote. In a harbinger of things to come, the major ethnic groups voted for their kinsmen: the Kikuyu for Kibaki; the Luo for Raila Odinga (the son of Oginga Odinga); Luhya for Michael Wamalwa; and Kamba for Charity Ngilu.

The results seemed to have a chastening effect on the

president. "My next government will be more sensitive to the needs and aspirations of the people," he said.[16] And, slowly, Moi began to keep his promise and loosen his grip. International pressure was growing again, this time from the United States and the Bush administration, focused squarely on political reform. When Secretary of State Colin Powell visited in May 2001, he urged Moi to allow the election of a new president and to step aside. The constitution prohibited him from running again, and though some urged him to do so, Powell appealed to his sense of legacy.

Knowing that he might have to step down, Moi tried to arrange the succession. He threw his weight behind Uhuru Kenyatta, the son of Kenya's founder. Uhuru was a dashing figure, young, Western-educated, and charismatic. But many Kenyans worried that he would just be a continuation of the Moi regime. The president didn't help his protégé by making it known that he would be around to help.

Kibaki succeeded in uniting the opposition in a "Rainbow Coalition." His platform focused on eliminating corruption and establishing the rule of law. Though there were sporadic reports of cheating by both sides and considerable violence, the elections were held on December 27, 2002. Kibaki won and Uhuru conceded. Kenya had reestablished a multiparty system and committed to a democratic path.

Another Opening but Kibaki Disappoints

Early on, observers of Kenyan politics gave Mwai Kibaki high marks for his personal qualities and commitment to a better Kenya. On inauguration day, he told Kenyans that he was "inheriting a country…badly ravaged by years of misrule and ineptitude."[17] It was not particularly gracious to say so with Moi sitting next to him on the dais. But it resonated with the Kenyan people, who had high hopes for their newly elected government.

To his credit, Kibaki launched a serious campaign against corruption. Just two months after he took power in 2003, the government suspended the chief justice and created an independent tribunal to investigate allegations that he had tortured opponents and engaged in corruption. A month later, the governor of Kenya's Central Bank stepped down in a major scandal. A private bank that held pension funds and proceeds from state-owned enterprises had collapsed, leaving the depositors with losses of almost $18 million. The same events brought down the commissioner general of Kenya's Revenue Authority, who was somehow, despite an obvious conflict of interest, the co-owner of the bank.

There were also wide-ranging probes of the judiciary. A special commission found evidence of corruption and misconduct implicating about one-third of the country's magistrates and about half of the judges on the high court and the appeals court. Kibaki himself declared, "The writing is on the wall. We are sending a clear message that the day of reckoning for those who engage in corruption has come."[18] Kenya was among the first countries to sign the United Nations Convention Against Corruption. The move was both symbolic and practical. The convention promised to make the seizure of assets across international lines easier—a promise largely unfulfilled to this day.

Kibaki also pursued populist policies like ending fees for

primary education. The government pleaded with its citizens to use their democratic institutions and petition for justice. And they obliged. One time, for example, 650 women were allowed to sue the Ministry of Defense. They claimed to have been sexually assaulted by British soldiers during joint exercises with the Kenyan military. The very act of bringing legal action against the state was widely praised by domestic and international human rights groups. And the government undertook prison reform, freeing thousands of young first offenders and working to reduce overcrowding and improve conditions for those incarcerated.

The president was a breath of fresh air, and he was celebrated internationally for his efforts. The IMF resumed lending to Nairobi on November 21, 2003, opening the way to accelerated international funding from a variety of donors. The country seemed to be well on course for economic recovery and political stability.

Kenya moved as well to institutionalize reforms by revising its constitution. A 629-member National Constitutional Conference spent months debating a new draft before eventually agreeing on the language. The reforms were intended to decentralize power to national, regional, district, and local levels. The executive was to be weakened by separating the functions of president and prime minister, who would choose the cabinet. A bicameral legislature, with women making up one-third of the members, was to be created. The reforms were breathtaking in scope. They were finally put to a referendum in November 2005. They failed.

That disappointment was a kind of watershed event for

Kibaki as reforms began to slow on a number of fronts. This was due in part to the president's worsening health. Shortly before the elections in 2002, he had been involved in a car accident but rallied to finish the campaign and win. He was left with far more serious injuries than he admitted at the time, though. In January 2003, he was hospitalized for high blood pressure and blood clots in his leg. The septuagenarian president never seemed to fully recover. When Kibaki came to the White House for a state visit in October of that year, he clearly struggled to walk and had trouble remembering the names of some of his new cabinet members. After Colin Powell met with him in January 2005, he reported that Kibaki was still having difficulty moving around and that his mental faculties were continuing to decline.

Moreover, even prior to the failed constitutional referendum in 2005, Kenyans were again growing impatient. Promised economic reforms were stalling and Kibaki's election pledge to create half a million jobs was now haunting him. Few if any had materialized. The heavily publicized campaign against corruption was slowing, leading to the resignation of the anti-corruption czar, John Githongo, who accused the government of continuing graft. His stand unnerved international donors, who yet again threatened to cut off aid.

And pressures were again growing for political reforms. In July, demonstrators took to the streets of Nairobi to advocate for changes in the constitution, particularly a weakening of the executive. They were met by riot police and one person died.

Kibaki had championed a weakened executive. Now in power, he and those around him retreated from the high-minded campaign promises to circumscribe presidential authority.

Instead, the new constitution submitted to the parliament created an essentially powerless prime minister, although it did give parliament a say in cabinet appointments. The vice president explained, according to the *New York Times*, that "presidents are father figures in Africa, and the voters would not put up with having someone outside the family rivaling the father."[19]

In fact, Kenyans begged to disagree. Kibaki managed to go from reformer to defender of the status quo within a matter of a few years. A challenger emerged in the person of Raila Odinga, a Luo minister in Kibaki's government who was appalled by the president's actions. He joined an effort to defeat the constitutional draft from inside the ranks of the president's own government. Kibaki thus found himself on the defensive among his supporters, calling those who opposed him "stupid."[20]

The younger, wealthy, and charismatic Odinga led an indefatigable campaign against the president. And he won. The referendum on the new constitution failed. Kibaki conceded defeat. But when people spilled into the streets to celebrate, the president tried to ban political protests. It didn't work. "Our rallies will go on," said a spokesman for those who had opposed the president.[21]

Kibaki was severely weakened by the events, and the opposition was emboldened. From that point on, after the crucible year of 2005, it was clear that an electoral showdown was looming.

"Save Our Beloved Country"

In 2007, Kenyans participated in what would be a landmark election that would pose a significant challenge to its fledgling institutions. Kenya's electoral law posed obstacles to the participants, but particularly to opposition figures. A candidate was required to win 25 percent of the vote in at least five of the country's eight provinces. The threshold was difficult to reach because multiple candidates split the vote. A third-party candidate, Kalonzo Musyoka, decided to stand for election instead of joining Raila or Kibaki, which denied them close to a million votes that would have created a clear victor. The rules set up a likely scenario of thin margins of victory and the potential for a runoff.

In the days leading up to the election, Odinga was the front-runner, but the race had tightened by election day. Early returns showed him ahead: A day after the election, with about half of the votes counted, he held a sizable lead. Several of Kibaki's key cabinet members lost their seats in parliament. It looked as if the government was headed toward defeat.

But as the counting continued into the next day, the margin began to shift in the president's favor. Odinga's lead was shrinking—nine hundred thousand votes, three hundred thousand votes, then less than one hundred thousand votes—and by the end of the day, the president's party was claiming victory. Odinga and his supporters cried foul.

We were watching Kenya closely in Washington. I checked in with the State Department operations center just before turning in for the night. The outcome was very much in doubt. I immediately called Jendayi, now assistant secretary for African affairs at State. "It's a mess," she said. "Everyone is accusing everyone else of cheating and it is really hard to know who really won." The next day she reported that the head of the ECK that had first called the election for Kibaki now wasn't willing to certify the results from his own organization. International electoral observers suspected significant fraud on both sides, but the vote was so close that it wasn't really possible to say whether it had mattered. "Maybe Kibaki did win. But maybe he didn't," one group reported.

Throughout the next two days, the embattled ECK tried to make sense of the vote count. Odinga was certain that the commission was trying to further alter the results. He called a press conference and made the charge publicly. Kenya was on the brink.

That Sunday morning, I followed my usual routine, talking to key aides and then to the British foreign secretary before heading to church. I suppose the weekly calls with the Brits underscored how special the relationship really is. I've always said that if the Brits weren't with you, you were alone. Sunday morning was a time to make sure we were on the same page, and somehow checking in with London just seemed like the right thing to do.

December 30 was all about Kenya. My phone rang at around 7 a.m. Jendayi was reporting that rumors were flying in Nairobi that the ECK was going to declare Kibaki the winner. "If they do that there will be blood in the streets," she warned. I called David Miliband, the British foreign secretary. The Brits too had heard the rumors, and, yes, chaos was about to break out across the country.

A few hours later, the commission chair, Samuel Kivuitu, came out and announced that Kibaki had won 4.6 million votes and Odinga 4.4 million votes. "Why," people asked, "would the

ECK declare a victor with a thin margin of two hundred thousand votes when not all had been certified?" Undeterred, Kibaki was sworn in at the State House under heavy guard. Odinga rejected the electoral outcome. It didn't help that some members of the ECK emerged to say that there had indeed been vote rigging on both sides. Kenya was plunged into political crisis and tribal violence. More than a thousand people would die over a period of a month. The *New York Times* wrote vividly that the "streets of Nairobi are beginning to look like war zones, with trucks of soldiers rumbling through a wasteland of burned cars and abandoned homes....Gangs of young men have built roadblocks between the neighborhoods of the Kikuyus...and those of the Luos."[22] By New Year's Day, Kenya was on the verge of civil war.

Another New Year's Day crisis, I thought as I read the morning papers. During my time as national security adviser and then secretary of state, I almost came to dread the holidays. Like clockwork something always seemed to happen right around Christmas and New Year's. In 2001 it had been the prospect of war between India and Pakistan. In 2004 it was a devastating tsunami in the Indian Ocean. The year 2005 brought Vladimir Putin's threat to cut off the gas supply to Ukraine. In 2006 it was Ethiopia's intervention in Somalia. Then in 2007 Benazir Bhutto was assassinated on December 27. Now, within twenty-four hours of that tragedy in Pakistan—Kenya was headed toward a meltdown.

I knew that the international community had to do something, but, frankly, it wasn't clear what to do. David Miliband and I issued a joint statement on January 2 urging calm. We welcomed the calls of the African Union (AU), the EU, and the Commonwealth for an end to the violence. And we pledged our diplomatic and political efforts to support reconciliation and national unity at this "vital time for Kenya and the region."

Then I kept doing what diplomats do in these circumstances—issuing statements, calling other foreign ministers to get them to issue statements, and ultimately having the president speak to the situation to lend weight to what we had been saying. It is hard to convey how frustrating these moments can be. You hope that your words will have an effect, but deep down you know that they probably won't.

More fruitfully, I sent Jendayi Frazer to Kenya to assess the situation and to represent me in working with the parties to calm the situation. I called Odinga and Kibaki on an almost daily basis, making clear that the United States was watching and ready to help. We tried to find leaders who could speak to both sides. John Kufuor, the president of Ghana and chairman of the AU, went to Nairobi to urge peace talks between Odinga and Kibaki. But the going was tough. Calling the proposed talks a "sideshow," Odinga added, "We want to meet with him but we don't recognize him."[23] Kufuor pushed Raila to recognize that his party's majority in parliament offered an important power center and counterbalance to the presidency in governing the country.

Finally, in consultation with the AU, we agreed that Kofi Annan, the highly regarded former UN chief, should go as a mediator. We had come to the conclusion that a government of national unity was the only way forward. The United States issued a statement saying that "irregularities in the vote tallying" had made the final result "impossible to determine with certainty." We reminded Kenyan leaders that the United States would not conduct business as usual until they sorted out their political problems.

At the beginning of 2008, I had a lot on my plate with Afghanistan and Iraq and North Korea and Israeli-Palestinian negotiations, but the secretary of state can't put an unfolding catastrophe on the back burner. We had invested so much time, energy, and resources in our policies toward Africa in general and Kenya in particular. The president and I had spent hours with African heads of state, trying to support democratic transitions; launched PEPFAR for AIDS relief, the single largest global health initiative in American history; and quadrupled foreign assistance to Africa. And now Kenya, one of the most stable countries in the region, was coming apart. I've often been asked how one sets priorities as secretary of state. Sometimes events do it for you. Kenya was now at the top of my agenda.

Every day the news just seemed to get worse. Annan succeeded in getting Kibaki and Odinga to meet. But within minutes, Kibaki was out publicly accusing his rival of stirring up violence. Odinga, for his part, returned the insult. The ethnic character of the unrest was becoming more marked, with revenge killings among the tribal groups. People were being driven from their homes to "purify" neighborhoods.

As fate would have it, President Bush was scheduled to visit Tanzania, Kenya's neighbor, on February 17. He had decided not to go to Nairobi, saying that he instead wanted to focus on the "success stories" of the region, especially U.S. policies for countering AIDS and malaria. The comment didn't go over well, sounding tone-deaf at that particular moment. But we knew that it made no sense for the president to go. The delicate talks were moving at a snail's pace. If the president were to visit, he would be expected to deliver a breakthrough. The stakes would be too high and the chances for failure were strong.

Instead, I would break off from the presidential party in Tanzania and go to Nairobi. I would try to help Kofi, who thought he was making a little progress. The Ghanaian-born diplomat had been on the ground in Kenya for nearly four weeks. I called and asked if he wanted me to come, not wanting to "bigfoot" him by swooping down as the American secretary of state. "Do come," he said. We had worked closely before in negotiating an end to the Lebanon War in 2006. I believed he genuinely wanted me there.

The night before I left for Kenya, I was sitting with the Tanzanian foreign minister and several other officials at the dinner in honor of President Bush. Somehow the conversation turned to Rwanda and the genocide that had unfolded there in 1994. "For a while," one of the officials who had been at the border said, "I thought the stories were made up about people being killed with machetes. It all sounded impossible. But then people started fleeing across the border." He lowered his head and his voice cracked a bit. "There they were. People with one arm, others with one leg—limbs had been hacked off in the most brutal fashion and the wounds were still open. I couldn't believe my eyes." That did it for me. Ethnic violence incites the worst and most uncontrolled passions in human beings. *Get on that plane tomorrow and make something happen*, I thought to myself. Then I prayed. *Just help us find a way.*

When I arrived, our very capable ambassador, Michael Ranneberger, met me. He pulled out a newspaper from January 3, 2008. "Save Our Beloved Country," it said. "This was the headline in every newspaper in the country and on every television and radio broadcast," Michael told me. "Civil society, the church, and the business community have been meeting and issuing statements to the protagonists. They are determined to force a solution," he continued. As we traveled along the road to the hotel where I would meet Kofi, people were holding signs with similar messages. It was a show of cohesion in civil society that defied tribal, social, and economic fault lines in the country. *We have something to work with*, I thought. I felt energized and encouraged. Kenyans wanted to save their democracy. Their leaders just had to respond.

After Kofi and I held a brief press conference, I headed off to meet Kibaki at one of the president's offices. The building was very old, and as we climbed the rickety stairs to the third floor, I found myself wondering how the crippled president had made it up them. I entered the room and shook his hand, bringing greetings from President Bush, and then sat down. Kibaki made a few rambling comments about wanting to unify the country and then looked to me.

"Mr. President," I said, "you led your country's democratic transition with your election in 2002. You have a wonderful legacy. But now we are all worried that the violence and anger is overtaking politics." He just nodded. But as I looked at the president, I heard someone break in. "He won the election," one of his advisers said. I ignored her, trying to stay focused on the president. Justice Minister Martha Karua continued by saying that a power-sharing arrangement would undermine democratic processes. The results of the election had to stand. "I am here to support Secretary-General Annan's efforts to bring about a unity government," I said. "The elections were very close and there should really be no losers." It seemed as if the president's level of consciousness was falling. It was hard to keep his attention.

I could feel the heat rising in the miserable third-floor room. But it was not just the weather on this African summer day. Kibaki's entourage was in no mood to compromise, and my mere mention of a unity government had raised the political temperature. At that moment it occurred to me that the septuagenarian president was perhaps the least of my problems. Those around him were determined to reap the spoils of electoral victory—no matter how narrow it had been.

As Kibaki's aides spoke more and more—and the president less and less—I wondered if they were really the power behind the Kibaki throne, manipulating the sick old man. I asked Jendayi. "Maybe a bit," she said. "But Kibaki is stubborn. They are doing his bidding. He believes that he won and deserves to be president."

After very pointed, at times hostile discussions with the president, we got back into the car and headed to our ambassador's house to meet with Odinga. The contrast in mood could not have been greater. We passed through the beautiful garden into a well-lit, air-conditioned room. Odinga was alert and challenging without being combative. He told me that he wanted to have real powers as prime minister. That would require the right to appoint and fire ministers, and he insisted that his party would hold at least one power position—finance or defense.

But then he turned stern and I became worried about his motives. His people would stay in the streets if compromise couldn't be found, he insisted. Though he personally disavowed violence, the implication was clear—he couldn't control all who were loyal to him. I wasn't at all sure he was willing to try.

I looked across the room at his young aides. Among them was Sally Kosgei, who had a PhD from Stanford. We had met when Moi first visited Washington in 2001. Sally, tall and imposing, was one of those people who commanded a room when she walked in, and it was clear that the president listened to everything she said. Uhuru Kenyatta's sister had also gone to Stanford with Jendayi. Suddenly my attention shifted back to the conversation with Odinga when he asked what I was proposing.

The key was to get Odinga to give up on the street and to get Kibaki to agree to share power. The sides had to move toward one another, and time was of the essence. I sketched out elements of a proposal for allocating ministries and shared it with Odinga. He agreed that it was a "good starting point." I gave it to Jendayi. "Stay and talk to Sally. Then go and talk to Uhuru. You know them both. Use the connections," I told her.

Before leaving, I joined a gathering of civil society leaders and listened to their pleas for a unity government. They were impressive people—university leaders, businesspeople, and human rights advocates. They were pressuring their leaders publicly and privately. I encouraged them to keep doing it and held a press conference with them to talk about the importance of civil society in democracy. I explained that the two sides were not too far apart and that only will was lacking. "It is the Kenyans who are insisting that its leaders and political class find a solution," I said to remind Kibaki and Odinga of their obligations to their people. But I added that the United States would be supportive if they agreed upon a path forward. "I don't want to talk about threats and sanctions," I said. Still, I made clear that the half billion dollars of annual American aid to Kenya was a part of the Bush administration's policy of rewarding those who embraced democracy.

Then I stopped off to see Kofi before heading to the airport. We reviewed the results of my meetings, and he thought the compromise might work. As I walked out of the room I thought to myself, *He looks really tired.* I wondered how long he would have to stay here to get this done. Kofi had been the director of UN peacekeeping during the Rwandan genocide. He knew that the stakes were very, very high. *He'll stay as long as it takes,* I thought.

Ten days later, after many ups and downs, he succeeded in closing the deal. A powerful prime minister post was created for Odinga, weakening the authority of the president. "I call on Kenyans to embrace the spirit of togetherness," Kibaki said. Our ambassador reported that Odinga was smiling widely at the ceremony. He had won almost everything he wanted.

I phoned the two Kenyans the next day to congratulate them, expressing my relief for their country. It was one of those rare really good moments when diplomacy works to forestall catastrophe.

Let me be clear: Kofi Annan did the hard work, staying in Nairobi for over a month to bring the sides together. But it helped to throw the weight of the United States behind the compromise. Odinga would later say that I had been tough and influential in getting the president to agree. People in the Kibaki camp conceded that pressure from "donor nations like the United States" had led to their change of heart. And who would have thought that connections made long ago at Stanford between members of the next generation might help too.

The power-sharing agreement allowed Kenyans to put the divisive election behind them and to get back to work, at least for the time being. Sometimes young democracies need breathing space, a chance to survive a crisis, to live to fight another day, and to get it right the next time.

It took two months for the camps to agree on the formation of a new government, but it was done with virtually no violence. Kibaki and Odinga jointly visited the Rift Valley in the west of the country, the scene of so much ethnic conflict after the flawed election. They appealed for unity. "Please forgive one another for what happened so that once again you can start living as Kenyans and build one nation," Kibaki said. Added Odinga, "We are here as leaders.... We can solve all the problems in order for peace to exist."[24]

Later that year, Prime Minister Odinga came to visit me at the State Department in Washington. He was on a trade mission to attract business to Kenya. "How is it going with the president?" I asked.

"I respect him as an elder," he said. "It works okay."

Still, the moments of unity could not mask the lingering

bitterness and desire to blame someone for the events of 2007. The Kenyans were reluctant to open the wounds, fearing that prosecutions would ignite new violence. But the issue could not be simply swept under the rug. Official commissions were launched to investigate the post-election violence, improve the country's electoral system, and promote reconciliation. The commission that investigated the violence recommended setting up a special tribunal to try those involved.

The Kenyan people also wanted to see the constitutional reforms agreed upon in 2008 passed and the fight against corruption reinvigorated. The Obama administration sent warning letters to several prominent Kenyans, including some government ministers, telling them that they would be denied visas to the United States if they did not act on these matters; take steps to root out corruption; and pass the constitutional reforms agreed upon in 2008.

Eventually, the internal demands and international pressure succeeded. The draft constitution was finally approved on April 2, 2010, putting an end to the "imperial presidency" that had characterized Kenyan politics since the country's founding. There were new and explicit guarantees of women's rights, minority rights, and efforts to reach out to marginalized communities. In addition to weakening the presidency, the document devolved power to regions and localities. People were hopeful that at least in political matters, tribal ties would become secondary. Sixty-seven percent of Kenyans voted in favor of the new constitution, and there was no violence and relatively few charges of fraud.

Kenyan democracy had survived the near-death experience

of the contested 2007 election, and political leaders, including Odinga and Kibaki, made good on the pledge to work toward unity in the country. Still, as Kenya prepared for the next election, observers wondered if the relative peace would hold. Kenyatta and William Ruto, who had been on opposite sides in 2007 and were allegedly implicated in the violence, announced an alliance to challenge Odinga, who was now planning to run for president. There was some isolated unrest in the country, but nothing on the scale of 2007. The election process was smoother and more orderly. Kenyans would even watch their first presidential debate. The national media sent a clear message that the violence of the last election should not be repeated. It gave voice to concerns about instability and defended the country's democracy by actively calling for the elections to proceed peacefully.

But the cloud of responsibility for the violence of the prior election hung over the new process. Kofi Annan had threatened to use the International Criminal Court if the parliament failed to set up its own tribunal. When it did not, he and others supported the ICC's decision to launch an inquiry. Even though the cases were eventually dropped for lack of evidence, six high-ranking political figures—three from Kibaki's side and three from Odinga's—were named in the investigation, among them Kenyatta. The government agreed to cooperate. Human rights groups wanted more, appealing to the Kenyan high court to disqualify politicians who were being investigated by the ICC. The court refused, saying that it had no standing to do so. Kenyatta was allowed to stand for election.

This time, despite technical flaws and delays, the Kenyan people experienced a relatively peaceful and smooth election day. The results were again close, but after two days Kenyatta was declared the winner. Odinga refused to admit defeat and appealed to the Supreme Court to overturn the results and hold new elections. Kenya was on edge as the court ordered a partial recount, allowing that there may have been some irregularities. Then finally, on March 29, three weeks after the balloting, the court released the retallied votes, showing that there had indeed been errors in the original count. A day later, however, the court unanimously ruled that the errors had not affected the outcome, upholding the original result. "The court has now spoken," Odinga conceded.[25] He wished Kenyatta well, though he did not attend the inauguration. Kenyatta declared, "Our nation has now successfully navigated the most complex general election in our history. Our journey began three years ago, with the promulgation of a new constitution, and ended eleven days ago, with a landmark Supreme Court decision."[26]

It was a good summary of Kenya's progress along the path toward a more stable democracy. There was a stark contrast in the reaction to a flawed election in 2007–8 and the response to a tight contest in 2012–13. This time the candidates for office put their faith in the country's institutions, which were respected as the legitimate intermediaries of political and social conflict. More important, the leaders accepted the outcome and encouraged their supporters to do so too. Perhaps they had learned from the events of 2007 that the Kenyan people expected no less.

This is not to suggest that Kenya's democracy is fully consolidated. The tribal basis of some of the country's regions, and its political parties, is a continuing challenge for stability. Corruption is still too prevalent and undermines the population's faith in their government. Moreover, political institutions are still suspect. Indeed, the devolution of authority as a result of constitutional changes in 2010 has exacerbated the problem. Local governors and regional leaders have used the new rules to ignore the central government in matters ranging from education to economic affairs. Federalism has been a double-edged sword, reinforcing some of the tribal tensions that threaten the country's unity.

Still, the hope is that over time the forces that lead people to vote in lockstep with their tribal affiliation will eventually break down. Kenyan leaders appeal to their people as Kenyans. But in times of challenge and adversity, the temptation to revert to tribal support has been irresistible. Breaking that pattern is the next step in Kenya's transition. Until then, every election holds the potential for violence and ethnic passion.

Kenya has come a long way in the sixty years since its independence, and perhaps the experience with peaceful elections and the constitution of 2010 will temper behavior the next time around—and again and again. Each time the country will get closer to stable democracy. And in time, the people will gain confidence that their faith in democracy is justified, whatever challenges lie ahead.

Chapter 6

COLOMBIA: THE ERA OF DEMOCRATIC SECURITY

"This is where Pablo Escobar was killed," my colleague Carolina Barco, now Colombian ambassador to the United States, said flatly. There wasn't much drama in her voice as we stood on the rooftop looking out over the city of Medellín. But there had been excitement and relief throughout Colombia when the notorious drug lord was eliminated in 1993. He had been the most wanted man in Latin America, responsible for thousands of assassinations and orchestrating an international drug empire that earned him more than $420 million per week at its height. In many ways, his life—a violent cocktail of drugs, money, and power—personified his country's troubled existence. And for many Colombians, his demise signaled the beginning of the end of the chaos. But it was just a beginning. A lot of work remained to be done.

Now, fourteen years later, we were in Medellín, a place that for decades had been synonymous with unspeakable violence. On the lovely summer afternoon, the city was dotted with green spaces and children playing on jungle gyms and swings. "It seems so normal," I blurted out to no one in particular.

"It is normal now," Carolina responded.

For so long in Colombia, normal meant something very different. The revered leader Simón Bolívar defeated the Spanish in 1821, establishing an independent republic of Gran Colombia that encompassed modern-day Colombia, Ecuador, Panama, and Venezuela. By 1830, only Colombia and Panama remained, and the country's political structures began to take shape.

Contested presidential and parliamentary elections, functioning courts, powerful business and agricultural groups, and a largely free press did exist. The Conservative and the Liberal political parties formed in 1849 and traded electoral victories for almost a hundred years. Yet these institutions and political practices, usually associated with stable democracies, belied the real state of affairs. They were unable to contain competing interests—rural and urban, rich and poor, social liberals and religious conservatives. The country would experience repeated civil conflicts throughout the remainder of the nineteenth century and the first half of the twentieth. At its worst, the terror known as La Violencia raged on and off during a nearly twenty-year period between 1946 and 1964, and was characterized by gruesome brutality. The country was in a near-perpetual state of war and civil conflict. Democratic institutions simply could not take hold.

For a short time, the violence lessened under the iron fist of Laureano Gómez, who took power in the deeply flawed election of 1950. But he did not last long, and Colombia, like so many of its Latin American neighbors, succumbed to a military coup in 1953. The seizure of power was originally seen as a liberalizing step, reversing the authoritarian rule of Gómez and the Conservative Party. But of course, the military regime of General Gustavo Rojas Pinilla was every bit as repressive as the one it overthrew—if not more so.

Sensing that he was personally in danger amid rising opposition, Rojas fled to the United States in May 1957, leaving a military junta in place. That summer, the Conservatives and the Liberals finally joined forces, creating a new political compact called the National Front to try to stem the violence.[1] The power-sharing arrangement between rival parties was approved by plebiscite in December and the coalition took power from the junta. This would indeed stabilize Colombia's political system for a time and give the exhausted country an opportunity to launch political and economic reforms.

Though the two parties dominated the political system, there were a number of interesting arrangements meant to prevent abuse of power. For instance, so that the ruling party could not pass laws favorable only to itself, a supermajority was required to pass legislation. A civil service was created to "eliminate the concept that the political winner has the right to the spoils of office," according to the agreement that established the National Front.[2] Economic reforms were far-reaching and partially successful in the industrial sphere. But the effort to improve agricultural efficiency by bundling small plots into larger ones displaced 40 percent of the farmers, ultimately exacerbating tensions between large landholders and rural peoples.[3]

And so the respite would be short-lived. As conflict between various interests grew, insurgents emerged willing to represent those factions through the barrel of a gun. One of the first of these, the ELN, formed in July 1964. Its leader, Fabio Vásquez Castaño, was inspired by Marxist-Leninist ideology, mobilizing peasants, college students, and priests who espoused liberation theology. They were inspired too by Fidel Castro's Cuban Revolution and opposition to business interests labeled as capitalist oppressors. Forming "independent republics" in the territories of their supporters, they organized these forces and armed them. In response, the government launched Operation Sovereignty and regained control of the areas. This pattern of insurgents taking and holding territory would be repeated several times in the next decades.

Despite the government assault, the rebel movement survived, pulling in new adherents with a narrative of armed struggle against the government. But the ELN would find itself outflanked by an even more violent and capable insurgent group. The FARC, or Revolutionary Armed Forces of Colombia, was born in 1966 with bigger ambitions than control of a few rural enclaves. They wanted to overthrow the Colombian government and replace it with a Marxist state. And they grew powerful quite quickly. By 1970, the president of Colombia was forced to declare that the country was in a state of siege.

The FARC was fueled not just by ideology but increasingly by the drug trade too. Over the years, the guerrilla movement slowly became intimately intertwined with the cocaine trade until it was finally indistinguishable from the drug cartel that it ran. The profits allowed the FARC to be financially self-sustaining. And though other Marxist groups would emerge, the FARC was clearly the vanguard of the revolution. It was admired in Havana and Moscow as well as in leftist corners of the West.

The Castro regime offered more than inspiration. It provided material support, and FARC leaders repeatedly sought refuge on the island nation. The group had Soviet connections from the time of its founding and it traded weapons and cocaine with the Russian mafia. Support cells raised money and even recruits from Marxist sympathizers across Europe and the Americas.

In Colombia, FARC was becoming a dominant force in political life. In the 1980s, its bombings, assassinations, and kidnappings became commonplace. Not surprisingly, a right-wing counterpart soon emerged. Landowners who did not trust the government to protect them began to buy security from armed groups. The United Self-Defense Forces of Colombia (AUC) now filled the void from the other side of the political spectrum. Brutal and uncompromising, the death squads terrorized rural areas and murdered people suspected of sympathizing with the insurgents. Moreover, the overmatched police and army were more than willing to look the other way. The right-wing paramilitaries had friends in high places, allowing them to act with impunity.

The government grew desperate, trying everything to stem the violence. Peace talks were launched, leading to the demobilization of some groups but doing nothing about either the FARC or the AUC. Thus the reign of terror continued. In the elections of 1990, three presidential candidates were assassinated. Seeking to strengthen the hand of the government, a constitutional convention was held in 1991, granting the president greater powers but to little effect.

The government continued to waver in its resolve, alternately confronting the insurgents and trying to make peace with them. When in 1998 President Andrés Pastrana decided to withdraw government forces from five municipalities, the FARC celebrated with a stepped-up campaign of terror in major population centers. Pastrana had inherited a mess from his predecessor, whose tenure was marred by corruption scandals, and likely felt that he had no choice. But he underestimated the FARC's growing strength and the degree to which his decision would boost the power of the insurgency.

By the end of the twentieth century, the Colombian military and police were unable to enter approximately 30 percent of the country. The weakened state could defend neither its people nor its territory. Right-wing paramilitaries and left-wing insurgents controlled the means of violence and had the will to use it. Colombia resembled a failed state.

Making and Remaking "Plan Colombia"

By the late 1990s, the U.S. government realized that it could no longer stand idly by as Colombia continued its descent into chaos. Originating in the Andean region in general and in Colombia in particular, drugs were spilling into America's cities as the FARC and other cartels found willing buyers across the U.S. border. The "war on drugs" was failing without a strategy to stem the flow from South America. Washington decided to intervene. President Clinton's team developed "Plan Colombia" and launched it in 1999 with bipartisan support in Congress.

The purpose of the effort was clear in some respects and cloudy in others. Obviously, the United States wanted to stop the flow of drugs and help Colombian authorities stabilize the country. This meant action against the cartels and their crops, using aerial spraying, interdiction, and capture-and-kill operations to break their hold on parts of the country. The program included development assistance to support farmers in the hope that they would turn their backs on the insurgents and grow alternative crops, not coca. In this way, the program tried to address simultaneously the underlying economic and security challenges driving the chaos.

The confusion in Plan Colombia, though, was rooted in queasiness about the degree to which the U.S. should take on the civil conflict itself and support the Colombian military in confronting the insurgents and armed groups. The members of the FARC were seen in some circles as freedom fighters against oppressive landowners. And there was another problem. The police and military forces that were recipients of U.S. aid were uncomfortably intertwined with right-wing paramilitary forces committing atrocities in the name of establishing order. The politics and violence of the insurgency were not easily separable from the drug trade. Plan Colombia was pursued earnestly and aggressively, assistance increasing nearly every fiscal year, without resolving the underlying question of whether to support the government in ending the insurgency by military means.

When George W. Bush took office in 2001, he believed that Plan Colombia was unsustainable without reconciling these tensions. Shortly after assuming office he asked me to lead a review of our Colombia policy through the National Security Council. But after the attacks of 9/11, questions about the state of Plan Colombia (and many other foreign policy issues) received less attention as we grappled with the urgent need to defend the country.

Inconsistency in Bogotá's approach to the problem also complicated American policy. On June 2, 2001, Pastrana signed a "humanitarian exchange accord" with the FARC, swapping prisoners for soldiers. Then, in October, the government and the FARC signed the accord of San Francisco de la Sombra, committing to negotiate a cease-fire. Pastrana agreed for the ninth time to continue the demilitarized safe zones, this time until January 2002. The zones had become havens for the FARC to train its forces and launch attacks with impunity. The government checkpoints around the zones were wholly ineffective and frequently the site of kidnappings for ransom.

Upon agreeing to extend the safe havens, though, Pastrana tried this time to use muscle as well as negotiation to send a message to the FARC. He increased the number of military checkpoints and surveillance flights around the demilitarized zones. The FARC responded by refusing to continue the peace talks. Pastrana then mobilized twelve thousand troops with air support. Before the government could act, diplomats from ten other countries and the Catholic Church negotiated a last-minute deal. Peace talks commenced.

With Pastrana's latest attempt at a peaceful solution backed by military might, President Bush decided to revisit the issue of military assistance in the winter of 2002. He wanted to give the Colombian government a stronger hand. The Bush administration had already classified the FARC, ELN, and AUC as terrorist groups. Now it wanted the flexibility to use counternarcotic funding against the insurgents as well. There was also a need to protect vital oil pipelines that had repeatedly been attacked by leftist guerrillas. Still, as the *New York Times* noted, this was a "sharp departure" from U.S. policy that had focused solely on the drug war.[4] From the administration's point of view, the two tasks—eliminating the drug trade and eliminating the insurgency—were inextricably linked. This gave clarity to U.S. policy. Subsequent events would change the thinking of the Colombian government as well.

A few days after that news report in the *New York Times*, four Colombian rebels hijacked a domestic flight carrying senior Senator Jorge Eduardo Gechém Turbay. This was the last straw for Pastrana, who announced a suspension of the peace talks. When the rebels ignored an ultimatum to release the senator, Colombian troops launched an offensive, taking control of major towns in the south of the country. Yet the FARC remained entrenched in the jungle and showed its muscle by kidnapping Íngrid Betancourt, a candidate in the presidential election of 2002.

Pastrana appealed to the United States for urgent military assistance. But congressional approval of a $1 billion anti-drug program for the Andean region specifically prohibited support to help the Colombian military put down the rebels. Many in Congress did not want America more deeply involved in what they viewed as an intractable conflict. And they questioned the Colombian military's record on corruption and human rights. Senator Patrick Leahy in particular criticized the administration's request as "proposing to cross the line from counter-narcotics to counter-insurgency." The new plan, he said, "is no longer about stopping drugs but about fighting the guerrillas."[5]

The president asked me to once again call together the NSC principals, the vice president, the secretary of state, and the secretary of defense to respond to Pastrana's request for military assistance. Colin Powell led off the discussion. "I'm skeptical of the prospects for success and not sure of Pastrana's willingness to stay the course against the FARC," he said. He added that the State Department believed that the millions of dollars the United States had spent trying to persuade peasants to plant alternative crops had failed in its objective. Everyone generally agreed, so I walked down to the Oval Office after the meeting and told the president that there was no obvious way out of the quagmire in Colombia. That is where our policy stood when Álvaro Uribe was elected on May 26, 2002.

Uribe had campaigned on a promise to bring "democratic security," as he called it, to the country. He was very clear: The Colombian government to this point had tried to negotiate from a position of weakness. That had failed. He would take a different course: Crack down hard on rebel groups, reestablish government control, initiate political reforms, and accept no less than the surrender of insurgents on both sides of the political divide.

Uribe's election, and his clarity of purpose, changed the terms and depth of U.S. engagement in Colombia. I got a sense of the man himself when the new president-elect came to my White House office on June 21, two months before he was sworn in. The national security adviser often meets with political leaders who are not heads of state, or in this case not yet inaugurated. Toward the end of these meetings, the president usually stops by. This is partly a matter of protocol, but it also gives the president a little distance from the moment—a chance to size up the visitor without the expectation of commitments.

As Uribe entered my office, I was immediately taken with the Colombian, who was short in stature but walked with unmistakable confidence. He impressed me as steely, determined, and serious, even slightly lacking in humor. I asked him what he meant by "democratic security." Uribe explained that "security" in Latin America had long been associated with right-wing dictators, and he wanted to differentiate himself. By democratic security he said he meant security for all Colombians, his political allies and adversaries alike.

We talked about the troubles in his country and about Plan Colombia. He emphasized the need for military assistance. "We can't fight them with economic assistance," he said. I demurred and started to explain that there were congressional limitations on what we could do. While I was in midsentence, my door flew open, startling the Colombians. The president doesn't have to knock. Uribe jumped up and remained standing while he talked about his hopes for peace in his country. President Bush listened and then asked him if he was serious about defeating the FARC. "Yes!" the president-elect shouted.

After his inauguration about two months later, Uribe returned to Washington. This time he was received in the Oval Office. Foreign leaders who enter this small but elegant bastion of democratic governance seem to sense the authority that dwells within it. They usually come trying to convince its occupant that the United States should support their cause—no matter how daunting the challenge.

Uribe accomplished that feat in a matter of minutes. He told the president that he would not waver in his fight against the terrorists, the FARC, invoking the language that President Bush had himself used after September 11. Admitting that the paramilitaries were also responsible for the chaos in the country, he pledged to demobilize the AUC and other groups or fight them too. And when the president gently raised the question of collaboration between the right-wing paramilitaries and Colombian authorities, Uribe didn't flinch. He promised to use the full weight of the judicial system to bring them to justice no matter how high-ranking they might be. This, he said, was the only way to restore confidence in the judiciary, the legislature, and ultimately the presidency.

President Bush had one final question, and, frankly, it made me squirm a bit. "Are you tough enough to kill their leaders? It is the only way to shut them down." Sitting on the sofa across from the Colombian foreign minister, I wondered if she and the other members of the delegation thought the president's question presumptuous. You had to be tough to survive Colombia's violent politics. And Carolina's own father had been president of the country, surviving multiple assassination attempts, trying to bring reform, and ultimately failing to do so due to violence. She was the embodiment of the Colombian experience. Who were we Americans to question their resolve so baldly?

Uribe didn't blink. "Yes, Mr. President," he said. "I give you my word." As the Colombians walked out, I knew that a real bond had been forged between the two men. The president-elect had convinced George Bush that he was the man to save his country, no matter how long the odds.

It didn't take long for those of us in government to see how long the odds really were, even if we had a new and determined partner. Underscoring the depth of Uribe's challenge, the FARC launched mortar attacks during his August inauguration, killing fourteen people in the capital. The Colombian president did not mention the violence in his speech but canceled public celebrations afterward, fearing assassination. In the following days, the right-wing paramilitaries killed more than a hundred people in retaliation.

Uribe did not back down. He declared a state of emergency but not a state of siege in the country. The distinction was important, since the latter would have allowed the suspension of civil liberties. The new president would tell his people and anyone else who would listen that he meant to bring security through democratic institutions: He would not subvert them. This was, for us, confirmation that he was committed to the *democratic* part of "democratic security."

Uribe found other ways to signal his determination. A few weeks after he took office, the government issued a declaration taxing the richest 300,000 Colombians and 120,000 companies to raise $800 million. The goal was to train and equip thousands of additional soldiers and police officers, and to create a new part-time security force of up to 100,000 recruits.

He was a serious man and he knew that he had little time to change the direction of his country. But he was determined to do it by rebuilding Colombia's political institutions and exercising power through them. In a sense, by helping the Colombian state regain its footing at this time of crisis, he was launching a transition to a new democratic future for the country.

Uribe's "Democratic Security"

As we have seen, Colombia had the institutions that form the basic infrastructure of democracy for decades. The presidency was constrained by Latin American standards, with a strong opposition party that was often just a few seats short of a majority in the legislature. Elections were held regularly and resulted in leadership changes. There was an independent judiciary. There were non-governmental organizations that could check the power of the executive, particularly business and agricultural groups. The army had been out of politics for five decades and the press was relatively free—though journalists were often targeted by violence from both sides.

Colombia's problem was not, then, the absence of institutions, but the weakness of them. The state had lost the monopoly on the use of force. Right-wing militias targeted labor leaders, and left-wing insurgents kidnapped and assassinated businessmen and government officials. The police and the army were viewed as worthless or, worse, complicit in political violence. The judiciary was seen as a tool to shield high-ranking officials from justice, not as an impartial arbiter of truth. And the presidency seemed unable to govern and protect the country. This institutional landscape that Uribe inherited makes it all the more remarkable that he succeeded in addressing Colombia's challenges through existing institutions.

First, the Colombian government had to provide security for its people. No state can thrive without a monopoly on the use of force. This meant that paramilitary and insurgent groups had to either disarm through negotiation or be disarmed by force.

Bolstered by greater military assistance from the United States, the Colombian administration set out to do exactly that. During a visit to Colombia in December 2002, Secretary of State Colin Powell announced that the United States would provide $537 million in annual aid, an increase of $125 million. The new American commitment put aid to Colombia at roughly the same level as aid to Afghanistan and Pakistan. But Colin also put the United States squarely on the side of eliminating the security threat to the country by military means. He stated that America viewed the war on leftist guerrillas and rightist paramilitary groups as a part of the Bush administration's war on terror. It was not just a counternarcotics mission; it was a counterterrorism mission as well.

I told the president that day that we had finally resolved the long-standing reluctance to take sides in the conflict. "We're taking a risk in saying that Colombia can gain the upper hand in the insurgency by military means," I said.

"But it's the right thing to do," the president replied.

The government's task was easier regarding the right-wing paramilitaries. Some would argue that the close connections between Colombian officials, the army, and these groups helped to explain the almost immediate response of the AUC to Uribe's election. On November 30, 2002, the AUC declared a unilateral cease-fire. "The government," the group declared, "is demonstrating its capacity and political will" against the insurgents.

The AUC reserved the right to respond to opportunistic attacks by the FARC. As a first step, eight hundred fighters from Medellín laid down their weapons. Over the next few years, larger blocs of paramilitaries would be demobilized: fourteen hundred fighters from Norte de Santander; two thousand from Antioquia, eleven hundred from Casanare, and so on.[6] In the end, some thirty thousand paramilitaries would lay down their arms after 2003.

For the most part, the fighters were transferred to halfway houses and put into job training programs. The terms of demobilization essentially constituted amnesty. The decision to forgo jail time for those who disarmed was of course controversial. International human rights groups, European governments, and more than sixty members of the U.S. Congress criticized the program as too lenient, allowing those with blood on their hands to go free. Some AUC leaders had been involved in the drug trade. Several had outstanding U.S. extradition warrants or trafficking charges. Some drug lords who had only tangential connection to the AUC used the opportunity to negotiate with the government and thus avoid punishment.

The decision to let violent people "walk" largely without consequence points to one of the hardest choices facing countries emerging from conflicts and insurgencies: When are societies' needs best served by forgetting the past, even if the guilty are not brought to justice? Many people have lost their lives. The families of victims want someone to be punished. It's fine to tell parents, wives, and children to move on, but they can't. It's too much to ask that they put the trauma behind them. Still, leaders have a national purpose to overcome the past and move the country forward. Facing this dilemma, the Colombian government opted for the chance to peacefully end the right-wing insurgency.

And while the demobilization of the paramilitaries was largely successful, sporadic, high-profile violence continued for some years. International attention was again drawn to Colombia when gunmen of one of these groups killed a vacationing Italian tourist in 2005—just a reminder that the paramilitaries were dangerous people.

If the paramilitaries' role in Colombia's violent landscape was subsiding, the struggle against the left-wing insurgency was proving more difficult. The ELN entered into on-and-off negotiations with the government, reducing one source of conflict. But the war against the FARC escalated. The Colombian army launched offensives against FARC strongholds. In retaliation, the FARC kidnapped more victims, including three American government employees after their plane crash-landed in the jungle.

The circumstances of guerrilla warfare are often murky, and there were multiple reports of atrocities by Colombian soldiers. One such incident garnered international attention when officials from the UN refugee agency accused the military of involvement in killing a peasant leader and seven villagers, three of them children, for suspected ties to the insurgency. The Colombian government initially denied the claim, but indictments were eventually brought against several high-ranking figures in the army's 17th Brigade, resulting in military trials, convictions, and jail terms. The Uribe administration pushed on with aggressive operations to root out the FARC. The Marxist rebels fought with equal furor, on one occasion killing seventeen Colombian soldiers in an ambush. The army commander called it a "terrorist, criminal act." In fact, it was simply an indication of how intense and violent the fighting had become between government forces and the FARC.

The violence reached a crescendo in the spring of 2007. Left-wing rebels blew up a truck carrying nine federal police officers on May 10. The next day, ten more soldiers were killed patrolling in the west of the country. Then, on June 18, a group of kidnapped lawmakers died. The guerrillas said the hostages had been killed in crossfire during a military attack. Many Colombians believed they had been assassinated by the FARC. More than a million people took to the streets of Bogotá, calling for the release of the hundreds of people being held hostage by the FARC. Among the captives were Colombian politicians, military officers, and U.S. military contractors. Such a protest would have been unthinkable only a few years earlier. Now, the Colombian people were fed up. They were no longer afraid and were willing to rally against the insurgency.

That same year I found myself face-to-face with the new foreign minister, Fernando Araújo Perdomo, who had been kidnapped by the FARC and had finally escaped after six years in captivity. He personified the sense that the Colombian government had turned the tide against the terrorists.

Uribe took seriously his pledge to President Bush to hunt down the FARC's leaders, and dozens of high- and mid-level guerrillas were taken out in the following years. In one particularly high-profile case, FARC leader Rodrigo Granda was captured by bounty hunters in the capital of Venezuela, leading to one of several disputes between the neighbors. Indeed, Uribe was insistent that Venezuelan president Hugo Chávez was harboring the FARC and permitting his territory to be used to launch operations against Colombia. While Chávez denied the claims, there was evidence to support Uribe's version of events. During a raid just across the Ecuadorian border (leading to a break in diplomatic relations with that country), Colombia killed Raúl Reyes, one of the most senior FARC leaders. The army recovered his laptop computer containing documents detailing Venezuela support for the Marxist rebellion. Caracas disputed the claim, but the United States supported Uribe.

The dispute between the Colombian president and Chávez was ideological as well. I remember first meeting the firebrand populist from Venezuela at the Summit of the Americas in 2001. He practically jumped across the table to shake the president's hand and talk about baseball. He was rough and almost clownish. The president turned to me afterward and said, "He's just a thug." Now he was also an active adversary of the United States. Given his support for leftist politicians from Nicaragua to Mexico, Chávez did not take kindly to the rout of the FARC that was under way. It was a considerable setback for his hemispheric ambitions.

By the time the FARC leader and founder, Manuel Marulanda, died of natural causes in 2008, the organization was a pale shadow of itself. While the FARC was able to carry out car bombings in several cities, the attacks were small and well outside the capital. The Colombian military was back in control of the country's territory. In July, the army's rescue of Íngrid Betancourt, who had been held in captivity for six years, underscored the government's success. The FARC was severely weakened and beginning to look toward accommodation with Bogotá.

The government refused direct talks with the FARC, continuing to chip away at the insurgency. Still, Uribe had to face the fact that it would be far harder to heal the deep and festering wounds in Colombian society than to secure military victory.

The Question of Justice

Rebuilding the reputation of the judiciary required showing that no one was above the law. And that would lead to some of the most challenging and dramatic tests of the political system.

The record of the Uribe administration was by no means perfect in investigating allegations and bringing people to justice. Still, many were indeed held to account. Questions surrounding the murders of journalists and labor leaders were brought out into the open. Uribe noted recently that before his election there had been only one murder conviction in relation to those events. By the end of his presidency there had been more than two hundred.[7]

The army, which had performed admirably against the FARC, was not immune from justice either. In late 2008, an investigation tied dozens of military personnel to the deaths of innocent citizens. The charge was that they had tried to inflate the number of insurgent deaths, increasing the body count by killing civilians. On October 29, President Uribe fired twenty-five officers, including three generals, in connection with the affair. A week later, the commander of the army was forced to resign as well.

By far the most sensitive issue was the continuing claim that members of the president's own cabinet, indeed, even the president himself, had been complicit in the right-wing violence that crippled the country. And the charges had an ideological tinge, many of the claims originating with organized labor and human rights groups that were sympathetic to the FARC.

The most serious and far-reaching allegations emerged in what would come to be known as the "parapolitics" scandal. The laptop of a former paramilitary warlord, "Jorge 40," contained evidence of collusion between Colombian politicians and right-wing death squads. When the story broke in October 2006, it was a national and international sensation. The Colombian Supreme Court acted a month later, ordering the arrests of Senators Álvaro García and Jairo Merlano; a member of the lower house, Deputy Erik Morris; and two other former politicians on charges ranging from supporting paramilitary groups to receiving campaign funds from them. All were strong supporters of Uribe.

Over the next few weeks, a steady stream of politicians were arrested or investigated. The Colombian inspector general charged Jorge Noguera, the former head of the Police Intelligence Service, with leaking operational information to the paramilitaries. The scandal would ultimately lead to the resignation of the foreign minister, María Consuelo Araújo, who resigned after her brother, a senator, was arrested.

The scandal failed to engulf the president, however. There was certainly a lot of smoke around him. Salvatore Mancuso, a notorious former paramilitary commander, had made a sensational claim. He said that during the 2002 election, Uribe enlisted his militia to engage in voter intimidation. Uribe denied the claim and openly defended himself in the press, leaving the judgment to his people. In the end, the Colombians supported him. He was reelected in May 2006 with 62 percent of the vote, the largest margin of victory in the country's history. At the height of the scandal his approval ratings never dropped below 60 percent.

Uribe was popular because he had returned Colombia to stability and a modicum of security. But he did not rule with an iron fist. He had done so through his presidential powers and his supporters' majority in the legislature. Right before his reelection, pro-Uribe coalition parties won 61 percent of the 102-seat Senate and 57 percent of the 166-seat lower house. The people were voting for his platform of keeping the pressure on the FARC. And his popularity was greatly enhanced by his partnership with the United States, which promised to bring not just security but also economic growth.

Partnership, Not Paternalism

The Bush administration and the Colombian government had more expansive goals in mind for Plan Colombia. At every opportunity, President Bush and I emphasized the larger picture—the potential triumph of democracy in Colombia and the shared values that underlay the bilateral relationship. The narrative of the United States in some parts of Latin America has not always been a positive one. Our history in the region, dating back all the way to our founding, has not always been one of equal partnership and respect, which at times has colored the way the region has viewed us and what we have tried to do. Cold War–era attempts to improve relations, such as President Kennedy's Alliance for Progress, were overshadowed by other actions, such as covert U.S. assistance in the overthrow of Chile's socialist government in 1973. Our goal in the Bush administration was to write a new narrative for the United States in the region based on our shared commitment to democracy and democratic development, and Colombia clearly demonstrated the promise of that approach. President Bush visited Bogotá in March 2007, becoming the first American president to do so in twenty-five years. It was a symbolic gesture of support and faith in Uribe's security efforts and his commitment to democracy.

The Colombians went all out with a lavish ceremony in the courtyard of the Presidential Palace. State visits are pretty much by formula, and this one was no different. There is a formal arrival ceremony. The presidents introduce the members of their delegations to each other. Both national anthems are played. There are some brief remarks—sometimes not so brief. And then there is a full review of the troops, a rather archaic ceremony complete with swords and flags. Yet, given the rebirth of the Colombian military, the ceremony carried considerable weight.

Walking along a red carpet, accompanied by martial music, the presidents receive the salute of unit after unit in what seems like an interminable slog. The American president is usually asked to acknowledge the troops in their native tongue—not so difficult in this case for George W. Bush, who speaks Spanish, but sometimes a bit of a problem in less familiar languages.

Standing in the courtyard of the Presidential Palace while all of this transpired, I remember thinking, *I hope this ends soon.* There had been multiple reports of terrorist threats against us and it was easy to see that there was a heavy security presence. I was anxious to get inside where it seemed a little safer. I'm pretty sure the Secret Service shared my view. Colombia was safer but not yet safe.

Uribe was determined to parlay the relationship with the United States into economic benefits for his country. After years of civil conflict, the Colombian economy needed growth. In the late 1990s, per capita GDP was in decline, falling from $2,814 in 1997 to $2,197 in 1999.[8] Meanwhile, the slowing economy started to shrink, contracting by 4.2 percent in 1999. Uribe's emphasis on security was part and parcel of a broader agenda that included promoting economic development and private investment. And it delivered on that front too. As the Colombian government regained control of its country, the economy boomed. GDP per capita increased during his time in office, from $2,376 in 2002 to $6,180 in 2010.

There was a larger hemispheric goal as well. Uribe was the most important bulwark against Hugo Chávez and his effort to remake Latin America in the image of his "Bolivarian Revolution." In his own bombastic and over-the-top way, Chávez promised and often delivered largesse to Latin American governments. Buoyed by high oil prices ($147 a barrel in 2008), he bought the election in Nicaragua, tried to do so and failed in Mexico, and gave concessionary oil deals to countries in the Caribbean.

Uribe and other friends of the United States, like Luiz Inácio Lula da Silva in Brazil, implored us to, as one put it, "steal away the social justice card from Chávez." So as we sought to rewrite the narrative of the United States in the region, and to center it on democracy, that became part of our language as well. It was not just about elections, free trade, macroeconomic soundness, and economic growth; it was also about making sure that democracies are accountable for something else. Are they delivering for their people? Are lives actually getting better? Are there improvements in education, health care, housing, and transparency in government? It was not about the language of the left or the right, but about the language of democracy.

The U.S.-Colombian Free Trade Agreement became the centerpiece of this economic strategy with Bogotá, and I visited Colombia in January 2008 with a U.S. congressional delegation. This trip was intended to generate bipartisan support for the agreement. We wanted to give members of Congress a chance to see the transformation of Colombia firsthand.

We found ourselves in Medellín, a city once associated with violence and chaos. Now there were glorious parks and a boom in construction. One moment seemed to sum up everything Uribe had tried to do. We visited a horticultural center where flowers were being grown to ship overseas. The FTA would greatly enhance access to our market for these products. Our guide was a woman, a demobilized paramilitary fighter, who could not have been more than thirty-five years old. She explained that she had joined the AUC when she was fifteen to "protect her village." Her unit had taken advantage of the chance to lay down arms in 2003. Now she was learning to read and had a job packing the flowers for shipment. Her teenage children came and helped out after school for a small wage.

I'm sure she was handpicked to impress us. But she did not look like a fighter to me, demobilized or not. She looked like a young woman whose life was almost ruined by civil conflict and who had a chance for a future because her country had been rescued from chaos. If that was the message the Colombians meant to send, it came through loud and clear.

We were unable to pass the FTA during our time in office, but President Obama succeeded in doing so in 2012. It cemented nearly thirty years of bipartisan American support for Colombia's journey from civil war to democratic security.

"Mr. President, It Is Time to Step Away"

One of the strengths of democracy is that it constrains even the most powerful and popular personalities. Legislatures, civil society, and the press all conspire to keep executive authority in check. So too do term limits. Those who govern democratically accept those constraints and act accordingly. Álvaro Uribe, who played such an important role in rebuilding faith in Colombia's democratic institutions, almost ignored that obligation.

Under the 1991 constitution, the Colombian president was barred from a second term. In 2004, at Uribe's urging, the Colombian legislature lifted that restriction and permitted the president to run again. The law survived eighteen challenges and was finally upheld by the Supreme Court, though not unanimously. Uribe argued that he needed to continue his fight against the FARC and complete the demobilization of right-wing armed groups. He was reelected with over 60 percent of the vote.

But when, in 2008, Uribe's supporters gathered five million signatures to call for a referendum on a third term, there was greater opposition. A bill cleared the lower house, but it would have required Uribe to sit out a term before running again in 2014. Many of the president's supporters persisted, committed in their belief that he should be allowed to stand for office in 2010.

Eventually, a second bill passed in September 2009 calling for a referendum on the question of amending the constitution. The approval of the Constitutional Court was required for the referendum to proceed. In a decision that could not be appealed, it refused to give its consent. The court's rationale cited substantial violations of democratic principles, irregularities in the financing of the campaign in support of the referendum, and its difficult passage through the legislature.

Many Colombians simply felt that a third term would place too much power in the presidency. A legislator summed up that position by saying, "In 2001, voters agreed Álvaro Uribe was the most qualified person for the job. But, like any other democracy, there are plenty of capable people for the job. And those people should get their chance."[9]

President Uribe was bitterly disappointed. He felt that he had delivered for his country—greater security, economic benefits, and stronger democratic institutions. In the end, it was ironically those democratic constraints that denied his dream of continuing to lead his country. "I accept and I respect the decision of the Constitutional Court," he said.

Uribe was a strong leader but not a traditional Latin American strongman. He was seen as a president who cared for all citizens and who governed with firsthand knowledge of the issues. During the height of the "democratic security" campaign, he and his cabinet members went to all corners of the country each week. They visited areas with the greatest security, economic, and social problems and held town meetings and discussions. In the end, his people appreciated what he had done. He left office with a 70 percent approval rating, after being elected twice. But it was really his success in rejuvenating Colombia's democratic institutions that should be remembered. And when those institutions told him that it was time to go, he accepted the verdict and vowed to continue in politics from a parliamentary seat instead.

All Wars Must End

Uribe's party did well in the legislative elections a month after the Supreme Court ruling. But it took his former defense minister, Juan Manuel Santos, two rounds of voting to win the presidency. Santos had been with President Uribe at that first meeting in the Oval Office. More than any other official, he was associated with the tough line against the FARC and the largely successful military campaign against the group.

The new president sounded very much like his mentor and

predecessor in his victory speech. Declaring that "time had run out" on the FARC, he said there would not be the "slightest chance of negotiations." This buoyed Uribe, who thought that his legacy would be preserved.

But within a few months, Santos started to move in a different direction. The Colombian press reported that he had initiated secret contacts with the FARC through a businessman. The FARC reciprocated by releasing a series of hostages, describing its move as a "gesture of peace" to the Santos administration.

Early in his term, Santos essentially followed a two-track policy: ready to negotiate but continuing the military campaign. But the blended approach was hard to sustain. The military dimension took a backseat to the political track of negotiations unfolding in Havana. The levels of violence fluctuated but never increased to the point of threatening Colombia's stability as in times past.

Slowly, the FARC and the government worked step by step toward an end to the conflict. The hardest issues were those of justice for past violence and the role of the FARC in the political process going forward. The two sides finally reached an agreement on transitional justice in September 2015. A few months later, they laid out a framework on how rebels would be punished in order to bring justice to the six million victims of the war.

This brought agreement on four of the five major issues. The remaining question was how the FARC would participate in the political process. In January 2016, the UN Security Council passed a resolution creating a political mission to monitor all aspects of the agreement. "The Security Council's decision means we are no longer going alone," Santos said, "but hand in hand with the UN, the entire world, towards the end of this war."[10]

In the summer of 2016, the two sides finally reached an agreement. It aimed to disarm and demobilize FARC forces within a matter of months. A UN peacekeeping mission would oversee the creation of twenty-three temporary zones where nearly seven thousand FARC rebels would relocate and begin the process of disarming and reincorporating into civilian life. Other provisions were more controversial, particularly the weak punishments for FARC leaders and the seats reserved for the group in the Colombian parliament.

When the peace deal was put to the people in a referendum in October 2016, it was greeted with mixed reactions. Domestic opposition was strong, led by none other than Álvaro Uribe from his perch as a member of the parliament. With a turnout of less than 38 percent, the deal failed to pass by half a percentage point, with 50.2 percent voting against. President Santos responded by vowing to resume the negotiations, and within weeks he signed a revised agreement with FARC leaders that aimed to address some of the concerns of its critics.

The polarization between left and right characteristic of Colombian politics throughout its history is once again intense as the country tries to end its civil war once and for all. It is a victory for democracy, though, that the contest this time is taking place within its institutions—not in the streets, villages, and jungles of a failed state.

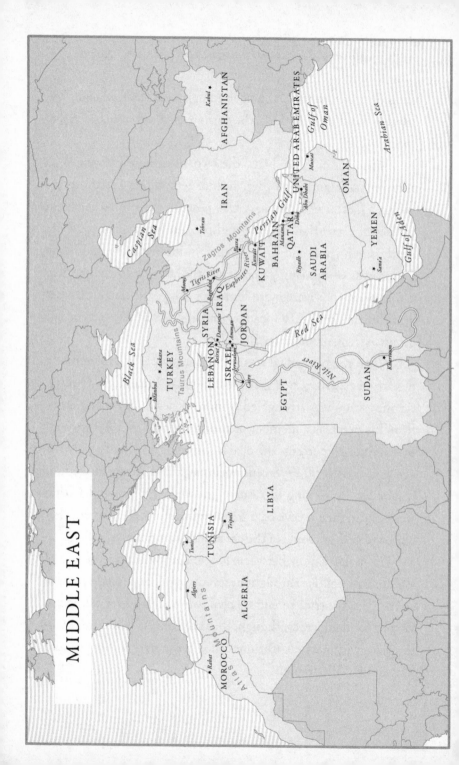

Chapter 7

THE MIDDLE EAST: CAN DEMOCRACY EXIST IN A CAULDRON?

Tsipi Livni, the Israeli foreign minister, was on the phone. "Hezbollah crossed the Blue Line," she said, referring to the border between Lebanon and Israel that had been established after Israel's withdrawal from its northern neighbor in 2000. "They killed three Israeli soldiers and kidnapped others." My heart sank. Another war in the Middle East was about to begin.

The Lebanon War of 2006 began on July 12 and would go on for six devastating weeks, shaking the Levant yet again. Within days, Israelis and Arabs and diplomats across the world were calling for the American secretary of state to find a solution. One night I watched as a snap poll on CNN asked whether people thought I would find a solution. (I believe 58 percent thought I would.) This was getting personal.

Facing pressure to do something, I tried to put the situation into context. "We are experiencing the birth pangs of a new Middle East," I told a reporter, hoping to signal that something good could still emerge from the chaos engulfing the region. It was a well-meaning comment, but it came across as insensitive. The cartoon of me pregnant with the new Middle East, blood dripping from my teeth, drove home the point. I quickly backed off the characterization. Yet the tumultuous events of the last decade have indeed torn apart the map of the area and cast aside the pillars of the old order. A new Middle East is emerging through war, unrest, revolution—and, in a few cases, reform.

⟳

Many tend to think of the Arab Middle East as uniform. The composite picture is one of corrupt, authoritarian governments, some of whom are kings. They oppress their women and behead their enemies. The region is *the* source of terrorism and wars and is wealthy only because of oil. It is a place that spells trouble, pure and simple.

But there is also another parallel reality. The historical, political, and social circumstances of the countries in the region vary greatly. Bahrain's ambassador to the United States from 2008 to 2013 was a Jewish woman. Jordan has five female ministers. The skyline of Dubai rivals that of Chicago. Lebanon's restaurants and nightclubs feel almost European.

And the political circumstances of the area—the institutional landscape—varies too. If we return to our earlier introductory framework, the Middle East has countries that fit into every category. Libya is a story of chaos after the overthrow of a totalitarian cult of personality. There were few institutions to speak of, and new ones are having trouble gaining traction. Egypt and Tunisia are examples of quite different outcomes after authoritarian presidents were deposed. The former is now ruled by the military, while the latter is now quasi-democratic, with a nascent institutional infrastructure struggling to survive. Iraq is trying to make young institutions work but under much more challenging security conditions and political divisions. The monarchs of Saudi Arabia, Bahrain, Kuwait, Jordan, Morocco, Qatar, Oman, and the UAE have different levels of tolerance for dissent and political activity—and the institutional landscapes reflect that. The challenge is to understand not just where these states stand today but what the building blocks might be for a better tomorrow.

This may seem a less than propitious time to think about a democratic future for the Middle East. The region is experiencing two upheavals simultaneously. The first is similar to uprisings around the world—people are fed up with authoritarian, corrupt regimes that don't deliver for them. This was the source of discontent that fueled the "Arab Spring," bringing down governments in Egypt and Tunisia and launching the civil war in Syria. Today, what happens in the village does not stay in the village, thanks to social media. Discontent is spreading across borders like wildfire. The second element, though, is unique to the Middle East—a backdrop of regional war and the splintering of an entire system of state borders.

The Middle East is cursed with a complex political geography. Egypt has existed for centuries. Modern-day Iran was once the core of the Persian Empire, and Turkey was the center of the Ottoman Empire. These states have strong and established national identities. Others in the region, however, emerged by diplomatic design in the early twentieth century. When the Ottoman Empire collapsed at the end of World War I, its four-hundred-year-old system of governing the Middle East collapsed with it. Britain and France, victors in the war, poured into the vacuum and redrew the borders, often without regard for the complexities on the ground. From this process emerged the modern boundaries of Iraq, Syria, Lebanon, Jordan, and what was then called Palestine. Monarchs and dictators held these constructed states together. Arbitrary lines crossed sectarian and ethnic divides, leaving a hodgepodge of Kurds, Shia and Sunni Muslims, and a smattering of Christian groups and other minorities within and across borders.

And often the leadership did not match the ethnic and religious mix. Iraq was ruled first by a Sunni king and later by a Sunni dictator, Saddam Hussein, though the Shia were 60 percent of the population. Bahrain's ruling family is Sunni, while the population is roughly 70 percent Shia. Eastern Saudi Arabia— 10 percent of the country and an oil-rich region—is largely Shia. The Sunni monarchs have historically neglected the needs of their populations, leading to widespread distrust. Bashar al-Assad is Alawite—a minority Shia sect. The broader Syrian population is roughly 75 percent Sunni, about 13 percent of whom are Kurds. Lebanon's population is about 27 percent Sunni, 27 percent Shia, and 40 percent Christian.[1] The country is governed by a fixed formula. The president must be Christian, the prime minister Sunni, and the speaker of the parliament Shia. Lebanese *Hezbollah*, meaning "Party of God," is also Shia and dominates the country's southern region and a big chunk of Beirut. It is almost purely an extension of Iran's Revolutionary Guard Corps— taking orders, money, and inspiration from Tehran.

The picture is further complicated by the relationship between Shia Iran and Saudi Arabia, the most important Sunni power. Sunni rulers—with some justification—accuse Iran of encouraging the disintegration of their states, of trying to build a "Shia crescent" from the Mediterranean to the Gulf and beyond. They resent the infiltration, as they see it, of Persian Iran into Arab affairs, a battle each side can trace back to the early days of Islam. Though there is no love lost between the Shia Arabs and the Iranians, Sunni leaders tend to lump them together—and to see Iran's influence everywhere. As a result, there has been a proxy war in Yemen, pitting Iran's allies against those of Saudi Arabia and the UAE. In Syria, Iraq, Yemen, and Lebanon, the regional powers vie for influence, complicating the already explosive domestic political circumstances.

So with the Middle East in flames, why even raise the question of democracy? Why not wait until the regional wars and conflicts subside? The answer is that the people of the region may not be so patient. The pent-up frustration that erupted in the "Arab Spring" has not gone away. The economic landscape, with slow growth and low oil prices, is forcing change. The populations of the Middle East are young, and recent surveys show that they remain unsatisfied with the status quo: More than two-thirds of Arab youth think their leaders should do more to improve their rights and freedoms.[2] And the landscape for the future is developing now in Tunisia, Egypt, Iraq, and the Gulf states. Eventually, peace will come in Syria too and will shape the institutional framework for that country.

Most important, the argument for the necessity of a democratic Middle East is as strong—if not stronger—than any place in the world. The case was made most effectively in a landmark manifesto by Arab intellectuals.[3]

The 2002 Arab Human Development Report painted a dire picture for the future of the Middle East. Written by Arab social scientists and academics, the report warned of an impending crisis if the region's leaders did not address three gaps—the freedom gap, the women's empowerment gap, and the knowledge gap. The study compared progress in the Arab world to that of the Asian Tigers and, somewhat surprisingly, to that of Israel. As the *Middle East Quarterly* stated in its summary, "The core assumption of the report is that poverty is not merely a matter of income."[4] It quoted Nader Fergany, the lead author of the report, as saying, "A person who is not free is poor. A woman who is not empowered is poor. And a person who has no access to knowledge is poor." And it concluded that "by all these criteria, the Arab region—even some of its wealthiest corners—could only be described as impoverished."

The report thus defined development not just by economic measures but by social and political freedom as indicators of progress as well. The message to Arab leaders could not have been clearer: Change or continue to fall behind the rest of the world.

I first read the Arab Human Development Report when a member of the NSC staff brought it to my attention. I was stunned at its candor and by the multiple taboos that it broke. I took a copy with me to the Oval Office one morning. "Mr. President, you have to read this," I said to him. And then I gave copies to others, including Donald Rumsfeld and Colin Powell, then the secretaries of defense and state. It was not the only factor, but it was a big one in shaping the Freedom Agenda—our belief that the United States had overlooked the absence of freedom in the Middle East for too long. In June 2005, I delivered a speech in Cairo that made that admission. "For sixty years, my country, the United States, pursued stability at the expense of democracy in this region here in the Middle East—and we achieved neither. Now we are taking a different course," I said. "We are supporting the democratic aspirations of all people." I went on to say that change was overdue. It was time for individual freedoms, fair elections, the end of violence and intimidation against citizens, and constitutional protections for all.

Despite regional circumstances less favorable today than in 2005, I stand by that statement. A stable Middle East will one day have to be a democratic Middle East. Only through institutions can people of all religious and ethnic groups find a way to peacefully protect their interests and rights. If dictators and authoritarian monarchs can no longer hold their countries together and make them prosper, democratic institutions have to take their place.

Iraq: When Tyrants Fall

I was sitting in my office, trying to put everything that had occurred over the last few days into perspective. The American military had met little resistance from Iraqi armed forces. The war that had begun on March 19, 2003, was, it seemed, just about to be over on April 9.

The television was on, but it was background noise. I was lost in thought, reviewing my to-do list. *Be sure to call Colin about getting the ambassadorial selection process going. He's also going to have to go back to the UN. Now that the war is over we'll have to try to bring the Russians and the French on board. [Treasury Secretary] Paul O'Neill ought to call his counterparts to talk about currency stabilization and debt relief. That can be a good icebreaker. Maybe the president should call Chirac and Putin. No—it's too soon.*

Suddenly, the commotion on the screen got my attention. The huge statue of Saddam Hussein was crashing to the ground, pulled down by angry young Iraqi men. *What a moment! I thought to myself. This feels like 1991 when statues of Josef Stalin were tumbling across Eastern Europe. The Iraqis have been liberated from a monster.*

In Iraq, though, that moment would turn out to be a bit of a mirage. Apparently the first attempt to bring down the likeness of the dictator had failed, leading someone—possibly an American soldier—to suggest that a rope might do the trick. And there was the awful moment when U.S. troops climbed up on the toppled statue to plant an *American* flag. Fortunately, wiser heads prevailed and the Iraqi banner suddenly appeared.

Maybe it was a kind of metaphor for the paradox of supporting a transition to democracy under occupation. American military power provided the opening. But the work of building a new state needed to be done by the Iraqis themselves.

Over the next decade and beyond, Iraqi leaders have struggled to make their people secure and to provide essential services. To their credit, they have tried to do the work *through* their new democratic institutions—contesting budget allocations and ministerial positions in the parliament and in the very free press. Several leaders have stepped down peacefully and the Iraqis have gone to the polls three times to replace them. Citizens have protested openly and sought to hold their government accountable. The country has been dogged by an existential question: What does it mean to be a federal Iraq? The Kurds have had one answer, the Shia another, and the Sunnis still another. And through it all, Iraqi leaders have had to learn to work together and trust each other. That has been hard.

In the pages that follow, we trace the Iraqi struggle to build and sustain democratic institutions under the hardest of circumstances. I do not intend to revisit the decision to invade Iraq, having done that thoroughly and as honestly as I know how in an earlier work.[5] It is important, though, to reiterate one point: We did not overthrow Saddam to try to bring democracy to Iraq at gunpoint. To do so would have been a misuse of American military power and I would never have advised the president to do pursue that idea.

In brief, the president and his national security principals believed that Saddam was a security threat. It was our belief—supported by the intelligence of multiple countries—that he had reconstituted his biological and chemical weapons programs and was well on the way to doing so on the nuclear side.[6]

That it was Saddam mattered. He had a history of aggression against his neighbors and a long record of seeking, building, and using weapons of mass destruction. He supported terrorists—not al-Qaeda, but numerous other groups. And, yes, we feared that he might transfer weapons of mass destruction or the technology to make them to some of them. Commercial airliners were used as missiles in the attack of 9/11—we ruled out no scenario in trying to protect the country. We had failed to connect the dots before that catastrophe, and we were not going to do it again.

After signing an armistice to end the first Gulf War in 1991, Saddam repeatedly ignored it. He tried to assassinate President George H. W. Bush. He claimed to destroy his prohibited weapons but refused to show proof—and was repeatedly caught lying. UN inspectors were kicked out of the country in 1998, unable to do their jobs as he played cat-and-mouse with them. His violations included shooting at our combat aircraft as they enforced a no-fly zone meant to protect his people from him. At one point in 2001, Defense Secretary Don Rumsfeld was told to develop plans should Iraqi air defenses succeed in bringing down an American plane. We were in a perpetual state of limited war with the Iraqi dictator.

The United States and thirty-two coalition countries decided that it was time for the international community to act. UNSCR 1441, passed in November 2002, had threatened "serious consequences" if Iraq did not comply with its terms. Those facts—or rather facts as we knew them at the time—were the sole reason for the invasion of Iraq.

The decision to give the Iraqis a chance at a democratic future was a separate one—and driven by a different logic. Some within the administration, including Don Rumsfeld, argued that we might be better off to install another strongman once Saddam was gone. Just find a general who wasn't implicated in his war crimes and let the Iraqis sort it out. It was a reasonable idea, but the president believed that America had done enough of that in the Middle East, with unacceptable outcomes. The freedom gap was in part to blame for terrorism and instability in the region. We knew the complexity of Iraq's ethnic and religious mix. It was precisely the complexity that demanded democratic institutions so that people could coexist while contending with their differences peacefully. The other option—someone oppresses someone else—was no longer a formula for stability.

The closest historical parallel to this view is American policy toward Germany and Japan after World War II. The United States did not enter those wars to bring democracy— it overthrew Imperial Japan and Adolf Hitler because they were security threats. But when the regimes were defeated, the Americans avowedly focused on building democratic successor states. There is a story—perhaps apocryphal—that as the war neared conclusion, Churchill was asked what he wanted to do about the vanquished Germany. "I like Germany so much that I want as many of them as possible," he is said to have remarked. In other words, break it up and keep it weak. It was classic balance-of-power thinking.

The United States, on the other hand, empowered men like Konrad Adenauer to rebuild the western part of Germany on the basis of democratic principles. Together they championed the inclusion of the Federal Republic of Germany in a political organization of democracies—the European Union and, in a collective defense treaty, NATO, with an American guarantee. Similarly, the basic tenets of the "Peace Constitution of Japan" bear a striking resemblance to those of the American one. And, once again, the United States provided for the defense of the country so that it would not need to fully rearm. In an early version of what political scientists call the "democratic peace," these leaders believed that democracies would not fight each other. France and Germany would never go to war again, and they believed that a democratic Japan would live in harmony with its neighbors. Let me be clear—we did not think that Iraq was Germany or Japan in terms of its readiness for democracy. But we did believe that a peaceful and democratic Iraq was better than an authoritarian alternative. That was the spirit that motivated the drive to give the Iraqis a chance at a democratic future.

An Institutional Landscape Like the Dark Side of the Moon

A few days after the statue fell, we turned to getting the country back on its feet and functioning again. We had engaged in multiple planning efforts for postwar Iraq, involving scores of U.S. government agencies. There was even a full-scale, all-agency dress rehearsal before the invasion. But the assumptions about the institutional infrastructure in Iraq were in large part wrong. The very opacity of Saddam's dictatorship meant that we could not know the likely unknowable: How precisely did he rule the country? And what would be left of those levers when he was gone? When a totalitarian regime is decapitated, the institutional landscape is barren. Iraq's resembled a moonscape.

We counted on institutions—like the civil service—that didn't have firm footing. And we trusted the returning diaspora—those who had lived in exile—too much. We undervalued some groups that did have standing—the Sunni tribes; Shia religious authorities led by the Ayatollah Ali al-Sistani; and the Kurds, who were competent and organized but ambivalent about a unified Iraqi state. All of these actors would play an increasing role as events unfolded. But misreading the institutional landscape early certainly cost valuable time at the beginning.

Under America's Flag

The chaos of the first weeks led the administration to tighten the reins on the occupation of Iraq rather quickly. As Americans with a more limited history of colonization than our European allies, we found the very idea of occupation distasteful. When commanding general Tommy Franks sent a draft of the decree he would issue once Saddam was defeated, I was horrified. "It sounds like Caesar," I told my communications director, Anna Perez. We revised it to sound more *collaborative*. We even asked our lawyers whether we had to call ourselves the "occupying power." The British were not so squeamish. They insisted that legally we had no choice. And I remember my British counterpart David Manning's warning: "You will be viewed as an occupying power anyway. The only question is will you be seen as competent."

In fact, we had envisioned a kinder, gentler approach through the Office of Reconstruction and Humanitarian Assistance (ORHA), led by retired general Jay Garner, who had led Operation Provide Comfort to protect the Kurds in 1991. Jay was to go in with a small team, find the civil servants who could run the country once high-ranking Ba'athists were fired, and coordinate the Iraqi Interim Authority (IIA)—composed of the Kurds and returning exiled Sunni and Shia leaders—in taking control of the country. There were a few potential leaders—very few—who had survived living inside Iraq. President Bush wanted to be sure that they too were included in the IIA.

The plan never got off the ground. The security situation began to deteriorate almost immediately. Criminal gangs looted the museum and the library, destroying antiquities; the oil fields were not functioning to provide revenue; basic services like electricity were dilapidated and breaking down. An insurgent group called Fedayeen Saddam suddenly appeared, engaging in hit-and-run skirmishes throughout the country. I cornered George Tenet, the CIA director, at the president's morning briefing. "What in blazes is Fedayeen Saddam and where did they come from?" I asked in a voice clearly signaling my alarm and displeasure. The intelligence agencies had significantly underestimated the strength of groups like this. George admitted that little was known about Fedayeen Saddam. They were clearly the dictator's supporters, but to this day, we don't really know much about them. In any case, despite the presence of two hundred thousand coalition troops, the Pentagon said that the security situation was too dangerous for ORHA to enter Iraq. Garner sat in Kuwait.

The military had defeated Saddam's forces decisively, but we needed a civilian presence on the ground to get the country functioning. Almost two weeks after Saddam fell, Garner finally arrived in Baghdad and was instantly overwhelmed. His organization was too small to sort out the tasks of bringing order to the country, let alone actually govern.

I called Margaret Tutwiler, our ambassador in Morocco. We

had been friends since the George H. W. Bush administration when she worked for James Baker at the State Department. She was simply capable, and that's what we needed—someone who was capable. "Margaret," I said, "I know it is asking a lot, but can you go and help Garner? He's hopeless." She confirmed what we all knew: The Garner mission was not going to work. The Pentagon, which had created ORHA, abandoned it. Rumsfeld recommended a new approach to the president: a fully empowered presidential envoy, reporting through the secretary of defense, to run the country. L. Paul "Jerry" Bremer took over as head of the new Coalition Provisional Authority (CPA) on May 13. The president's orders gave him all executive, legislative, and judicial functions in Iraq. Iraq was now controlled by a two-headed hydra: the military commander for matters of security and the CPA for civilian reconstruction.

The CPA was twice as large as ORHA, and its mandate far more sweeping. On one hand, this gave Jerry Bremer the authority to do what Garner had been unable to—bring a semblance of order. On the other hand, it meant that the Iraqi institutions, both new and old, sometimes felt stymied in finding a role in the affairs of the country. This was especially true as the CPA set up the Iraqi Governing Council (IGC), comprising Kurdish, Shia, and Sunni parties. Each group brought its own strengths and considerable weaknesses to the endeavor.

The Kurds were by far the most competent and coherent group in post-Saddam Iraq. They were an ethnically distinct minority population that lived dispersed within the boundaries of the constructed states of the post-Ottoman Middle East. Turkey was about 18 percent Kurdish, Syria about 10 percent, and Iraq about 15–20 percent. The worldwide Kurdish population is about thirty-two million. As a people they had long suffered discrimination and persecution at the hands of Arabs and Turks and dreamed of creating an independent Kurdish state. They were closest to realizing that desire in Iraq, where they had existed as a state within the state since the end of the first Gulf War in 1991, protected by the United States and Britain under UN mandate.

From 1991 to 2003, the Kurds used their status effectively. They built a relatively well-functioning system in the rough mountainous territory of northern Iraq. The region is oil-rich and the economy was relatively strong compared to that of the rest of the country. There was considerable corruption, but the Kurdish lands functioned efficiently. The infrastructure was far superior to much of Iraq's, with good roads and even a fairly modern airport.

Kurdistan, as it was called, had another problem, however— the animosity between its two dominant political forces. Masoud Barzani led the KDP and Jalal Talabani the PUK. The conflict was sometimes violent since both maintained militias. And neither controlled the PKK (the Kurdish Workers' Party), a third group that carried out terrorist attacks across the Turkish border. The tensions between the two clans grew so great that the United States finally stepped in and brokered a governing agreement in 1998. They kept their rivalry under control and even jointly commanded a security force, the *peshmerga*. The "pesh" were fierce fighters—male and female—who took their orders from the two in a relatively harmonious fashion, though divided loyalty was certainly evident from time to time.

When Iraq was liberated from Saddam, Barzani and Talabani were asked to join the IGC. The two men could not have been more different, and their responses to the call showed it. Jalal came down from Kurdistan to take up residence in Baghdad. You had to like this man who was as wide as he was tall. He was jovial and always joked in heavily accented but very good English. When one was invited to dinner at Jalal's house, as I often was as secretary of state, you had to eat—and eat—and eat. Jalal for his part would dine with both hands, shoving food into his mouth with one hand and onto your plate with the other. From the very start he warmed to the role of "founding father of a new Iraq." He was smart and effective and largely trusted by the other members of the IGC. Jalal Talabani was by far the shrewdest politician in the country and, ironically, this Kurd would become a unifying figure in Iraq.

Barzani, on the other hand, refused to live in Baghdad. On my first trip to Iraq, I therefore went to see him. When I arrived, Barzani's aides greeted me at the helicopter. They were tough-looking men who I assume doubled as bodyguards. The Kurd was waiting for me on a red carpet with the Kurdish national flag behind him. We stood at attention while the Kurdish anthem was played. There was no sign of the flag of the united Iraq.

Barzani's remote mountain home was at once palatial and rough-hewn. We ate a lot too, but Masoud was an active man, riding horses and herding his own farm animals. He appeared fit and looked as if he would have been right at home on America's western frontier in the nineteenth century.

It should now be clear that the Kurdish region had good raw

material for a transition. They were wildly enthusiastic about the overthrow of Saddam (who had murdered legions of their kin) and grateful to the United States for having done it. Yet their very competence made the politics of the country more complicated. The international community was united in its view that Iraq had to be a single, unified state. Anything else would have destabilized the delicate geopolitics of the region, particularly with Turkey, whose own Kurdish population also harbored ambitions for self-determination. The Kurds waxed and waned in their enthusiasm for a unified Iraq, and not just because of national aspirations. There was money at stake too. The Kurds wanted control of their own oil wealth, and so did Baghdad.

The Shia also had effective leaders and organized political parties. They were Arab, but as subjects of the Sunni-led states, they experienced deprivation and persecution. In Iraq they were about 60 percent of the population, with large concentrations of them living in the south of the country. Saddam had been especially brutal toward them, using chemical weapons to wipe out rebels near the holy cities of Karbala and Najaf in 1991. It was estimated that up to 180,000 Iraqi Shia died in the crushed rebellion. After the war, mass graves holding more than 300,000 souls were discovered in the country, the great majority of them Shia.

Not surprisingly, the Shia were also buoyed by the overthrow of the dictator. But relations were complicated with them by two factors: splits within the Shia community and the role of Iran. In post-Saddam Iraq, two secular figures vied for power: Iyad Allawi and the late Ahmad Chalabi. Both had lived in exile in London, spoke perfect English, and were partial to Savile Row suits. And though they looked like modern politicians, they played an insider's game, rarely seeming to connect with the concerns of ordinary Iraqis. We found Allawi to be relatively reliable. We would eventually learn that Chalabi was both cunning and dishonest.

The other heavyweight in Iraqi politics was a Shia religious coalition. Its leader, Abdul Aziz al-Hakim, wore the white robes of a cleric and an ayatollah's black turban. He was polite and pious, did not speak much English, and maintained close ties to Tehran. Still, there was much to like about him, and he could be surprisingly sentimental. I will never forget one really difficult meeting after which he asked, "Will you do me a favor?"

A favor? I thought, not knowing what to expect.

"My thirteen-year-old granddaughter loves you. She watches you on television. Will you meet her and her mother when they come to Washington next month?"

Several weeks later, the Hakim family arrived and the granddaughter walked right up to me and said, "I want to be foreign minister too." I remembered how her grandfather had beamed when he talked about her. Maybe he wasn't so reactionary after all.

Hakim kept his distance from the rough-and-tumble of daily politics, delegating much of that to Adel Abdul Mahdi. He too had been in Europe as an exile but seemed to have a better feel for the politics of the street in Iraq. In many ways, he was our best interlocutor on the Shia side.

It was challenging to manage the personalities. But unresolved issues dating far back into the history of Islam made it even harder. In AD 632, when Islam split into two confessional groups in a fight over who should lead the faithful after the Prophet Muhammad's death, the Shia were unified under a single authoritative leader—a figure whose writ was not unlike that of the Holy Father in the Catholic Church. For centuries that leader was a member of a religious council operating in Najaf, now in modern Iraq. But as Sunni leaders cracked down on Shia in the country, the council had to operate underground and could not be a source of inspiration for the people. Some of the putative leadership of the Shia shifted to Qom in modern Iran. Though Persian, the ayatollahs, the latest of whom is the Ayatollah Khamenei, sought to speak for Shia wherever they lived. This, along with Iran's more traditional Persian geopolitical aspirations, is at the core of the Sunni concern about a rising "Shia crescent."

When Saddam was overthrown, Najaf was reborn. The man whom Iraqi Shia saw as the rightful heir to leadership—the Ayatollah Sistani—emerged. He was a powerful presence and wielded enormous influence. But he would very rarely meet foreigners, and no American official ever saw him. He spoke through his son, who issued statements on his behalf.

While this might have been a challenge, it turned out to be a blessing—a remarkable gift. This cloistered cleric had democratic instincts far beyond those of many of his countrymen. His first edict was to declare that clerics should not serve in government. There needed to be a separation of religion and politics. We often found ourselves in the odd position of *wanting* this religious man to say something political.

Unfortunately, he was not the only religious figure in Iraq.

Muqtada al-Sadr, a rival of Hakim, was a minor cleric who had not completed his theological studies and thus lacked religious standing. But he was a fire-breathing nationalist whose father had been murdered by Saddam. He was virulently anti-American and directed a violent militia that targeted our forces all of the time and often the security forces of his own country. Many Iraqis said that he was crazy. Maybe—but he was a power to be reckoned with in the landscape.

Sorting out the politics of the Shia was thus really difficult. One man, one vote promised to create a Shia-led Iraq. That was a red flag for Sunni Arabs—those living in the country, and those who led the powerful countries of the region.

We so wanted the Sunni states to embrace Iraq—in part as a counter to Iran's influence. After several attempts, I finally managed to get the Iraqi foreign minister invited to my meeting with the Gulf Cooperation Council (the Arab monarchies), Egypt, and Jordan in 2006. Hoshyar Zebari, a highly regarded Kurdish leader, entered the room proudly. But after listening to harangues from his colleagues about instability in Iraq, he had had enough. "You treat us like a virus," he said. I held my breath for what he would say next. "I'm not sure if you're more afraid of the Shia part or the democratic part," he said. *That was brilliant,* I thought to myself. But it really underscored the problem. The Sunni states felt vulnerable on both fronts, which caused them to vacillate between resignation and aggression.

To make matters worse, the Iraqi Sunnis lacked coherent leadership. Before the war, Sunnis had been 20 percent of the population, and one of them—Saddam—had held 100 percent of the power. In truth, they too had been tortured by him, persecuted and exiled by him, and subjected to his misrule. But dictators rarely rule just by fear. They have their ways—bargains that make it easier to control the population. Some Sunnis had benefited from those arrangements.

And the deteriorating security situation complicated matters further. It was sometimes difficult to tell when the Sunnis were part of the solution and when they were part of the problem. In this complex environment our military could not stem the violence. The chaotic situation on the ground robbed our political strategy of needed breathing space to mature.

The Disaffected Sunnis

The institutional landscape among Sunnis consisted of four groups: a few exiles who had lived principally in Europe; Sunni tribes who inhabited territorial enclaves, some of whom had been protected by Saddam and others who had simply been left alone; the army, which Saddam had shaped to serve him and no one else; and a few men who had run afoul of the dictator enough to be imprisoned but not enough to be killed.

When the Iraqi transitional government was formed, everyone understood the importance of Sunni representation. In the lead-up to the war, we were worried about revenge killings and were determined to protect the Sunnis as best we could to make sure that they had a place in the new Iraq.

A few Sunni exiles did play prominent roles in the occupation period. For instance, Tariq al-Hashemi, who, like several others, had lived in exile, was relatively effective. He too liked fine suits and spoke perfect English. But he had an impeccable Sunni lineage—the grandson of a former general in the Ottoman army and a nephew of the tutor of Iraqi king Ghazi. He had attended the military academy but insisted that he had never joined the Ba'ath Party. Hashemi was always cognizant of how his fellow Sunnis viewed him. He craved the approval of the tribes and feared backlash from Sunni terrorists. He had good reason for concern. His sister was gunned down in Baghdad in 2006, one day after he had stood with Shia and Kurdish leaders and called for the insurgency to be put down by force.[7] Two of his brothers were killed in the same year.

The interim government also included a few Sunnis who had been imprisoned by the Ba'athist regime. The man who would become speaker of the parliament, Mahmoud al-Mashhadani, came from this background. When we met at our ambassador's house in 2005, he flashed a smile adorned with several gold teeth. "I know who you are," he said to me. "I've known who you are for a long time." I admit that I was getting a bit uncomfortable and wondered where the conversation was going. "When we were in prison," he continued, "we heard about the things you were saying about Saddam. During the war, we found a picture of you and hung it up on the wall. All the prisoners loved you. You liberated us." That frankly gave me the creeps, and I'm not even sure the story was true, but I was grateful for the sentiment he was trying to express.

These men—exiles and ex-prisoners—were entrusted with representing Sunnis during the occupation and several years beyond. But they lacked deep roots in the community. It is fair to say that they were the weakest element of the institutional landscape. Yet we largely depended on them to give Sunnis a voice in the new Iraq.

Unforced Errors

The fact is that we made a number of mistakes throughout the occupation that cost us and cost the Iraqis. From the very start of the war, we simply did not have enough forces on the ground to occupy a country the size of Iraq. We defeated Saddam's army but we couldn't secure the country. Colin had been concerned about it and brought it to the attention of the chairman of the Joint Chiefs, Dick Myers. Steve Hadley and I had repeatedly asked the Pentagon to plan for "rear area security," to protect liberated land as our forces raced through the country.

The president finally raised the issue in an NSC meeting several weeks before the invasion. "Condi is worried about this," he said, leaving the impression that he was not. After that meeting Steve Hadley came into my office. "I would resign. That was unfair." "I know," I said. "I'll talk to the president, but we'll just have to keep hammering away at the issue." He did subsequently discuss the issue again with the secretary of defense. In a meeting with the Joint Chiefs of Staff, he asked again. And he got the same answer—the Pentagon expressed confidence in the plan and the sufficiency of the troop totals. They were wrong. That made everything else that we did an uphill climb.

And we compounded that problem with other missteps, particularly with the Sunnis. In the fall of 2002, President Bush was trying to better understand the lay of the land in Iraq. He asked to meet with as many Iraqi nationals as possible, and on this particular day we had an Iraqi Shia academic, a businessman in exile, and a former army officer. All had escaped Saddam and were thrilled to be in the Oval Office with an American president who might finally deal with the dictator.

The former army officer had a different take on the message, though. He was a man of about fifty who fled the country in the chaos of the 1991 Gulf War. I kept wondering how he had gotten out alive—but there he was. "Mr. President," he said, "don't underestimate how important the army can be in helping you. Most of them hate Saddam. He tortures his own officers. If you treat them well, they will help you." The president was deeply affected by that exchange and wanted to make sure that we took this view into account.

Our visitor that day was not the only one who advised us about the army. It made sense, of course, since it is generally not a good idea to alienate men with guns—at least until you disarm them. Moreover, lower-ranking officers could be useful. The challenge would be to distinguish those who had really been *with* Saddam from those who had simply had no choice but to serve him.

"Have You Seen the Order?"

Colin Powell was on the phone, somewhere between annoyed and alarmed. "Have you seen the order that Jerry sent out in Baghdad?" I said that I had not. "He disbanded the army!"

I was shuffling through papers on my desk trying to see if I had anything to that effect. "I'll get back to you," I said and hung up the phone.

"Steve," I yelled to my deputy in the next office. "Do you have the order?" After some back-and-forth we learned that Colin was right. We had disbanded the army. I tried to get Jerry on the phone but couldn't. Realizing that I hadn't told the president, I headed down to the Oval Office. "He is going to be furious," I told Steve as I started down the hallway. But the president was calm. "Well, that wasn't the plan, right?" I acknowledged that and went back to my office to see what had happened.

Indeed, the plan was just the opposite of disbanding the army. It was to keep 150,000 forces instead. They were to be vetted, tried out on reconstruction-type work, and then used for security. Needless to say, that plan had been abandoned with the CPA order to disband the army.

To be fair to Jerry, the Iraqi army, like so many other institutions, seemed to have vanished into thin air by the time the order came down. It didn't remain coherent; whole units disappeared, and in a sense the army kind of disbanded itself. Still, the assault on the men with guns backfired. Not only did we forgo their help, but we threw hundreds of thousands of armed people off the payroll and onto the streets. It was one of the biggest blunders of the post-invasion period.

Jerry was empowered to make decisions on the ground. He did so under time pressure and difficult circumstances. But a decision of that magnitude needed full NSC review. This case was emblematic of communication breakdowns between the Pentagon and the CPA and between the Pentagon and the White House. I felt that I had failed to wire the various parts together into a cohesive whole. The national security adviser has to do that on behalf of the president. After several of these "failures to communicate," I started to talk directly with Jerry almost every day.

Don was furious, believing that I was usurping his authority and interfering in his chain of command. At one of our weekly lunches, he informed Colin and me that he was washing his hands of the whole thing. "From now on Jerry reports to the White House," he said petulantly. Colin rolled his eyes. I tried to protest that I was just trying to get better coordination. But Don insisted on his stance. I decided that his pique was worth it if we could avoid screwups like this.

The mistake of disbanding the army was exacerbated by the broader policy of de-Ba'athification. This was an extremely sensitive issue because it threatened so many ordinary Iraqis. People often joined the Ba'ath Party because it was the only way to keep a job or get a promotion. There were thousands of teachers, university professors, civil servants, and scientists, among others, in this category. I understood this from studying the Soviet Union. Membership in a totalitarian party was often the way to get ahead—not a sign of ideological purity. The State Department and the intelligence agencies did careful analysis, suggesting the appropriate level at which people might be trusted. Again, there was room to review individuals on a case-by-case basis.

The question was how to carry out the process. Jerry believed—rightly, in my view—that this sensitive matter had to be handled by Iraqis themselves. It was entrusted to Ahmad Chalabi, but he was not just any Iraqi. He turned out to be a determined and opportunistic politician. Chalabi used the committee to carry out a vendetta against the Sunnis, giving him cachet and enhancing his popularity among the Shia. Or at least that is how he saw it.

In the end, the Iraqis had to undo much of the work that the committee had done. In June 2004, about a year after de-Ba'athification began, Bremer dissolved the commission and Interim Prime Minister Iyad Allawi allowed thousands of vetted Ba'athists to return to the government and military. But the damage had been done. The Sunni population felt disenfranchised and collectively punished for Saddam's crimes. It was really difficult to keep them engaged in the effort to build a new Iraq.

The Tribes

Nor did we work effectively with the tribes early on. Iraq's tribes were not *tribes* in the sense of Kikuyu in Kenya, with different languages and ethnic backgrounds. Rather, they were highly structured familial groupings—clans—that kept order and managed the affairs of territorial enclaves throughout the country. The most powerful of these were the tribes of al-Anbar province. There were about 150 tribes in all.

As with the army, we knew that the tribes were important to the future of Iraq. Our initial idea was to supplement Jay Garner's mission with tribal engagement, led by Zalmay Khalilzad. Zal had been born in Afghanistan and had come to the United States to get his PhD. He later became a citizen and taught at

Columbia. He had been our ambassador to Afghanistan and was very successful there. But he knew Iraq too. He first visited Baghdad while serving in the Reagan State Department, and he was director of policy planning at the Pentagon during the Gulf War and its aftermath. Zal was well liked among people of the region. I don't believe that cultural affinity is a result of ethnic heritage—and Zal was, after all, an Afghan. But there was something about Zal—he was at home with leaders in Baghdad and they were at home with him. I once asked him about it. "Well, you have to sit and drink tea—not hurry, take time," he said. "That's as true in Baghdad as in Kabul."

We wanted Zal to use that affinity to bring the various factions into Iraq's postwar governance. In December 2002, he took the lead in our efforts to work with the Iraqi opposition, attending several meetings abroad including an opposition conference in Iraqi Kurdistan in February 2003. As the war began, he was in Turkey, working to identify external and internal Iraqi leaders who could form a provisional government, and he was ready to enter the country as soon as the security situation permitted.

When Jerry Bremer was appointed, I went to the president and told him that we should go ahead with Zal's mission. He was reluctant, having just entrusted Jerry with enormous authority in Iraq. "Ask Jerry," he said. "It would have to be okay with him." I did. Jerry demurred, saying that he wanted to engage the tribes himself. Perhaps there could be a role for Zal later.

We will never know whether the different approach would have worked. I don't think that Jerry was incapable of working with the tribes. But he was so busy in Baghdad. And these were not people you summoned to the capital. You had to have tea with them where they lived.

That was not the only problem in engaging the tribes, though. The insurgency in Sunni provinces that was fueled by a coalition of Saddam's officers and disbanded army personnel found many tribal allies who also feared exclusion. All of this was exacerbated by the rise of Sunni terrorists who took the name of al-Qaeda in Iraq. Led by the clever and diabolic Abu Musab al-Zarqawi, they carried out a violent campaign in the Sunni provinces. They found ways to accommodate the tribes when possible and to coerce and compel their cooperation when necessary.

We saw this most clearly in Fallujah, where our conventional military tactics did little to stem the tide against any of these forces. As it became obvious that we could not stop the violence, the tribes became even more tolerant of the terrorists. These rough, secular men did not have much in common with Zarqawi's religious zealots—but they were not going to risk confrontation when we could not protect them.

Further, our military tactics were not defeating the terrorists, but we were angering the population. Raids with heavy military equipment destroyed too many houses and killed too many tribesmen. Saddam had, we learned, never made that mistake. An Arab leader asked me one day, "Why did you try to pacify Fallujah? Saddam never tried to pacify Fallujah. He knew the tribes were smugglers and gunrunners. He just said, 'You leave me alone and I'll leave you alone.' That is what you should have done." As I said, even dictators have their ways of ruling—that was one that had not occurred to us.

And sometimes our efforts were undermined not in Washington but by incidents in the field. None was more damaging in that regard than Abu Ghraib.

Don was contrite as he briefed the president on the horrific story that was unfolding at the Iraqi prison. "I have seen the photographs," he said, "and they are awful." American soldiers had been involved in abusing and humiliating Iraqi prisoners and the full, awful story was about to hit the news. The president said that we would admit wrongdoing and punish those responsible. "I just don't want to sully the reputation and honor of all of our people," he said sadly. Don asked if he could speak to the president alone. When I came back into the room, the president told me that Don had offered to resign. "I didn't accept it," he said. It was the right call because what had happened at Abu Ghraib was not Don's fault. But we never recovered fully from the fallout. The images lasted and reinforced Sunni suspicion and distrust of the United States.

A Glimmer of Hope

Despite the difficulties and missteps, we made progress on the political front. Jerry Bremer helped the many Iraqi factions to agree on a set of laws for ruling the country. The Transitional Administrative Law (TAL) formed the basis for democratic governance and laid out the principles that would later be enshrined in the constitution. The TAL guaranteed fundamental political rights for Iraqi citizens, including freedom of speech, religion, and assembly, and outlined the process by which power would be transferred to a three-branch transitional government, which would then be responsible for drafting a permanent constitution for approval by referendum.

I was at a seder at the home of the Israeli ambassador, Danny Ayalon, when I got a call from the Situation Room. Jerry Bremer was on the phone. "We got it," he said. "Everyone has signed off and there will be a ceremony on Friday morning after prayers. The leaders will all be there with their wives and children. Some of them with several of their wives," he joked.

I felt a deep surge of emotion. There weren't many times in 2003 when things had gone right in Iraq. This was one of them. I congratulated Jerry, who had taken so many slings and arrows. Then I called the president even though it was pretty late. He too was kind of emotional. "It is their first baby step," he said. I silently filled in the rest of the sentence—*toward democracy*.

On Friday morning, I waited for television coverage of the ceremony, but something was wrong—the start of the event was well overdue. Just as I was about to call him, Jerry called me. "What's going on?" I asked before he could say anything. "Well," he said, "the Shia aren't here. The children's choir has already performed all of the songs they know—twice." It turned out that there had been a last-minute disagreement about some of the language. Everyone returned the following Monday morning; the children's choir sang; and the TAL went into effect.

Still, the successful experiment in governance led the Iraqis to desire more: They wanted sovereignty. We had long discussions in Washington about whether they were ready. The security forces were in their infancy and completely dependent on coalition forces to keep a semblance of peace. The terrorists practically owned Anbar, and Sadr's forces were a constant threat to destabilize the south of the country. Efforts to rebuild the infrastructure were slow, often held hostage to the security situation. The unreliable electrical grid had become a focal point for our reconstruction efforts and a source of tension with the population. This was due to another unpleasant surprise about how Saddam had run the country. Most of the generating power had gone to Baghdad, leaving the rest of the country with long periods without service, or with partial service. When the CPA tried to even out distribution, we learned that there was not remotely enough power to light the whole country. Baghdad residents lost their privileged position and complained loudly about the deterioration of their services.

In other words, the Iraqis were not really ready to run their own affairs. But their leaders believed that ending the occupation could help stabilize the country. We believed that they would not tolerate the occupation much longer. Together, we set in motion a plan to make Iraq sovereign on July 1, 2004—a little more than sixteen months after the war had begun.

The blueprint from Jerry Bremer and the CPA entailed a handoff to an interim government that would write a new constitution. There would then be elections for a permanent government based on the new document. This seven-point plan appeared in the *Washington Post* on September 8, 2003. The first three steps had already been taken: The Iraqi Governing Council had been established earlier in the summer; it had formed a committee to determine how to draft a new constitution; and it had appointed Iraqis to head all twenty-five public ministries.

The next three steps were still to come: drafting a new constitution, ratifying it by popular vote, and electing a new permanent government. The final step, to be taken after the election, was to disband the coalition authority.

Jerry's plan broke in the press before we could fully debate it in Washington. But frankly, it didn't seem like a bad road map for the way ahead. At least to us.

Ayatollah Sistani did not agree. He issued a blistering statement saying that it was unthinkable to have the Iraqi constitution written by people who had not been democratically elected. There would have to be elections first, and then the drafting of the founding document.

The president called the National Security Council together to talk about the situation. One by one everyone extolled the virtues of writing the constitution *before* the elections. I no longer remember why except it seemed to make sense to have electoral rules before you had an election. The president interrupted: "How did I get on the wrong side of people wanting to elect their leaders?" he asked. That quieted the debate. The Ayatollah Sistani had an important ally—the president of the United States. The Iraqis would have their elections and then write their constitution.

"Iraq Is Sovereign"

On June 28, I was attending a NATO meeting in Istanbul with the president. Only a few Americans, Brits, and Iraqis knew that Iraq was about to become sovereign. The official date of the handover was to be July 1, but we had secretly moved it up to wrong-foot terrorists who might want to launch an attack. I was called out of the chamber and told that Jerry Bremer was on the phone. He had handed the letter abolishing the occupation to Allawi, who was president of the IGC. I returned to the meeting and gave President Bush a note. "Iraq is sovereign. The note was passed from Bremer at 10:26 Iraqi time," it said. He wrote on the bottom of it, "Let freedom reign!" and handed it to British prime minister Tony Blair. The men were sitting next to each other simply by virtue of alphabetical order. They shook hands firmly and turned back to the affairs of NATO.

Elections to a National Assembly were held six months later. The United Nations did splendid work with the Iraqis to help them through the process. The country seemed to have a sense of common purpose, at least for a brief time. In January 2005, the front pages of newspapers and television screens throughout Iraq, the Middle East, and the world showed proud Iraqis voting for the first time. The finger dipped into purple ink used to certify that one had voted became an instant symbol of the new democracy. People turned out in significant numbers— 58 percent overall, though Sunnis less so. The security situation made voting difficult and terrorist threats did keep some people away. We worried too that there were some Sunnis who were signaling that this was not their election.

And the voting broke down roughly—though not completely—along sectarian lines, both geographically and in terms of vote totals. This was, I suppose, to be expected in a first election. The main Shia coalition dominated in the south and came in first overall, with 47 percent of the vote; the Kurdish coalition dominated in the north and came in second with more than 25 percent of the total; and a smattering of smaller parties, representing secular and Sunni factions, took the remainder.

The new transitional leadership of Iraq reflected the rough makeup of the country: Talabani the jovial Kurd became president. His vice presidents were al-Mahdi and Hashemi, a Shia and a Sunni, and the speaker of the parliament was a Sunni, the former prisoner Mashhadani. By virtue of their numbers, the Shia parties would select the new prime minister. The competition was fierce and in the end a consensus candidate, Ibrahim al-Jaafari, won—more because he was not hated than because he was admired. To be fair, everyone thought he was honest.

He was also really odd. In my first meeting with him, he took me on a verbal tour of his encyclopedic—and quite wrong—knowledge of American history. Mixing up presidents along the way—Abraham Lincoln was apparently a Founding Father—he was trying to make the point that democracy required selflessness. I sensed that he lacked focus and a program for governing. But his job was to do one thing and one thing only: shepherd the writing of the constitution and the referendum afterward to get it approved.

He and the other leaders managed to do that, but not without considerable difficulty. With the help of constitutional experts assembled by the UN, the Iraqis produced a document. The initial draft bore the mark of compromises between Islamic law and liberal tenets. For instance, one provision stated that no law could contradict Islamic principles; another that Iraq's Supreme Court would include a number of experts on sharia law. This sent Sunni Arabs into the streets to demonstrate against the draft. Moderate Sunni parties were mollified when the transitional assembly agreed to consider changes once a general election was held.

The document created the structure of the new government as a mixed system with a president who was more than ceremonial but without a well-defined portfolio. The parliament was to be bicameral, with a quarter of the seats in the lower house held for women. The prime minister would hold most of the authority, including command of the armed forces, but would be subject to recall by a majority vote in parliament. Like the TAL, the constitution enumerated the rights of citizens and limited the power of the government. Freedom of the press, assembly, and religious conscience were enshrined. The independence of the judiciary was to be respected.

And the country was established as a unified and federal Iraq with broad powers flowing to the provinces. Many of the laws that would make this system function were to be drafted later by the parliament. A national army was created and was to take its members from all parts of the country. The police were to be recruited locally. The *peshmerga* were grandfathered in.

Private property rights were enshrined too and a budget law (essentially an appropriations bill) had to be passed each year. The parliament was charged with writing and passing a law on sharing oil revenue. This was a litmus test for just how much power would reside in the provinces. For the Kurds in particular, this was the sine qua non for participation in a federal and unified Iraq.

The referendum passed in October 2005 with support from 78 percent of voters. The provinces dominated by Kurds and

Shia—twelve of the sixteen—voted overwhelmingly in favor. The Ayatollah Sistani had issued a statement of support: "His highness favors the participation of citizens in the referendum and their voting 'yes' for the constitution, despite the failure to eliminate some of its weaknesses." Americans tend to be made nervous by the involvement of religious figures. But I was really happy to see the statement, even if the ayatollah's followers considered it a fatwa and therefore compulsory.

Sunni support was far weaker. A veto provision designed to protect minority interests meant the constitution would fail if two-thirds of voters in any three provinces voted against it. "No" votes exceeded two-thirds in two Sunni provinces, with 82 percent voting against in Salaheddin and 97 percent in Anbar. Fortunately, Nineveh, a mixed Kurdish and Sunni Arab province, voted 56 percent "no"—below the two-thirds threshold. The referendum passed and the constitution was adopted. There was obviously a lot of work to do with the Sunni Arabs.

I was visiting Tony Blair at Chequers (the prime minister's equivalent of Camp David) the morning after the voting. We sat in his lovely garden eating a mostly British breakfast (I skipped the kippers), waiting in suspense until the outcome was assured. When word came that the referendum had indeed passed all the requisite tests, we both felt that Iraq had turned a corner. In some sense it had. The structure that Iraqis affirmed is the one that has largely held since 2005.

National elections for a permanent government were held six weeks later, in December 2005. This time, Sunni leaders implored their constituents to participate in the process.

"I'm Tired of Doing Their Dirty Work"

In the early days, the most common response when Iraqi leaders fell out of favor with one another was to call the American ambassador—or if the situation was really intolerable, the American secretary of state. I felt at times as if I were keeping the peace among teenagers hurling insults at one another and periodically threatening to quit. In part, they had trouble telling each other the truth face-to-face: all smiles when they were together and ripping each other apart behind each other's backs.

This behavior reached its height when, after the 2006 national election, Jaafari's party nominated him to be prime minister. The process of forming a government had dragged on and on. Iraqis were losing patience with their new leaders and the levels of violence were not abating, though there had been some hope that they might after the elections. In February, the country experienced a devastating attack—Sunni terrorists bombed the Golden Mosque of Samarra, one of the holiest shrines of the Shia. To their credit, leaders from all confessional groups condemned the attack, and some traveled to the shrine in a show of solidarity. It was one of those moments when the Iraqis seemed to be maturing and understanding the demands of leadership.

But the renewed sense of purpose didn't help them break the logjam on government formation. Zal explained that no one really wanted Jaafari to be prime minister.

"Then why did they nominate him?" I asked.

"Well, no one else has the votes either, so they just left it with the status quo. But he'll never get the support of the parliament," he added.

"Have you told him that?"

"About a thousand times," he said.

So Prime Minister Blair and President Bush decided to send Foreign Secretary Jack Straw and me to tell Jaafari to step down. I told the president that I didn't like having to do the Iraqis' dirty work. But Jack and I boarded a plane for Baghdad and upon landing went directly to see Jaafari. We sat down and he immediately launched into a long monologue on his plans as Iraq's first freely elected prime minister.

Jack tried, politician to politician, to explain that it was unlikely he would actually be able to take up the post. "Sometimes it's time to step down and do the best thing for the country," he said. Jaafari was having no part of it, noting correctly that the democratic process had produced *him*. "Who am I to step aside when my fellow citizens want me to serve?" he asked plaintively.

We weren't getting anywhere, and thirty minutes or so into the conversation, I decided to try a different tack. "You aren't going to be prime minister," I blurted out. "You have to step down. This isn't because the United States wants it this way. The Iraqis don't want you, and that's what matters." Jack was a bit shocked, I think, by my tone. As the translation rolled forward, Jaafari looked a bit hurt. But he kept insisting that he would be prime minister.

We then went to see other Iraqi leaders. "Did you convince him?" they asked. *Can't you people see that democracy is hard work? Sometimes you have to do unpleasant things*, I thought to myself. We shuttled back to Jaafari and delivered the message again. This time there was no one in the room except the three of us and an interpreter. He finally seemed to get it. After our trip he began to suggest publicly that he might withdraw, and then, three weeks later, he did. The Iraqis took it from there and resumed their search for a new prime minister.

Zal called a few days after Jaafari stepped down to say that the process was still dragging on. "They just can't agree. It looks like al-Mahdi might win, but it will be close." That was music to my ears because we all liked the affable and competent man— even if he was essentially Hakim's lieutenant.

A few hours later Zal called to say that Mahdi had lost by one vote. "Great. So what now?" I asked in exasperation.

"Some people are talking about Nouri al-Maliki," he responded.

"Who?" I asked.

Zal laughed. "We don't know much about him, but he might be the last man standing."

Maliki was a compromise candidate and came not from one of the major parties but from Dawa, a group that had been forced to operate in a secretive, cell-like fashion during Saddam's reign. Maliki had fled the country in Saddam's day, seeking refuge first in Tehran and then in Damascus. We were told that he hated the Iranians. That, of course, endeared us to him. He turned out to be a good fit for the country at that moment.

I traveled to Baghdad with Don Rumsfeld to meet the new prime minister. We both liked him, principally because he seemed to know what he wanted to do. Iraq was descending into chaos after the bombing of the Golden Mosque. Shia militias were engaging in revenge killings against Sunnis—and Sunnis were returning the favor. The country had been deprived of leadership during the long process of government formation. It was a relief to finally have a prime minister.

Later that evening, Maliki and I met alone in Zal's living room in Baghdad. As he entered, he impressed me as so different from many of those who had returned from exile. For one thing, he was wearing a really bad brown suit. *No designer suits for this man*, I thought. I don't know why, but I found that reassuring.

Maliki spoke almost no English, but he was animated in conversation. He talked about gaining the confidence of all groups. We talked about the problems with the police, who were overwhelmingly Shia and were often complicit in violence against the Sunnis. I told the prime minister that I knew what it was like to be at the mercy of police whom you did not trust. Telling him about growing up in Birmingham, I recalled what it was like to live in a neighborhood when Bull Connor's henchmen came through. "Seeing the police in your neighborhood if you were black was not a reassuring sight," I said. Maliki didn't miss a beat. "I don't even want to see some of them in my neighborhood," he said, chuckling. Then he turned serious. "A lot of them are just thugs."

Nouri al-Maliki served as Iraq's prime minister for eight years—a remarkable run in the rough-and-tumble of Iraqi politics. The members of the ruling group that included Talabani, Hashemi, and Mahdi (a surrogate for Hakim) disliked Maliki and tried on more than one occasion to get rid of him. Of course, they wanted *us* to do it for them. Our response was that they had elected him—now they would have to work together.

When President George H. W. Bush visited Solidarity's birthplace of Gdańsk, Poland, alongside its leader, Lech Wałęsa, in 1989, they were met by thousands of dockworkers chanting, "Freedom! Freedom! Freedom!" It must not have been what Karl Marx had in mind when he said, "Workers of the world, unite!"

Italian dictator Benito Mussolini coined the term *totalitario*, meaning "All within the state, none outside the state, none against the state." Totalitarian regimes prohibit life outside the state. Authoritarian regimes allow some free space, but none for politics. Quasi-democratic regimes have a semblance of democratic institutions, but they are weak and corrupted. Only democracies have institutions that are resilient enough to protect their people's rights in the long run.

The signing of the Declaration of Independence was a milestone in human history. In addition to its assertion that "all men are created equal," the document contains emotional and even hyperbolic criticism of British rule, reminding us that a revolutionary moment is not always the most propitious time for a rational discussion of how to secure newly won rights.

America's founding documents served as inspiration for the Universal Declaration of Human Rights, adopted by the United Nations General Assembly in 1948. "All human beings are born free and equal in dignity and rights," it says. Spearheaded by former first lady Eleanor Roosevelt, the declaration details the fundamental rights that all people deserve—and that only democracies can deliver.

Dred Scott was a slave who was taken to a free state by his owner. He claimed he should therefore be free. Ruling against him in 1857, the U.S. Supreme Court said African descendants, free or enslaved, were never intended to be protected by the Constitution.

The integration of the University of Alabama in 1963 was an important moment in the civil rights movement. It also vivified conflicts over federalism and civil-military relations. Here, General Henry Graham of the Alabama National Guard, acting on orders from President John F. Kennedy, instructs segregationist governor George Wallace to stand aside from the schoolhouse door.

Russian president Boris Yeltsin confronts weakened Soviet leader Mikhail Gorbachev on August 23, 1991, shortly after Gorbachev suffered a coup attempt by communist hard-liners. The simultaneous collapse of Soviet institutions with the rebirth of the Russian state hampered the subsequent attempt to establish democracy.

Vladimir Putin has returned Russia to its authoritarian roots. Yeltsin chose Putin to succeed him in part to protect the ill-gotten gains from his presidency. Not content with snuffing out hopes for democracy in Russia, Putin has worked to undermine democratic governments around the world.

Electrician Lech Wałęsa rallies support during the 1980 strikes at the Lenin shipyard in Gdańsk, which gave rise to the independent trade union Solidarity. Polish communists eventually cracked down on the group and declared martial law. Solidarity nevertheless survived underground and was prepared to take the reins of power when the opportunity arose in 1989.

Ukraine has had three revolutions since its independence in 1991. Pictured here are the leaders of the 2004 Orange Revolution, Viktor Yushchenko and Yulia Tymoshenko, who went on to be president and prime minister, respectively. Yushchenko was poisoned during his run for the presidency, and Tymoshenko was jailed for several years after her term.

Non-democratic rulers often hold sham elections to portray a façade of democracy. That was even the case in Saddam Hussein's Iraq, where political dissent was often met with a death sentence. Shown here, Iraqis vote in their first free national elections in January 2005. They have held several free elections since.

Elections sometimes have consequences even if they are not free and fair. Thousands of Iranians defied a protest ban in June 2009, after what they said was the rigged reelection of President Mahmoud Ahmadinejad, whose victory was announced almost as soon as the polls closed. It was the largest uprising since the 1979 revolution, and the regime cracked down brutally in response.

Dueling claims of victory after Kenya's second free presidential election led to ethnic violence and more than one thousand deaths. Under a power-sharing deal brokered by Kofi Annan (left), President Mwai Kibaki (center) secured a second term, and his challenger, Raila Odinga (right), joined the government as prime minister. Five years later, Odinga ran for president once again. When he came up short, no violence followed, and he accepted the result after it was certified by the Supreme Court.

After decades of battling a narco-terrorist insurgency, Colombia has turned the corner toward peace. Former president Álvaro Uribe promised "democratic security" and worked tirelessly to strengthen the institutions of the state. He is pictured here in 2005 with Carolina Barco, former foreign minister and ambassador to the United States.

Liberian president Ellen Johnson Sirleaf, called "Ma Ellen" by her people, has been determined to strengthen Liberia's institutions while delivering for the population. She is the first female head of state in Africa. Here we are at a development event in 2007.

At my swearing-in ceremony at the State Department in 2005, I was accompanied by my uncle Alto and aunts Mattie and Gee, as well as President George W. Bush. The oath of office was administered by my Watergate neighbor Ruth Bader Ginsburg, with a portrait of America's first diplomat, Benjamin Franklin, hanging in the background.

Most of the focus was on trying to pass a budget and an oil law; build security forces; purge the police of sectarian elements; and deliver essential services like electricity to the population. The U.S. Congress even insisted on a set of benchmarks for governing in exchange for the substantial assistance that Iraq was receiving. The Iraqis resented the notion of being graded on their performance, a point we tried to make to the Congress. But we dutifully reported on how Baghdad was doing. There seemed to be little recognition of how hard it was to make new institutions actually work. To their credit, the Iraqis were trying to use their democratic processes—passing legislation rather than ruling by decree. In such a divided country, this was a very hard task indeed.

"Pretty Soon You Will All Be Swinging from Lampposts"

The governance problem was exacerbated by the horrible security situation. Revenge killings were occurring almost daily as sectarian violence worsened considerably throughout 2006. It was a period of nearly full-scale civil war as neighborhoods and communities were being cleansed on a sectarian basis. Visiting Baghdad again late in 2006, I asked to meet with Sunni leaders—including some tribesmen—and then separately with Shia.

Before I could say a word, the Sunnis handed me grotesque pictures of children with severed heads and limbs. I think it was meant to shock me, but unfortunately, it wasn't the first time I had seen photographic evidence of atrocities. "Let me tell you something," I said to them. "We have a saying in the United States. We can hang separately or we can hang together." I paused and let the interpreter say the phrase a couple of times. "Do they understand?" I asked.

He nodded. "Well, you can stick together or the next time I come you'll all be swinging from lampposts."

"Did they get that?" I asked.

"You bet," he answered.

About an hour later, the next group made the same photographic presentation—but this time the victims were Shia. I wanted to make the point that turning on each other was not the answer. Either they had to pull together to solve their problems or they would be devoured by the chaos.

The morning after returning to Washington, I went to see the president and told him about all that had happened. "I'm not sure they are going to make it," I said. He could see that I was pretty despondent and really tired. "Well, what should we do?" he asked. Throughout my time with him, I had tried not to dump a problem in his lap with no answer. But this time I had nothing to say. "Let me go and think about it, sir." It was the low point for me—professionally and personally.

Another Chance to Govern: The Violence Begins to Subside

Late in 2006, intelligence reports continued to be bleak, yet we now know that things were starting to turn slowly in favor of a more stable Iraq. John Taylor, a colleague from Stanford who had been undersecretary of the Treasury in the first term, called me one morning. "My son is serving in Anbar and he has sent a note that I think you ought to see," he said. John sent a copy of the e-mail to my executive assistant, who passed it on to me. It was a revelation. The young Marine talked about how cooperation with the tribes was improving. Our soldiers were being treated well by the tribesmen and their families, he reported. The insurgents were losing ground.

Indeed, a few months earlier, I had received news on June 7 that Abu Musab al-Zarqawi had been killed in a U.S. airstrike. He had been the mastermind of al-Qaeda in Iraq and had orchestrated the February bombing of the Golden Mosque. He hoped to plunge the country into civil war, and he had succeeded. I have reflected on how I became hardened enough to celebrate the demise of another human being with absolutely no remorse. Today, a gruesome souvenir occupies a treasured space on my bookcase. The unit that killed Zarqawi gave me a stone from the house where he met his demise. The gray-and-black piece of slab has jagged edges—clearly the result of an explosion. It says simply *AMZ: 6-7-2006*.

And on the ground in Anbar, just as John's son had predicted, we began to get reports of offers from the tribes to cooperate with us. Apparently, Zarqawi's fighters were very bad guests—compelling cooperation through brutal tactics, delivering the severed heads of children to their parents, and marrying their daughters off to al-Qaeda fighters. Zarqawi's successor, Abu Ayyub al-Masri, was even more demanding and escalated these practices. The sheikhs had eventually had enough. They might not have liked us, but we were, at least for the time being, the lesser of two evils.

In time, though, the cooperation would become real and deeper. First, we finally created a mechanism for tribal engagement that worked. We dispatched teams of diplomats, aid workers, and security experts to live among the tribes and help them in matters of governance and reconstruction. These Provincial Reconstruction Teams (PRTs) gave us a structure for real engagement in the Sunni heartland.[8] They didn't have to come to Baghdad—we went to them.

On one occasion, an American diplomat, Jason P. Hyland, welcomed me to the PRT in Mosul. It was a fine example of what we were trying to do. In this case, Hyland had helped the Iraqis to form a town council made up of elected officials who met to resolve the city's problems. The job was made difficult by its ethnic and sectarian mix. It was a majority Sunni Arab city with significant populations of Kurds and other minorities. After greeting the participants I said, "I'm here to listen and to help in any way that I can. I'll report your views directly to the president." Much to my amazement, the meeting wasn't at all about what the United States could do. The Sunni sheikh, his deputy, and the ten or so members of the council were much more engaged in debating each other. That was a good sign. But you could see that they were struggling to be civil. The chairman in particular was trying to restrain himself as he listened to the deputy go on and on about Kurdish rights. But he did restrain himself. In fact, he asked each member of the council to speak, telling me that everyone had a right to an opinion. I'm not sure he really believed it—and I did wonder if that was his practice when I wasn't in the room. Hyland assured me that it was always the case. They weren't being civil just for show.

The situation was improving too, because the tribes organized to work with us to expel al-Qaeda from al-Anbar province. They were fierce fighters and with training and American airpower turned out to be a formidable force.

Still, the tide was not turning quickly enough and levels of violence remained unacceptably high. The big problem was in the central part of the country, where the population was a mix of Sunni and Shia. The military used to say that 80 percent of sectarian violence in Iraq occurred within thirty miles of Baghdad. The south of the country was relatively free of that kind of violence because it was almost all Shia, but it was nevertheless extremely dangerous for our soldiers. Tehran was helping radical Shia militias—including those of Muqtada al-Sadr—to kill our troops. Too many Americans were dying. Too many Iraqis were dying.

Each morning I opened the *Washington Post* to "Faces of the Fallen." The *Post* had begun the series in 2003 to memorialize Americans killed in the war. I made myself look at every one of the photos—a harsh reminder of the costs of the war. All of our top national security officials met with Gold Star families and visited Walter Reed and Bethesda Naval Hospital.

I tried to visit wounded soldiers at least a few times each year. On Good Friday, I would go to noon services and then in the afternoon go to one of the hospitals. During one visit, the doctor accompanying me asked if I would visit a particular patient's mother who wanted to meet me. "Of course," I said. He told me that it would be rough going. The young man—an African American in his midtwenties—had sustained a brain injury and cried out uncontrollably. "Be prepared," the doctor said. I opened the door and entered the room. His mom came over. All that I could say was, "I'm so sorry for your sacrifice and I'm praying for your family." She thanked me for coming and asked if we could take a picture. "He'll be all right," she said. I knew that he probably wouldn't be. At times like that, no goal, no matter how worthy, seemed worth the sacrifice. But I had to hope—and still do—that one day a stable, secure, and democratic Iraq would honor soldiers like that young man.

The Iraqis were taking huge losses fighting the insurgency too. Sitting in my office one day, Steve Hadley said something really profound. "The Iraqis have to win their freedom," he said. "We can't do it for them." By 2006, the Iraqis were doing just that—with their own blood, not just that of Americans. They had a very good defense minister who was making progress in training the army, particularly the special forces. But they were overmatched and we didn't have the strategy or the numbers to help them.

Pete Pace, the chairman of the Joint Chiefs of Staff, asked to see me one afternoon. He was a Marine—the first to be chairman. Pete was a soldier, not a Washington bureaucrat. "I've been thinking," he began. "If the number of trained Iraqi troops is increasing and we're making progress—why is the security situation getting worse?" Pete said that he had quietly (meaning without Don's permission) asked a group of colonels to take a fresh look at our strategy in Iraq. I wanted to jump up and hug him.

For three years, I had listened to the Pentagon brief the president, using largely useless metrics, like ammunition dumps destroyed and a version of a "body count"—how many terrorists had been killed. I kept thinking back to Vietnam where metrics like these had given Lyndon Johnson a false sense that the United States was winning the war.

And I had listened with growing concern and anger as the State Department was blamed for not finding a political solution. In one session, the U.S. commander in Iraq, George Casey, asked for more civilian personnel. "The State Department needs to bring me as many civilians as possible," he said to the president.

I don't know why, but I snapped. "General, when you can protect them, I'll send them," I barked. The room fell silent.

Later, after the meeting, Steve Hadley called me and asked me to talk to George. "You embarrassed him in front of the president," he said.

"Yes, I know. I will call him because he's a good man. But I meant what I said, Steve. And I won't take it back."

We were all coming to terms with our failing strategy. The security situation, the Pentagon would say, would improve when the political situation improved. Steve put it best. "Sometimes a security problem is just a security problem," he told the president.

All In

In November 2006, President Bush decided that it was time to change direction. He asked Don Rumsfeld to step down as secretary and brought Bob Gates to head the Pentagon. George Casey returned to Washington, and David Petraeus deployed to

Baghdad to head the military effort. Though John Negroponte and Zal had been excellent ambassadors, we decided to bring in fresh legs in Baghdad. Ryan Crocker, one of the best officers in the Foreign Service and our ambassador to Pakistan—one of the toughest posts in the world—headed to Iraq.

But change in personnel was not enough—we needed a change in strategy too. The generals who had fought in Iraq after Saddam was overthrown—Petraeus, Pete Chiarelli, Ray Odierno—returned to Washington in 2004 with a chance to reassess what they had done. The military is very good at exercises in "lessons learned." These generals and Pete Pace's group of colonels, which included H. R. McMaster, developed a new approach. In order to help with the Iraqis, you had to live with them, train with them, and fight with them. It was dangerous work and it took many more people than we had on the ground. Together with aid workers and diplomats deployed in the PRTs, American soldiers went right into the heart of the fight.

The president's new policy became known as "the surge." It was a gut-wrenching decision for him—and frankly for all who advised him. I was really skeptical at the start, believing that we might achieve little and yet lose more American lives. When the NSC met on December 8, 2006, to consider the policy, the president and I argued publicly in an NSC meeting—the first time we had ever done so.

"Mr. President, if you send more troops in and don't change *what* we are doing, we will just have more people killed. And if the Iraqis keep up their sectarian ways, nothing will work."

"So what's your plan, Condi?" the president asked. "We'll

just let them kill each other, and we'll stand by and try to pick up the pieces?"

"No, Mr. President," I said. "We just can't win by putting our forces in the middle of their blood feud. If they want to have a civil war, we're going to have to let them."

I was furious. But he was the president and I wasn't going to argue further with others in the room. After the meeting, I followed him into the Oval Office. "You know I've been all in. No one has supported this war and worked harder than I have," I said—the *how dare you* unsaid but clearly meant.

"I know," he said quietly. I felt so awful at that moment. This war was "his" war, and he was not prepared as president to lose it and repeat America's tragic retreat after Vietnam. I started to see that he believed surging U.S. forces was his best chance to avoid Johnson's fate.

The personnel changes that the president had made reassured me that we might succeed. Bob Gates and I were friends. We had gone through the extraordinary events of the end of the Cold War together while serving on George H. W. Bush's NSC. There were few people I trusted more. And David Petraeus was one of the best minds in the American military. We had dinner together one night at the Watergate. "I tried to have this conversation back in 2003 when you were national security adviser," he said. I didn't understand what he meant. "Don Rumsfeld canceled the meeting," he explained. He went on to talk about how much we needed close cooperation between civilians and the military if we were to succeed.

And I had done one other thing: I stepped outside of

channels and called General Ray Odierno, who was now commanding our forces in Anbar. Ray, a giant of a man with a shaved head and a tough persona, had been my Joint Chiefs liaison in my first two years as secretary. He had helped me develop the Provincial Reconstruction Teams.

"Ray," I said, "you and I are not having this conversation. But tell me. Will the surge do as advertised?"

"It is our best chance. And I think it will work," he answered. That was enough for me.

At the very end of 2006, the national security team was at the president's Crawford ranch for a series of meetings to review Iraq. A couple of hours before dinner, I saw the president standing at the fishing pond near the end of the property. The sun was setting on an unusually warm day, and at first I thought, *I should just leave him alone.* But something told me to go ahead and join him. He was looking out over the plains and motioned for me to come on down. "Can you support me on this?" He didn't need to fill in the antecedent. "I can," I said. "But you know that this is our last card."

The president had done his homework on whether the Iraqis were really prepared to win their own peace. This time there could be no excuses—no blaming America for every shortcoming, and no blaming each other. Before he made the decision to surge forces, the president met with Maliki in Amman, Jordan, in November 2006. The Iraqi prime minister was well prepared. He had a military plan of action—a fairly sophisticated briefing—that he handed over to the president. The problem was that Maliki wanted to execute the plan himself, which is not a bad thing in its own right, but our commanders did not think the Iraqi military would be ready for such an operation for at least another year. President Bush knew the surge could not wait. He met privately with Maliki, and told him, "Let me lend you some of my forces." We were all in.

Histories will be written for years to come about the surge and its success. Anbar was taken back from al-Qaeda, the black flag of the terrorists torn down by local tribesmen as they chased them from town after town. Most important, sectarian violence in and around Baghdad and in the center of the country declined dramatically and tailed off over time. Al-Qaeda in Iraq continued its attacks but at a level that did not threaten the government. And in the south of the country, with more American forces on the ground, the Iranians faced a tougher task.

We had told the Iranians that we knew they were providing the weapons and the training that were killing our soldiers. The Russians carried the message for us. "We won't cross the border, but if we find your people in Iraq, we will capture or kill them." In a stroke of good fortune, we caught the deputy commander of the Quds force inside Iraqi territory. He was taken to Irbil and questioned. We told the Iranians that he was "singing like a bird" about everything they were doing and exposing their operations. They were less active after that.

Maliki proved to be an able commander in chief during this period. At one point, in March 2008, he ordered Iraqi security forces to take back the refinery in Basra from Iranian-backed Shia militias. American generals objected, telling him that his forces were not ready. Maliki launched the operation anyway.

As we sat in the Situation Room at the White House, every one of us proclaimed the stupidity of the prime minister—everyone except President Bush. "He is showing that he is in charge. It is an important message to his people," he said.

The president, a politician himself, understood what Maliki was trying to do. The Iraqi prime minister entered the liberated area on the back of an Iraqi tank. He was, for the moment, a symbol for his people—of what Iraq could achieve.

The improving security situation gave the Iraqis some breathing room to take on the other tasks of governing. Here the picture was decidedly mixed—but not without some successes.

The parliament's two big tasks—pass a budget and pass an oil law—were intertwined. And both were proxies for the limits of federalism. The relationship was this: The budget had to be based on revenue, mostly from oil. But the formula for sharing oil revenue between the Kurdish region and Baghdad was a test for the political arrangements between them.

The Iraqis were caught in an endless loop—until they could sort out revenue projections, they couldn't pass a budget. That slowed the allocation of funds to important tasks like paying the army or letting contracts for building electricity plants. Sunni areas, largely without oil production capability, had also been promised funding for various projects.

One project, the building of a new military academy, became symbolic of the political tensions between Baghdad and its regions. On one of President Bush's final trips to Iraq, he met with Iraqi leaders and the Sunni tribesmen who had successfully expelled al-Qaeda from Anbar. The tribesmen were a tough lot, unshaven, with rough, dark skin. I remember thinking back to the Arab diplomat's advice. *Why did we try to fight this bunch back in 2003?* It was surely better to have them on our side. And now they were.

Maliki seemed more uncomfortable with these men than the Americans did. He didn't take the center seat saved for him, but a corner chair at the end of the table. His body language was just terrible. He was almost in the fetal position. *He's just not a natural politician,* I thought.

On the other hand, Jalal Talabani—a terrific politician—was in his element. "The brave sons of Anbar," he intoned, "have played an essential role in saving Iraq. You shall have your military academy." I remember thinking that Jalal would have been great in American pork-barrel politics. Unfortunately, the funding for the academy was not forthcoming for several more years.

The Iraqis did find other ways to appease the Sunnis, though. In 2008, large numbers of former Ba'athists were allowed back into their jobs and thousands of prisoners were granted amnesty. The country finally passed the "Law of the Supreme Commission for Accountability and Justice," which tried to give a modicum of protection to innocent Sunnis while acknowledging the crimes of the Ba'ath Party.

Still, Iraqi leaders continued to struggle with all of the major issues of governance, and admittedly it was frustrating. Our Congress was brutal in its assessment of their incompetence. There seemed to be little sympathy for how hard it is to make democratic institutions—especially new ones—work. On one occasion, when testifying before the Senate Foreign Relations

Committee, I almost lost it. As one senator droned on and on about how the Iraqis still hadn't passed a budget, it took all the self-control I could muster not to retort, *And neither have you.* The legislature of the mature American democracy had failed to pass an actual budget in 2003, 2005, and 2007. The Iraqis finally did so in 2008 with a budget law authorizing $48 billion in expenditures. They finessed the oil revenue question, with the Kurds agreeing to a budget formula in lieu of an oil law.

A hydrocarbon law was indeed drafted in 2007. According to the constitution, "Oil and gas are owned by all the people of Iraq," but it does not say what the autonomous regions are and are not allowed to do. In the absence of firm rules, the Kurds have passed their own regional law and attracted considerable foreign investment, despite the jurisdictional uncertainties. The Kurdish deal terms are significantly more oriented toward the free market and thus more favorable to business.

Shia parties sometimes support the Kurds since they want to maintain some flexibility for the south—also an oil-producing region. Obviously, the big loser would be the central government and particularly the Sunni region, which has virtually no oil production.

In my class on political risk at Stanford's Graduate School of Business, we give the students a hypothetical case: whether to invest in an oil field in Kurdistan even though Baghdad objects. About 70 percent of the time, these future business leaders take the chance. That's the sentiment the Kurds are counting on, and so far it has served them well.

The Iraqis have made some progress on other sticky problems as well. One ticking time bomb for Iraq was the status of

Kirkuk—a region that sits partly in Kurdish territory but has a very large Sunni population. The Kurds had routinely threatened to annex it, giving provincial elections added importance. The passage of a 2008 provincial electoral law was hailed as a milestone. And at the end of 2009, the Iraqis passed a critical national elections law, stepping back from a constitutional crisis that threatened to delay balloting. Dr. Haider Ala Hamoudi, an expert on Iraq, has noted that the United States did not draft any of the amendments. The Iraqis managed to do so in a process that he said was "messy but worked."[9]

When the Bush administration left office in January 2009, Iraq had been the most trying and the most dominant issue. But in the end, despite all the trials and sacrifices, I felt that the Iraqis were ready to embrace their chance at democracy. Sometimes they should have taken our advice—but often things worked out even when they didn't. President Bush had met weekly with Maliki by video, elected leader to elected leader. It was affirming for the Iraqi prime minister and a good way to gently prod him in the right direction. Now it was up to him.

The country had come a long way—it was more secure, and for that I was grateful. I had personally experienced some scary times in Iraq. I always flew to a U.S. military base, usually in Turkey. From there I would take a C-130 to the Baghdad airport, sitting in the cockpit with the young pilots, who were often members of the National Guard. Then we would take a Black Hawk helicopter, machine gunners hanging out of the windows, into the Green Zone, the protected enclave for the international community and a number of high-ranking Iraqi officials.

On one trip, as we were about to land, the plane suddenly

pulled up. "What just happened?" I asked, hoping that my heart rate would come down so that I could breathe.

"Oh, ma'am, there was some mortar fire. But we're not sure if it was just random or meant for you," the young man said.

"I guess it doesn't matter," I replied.

Another time, a sandstorm prevented me from taking a helicopter into the Green Zone. We had to drive along what had been dubbed the "highway of death," because explosions along it were frequent. We made it without incident, but as the car moved slowly among stalled trucks and automobiles, I tried not to focus on the stricken faces of my security guards.

My last trip to Iraq showed me just how much had changed. I made the rounds with the politicians and joined them for lunch at Talabani's house. But Hakim was ill and asked if I would come to see him. He lived in the "red zone." I would travel into territory where a year before I could not have gone.

As we slowly made our way to the cleric's home, signs of conflict were everywhere. The streets were pockmarked with holes made by mortar fire, and there were more than a few bombed-out buildings. Iraqi soldiers patrolled on foot, and helicopters appeared above periodically. But things were finally quiet and people went about their daily tasks—shopkeepers selling goods and customers buying them, and youngsters playing in the streets.

As my armored motorcade passed those places and people, I felt a surge of satisfaction and hope. Perhaps one day the Iraqis who had endured so much chaos would enjoy a peaceful and democratic future. I felt that we had given them a chance.

After the Islamic State Is Defeated

In 2011, President Obama fulfilled his campaign promise to pull all American forces out of Iraq. The Status of Forces Agreement (SOFA) that we had signed in 2008 was set to expire. In truth, the firm 2011 date had been a compromise with Maliki, who wanted to show that Iraq could stand on its own two feet. Elections were coming up in 2009, and he thought that it would be a popular move. Everyone, including Maliki, thought that the SOFA would be renegotiated or extended. He told President Bush that he would be able to do so after the elections—he meant his, not ours.

The Obama administration did not succeed in extending the SOFA. The same terms that had been acceptable to the Pentagon in the prior agreement should have been acceptable in a new one. Bob Gates, secretary of defense for both Presidents Bush and Obama, said the following: "The only chance we would have had for an agreement would have been with [President Obama's] intensive involvement personally, and that didn't happen."[10]

It is a pity, because Iraq was on its way to a better future. The American sacrifices—and those of Iraqis—were beginning to pay off. Whatever one's view of the decision to invade Iraq in 2003, the hardest work had been done and the ground was prepared for a decent outcome for Iraq and the region. In 2010, in the final elections before American forces left, Iraqi voters delivered a remarkable result: Iyad Allawi, a Shia, won the largest share of the vote as the head of an avowedly non-sectarian party, with considerable Sunni support. The political system was beginning to mature and the violence had subsided.

I have been asked repeatedly, "Knowing today what you do, would you still counsel the invasion of Iraq?" Well, of course, what you know today cannot affect what you did yesterday. That said, had I known that we would not be prepared to keep forces in the country—in small numbers—to help the Iraqis find democratic stability, the decision would have been much harder for me.

When U.S. forces departed, Vice President Joe Biden declared Iraq stable and free. He was right about half of it. Within a year, the civil war in Syria became a new front against stability and peace. The remnants of al-Qaeda that the surge had defeated in Iraq regrouped across the border. Now, with the chaos that obliterated national lines, they came back and eventually formed the core of a new menace—the so-called Islamic State, or ISIS. Our intelligence agencies have admitted that they did not see the threat emerging. And the Iraqis were ill-prepared to handle the challenge on their own. ISIS poured into the vacuum.

Without the steadying hand of American influence, Maliki gave way to his own worst instincts. He was a proud and prickly man who cataloged every slight, perceived or real. In a matter of months, he was using his power to go after his enemies, particularly Tariq al-Hashemi, whom he accused of trying to overthrow him. That alienated Sunnis, and increasingly he gave in to his sectarian streak—firing competent commanders in the security forces and the police and replacing them with those loyal to him. They were mostly Shia, of course, exacerbating tensions between the sectarian groups.

After almost a decade in office, Maliki was a spent force. Despite his success in the 2014 elections, many Iraqis no longer trusted or respected their prime minister. He had lost the confidence of the United States too, especially after the Iraqi army lost control of Mosul. Reminiscent of Jaafari years before, at first he tried to hang on. He threatened to take his supporters to the streets. But the ploy didn't work and he soon stepped down, saying that he would return to the parliament and work for the causes that mattered to him. He was given a ceremonial title of vice president and accepted the face-saving compromise. It was a mature response from a mercurial man. Arab strongmen didn't usually step down. This was a sign that something had changed in Iraq for the better.

The country continues to function in a quasi-democratic fashion—the institutions are weak but at least present. The parliament meets and then disbands due to boycotts by one group or another. Then they reconvene, unable to do much work, but they do keep trying. Prime Minister Haider al-Abadi has survived multiple no-confidence measures. And he keeps at it, re-forming his cabinet and shaking up his government in hopes of finding a workable formula. The people protest the incompetence of their leaders, and—after one bloody incident a year or so ago—the state no longer interferes.

The government respects the basic rights of Iraqi citizens, according to Freedom House. There are a dozen private television stations in addition to 150 print publications. The Internet is not restricted and Arab satellite TV is readily available, though journalists have complained more in recent years about harassment from sectarian groups. Iraqi athletes participate in world competitions like the Olympics. They no longer fear reprisals from a brutal dictator if they lose.

Women make up 25 percent of the parliament thanks to a formula passed in the 2009 electoral law. Iraq is a conservative society and women still face obstacles, but they are not legal, governmental restrictions. Forty-five percent of university students are women, as are one in three university professors.[11] That is a step forward.

Freedom of religion is guaranteed and there is no official religious body to interfere. Yet religious minorities are being driven out of the country. This is not due to policy but because the government cannot protect them from sectarian militias and terrorists. And, sadly, the Iraqi state cannot yet secure its citizens more generally. Bombs go off with regularity in the streets of Baghdad—the work of ISIS, which still occupies a swath of the country's territory.

Slowly, though, ISIS is being beaten back by Iraqi security forces, the Sunni tribes, Kurdish *peshmerga*, and American airpower and advisers. As of late 2016, the United States has more than five thousand troops in Iraq—about half the number the generals wanted to leave behind in 2011 when Iraq was stable.

A positive outcome in the war against ISIS is by no means assured. But there is a good chance that the so-called Caliphate they hoped to establish will fail and that the extremist group will be defeated. The larger question is whether a unified Iraq will survive. When the war is over, the Kurds will most assuredly push for greater autonomy. They have expanded their territory by about 40 percent since 2014 and taken a number of villages around Mosul, as well as Kirkuk. Barzani has taken a tough line rhetorically, saying that land won with Kurdish blood should never again be ruled by Baghdad. Many observers think that he is staking out ground from which to bargain when the war ends. Others take him at his word. One thing is clear: The Kurds have built a relatively peaceful and prosperous region within an unstable Iraq. It remains to be seen whether they will demand distance from Baghdad or a divorce.

The Shia in the south will have to find a way to resist the pull of the "Iranian crescent." Iranian-backed militias will claim—with some justification—that they too contributed to the defeat of ISIS. Tehran will be influential, but how influential? As one former ambassador said, "If Iran were really calling the shots, the Iraqis wouldn't be pumping four million barrels of oil a day—and keeping the price of oil low when Tehran needs the revenue." Iran could not have wanted to see American forces, even in limited numbers, back in Iraq. The Iraqi Shia are Arab, not Persian, and that has always been a limiting factor in Tehran's influence. The Iranians will have free rein if there is no American counterweight. The scale of Tehran's writ will be determined by policy choices—ours as well as theirs.

Iraq's institutions will bear the mark of what the country has gone through to defeat ISIS. Perhaps there will be a new "Articles of Confederation" that reflects the geostrategic reality of the country. As long as it is a democratic one, something will have been gained. And at this moment, Iraq and Tunisia are the only Arab countries that have quasi-democratic institutions on which to build. When the Middle East settles down, there may be a new democratic opening. This time there will be something there that was absent before—political institutions, weak though they may be—that might be able to mediate differences between peoples, peacefully.

Egypt and Tunisia: When Old Men Fail

It had been a really strange trip. I slept fitfully that September night in 2008 after my visit with Muammar Qaddafi in the Libyan capital. My meeting with "the Leader" had gone later into the night than planned—my security detail sitting anxiously outside the door, banned from joining me in the room. I had arrived in Tunis well after midnight. Now, startled by my alarm, I awoke with that sensation one has after a bizarre dream. *Did I really just sit in his kitchen and have dinner with his female security guards who many believe are also his daughters? Did he really give me a video—with pictures of me set to music—called* Black Flower *in the White House? Okay. Whatever his weird affection for you, thank the Lord, that visit is over. Time to move on. Get your mind around what you need to say to Ben Ali.*

The meeting room in Tunis was palatial, as they all are in the Middle East. There was enough malachite and gold to make the Russian Winter Palace seem modest by comparison. The Tunisian president, Zine al-Abidine Ben Ali, hair dyed jet-black, was cordial but distant, and I quickly realized that the longer I talked, the less he engaged. I was trying to make several points about cooperation in fighting terrorism and the more contentious one that Tunisia had a responsibility to take back some of its citizens who were prisoners at Guantánamo. Ben Ali kept insisting that it had already done so. But they hadn't, and none of his entourage seemed anxious to tell him that he was wrong.

He was befuddled and slow, slipping in and out of genuine attention to what I was saying. *This reminds me of meeting with Hosni Mubarak, I thought. He always told those tired stories—sometimes repeating the same one within a matter of minutes in the same meeting. These are failing old men who are out of touch and shielded by those who won't tell them what is going on. It really is sad.*

Three years later, as I watched the events of the 2011 "Arab Spring" explode into the world's consciousness, I thought back on those meetings with Mubarak and Ben Ali. They never saw it coming, but they should have. The level of discontent in their countries was high. Unemployment and corruption and a sense of powerlessness oppressed the populations as much as the brutality of the security forces. A citizen could largely avoid the ire of the police by keeping his mouth closed. The daily humiliations—hopeless poverty, imperious bureaucrats, and the anger they engendered—could not be ignored.

"Mr. President, Reform Before Your People Are in the Streets"

As we have noted, authoritarian regimes do not dominate all of society in the way that totalitarian/cult-of-personality rulers do. There is space for independent organizations—business groups, universities, and civil society. And the size and robustness of that space varies from country to country and at different times within a country. The chance for reform is present because there is a nascent infrastructure on which to build.

But in the case of Egypt and Tunisia, the regimes did not

take that opportunity, though Egypt came close in 2005. In fact, Egypt provides an object lesson in what could have been. The story below is one of arrested reform. The regime almost did the right thing, making hesitant but significant changes in the way that politics was practiced. And then Mubarak panicked and pulled back at the end of the year. That sealed his fate and the fate of his regime when in 2011 the Egyptian people—and the people of the region—said they had had enough.

Freedom's "Indian Summer"

I was sworn in as secretary of state on January 26, 2005. The timing could not have been more fortunate. People seeking freedom seemed to be winning everywhere, and I felt like there was really a strong favorable wind behind them—and us. The Orange Revolution in Ukraine, the Rose Revolution in Georgia, and the Tulip Revolution in Tajikistan were in full bloom, with pro-Western governments emerging in all of them. But it was the stunning events in the Middle East that suggested the Freedom Agenda was indeed on the right side of history, even in the world's most troubled region.

In January 2005, the Iraqis held successful "Purple Finger" parliamentary elections, with large turnouts even in areas threatened by terrorism. The iconic picture of newly freed citizens holding up their hands, their fingers stained with purple ink—the equivalent of a sticker saying "I voted"—swept across the world's media. The moment was emotional for me and for all of us who had been involved in the decision to overthrow Saddam Hussein.

President Bush invited representatives of the Purple Finger Revolution to the first lady's box at the State of the Union address. The sustained, bipartisan standing ovation for these Iraqi patriots was stirring, and for that moment, a sense of pride in what America had done echoed through the chamber.

In Lebanon, Rafik Hariri, the wealthy businessman who was the country's prime minister, was assassinated in February of the same year. This created a revolutionary moment as more than a million people spilled into the streets of Beirut to demonstrate against the Syrians and Hezbollah, who were suspected of complicity in his death. They demanded the removal of Syrian forces that had occupied the country since the 1970s.

I watched those events on TV in London from my room in the Churchill Hotel. Earlier that morning, the French foreign minister and I had issued a joint statement on the events in Lebanon. Jacques Chirac and George W. Bush didn't agree about most issues in the Middle East, most especially about Iraq, but regarding Lebanon they had found common purpose. In 2004 they jointly engineered a UN Security Council resolution calling for the withdrawal of Syrian forces.

Watching the television coverage from Beirut, I thought back on the events that secured that international agreement. It was August 2004 and we were in New York for the Republican convention that nominated the president for a second term. I was in my room at the Waldorf Astoria, my attention split between his speech on TV and my telephone calls to our UN ambassador and the French foreign minister. When the president returned to the hotel that night he asked me to come to his suite. "Do we have the votes?" he asked. "I think so, as long as everyone holds firm," I said. I returned to my room and waited for my appointment to call the foreign minister of the Philippines—at 3 a.m. He promised to "look into it." The Philippine ambassador would eventually abstain, but we would win the vote, nine in favor and six abstentions. I told the president that the resolution would pass. He smiled and said, "I should call Chirac."

Now, in March 2005, that resolution gave the force of international law to the Lebanese people's demand that the Syrians get out. The Saudis, who loved Hariri, leaned heavily on Syrian president Bashar al-Assad. Amazingly, Damascus relented. Though everyone knew that Assad would leave his secret security network behind, the pictures of Syrian forces humbly and hurriedly leaving Lebanon was exhilarating.

The pro-Western "March 14" movement (named for the day of a massive rally protesting Hariri's assassination and led by his son, Saad) took power in subsequent elections. Hariri's long-time friend, technocrat Fouad Siniora, became prime minister. The Lebanese people had won the day.

So I was confident and excited when I headed to Egypt in June of the same year to give my speech on freedom at the American University of Cairo. Egypt was a regional heavyweight, culturally, politically, and historically. I wanted to argue that just as Anwar Sadat had led the region to peace in his landmark opening to Israel, Mubarak could lead the region to democratic reform. I wanted to challenge but not embarrass the Egyptian president.

Before giving the speech, I asked to meet with Mubarak. At least it was morning and he was alert. I had learned to always meet the Egyptian early in the day. He experienced what physicians call "sundowning." As the day goes on, some older people have more trouble concentrating. That was the case with Mubarak. And I always tried to sit on his right side, as he was nearly deaf in the other ear.

Our ambassador had given the president's staff a heads-up before I saw him. I foolishly thought that Mubarak might be in a mood to listen given all that was happening in the region, including in Egypt. Before I could say anything beyond "Good morning," he preempted. "Go ahead and give your speech," he said.

I persisted, trying to preview the content of my remarks for him. "Mr. President," I said, "I just don't want you to be surprised by what I am going to say."

"Go ahead and give your speech," he repeated. "The Egyptian people need me. They need a strong hand. Don't you understand that all that stands between the Muslim Brotherhood and Egypt—is me!"

I tried to interject that I was not calling in any way for him to step down, but just to bring change. "Mr. President," I concluded, "reform before your people are in the streets." The meeting ended on that note.

Egypt badly needed to change its stagnant politics and its underperforming economy. From the time of Sadat's assassination and the rise of Mubarak in 1981, three groups fought to define Egypt's future. Civil society—human rights advocates and intellectuals—tried to carve out a little space within the political sphere. At times they could be relatively influential, mostly by appeal to international opinion and, in the case of the universities, by demonstrations, strikes, and riots. Islamists were also a factor due to their discipline, support among the rural and pious populations, and, at times, their resorting to violence. And finally, there was what some call the "deep state"—embedded constituencies resistant to change that largely helped to prop up the regime. The military, large family businesses, and the governmental apparatus—particularly the security forces—fit that definition.

The country was perpetually in economic difficulty. Bread riots broke out periodically when the government tried to end expensive and crippling food subsidies to the population. The number of people living in poverty increased from fifty-eight million to seventy-eight million between 1990 and 2008.[12] The business community consisted in large part of big family conglomerates that were very close to state officials and thus a ready source of corruption. For many years, ordinary Egyptians saw no rise in their real incomes—or worse. Per capita income fell by 8.7 percent between 2005 and 2009.[13]

Mubarak ruled this complex country for thirty years. He treated his supporters well, particularly in the business community and the security forces. The opposition was kept at bay by constantly raising the specter of an Islamic takeover—a narrative that Egypt would become like Iran.

"You will not see a single veiled woman," the Egyptian foreign minister, Aboul Gheit, told me as he introduced me to his staff in 2005. "I have a lot of women working for me. They are smart and educated and they would never wear the hijab," he intoned. On another occasion, the minister arranged a dinner after a conference on Iraq. He had intended to have the Iranian foreign minister sit next to me, hoping to start a dialogue between us. When I arrived, Aboul Gheit explained that the Iranian had left. "He was offended by the violinist," he said, laughing. Onstage a Ukrainian violinist in a skimpy red dress was performing show tunes. "That's the problem with these people," he said. "They just can't have any fun."

The sarcastic comment masked a more serious point about the political landscape in Egypt. The tensions between secularists and Islamists were unresolved in the country. Most urban dwellers and educated people valued the president's ability to keep the religious authorities out of their lives. But the Islamists had their own following among some intellectuals and also in the countryside. The most important Islamist group, the Muslim Brotherhood, was founded in 1928 but had been banned for decades after coming into conflict with the state. One of its most prominent members, Sayyid Qutb, was executed in 1966, but his extremist ideology inspired generations of terrorists who followed. Another member, Ayman al-Zawahiri, split from the group in 1979, believing it had become too moderate and too interested in the political process. Zawahiri would later merge his new organization into al-Qaeda and, after the death of Osama bin Laden, become its leader.

Elections in the country were essentially for show—the reaffirmation of Mubarak's rule. But in the lead-up to the elections of 2000, something began to change. Pockets of opposition to the president were emerging. Mubarak was particularly alarmed by the growing power of the Islamists. He responded by arresting two hundred members of the Muslim Brotherhood and banning them from politics. So adherents ran as independents and won significant representation in that election and in subsequent ones. Despite the formal ban, the group remained tightly organized, providing alms in poorer parts of the country where the government was failing. The Muslim Brotherhood could not operate in the open, but they did so in mosques and madrassas. They were the most structured and effective political opposition, even though technically they had been excluded from politics.

On the other hand, secular pro-democracy forces had trouble finding their footing. In 2001, Ayman Nour, a young legislator, formed the Al Ghad ("Tomorrow") Party. It was a promising step, supported by university students, human rights activists, and even some members of the business community. Nour was finally able to register his party three years later in 2004. Then he declared his intention to run for the presidency. Within three months, prosecutors had accused him of falsifying signatures and he was arrested.

The president did not see that these secular democrats could have been allies for him in tempering the influence of the Islamists. He saw only adversaries and opposition to his goal of extending his rule. He vacillated between repressing the Muslim Brotherhood and tolerating them. On the other hand, he constantly harassed the liberals, closing their offices and jailing their leaders. It was now largely a matter of holding on to power for the aging president. And anyone who challenged his right to do so was the enemy.

But when in 2004 he made clear his intention to seek a fifth six-year term, and some hinted that his son Gemal might succeed him, the Egyptian people responded. A broad movement of intellectuals and human rights and democracy advocates formed Kefaya ("Enough"). Earlier reform efforts had focused on lifting the state of emergency, reining in police powers, and updating the constitution. This time the movement went right to the heart of the matter—the need to limit executive power and the term of the president. The coalition that included Nour's party also welcomed moderate Islamists into its ranks. Their platform demanded lifting the state of emergency so that there could be free assembly, removing restrictions on the formation of political parties, and the release of political prisoners.

The unfolding events in Egypt complicated U.S.-Egyptian relations. Mubarak did not trust President Bush and resented the Freedom Agenda. He took the calls for reform in the Middle East as a personal insult. In fact, the Egyptian visited the United States in 2003 and did not return throughout the president's tenure. Matters reached a crucial point when Nour was jailed on January 28, 2005.

I met with the Egyptian foreign minister in Washington on February 15, 2005. The meeting focused on Lebanon, Sudan, reconstruction in Iraq, and some matters relating to the Israeli-Palestinian peace process. But everyone knew that tensions between us were high. I was scheduled to go to Cairo the next week for a Group of Eight meeting with the Arab League.

"Did the status and imprisonment of Ayman Nour come up in your conversation?" a journalist asked at the press conference following the meeting.

"Yes, I did raise our concerns, very strong concerns about this case," I replied.

"Are you going to Cairo?"

"Our delegation has not yet decided, but I'll get back to you."

That was a thunderbolt as speculation spread that I had told the Egyptians that I was canceling the trip to protest Nour's detention. In fact, I hadn't decided, hoping to use the trip as leverage to get him released. The Egyptians refused to budge on Nour, and on February 22, I told them that I was not coming, making the public announcement on February 25. The Egyptians fumed and vented loudly. As the *New York Times* reported, they "rejected any foreign interference in Egypt's internal affairs." Then the government petulantly announced that it was *they* who had canceled the trip. That statement was not true.

Mubarak Opens a Path to Change: The Events of 2005

Pressure was building on Mubarak at home and abroad. Television screens across the world were filled with images of Egyptians protesting their government in general and their president in particular. Remarkably, he responded with a plan for change. On February 26, he "requested" that the parliament take up the issue of electoral reform. Though Mubarak's party dominated the legislature and could protect him, it was still a significant move. The proposed legislation included the direct election of the president by secret ballot; the opportunity for political parties to run candidates; and "more than one candidate for the people to choose from with their own will." Nour welcomed the announcement from prison. On March 12, Ayman Nour was freed and declared his candidacy for the presidency.

The referendum that established the rules for the elections was a disappointment to the opposition. Strict limitations on who could run, including a requirement that any party would have had to be in existence for five years, stacked the cards in the president's favor. The balloting was to take place in one day, making it difficult to have enough judges to oversee the polling. Independent candidates had to be supported by 250 members of the People's Assembly, the Shura Council, or local elected councils—bodies dominated by the president's party. And during the voting on the referendum on May 25, the government resorted to violence, beating opposition figures and reportedly assaulting women. The actions of the government only served to energize the opposition, however, as protests continued.

The worried leadership again turned to undermining Ayman Nour, who was widely regarded as the most likely threat to Mubarak despite the limiting electoral rules. After my speech in Cairo on June 20, I met with Nour. He was clearly suspicious of American intentions, did not want to be associated with the Freedom Agenda, and at the same time insisted that we help more. This was the dilemma that we faced time and again in the region. No opposition leader wanted to be seen as doing the bidding of the United States. But they needed us to advocate for them and wanted us to punish their governments. It was a delicate line to walk.

Nour's trial began on June 28, but with the key witness against him recanting his earlier testimony, the government's case was in tatters. Rather than let Nour be exonerated and stand for the presidency free of the legal issue, the state requested a delay until September 25. The election was to take place on September 7.

With all of the constraints and trickery, it was unlikely that anyone would defeat Mubarak. And to be fair, the president was supported by large parts of the population. But even this limited experience with contested elections was a heady one for the people of Egypt—and the president of twenty-four years seemed ready to embrace the moment.

Omar Suleiman was in town, and he asked to have dinner with Steve Hadley, the national security adviser, and me. It was a quiet July evening at the Watergate restaurant, and we expected to talk about Hamas, the Israelis, and other matters of that kind. He was, after all, the head of the security services—feared by his adversaries and trusted by Mubarak: the Egyptian president's right-hand man.

Imagine our surprise when the conversation turned to the elections. "What do presidents do to get reelected?" Suleiman asked. Steve and I looked at each other and at him as he asked about the details of carrying out a free election. "How do security forces keep order but not be seen to interfere in peaceful protests?" he continued. As he kept going, I was stunned by the nature of the questions from this hardened police chief.

Steve and I related various experiences on the Bush campaign. And then Steve said something that seemed to lighten Omar's mood. "President Bush enjoyed campaigning." I'm not sure Suleiman could imagine Mubarak "enjoying" the process, but he clearly liked the notion. It was a strange conversation, because Mubarak was *going* to be elected. His party dominated the rulemaking; he had a huge financial advantage; and there would be no electoral monitors to catalog the inevitable fraud. Even so, Omar seemed genuinely interested in having the president actually *win* the people's trust.

During the ensuing monthlong campaign, Mubarak acted as if he actually wanted to convince people that he *should* be elected. He gave speeches, traveling around the country and laying out a governing agenda for the next six years. And he seemed to enjoy it.

For their part, other candidates made their case with little intimidation. Even the Wafd Party, which adopted as a slogan a single word that meant "We have been suffocated," did so openly. Ayman Nour traversed Cairo in an open horse-drawn carriage on the first day. He gave remarkable, defiant speeches. "We are a nation of freedom and democracy in our roots. But this nation has been transformed into one person and not a nation, to one person, and not Egypt."[14] The Muslim Brotherhood was oddly passive, urging people to vote but not endorsing a candidate.

Our ambassador reported almost daily on events in Cairo. "I actually saw a story today," he told me, "that accused Suzanne Mubarak [the president's wife] of corruption. The cafés are full of people debating politics. It seems as if fear has broken down and the atmosphere is almost festival-like," he said.

Mubarak won, of course, with 88.6 percent of the vote. But he was terribly disappointed at the low turnout, suggesting that Egyptians had not considered the entire enterprise worthwhile. Still, those who did participate witnessed a new openness in Egyptian politics that might have laid the foundation for further progress. The election was obviously imperfect, but it was the first truly contested presidential election, a significant fact in post-Mubarak Egypt.

Unfortunately, the presidential election was the high-water mark. Two months later, in November 2005, parliamentary elections were held. The Wafd Party and Tomorrow (Nour's party) were unable to sustain their momentum, again hounded by the government and denied resources. The big winner was the Muslim Brotherhood, which claimed more than half the seats it contested through independent candidates. The National Democratic Party (of Mubarak) held 324 seats and the Brotherhood 88. All others held just 30.

Mubarak was alarmed by what had happened in the elections. At my next meeting with him early in 2006, he all but accused the United States of strengthening the hand of the "Brothers," as he called them. He looked directly at me and asked, "Are you satisfied?" *Satisfied with what?* I thought. He was referring to the election result.

Then I remembered a conversation that explained that comment. During a meeting with Saudi king Abdullah, he told me that he now trusted me. He had come to believe, he said, that I didn't want the Muslim Brotherhood to rule the Middle East after all. *Where did that come from?* And then I realized that it had come from the Egyptians. "I'm all that stands between the Muslim Brothers and Egypt"—that was always Mubarak's trump card in any conversation about the virtues of democracy. He seemed honestly to believe that we viewed the Muslim Brotherhood favorably.

In light of the electoral results at the end of 2005, the

Egyptian government began backpedaling from the modest reforms it had made. In response to the jailing, once again, of Ayman Nour, I postponed consideration of the U.S.-Egyptian Free Trade Agreement. Doing so was a double-edged sword, because FTAs tend to empower more liberalizing elements in a society—opening the economy, undercutting corruption, and sometimes helping young people looking for opportunity.

During a press conference with the Egyptian foreign minister, Glenn Kessler of the *Washington Post* asked the question that I dreaded: "You met Ayman Nour here on your last trip here and now he faces a prison term after a trial on what appears to be trumped-up charges. His party is destroyed. How disappointed are you by that result, and what will you say to civil society representatives tomorrow as they struggle to develop under this authoritarian government?"

I answered that I was of course disappointed. But I essentially said that I would tell them to keep trying, that progress is not always a straight line, and that we would support them.

During a question on the postponement of the FTA, my mind wandered. I knew that my answer to Glenn had not been very satisfactory. So I took another crack at it. "Let me go back.... The president made very clear in his State of the Union that the United States would stand for the right of men and women in every corner of the earth to have the same rights and indeed the same responsibilities that we as Americans are fortunate enough to enjoy.... I came here to Cairo to give that speech because this is a central, perhaps the central, place in Arab civilization in terms of history, culture and scientific progress.... Egypt can and I think will lead this entire region in terms of economic and political reform.... That, I think, is a statement not just of hope but confidence.... We're going to stay on course, continuing to discuss reform and the need to move forward toward democracy... and listen to all voices in Egyptian society, because it is really very critical that Egypt lead in this area."[15]

I looked out at the members of my traveling press corps—Glenn, Helene Cooper of the *New York Times*, Janine Zacharia of Bloomberg, Anne Gearan of the Associated Press, Arshad Mohammed of Reuters, and Andrea Mitchell of NBC, to name a few. They had watched March 14 rise in Lebanon. They had covered the Purple Finger election. They had seen the awakening of politics in Egypt. Now, at this disheartening moment for freedom in the region, I saw in these tough and skeptical journalists signs of empathy.

They, like me, knew that Mubarak would not lead the region to change. Indeed, the regime doubled down on repression. The hated law on emergency powers was extended for two years. Most had expected that it would be lifted. A new constitutional referendum in 2007 further tightened the requirements for independent candidates to run, hoping to stall the progress of the Muslim Brothers but limiting other political forces as well. Violence spiked against opposition rallies and detention of activists of all stripes increased. Mubarak systematically stripped away the nascent institutions that might have helped Egyptians—many of whom shared his secular orientation—to make a democratic transition.

This would turn out to be his last chance for peaceful change. The president sealed the fate of his regime when he backed away from the political opening of 2005. Now it was only a matter of time until the tired and illegitimate regime could no longer hold power.

The denouement came in December 2010, when a fed-up street vendor in neighboring Tunisia set himself on fire. His death sparked a social-media-driven revolution across the Middle East, as popular protests forced the departure of Tunisia's Zine al-Abidine Ben Ali—a first in Arab history. Now there was nothing standing between the octogenarian Egyptian president and his angry and despondent people. They turned on him, calling for his ouster. "*Erhal!*" ("Leave!") became the slogan of the day.

The young people in the streets desperately wanted to embrace a democratic and brighter future. The population in the region had doubled over thirty years: 60 percent of Middle Easterners were twenty-five years old or younger. Tired, corrupt governments could not provide for them. The *Middle East Monitor* spoke of "a visceral sense of national humiliation and lack of self-esteem."[16]

A Second Chance for Democracy

As frustrated citizens poured out into places like Tahrir Square, there was another momentary opening for democratic change. But the energy in Cairo and other major cities was without direction and political purpose. Ayman Nour tried to channel the passions of the moment, and so did Kefaya, but they were spent forces—wasted in earlier struggles with the government.

The Nobel laureate Mohamed ElBaradei came home, but he had been out of the country too long—doing important work at the IAEA, but disconnected from Egypt's aspirations. The secular forces that the president should have nourished years before were unable to cohere at this crucial moment.

Mubarak tried belatedly to save his regime. He fired his cabinet but refused to step down, appointing a vice president for the first time in his presidency—Omar Suleiman. Clashes between government and anti-regime forces took place daily as security forces failed to maintain order.

Two months into the crisis, Mubarak continued to insist that he would hold power until elections could be called. In a dramatic speech on February 10, 2011, he finally said that he would not run in the next election, though he would discharge his duties until then. It was too late—the Egyptian people were calling for his immediate ouster, and some for his head. He resigned the next day, transferring power to the Supreme Council of the Armed Forces. The military would then oversee a hurried process to write an interim constitution. Many worried that the rapid move to elections would give secular forces little time to gather themselves and compete. They were right. The well-organized Muslim Brotherhood—now legal as a political party—won an impressive victory in peaceful elections across the country. When the several rounds of parliamentary balloting were done, the Brotherhood controlled 47 percent of the seats. A second and even more conservative Islamist party controlled another 24 percent. Though the Brotherhood had promised not to run a presidential candidate, it did. Mohamed Morsi won, the first Islamist to be elected head of state in the

Arab world. Mubarak's nightmare had come true—and it was, at least in part, his own doing. He more than any single figure was responsible for the barren political landscape and the dominance of "the Brothers."

Of course the story did not end there. The Muslim Brotherhood's brief reign in Egypt was tumultuous and incompetent. The country was in serious economic trouble, experiencing catastrophic declines in foreign reserves and a slide in the value of the currency. Morsi begged for assistance, promising economic reforms to meet IMF conditions for a $4.8 billion loan package. The United States granted Egypt $250 million but told the president it would closely monitor how he governed.

While seeking foreign assistance, however, Morsi seemed intent on doing everything to drive a wedge between his government and millions of secular Egyptians and religious minorities. The draft constitution did not provide safeguards for the rights of women. And, according to Morsi's critics, the document would have given Al-Azhar, Egypt's oldest university and one of Sunni Islam's highest authorities, power to pass judgment on the religious merits of the nation's laws.

Under pressure, Morsi kept pledging compromise, but the Islamic and autocratic tilt of his policies and their effects continued. He was blamed, whether fairly or not, for attacks on religious minorities and those seen as insufficiently respectful of Islam. The arrest of a popular television satirist, Bassem Youssef, on March 30 for insulting Islam and Morsi seemed to demonstrate an inextricable link between the president and his religious beliefs. Less than a week later a group of Muslims attacked the main cathedral of the Coptic Orthodox Church where a funeral for Christians killed in sectarian violence was being held. The head of the church, Pope Tawadros II, blamed the president for not protecting them.

Morsi did nothing to quiet his critics. In fact, he seemed to double down, increasing the influence of the Muslim Brotherhood. He appointed Islamists to thirteen of the twenty-seven governorships in the country. If he had any intention of bringing Egyptians together to bridge their religious differences in democratic institutions, he hid it well. Violent protests again swept the country, with millions of Morsi supporters and millions of his critics facing off as the future of Egypt hung in the balance.

On July 1, the army gave the president forty-eight hours to engage the opposition and find a solution. He did not, and on July 3 he was ousted. Thousands of demonstrators cheered the military takeover. Thousands more protested it. Violence continued for several months more, but in time, the army reestablished order.

Presidential elections, reminiscent of an earlier time, were held. Just two candidates participated and General Abdel Fattah el-Sisi won. Leaders of the Muslim Brotherhood were arrested, and many, including Morsi, sit in jails today, a death sentence on their heads.

And that is where Egypt now stands. For the fourth time in its modern history, a military man rules the country. As for most of the past sixty years, the state of emergency is in full force. The parliament is largely a rubber stamp. NGOs, especially those with foreign donors, are under siege. And the Muslim Brotherhood is jailed, while some of its adherents have gone underground—a fifth column within Egypt promoting violence and engaging in terrorism. The democratic openings of 2005 and 2011 seem very far in the past.

Yet, despite these dark prospects and the repression unleashed by the Sisi regime, the dream of a freer and more democratic Egypt lives on. It can be seen in the stories of activists who, at great personal risk to themselves, continue to advocate for reforms. One such figure, a young Egyptian woman who studied law and human rights in the West, returned to Egypt in 2011 to help her country realize its full potential. She and her colleagues— and millions of like-minded Egyptians—persevered through the roller-coaster ride that followed Mubarak. In 2014 she was arrested for taking part in a protest outside the Presidential Palace. It was a rally against a harsh new ban on protests. Her case drew public attention when she was sentenced to three years in prison, and she used it to shine a spotlight on the thousands of prisoners who suffer unnoticed, facing worse conditions and even abuse. Sisi eventually relented to international calls for her release, but not before she had spent more than 450 days behind bars. In doing so, she joined the long line of democracy activists, from Gandhi to Mandela, who have paid the high price of imprisonment in order for their country to have a better chance at freedom.

Now released and undeterred, this young activist and others like her are the reason to have hope for Egypt. They have learned hard lessons about the challenges before them, and they have proved themselves willing to bear the burdens of their cause. Someday Egypt's future will be brighter, and they will have another opportunity to build their dream. It might be a far-off and distant future. But those who think otherwise discount the human yearning to live free.

Tunisia Shows the Way

Mohammed Bouazizi set himself on fire to protest tyranny and injustice under the Ben Ali regime. He was a simple man who was fed up with the daily humiliation of paying bribes to keep his small business alive. His country has had challenges since Ben Ali fell in January 2011. But, unlike Egypt, Tunisia has overcome the obstacles in its path—at least so far. It has approved a new constitution with support from secularists and Islamists. It has found a place in the new system for people who had been exiled by the old regime, as well as former members of that regime. It has held several free and fair elections at the local and national levels. And, in the years following Ben Ali's ouster, it has peacefully transferred power from one party to another on more than one occasion.

Ben Ali and Mubarak looked like carbon copies of each other—tired, isolated men who had lost touch with the problems and aspirations of their people. So why has Tunisia succeeded thus far where Egypt failed?

Like Egypt under Mubarak, Tunisia under Ben Ali had a prominent Islamist organization that was banned by the government but survived underground. Like the Brotherhood, Tunisia's main Islamist group, called Ennahda, reemerged to play a central role in the attempt to form a new and more democratic government. But unlike the Brotherhood, Ennahda has so far adopted a more conciliatory approach to its political rivals, and it has demonstrated a willingness to share and even relinquish power. This is not simply because Tunisian Islamists are more moderate or prone to compromise, although that may be part of the explanation, particularly among the top leadership. It is also because Ennahda and the other actors in Tunisian politics face an environment in which compromise offers the best alternative to conflict. There are multiple forces that balance each other. As some scholars have argued, the most important reason why Tunisia has been more successful than Egypt is not because "all sides wanted democracy, but rather that all sides had no choice but to settle for democracy."[17]

The Tunisian institutional landscape is richer than that of Egypt. Ennahda is one of several organizations competing for power. It has had to contend with a variety of other actors— from an independent national labor movement, to a new political party backed by allies of the old regime, to a populace willing to return to the streets if it feels the "revolution" has been betrayed—all of which have been powerful forces in preventing Ennahda from asserting its dominance in the same manner as the Brotherhood attempted to do.[18]

In Tunisia, an influential player in post-2011 politics has been the country's national labor union, which was part of a coalition of civil society groups—including lawyers, human rights activists, and others—that won the Nobel Peace Prize in 2015. Tunisia's national labor union played an integral role in the country's independence struggle of the 1950s and has always maintained some autonomy from the ruling regime. Egypt's national labor union, conversely, has always been more or less an extension of the state, and it lacked the nationalist legitimacy required to play an effective independent role after 2011. If Mubarak had opened more political space in the mid-2000s, and done more to foster the independence of institutions like labor unions and the judiciary, Egyptians would have been better positioned to take advantage of the opening they created in Tahrir Square in 2011. Instead, at least for now, that moment has passed.

But just as Mohammed Bouazizi's self-immolation was a spark that set the region ablaze, the story of Tunisia's struggle for democracy continues to reverberate outside its borders, and nowhere more so than in Egypt. Tunisia's victories are fragile, and its future setbacks are certain. But its experience offers lessons for pro-democracy forces around the region.

The Tunisian example demonstrates the importance of a diverse institutional landscape. The country has a vibrant civil society that has been actively engaged at every stage of the post–Ben Ali transition. Often, pro-democracy forces are isolated from the larger population, led by intellectuals and operating largely in major cities. In Tunisia, the nationwide labor union, reminiscent of Solidarity in Poland, gave the opposition stronger footing and legitimacy with the population as a whole. The richness of the landscape was a check on more extreme factions— particularly among the Islamists. When draft language limiting the rights of women was being debated for the constitution, an uproar among women's groups and other members of civil society forced its proponents to retreat. The Nobel Peace Prize was awarded to a quartet of Tunisian civil society groups because of their role in mediated disputes during the tumultuous process of establishing a democratic government. Although that process continues to this day—and will hopefully continue well into the future—it was a timely recognition of the power of these groups and the important role they can play.

Tunisia still faces many dangers ahead. It has produced more ISIS terrorists than any other country, and it has also experienced terror attacks at home. Yet its story suggests a way forward in laying the groundwork for democratic openings in the Middle East and elsewhere: Find constituencies with deep roots in the society and the breadth to reach outside of urban areas. The lesson is that democracy is strongest when its base is widest. Tunisia's fate—like that of any young democracy—still hangs in the balance. But little by little it is building a stable future and providing a path ahead that others may follow.

Arab Monarchies: Will They Reform?

The countries most affected by the 2011 unrest in the Middle East share a common trait. Egypt, Tunisia, Libya, Syria, and Yemen were all founded as Arab "republics" in the mid-twentieth century. Yet, while the unrest seemed to spread from one "republic" to the next, it appeared to skip over the region's monarchies, with the exception of the small Kingdom of Bahrain. In one sense, this is not surprising. The "republics" were never really republics, after all, and it is not as if their populations didn't notice. Arab monarchies do not rule with regard to formal democratic procedures, but they do by and large enjoy some legitimacy. The republics, on the other hand, have long experienced a fatal gap between what they claim to be and what they really are, and in 2011, fear broke down and their people finally called them out on it. They no longer wanted a "president for life," they said. They wanted their "republics" to live up to their name.

Although the Arab monarchies, especially those in the Gulf, have so far withstood calls for political reform, they do not have time to rest comfortably. Louder demands for change will eventually come their way too. The question is, Will they be ready? The challenge for them today is to prepare for that day now.

Education Reform: A Substitute for Political Rights?

The monarchs have for the most part tried to modernize their societies through progress in areas other than politics. They remain repressive of political dissent, as evidenced most brutally in Saudi Arabia by the harsh punishments for even minor bloggers. Yet, in addition to the freedom gap, the Arab Human Development Report noted that the Arab world risked being left behind due to shortcomings in two other important areas: education and women's empowerment. These two areas have become increasingly linked in the changes taking place in the region. Education reform has emerged as a safe way to address gender issues—at least for now.

Ironically, the monarchs' wives have led some of these efforts, despite the patriarchal nature of the societies. In Qatar, Sheikha Mozah is an outspoken advocate for this cause, creating partnerships with American universities like Texas A&M. She travels across the world speaking about the subject. The widow of the founder of the United Arab Emirates (and the mother of the ruling bin Zayed brothers) has not only educated her daughters but pushed for opportunities for women across the country.

Sheikha Fatima of the United Arab Emirates wears an abaya and a silk mask that covers all but her eyes and will not see men outside of her family. And so it was very good to be a female secretary of state. She always made time for me, gathering her daughters, daughters-in-law, and other women for a conversation over tea. I would listen intently as they traded stories about the region and the circumstances of various leaders. You see, there was a wives' network that stretched from Cairo to the Gulf, and it was an amazing source of insight into the complex relationships dictating the direction of politics in the region.

The UAE has relentlessly pursued the cause of women's education. Emirati women play a wide role in the economy and society. They serve in appointed positions in politics, diplomacy, and the judiciary. And they are educated in fine universities. I have taught several of them in my undergraduate and MBA classes at Stanford. According to the government, women make up more than 60 percent of the students enrolled in higher education and more than 70 percent of total graduates. The ruling families of the Emirates with their small indigenous populations see economic development and women's empowerment as inextricably linked.

In Saudi Arabia, the most conservative of the monarchies, the advocacy for education reform is most closely associated with the late king, Abdullah bin Abdulaziz al-Saud. I saw this firsthand during my many visits with him. One met the king very late at night—no earlier than 11 p.m. After intensive discussions of the long political agenda in the region—Iraq, Lebanon, Iran, and the Palestinians—Abdullah would ask if we could take a little break. By this time it was already one o'clock and I knew that we would spend at least another hour or so together.

After the brief pause, he always seemed more relaxed. We were essentially alone—with only my interpreter, Gemal Helal, whom the Arabs trusted completely, and sometimes Adel al-Jubeir, the king's closest aide. The conversation would turn quickly to the broader philosophical challenges facing the kingdom. Abdullah was fascinated by American education and would ask questions, usually prefacing them with, "You teach in a university."

Abdullah had a very nuanced understanding of the educational landscape in his country. He explained that Saudi students had once gone abroad in large numbers, studying in the United Kingdom and the United States. His foreign minister and nephew, the late Saud al-Faisal, was an example. Educated at Princeton, he was at ease in any cultural setting. The next generation, forty-somethings, Abdullah noted, largely stayed home. They didn't speak foreign languages and they took a curriculum at King Fahd University that was heavily weighted toward religious studies. "They have no useful skills," he said. *That's quite an admission from a deeply pious man*, I thought to myself.

Abdullah told me that Saudi Arabia could not afford to lose another generation and had insisted on sending students abroad. But after 9/11, the number of Saudis studying in the United States dropped precipitously. Several of the suicide hijackers had gone to college in the West. This made intelligence agencies—and especially the Congress—wary of foreign students. And many Saudis were afraid to come. They were not alone in facing barriers to university study in the United States. Stricter screening and cumbersome tracking rules caused a plunge in American exchange student programs across the world.

In every meeting with the president, foreign leaders would complain about this. I will never forget one encounter with the prime minister of Singapore. He asked each member of his delegation, "Where did you go to school?" Every one of them had attended an American university. "Mr. President," the prime minister said, "you are shooting yourselves in the foot. Educating these people in the United States is more valuable than anything else that you do." The president was moved, and I took responsibility for trying to get the numbers back to the pre-9/11 level. By 2007 we achieved that goal, including in the Middle East.

Still, Abdullah did not want to depend solely on foreign institutions to train future generations. And so he launched a plan to build a world-class university in the kingdom. King Abdullah University of Science and Technology was established with a $10 billion endowment. "It will be like Stanford," he said, perhaps flattering me a bit. "Strong in science, medicine, and technology." I knew the king well enough to ask the next question. "Will women attend, Your Majesty?" I asked. Abdullah laughed. "Of course." I didn't want to ask if they would have to sit in separate classrooms. But if I had, I would have been pleased to learn they do not. Today in Saudi Arabia, more women graduate from college every year than men.[19] Saudi women are entering the workforce in greater numbers, with female employment rising 48 percent between 2010 and 2015.[20]

Still, conversations with the late king about women's rights were always a bit contradictory. On one occasion he told me flatly that women would vote in ten years. That was 2005, and in 2015 the franchise—such as it was—was extended to female citizens. Abdullah went to great lengths to receive delegations of women, something that his predecessors had not done. Although women were not allowed to vote or run for a seat when the first elections were held for municipal councils, they won those rights in 2011, and exercised them for the first time in 2015. Saudi women went to polling booths just as Saudi men did (but at different locations), and by the next day, twenty Saudi women had won seats on the municipal councils.

On the other hand, Abdullah just didn't see why the prohibition on women driving was an issue. He once explained that it wasn't really safe to drive in Saudi cities. The logic of that answer escaped me, but I didn't push. And, of course, despite some of the changes, women remain second-class citizens in the kingdom—dependent on a male guardian's permission to marry, apply for a passport, travel abroad, pursue certain jobs, and carry out other basic life activities. Every day, they face social pressures and public dangers if they stray from the strict rule of the hated religious police.

Still, one senses that the monarchs are searching for a way to get ahead of the demands for reform. In a few cases, there is even some movement on the political front.

The UAE has created a parliament-like *majlis* that advises the government on matters of policy. Half of its forty members are indirectly elected through an electoral college and the other half are appointed by the government. The *majlis* does not have the kinds of powers we traditionally associate with a parliament. But compared to the situation before its establishment in 2006, steps like these mark progress.

Morocco and Jordan have young monarchs who are relatively popular. In fits and starts, they have reformed the civil service, strengthened rule of law, and ceded some power to prime ministers. Morocco has now held several relatively free elections in which a moderate Islamist party has performed well. That party has even gone on to do a reasonably good job in government, hoping to get reelected the next time.

The al-Sabah family in Kuwait has also engaged in reforms. The Kuwaiti parliament functions as a check on the government in real ways. Comprising fifty members who run in elections, it serves as a national stage for debate, where the government's policies face regular scrutiny and criticism. It can be dismissed at any time, and there are no political parties, but different groups are represented by different blocs, with one bloc for liberals, another for Sunnis, another for Shia, and so on. Parliamentarians cannot initiate legislation, but they play an important role in overseeing ministerial appointments, in effect giving the people a voice in deciding who serves in some of the highest offices. Kuwaiti women were granted the right to vote and run for office in 2005, and the first female candidates were elected to parliament in 2009.

I was in Kuwait shortly after the first elections in which women were allowed to run, and I talked with several female candidates who had failed to win. They were crushed. I did my best to lift their spirits, reflecting on the long road to democracy. "Women didn't get the right to vote in the United States until

1920," I said. "And now I'm secretary of state." They were inconsolable, though. They didn't give up and ran in larger numbers in the next cycle. This time, they campaigned and pushed their message with men—reminding them that they too had mothers and sisters and daughters. Four won.

A week or so later after my visit, I opened a package at the State Department. It was a T-shirt that I had been presented in Kuwait—a gift from those who had met with me. "Half a democracy is no democracy at all" was emblazoned in white and light blue. I turned to Brian Gunderson, my chief of staff. "Truer words have never been spoken," I said.

For the most part, the monarchs are trying to address the three gaps that the Arab Human Development Report identified—on freedom, knowledge, and women's empowerment—as if they were separable. But they cannot likely be solved fully in isolation from one another. They are intertwined. Yet progress on any one of them brings the Middle Eastern monarchies closer to building a favorable institutional landscape. These are unlikely to ever become constitutional monarchies of the kind that helped ease the transition to democracy in Spain.[21] But the role of these leaders is shifting, albeit very slowly. Continuity is not a bad thing if it is paired with a willingness to change.

In this regard, the biggest question is one of how these societies will balance religious beliefs and individual liberty. In many of them, particularly Saudi Arabia, religious reactionaries are a power in their own right. The bargain struck years ago between the Saudi monarch and the clerics is an impediment to change. At the time, "We'll leave religion to you and you leave politics to us" must have seemed reasonable. Shaken by the Iranian

Revolution of 1979, the Saudis took a shortcut to stability. In exchange for peaceful coexistence with the Wahhabis, followers of a puritanical strain of Islam, the kingdom ceded moral authority to the clerics. They, in turn, came to infiltrate larger and larger domains—including the export of their radical ideas abroad under the Saudi flag.

For years, the Gulf monarchies thought that the radicals would target only foreigners. They tolerated them and looked the other way, buying their loyalty with state funding. During one visit to Saudi Arabia, Steve Hadley and I were taken on a tour of the king's extraordinary aquarium. As we walked through the glass tunnel, fish swimming all around us, Steve and I both noticed that there were not just tropical fish but also sharks. "How do you keep the sharks from eating the fish?" he asked. "Oh, if you feed the sharks enough, they don't bother the fish," our guide answered. Steve whispered to me, "That's what they thought about al-Qaeda."

Indeed, the Frankenstein of the Wahhabis—al-Qaeda and its kin—turned on those who had fed them. The bombing of residential compounds in Riyadh in 2003 was a turning point. Gulf rulers, particularly in Saudi Arabia, have tried to rein the clerics in, closing mosques and schools known for radicalism. But it is difficult to root out such entrenched influence. The society remains deeply conservative and, in many cases, at odds with the demands of modern governance.

Just consider this: Saudi Arabia wants to decrease its dependence on oil and modernize the economy. The young deputy crown prince Mohammad bin Salman has launched a plan—Vision 2030—to transform the economic landscape in the country. The plan aims to increase the share of non-oil revenue in public finances by 70 percent, reduce subsidies for water and electricity prices to zero by 2020, increase female participation in the workforce, and limit the growth of new jobs in the civil service. Another goal is to increase tourism beyond that associated with the hajj. The Saudis hope to attract more foreign businesses and the people who come with them. But life in Saudi Arabia can be grim, given the social restrictions. So they have proposed to create large gated communities—almost the size of cities—where foreigners, and maybe some Saudis, can pretty much do as they please. This odd compromise may be the best that they can do for the moment. But in the long run, the relationship between religion, politics, and society will have to be addressed more forthrightly.

The monarchs are not alone, though, in needing to find a way to reconcile religion and politics. The region has seen two extremes: the complete marriage of Islam and the state and, on the other hand, enforced secularism. Neither has worked very well.

Secularism as practiced in Egypt and Turkey led to the disenfranchisement of large segments of the population, particularly rural people. This was a boon to groups like the Muslim Brotherhood and at the root of the success of Recep Tayyip Erdoğan's AKP party. Religion and politics don't mix easily—but the exclusion of religious people from politics doesn't work either.

The Europeans fought wars for two centuries in order to finally expel religious authorities from the political space. The American Founding Fathers had a different answer, insisting that religious freedom could be guaranteed only through the separation of church and state. Neither of these roads seems particularly likely in the Middle East. But the region desperately needs an answer to the challenge. Institutions that recognize the rights of the individual citizen to make choices in this most personal of realms—religious belief—would be a good start.

Today's Middle East is going in the wrong direction in this regard. Religious minorities, particularly Christians, are literally being driven from the region because governments cannot or will not protect them. This has been especially true in Iraq and Syria, but it is also a regional phenomenon, affecting Egypt, Lebanon, Palestine, and others. Secularists in Turkey hold their breath to see how far the reach of religious conservatives will spread after the coup attempt against Erdoğan in 2016. Religious people in Egypt wait anxiously to see whether all Islamists, no matter how moderate, will be branded Muslim Brotherhood and excluded from the political square. It is a gross understatement to note that the region has found no way to address the question of proper balance between religion and politics.

The uncomfortable question in the Middle East is whether Islam and democracy's protections for individual liberty can coexist. Some would say that Islam's claim to govern every aspect of an adherent's life makes societies vulnerable to totalitarian-like impulses. Certainly, the Muslim Brotherhood's brief reign in Egypt or Hamas's reign in the Gaza Strip would support this view. On the other hand, Islamists in Tunisia have found a way to work with others who are not like-minded and Iraq's parliament houses both religious and secular politicians. Further afield, India and indeed the United States show that Islam and democracy are not irreconcilable. Even Indonesia, younger in its democratic journey, has largely succeeded in containing extremism and embracing a multi-religious future, although not without difficulty.

This suggests that if there is to be a future for a democratic version of political Islam, it rests in the institutional context in which it operates. In other words, there is nothing inherently undemocratic about Islam as a faith—but individual citizens have to be able to make choices about how deeply religion will influence their lives. Essentially, it cannot be the business of the state to dictate this matter of conscience.

The Middle East is a long way from that place. Still, if it is to be found, it is more likely to come through free political discourse. At least then the questions will be debated in the open. That is the only way to temper the power of extreme elements on both sides—those who would ban religious people from the square *and* those who would insist that religious belief must dominate the political and social landscape.

Containing the Fire Next Time

The people of the Middle East have shown their impatience with the freedom gap, the lack of democracy that sets their region apart. Still, a chasm remains between the populations of the region and their rulers—and the efforts to address it are sporadic and hesitant. Weak democratic institutions exist in Tunisia and Iraq, but they are challenged every day by the ills of the region—sectarianism, terrorism, and violence. Beyond this, other countries lack even these fragile reeds to build upon in the future. So, to quote Lenin, "What is to be Done?"

The task now is to lay a foundation for the time of the next democratic opening. The institutional landscape needs to be richer and more diverse. This requires acknowledging three realities: Education is one answer but it is not enough; women's empowerment and political liberalization need to go hand in hand; and liberal, pro-democracy forces must engage the entire population—including religious people and rural constituencies. Political change divorced from this broadened landscape is likely to backfire.

The Special Problem of Elections

In fact, the reality is that the most organized and capable political forces in the Middle East at the moment are the Islamists. While regimes repressed civil society—intellectuals, human rights groups, social entrepreneurs, community-based organizations, and journalists—the Islamists across the region organized in radical madrassas and radical mosques. They did the hard work of courting the disenfranchised and taking care of their needs. Hezbollah, Hamas, and the Muslim Brotherhood all provided alms to the poor, stepping in where incompetent authoritarian regimes failed. And their worst elements have motivated too many young men (and even women) to prove their manhood on a battlefield. Their strength is no accident of history—it is a direct outcome of the policies of those who have ruled the Middle East.

This has made "one man, one vote" fraught with danger for liberal, democratic values. We learned this lesson the hard way in the 2006 elections in the Palestinian territories. In the run-up to the elections, the reporting from our embassies and from intelligence sources suggested that Mahmoud Abbas's Fatah Party would win a close election. I went about my work that day, keeping tabs on what was happening but not really worried about the outcome. Not long before I was to be leaving for the evening, Liz Cheney, the deputy assistant secretary for the Middle East, stopped by. "Our people on the ground are reporting that the green flag of Hamas is flying everywhere. And Hamas is polling well in some of the Fatah strongholds," she said. Liz's news shook me a little, but I gathered my things and went home—still expecting the Palestinian Authority to win.

The next morning I went to the door of my Watergate apartment and picked up the *Washington Post*. The headline was as expected—"Hamas Makes Strong Showing in Vote; Exit Poll Shows Party Winning Near-Parity with Fatah in Palestinian Assembly." "Whew! That was a close call," I said out loud. Then I went upstairs to the gym for my daily exercise.

The 5 a.m. news was just starting and I noticed the runner at the bottom of the screen. "Hamas victorious. Palestinian Authority officials resign," it said as it scrolled across. *That can't be right. I just saw that the PA won.* I kept pedaling the elliptical—my heart beating a little faster after the bulletin. The runner at the bottom kept returning, each time heralding Hamas's victory. Finally, I got off the machine and called the Operations Center. "What happened in the Palestinian elections?" I asked.

"Oh, Hamas won," the young watch officer said calmly.

"Hamas won?" I repeated.

"Yes ma'am."

Startled, I asked to speak to Jake Walles, our consul general in Jerusalem, who effectively functioned as our ambassador to the Palestinians. But instead I mixed up his name with our ambassador in Lebanon, Jeffrey Feltman. Jeff was a little surprised to hear from me, but he confirmed that the whole region was in a state of shock. Needless to say, Jake and Dick Jones, our ambassador in Tel Aviv, were as well.

When I arrived at the office and called the president, he said, "So what do we do now? They won the election—by all accounts fairly."

"Let me talk to the Israelis and Abbas," I said. By the end of the day, I had also convened the Middle East Quartet—the United States, Russia, the European Union, and the UN. We issued a statement that affirmed the outcome of the election but set conditions on dealing with the new Hamas-led government. They would have to accept the terms that Yasser Arafat negotiated in 1993: recognize the right of Israel to exist; renounce violence; and accept all agreements that the Palestinians and the Israelis had signed. Hamas never did. They remained isolated from the international community and proved to be completely incompetent at governing. As a Palestinian friend said, "Now people can see that they aren't the glorious freedom fighters. They are just a bunch of politicians who can't make the sewer system work either."

The experience with elections that brought Hamas—branded by the United States and Europe as a terrorist organization—to power was chastening. It pointed to the danger of elections before liberal parties could find their footing. The Muslim Brotherhood in Egypt benefited in the same way.

But it is often difficult to delay elections until the landscape is broader—even if theoretically it would be better to do so. Voting is the single most important and symbolic act of a liberated people, and they are reluctant to wait. The circumstances of the first elections are not likely to favor liberal forces. Still, the electoral process brings challenges for radical forces too—forcing them into the democratic process where the people can judge them peacefully. Is it better, to quote my friend, to show that "they can't make the sewer system work either"?

On the one hand, some elected Islamist parties have shown little regard for the democratic process that brought them to power, which appears to be their only goal. We have seen how the Muslim Brotherhood overstepped its mandate and sought to enforce Islamist values in Egypt, running roughshod over the interests of religious minorities and more secular forces. Hezbollah is not just a party; it is an armed militia. It has used the political perch in Lebanon to terrorize the region, with the support of Iran.

This is a warning that, at a minimum, armed groups should not participate in the electoral process. It goes without saying that an armed militia has an unfair advantage due to its ability to intimidate and threaten. There are multiple cases of post-conflict transitions in which political groups were allowed to participate only after disarming.[22]

Still, when Hezbollah turned its arms on Lebanese citizens in 2008, forcibly taking over parts of Beirut in a dispute with the government, it lost the claim to "armed resistance against Israel."

The Lebanese people punished them in the 2009 elections, leaving Hassan Nasrallah to fume that he had won the popular vote but the drawing of the electoral districts was flawed. Elections are about the only way that the Lebanese people can voice dissent against Hezbollah. There is also some evidence that the group's foreign adventure in Syria is playing poorly at home.

Islamist parties in Morocco, Jordan, Kuwait, Iraq, and Tunisia have been less able to bend politics to their will. It is worth noting that all of them face real competition from organized secular forces. This suggests that it is not a question of having Islamists participate or not participate in elections. Elections will be held. The question is the institutional landscape in which they take place: the richer the better.

So it comes down once again to nurturing a diverse set of institutions. That means empowering entrepreneurs and businesspeople; educating and empowering women; and encouraging social entrepreneurs and local civic organizations. In 2016 the Atlantic Council gathered a group of experts and former leaders to assess the state of the Middle East and what to do about it. Their recommendations read like a road map for a richer institutional environment.[23] And there is already some progress. In the summer of 2016, I met several young entrepreneurs from the region. There was a Jordanian man who founded an Amazon-style website for selling Arabic-language books; a social entrepreneur from the UAE who founded programs to empower youth and protect victims of sex trafficking; and an Egyptian scientist who founded a tech start-up that, in her words, aimed "to bring emotional intelligence to our digital world." These visionaries are not alone in wanting to build a different future for their region. Human rights advocates, women in politics, business and social entrepreneurs, and intellectuals are the vanguard of a new energy—bottom up—for change.

These people, many of them young women, are determined but, in many countries, hunted. A blogger in Saudi Arabia is flogged for mild criticism of the regime. A journalist in Egypt is jailed for advocating for press freedoms. An activist in Bahrain goes on a hunger strike to protest her indefinite detention. It is reminiscent of another time in another part of the world—the Soviet Union and Eastern Europe—when it seemed unlikely that protesters would ever be heard.

We know now that in international organizations like the Commission on Security and Cooperation in Europe (CSCE) these dissidents were finding their voices. There were safe places for them to meet and influence the rest of the world. When they returned home they often faced intimidation and, in some cases, arrest. But they kept meeting and speaking out, and when the opening came, they led democratic transitions—some more successfully than others.

In 2004 we created the Broader Middle East and North Africa Initiative, which sought to support civil society. We hoped to model it on the CSCE. To be frank, Iraq clouded the effort, but nineteen countries participated, as did dozens of civil society groups from the region. At one of the meetings, a young activist confronted the foreign minister of Bahrain about press restrictions. Another spoke in guarded terms about women's rights in the Gulf monarchies. And at the press conference, a young Syrian challenged me. "Why do you talk about freedom in Iraq and never in Syria?" he asked. I made a note to speak out about the regime in Damascus the next time I had a chance.

In today's Middle East—some ten years removed from those exchanges—it is difficult to imagine a gathering of that kind. The Bahrainis have stopped listening to dissent, cracking down hard instead. The civil war in Syria has become the worst humanitarian catastrophe of our age, haunting us with images of children being pulled from bombed-out rubble, or dying in dimly lit hospitals, suffocating from the effects of chemical weapons. I can't help wondering what happened to my Syrian questioner.

The larger political context has changed in the region too. There was a time when the talisman against dissent was to invoke the Palestinian-Israeli issue. So many times the Arabs would say, "My street"—meaning their people—"is up in arms about what the Israelis are doing." I had to hold my tongue, because I wanted to say, *How do you know what your street thinks? Why don't you hold an election and find out?*

Still, the region cannot be truly stable without a solution to the Palestinian problem. I traveled to the West Bank and Jerusalem twenty-three times as secretary trying to find one. But the story of the sadly unfinished business of delivering a two-state solution is not just a matter of getting the final-status issues right. Yes, the borders of the Israeli and Palestinian states will have to be settled and security arrangements will have to be put in place to protect both peoples. There will have to be a solution to the "right of return," the insistence of Palestinians now generations removed from 1948 that they must be allowed to return to their homeland, which is now inhabited by Israelis. And the emotional issue of dividing the holy city of Jerusalem, claimed as the capital by both peoples, must be solved too.

For the eight years of the Bush administration, we tried to ease the way to the solution of these core issues by helping the Palestinians build decent political, economic, and social institutions. Hamas, we believed, could be finally defeated only if the Palestinian people saw an alternative—a Palestinian Authority led by Mahmoud Abbas that had thrown off corruption and found a way to govern wisely.

The Palestinians made a great deal of progress, thanks in part to the help of the United States, Europe, and Canada in building effective security forces that even the Israel Defense Forces recognized as capable. And thanks to the enlightened leadership of men like Salam Fayyad, they made progress in building political and social institutions too.

I will never forget my first extended conversation with Salam in Sharm El Sheikh, Egypt, in 2003. President Bush had convened a meeting of Arab leaders to discuss the peace process, in advance of a meeting between Israeli prime minister Ariel Sharon and Abbas in Aqaba, Jordan. We were waiting for King Abdullah of Saudi Arabia to arrive—holding our breath as to whether the "Keeper of the Holy Mosques," as he is called, would overcome his reservations and attend. It was an interminable wait, feeling much longer than the actual two or so hours that passed.

Salam walked over to me and immediately started to talk about American football. He was an economist, trained at the University of Texas. After a few shots at the Notre Dame Fighting Irish, he turned serious. He already had ideas about improving transparency in the Palestinian Authority—putting the budget online, cleaning up the security services, which he called a bunch of gangsters, and improving the lives of his people. He would be prime minister twice.

Under his leadership, the battered Palestinian economy showed new life, with an influx of foreign aid and an increase in real GDP, which grew at an annual rate of more than 7 percent from 2008 to 2011.[24] I remember well going to Bethlehem in 2008. It had been the site of horrible violence in 2001 when an Israeli tank shell blew a hole in the Church of the Nativity. Now we walked through a new and elegant hotel—the site a few weeks earlier of a successful outdoor dinner for potential investors. Salam gained the respect of everyone, including the Israelis.

Salam was thick-skinned—you had to be to tolerate the slings and arrows from those whom he challenged inside the Palestinian Authority. Abbas himself waxed and waned in his support of his prime minister, firing him twice, only to bring him back when there was no other alternative. I asked Salam how he put up with it all. He didn't hesitate: "I am determined to build our democratic state—even if we have to do it under occupation." And he set out to do just that.

Today, the Israeli-Palestinian conflict has taken a backseat to the region's troubles with ISIS, Syria, Yemen, and terrorism. Still, a stable Middle East will need a solution for the Palestinians too. And if they are ever to gain a homeland—the independent state that they deserve—it will be because they built democratic institutions despite the odds.

The Palestinian question has also receded due to the rising

challenge of Iran. For the Arab regimes, a militant Iran is *the* threat of the age: a Persian power with designs on their borders, aggressively pursuing its interests with a latent nuclear capability in its pocket. Tehran's behavior begs the question of whether Iran itself might one day—sooner or later—face a moment of truth, a democratic opening.

The Green Revolution and What Might Have Been

The powerful image of a bloodied young woman came to represent the tragedy of Iran's people. Thanks to social media, the world got to observe their plight. For a few days in the summer of 2009, the mullahs who had ruled Iran for three decades seemed vulnerable.

Iran's electoral system is not free and fair. Races are competitive and the franchise is open to women, but candidates are forced to undergo a rigorous vetting process and must be approved before being allowed to run. In practice, this process is led by conservative hard-liners who filter out anyone who would provide genuine opposition to the government. Most reform-minded candidates, as well as any others deemed insufficiently loyal to the regime, are disqualified and blocked from the ballot.

But in 2009, when the regime violated even these limited rights, cooking the electoral results to favor conservative candidates, they set off a firestorm. There is a lesson in this. Even elections that are not free and fair can have consequences. In this case, the result was a massive protest movement because the Iranian people had had enough. The sad spectacle of Iranians appealing for help from the West reminds us that the international community cannot ignore the plight of people seeking freedom. The Obama administration said nothing at first—and very little later on. The president apparently did not want to contaminate the revolution with outside interference. The brave protesters were carrying signs in English. They appeared ready to take the risk of associating their rebellion with America.

The opening did not last. The regime cracked down hard. The mullahs survived the scare of 2009 and continue to hold back pressures for change, at least as of this writing. There may be no greater gap in the entire region between the aspirations of the people and the posture of their government.

Iran's population is young—70 percent of them are under the age of thirty. They are well connected to the outside world, and in the cities well educated and urbane. In many cases, they are remarkably pro-American. Jared Cohen traveled to Tehran and five other Iranian cities in 2004. At the time, he was a Stanford student, but he would later go on to head social media outreach at the State Department for me and then for Hillary Clinton. When Jared returned from his Iran trip he got in touch with me at the White House. "I couldn't believe it," he said. "When I said I was American, no one would let me pay for anything."

I would later witness the same phenomenon. As secretary, I decided that we had to try to end the isolation of the Iranian people, even if we could do nothing about their government. With the president's blessing, we established a modest exchange program. The first installment brought members of the Iranian equivalent of the Centers for Disease Control to Atlanta to meet their counterparts. Then we brought a group of young artists, all below the age of forty, to exhibit their work. I greeted them at the Meridian International Center in Washington and made remarks about the universality of the arts—careful to avoid anything political that might embarrass or endanger our guests.

Finally, the Iranians agreed to allow Americans to come to them in the person of the U.S. wrestling team. On game day, the fans waved American flags. At first I thought that the government must have encouraged it. That was decidedly not the case. After that show of affection for the United States—a spontaneous one, it turns out—Tehran decided that it had had enough of "people to people" exchanges.

The Iranian people crave freedom. The theocratic regime of the Ayatollah Khamenei refuses to bend. While some in the government seem to seek a more moderate course, they too are not truly moderates. They may want to shave the hard edges from the regime's relationship with its people: Perhaps women should not have to fear the religious police if an ankle shows; certainly there ought to be enough trade with the West to fill the shops with foodstuffs and other goods; and why shouldn't Iranians travel and study abroad? But the context is the same. Service in the Iranian government requires fealty to the tenets of the regime—religious orthodoxy; brutal repression of dissent; and a foreign policy that is messianic, reckless, and xenophobic.

No single revolutionary development could transform the Middle East more than the end of theocracy in Iran. While there appears to be no democratic opening on the horizon, regimes of this kind are brittle. Aging men head the theocratic regime. Khamenei, the only real power in the country, is nearly an octogenarian and is reportedly ill. The regime's base of support is outside the cities with older people, the less educated, and rural populations. The Revolutionary Guard Corps and its fist, the Quds Force, protect the interests of hard-liners at home and abroad.

Prior to the nuclear arms deal with the United States and other international powers, the Iranian economy was in terrible shape, suffering from mismanagement and the effect of a decade of sanctions. GDP shrank by almost 10 percent between 2012 and 2014.[25] Unemployment hovered around 20 percent, although many believed it was underreported. Prices rose for everyday goods as the value of the rial plummeted. The mullahs undoubtedly believe that they have bought time with a promise of reentry into the international economy.

Whether that greater engagement staves off decline and dampens pressures for change or accelerates them is impossible to know. But one thing is certain—if a democratic opening comes, Iran has an educated and young population that could take advantage of it. It does not, however, have independent institutions to help channel change. That is why the regime is determined to prevent the rise of civil society. This may for a time prevent the Iranian people from rising against their government, but it almost ensures that when they do, the landing will not be a soft one for the regime or the country.

Chapter 8

ARE AUTHORITARIANS SO BAD?

I was driving home from school with my uncle Alto that November afternoon. It was Election Day and we passed long lines of black citizens standing in line waiting to vote. George Wallace, the segregationist candidate for governor of Alabama, was on the ballot. I had heard my parents talk about him and I knew, in my innocent way, that he was bad news for us.

I turned to my uncle and asked, "If all those black people vote, how can Wallace win?" My uncle answered that blacks were still the minority (a large minority to be sure) and wouldn't be able to stop Wallace from being elected.

"Then why do they bother?" I asked.

"Because it is your duty to vote," he answered. "And one day that vote will matter."

I asked him, "Are you going to vote?"

"I did this morning," he answered, "and so did your mother, daddy, grandmother, and Daddy Ray."

Seems like a waste of time, I thought. But I never forgot that sentiment. *One day that vote will matter.*

Voting for the first time can be an emotional experience, especially if it has been a right denied for a lifetime. "At last, we are human!"[1] That's how one elderly woman from Kandahar explained her feelings as she stood in line to vote in the first presidential election in Afghan history in 2004. Millions of men and women braved Taliban threats to cast a ballot. From the poorest rural villages to the neighborhoods of Kabul, citizens waited through long lines and unseasonable cold to make their voices heard.

Moqadasa Sidiqi, a nineteen-year-old student, cast her first vote. "I cannot explain my feelings, just how happy I am," she said.[2] Among her options on the ballot was Masooda Jalal, a pediatrician and mother of three. Just a few years earlier, women had been prohibited from working, getting an education, or leaving their house alone. Those who ran afoul of the Taliban's strict moral codes were publicly executed in a soccer stadium. Now they were voting and running for president.

Ahmed Rashid, a journalist who had spent many years covering bloodshed in Afghanistan and was no cheerleader of U.S. policy, described the election as "the most moving and memorable day of my life."[3] The emotion of the event was inescapable, he wrote, as he visited polling places with a fellow journalist. "We were so amazed by the huge turnout, the orderly queues, the patience of the women holding little children, the good humor and joking as people waited, the stories they told of their loss and hardship, that we burst into tears," he wrote.[4]

Similar scenes were evident in Iraq during the elections for a transitional government in January 2005, the country's first free vote in five decades—if ever. Despite sporadic violence and a boycott by some Sunnis, voter turnout was high across the country, with voters even queuing in the volatile city of Fallujah. Some families went to the polls together, sometimes bringing elderly relatives along in wooden carts. Parents stood in line while children played soccer in the streets. Voters emerged from polling booths and dunked their fingers in indelible ink to prevent fraud. "A hundred names on the ballot are better than one," said Fadila Saleh, a middle-aged engineer in central Baghdad, "because it means that we are free."[5] It could not have been more different from the "elections" held under Saddam Hussein.

As I have watched long lines of Afghans and Iraqis and Liberians waiting to vote, I understand that deep inside they believe that *one day that vote will matter.* By the way, I have never missed the chance to vote. It would be an insult to my ancestors who struggled for almost a century after emancipation to gain that right.

There is an emotional attachment to "the vote," and it has to be satisfied. It means that the first condition of democracy has been met. People can choose their leaders and change them peacefully if necessary. It is an important beginning—but just a beginning. The time when that liberating moment is translated into functioning institutions and effective governance is still in the future. The opening for democracy is just that—an opening—and it can be fleeting if it is not used well.

Most would agree that a functioning democracy is preferable to an authoritarian fiat. The skeptics would say, though, that democracies are failing while some authoritarians are delivering for their people. For skeptics, the preference for democracy is not so obvious, at least in the short term. Perhaps it is better to govern effectively. Democracy can come later.

Two countries come to mind in support of this argument: Singapore and China—one of the world's smallest countries and the largest. Singapore is a city-state of about six million people, and it was governed for decades by the iron hand of Lee Kuan Yu, the father of the country. He transformed a resource-poor plot of land into a prosperous state. And today Singapore is freer, clean, and safe. The retort, of course, is that it is tiny and that Lee Kuan Yu was a wise man, ruling in another time when democratic values had not spread across the world.

The Asian Tigers, also admired for iron-fisted rulers who modernized their economies, are in reality a mixed bag. South Korea eventually succeeded in building a stable democracy. But there was nothing benign about the military rulers who led the country for three decades. And the South Korean people do remember that dark past.

I attended the inauguration of South Korean president Lee Myung-Bak in 2008. The ceremony was an affirmation of democracy, celebrated at the end by a stirring rendition of Beethoven's "Ode to Joy," from the Ninth Symphony. Yet nothing linked the past to this triumphant moment like the troop review. The South Korean president stood at the podium, units of his troops saluting him one after another. I noticed the emotional response of everyone around me—especially the foreign minister, who was a few seats away. South Koreans knew that they were affirming democracy. From now on, civilians would command the armed forces, laying to rest a time when violent and repressive military rulers helped to make them prosperous, but at a price—the loss of freedom and national dignity.

In fact, most countries have failed to find benign, wise autocrats to rule them. Just ask the people of Zimbabwe or Venezuela. Cambodia and Laos are neither democratic nor particularly prosperous. The myth of the authoritarian who transforms his country, makes it rich, and then steps aside is rare in reality. Most of the time, as in South Korea, the country has struggled—often violently—before people have gained political rights and enjoyed economic prosperity. And there have been plenty of corrupt tyrants who can't govern at all.

China is, of course, the most obvious case of authoritarians who have delivered well-being. The Chinese communists have lifted hundreds of millions of people out of poverty, built gleaming cities, created excellent infrastructure, and launched world-class companies. By all measures, the country has had effective leaders who can get things done.

In a sense, China made a successful transition—not to democracy but from totalitarianism to authoritarianism. After the revolution, China fit perfectly Mussolini's *totalitario*. In the 1960s, everyone had a copy of Mao's "Little Red Book," chanted his slogans, and wore his iconic tunic—both men and women. Color choices were pretty much limited to gray and blue.

In 1982, our first contingent of Chinese scholars arrived at the Stanford program on Arms Control and Disarmament. One of them was Madame Zhou, whose scholarship interests were always a little vague. She showed up every day in her navy Mao jacket but didn't seem very interested in intellectual exchange. She walked into my office one day and said that she had seen *Gone with the Wind* the night before. It was, she said, a perfect representation of the capitalist oppression of black people. Not wanting to get into an extended conversation on slavery, I simply asked if she found the plight of black people interesting. "Not really," she said and walked away. We later figured out that Madame Zhou was the political commissar—sent to keep an eye on everyone else in the group. She was the quintessential product of totalitarian China.

Several years later, in 1988, I visited China for the first time. Mao jackets had been replaced by colorful clothing and no one mentioned the Little Red Book. But our trip to the opera demonstrated that the "red" arts were still very much in vogue. The story was something about the Long March, the legendary victory of Mao's troops against the Kuomintang. I didn't understand the words—even with translation—but the message got through: The glories of the Communist Party were to be celebrated in every aspect of life.

If one visits China today, these vestiges of *totalitario* are long gone—cast aside some three decades after Deng Xiaoping opened the economy to capitalism. Chanel, Armani, and Nike dot the major boulevards, and their customers are well-to-do Chinese. Pianists and violinists from the country grace the world's concert stages, playing the occasional Chinese folk song, but mostly delivering exquisite renditions of Brahms and Beethoven. Alibaba and Tencent are among the world's most highly regarded tech companies. So far the leadership has managed to open cultural and economic space *and* protect its monopoly in politics. The question is whether that separation can be maintained.

On the one hand, the last real threat to the party's authority perished at Tiananmen Square in 1989. The movement of students and intellectuals—mostly young people—was crushed, literally. The iconic images of a young man standing in front of a tank and the makeshift replica of the Statue of Liberty belong to the past. Widespread purges and arrests sent a very strong message: Politics is the purview of the Communist Party. Do not cross that line again.

Since then, the regime has faced no organized challenge. The party leadership is fortunate, because it is playing a strong hand in two important ways. First, it enjoys legitimacy based on prosperity. In today's China, almost all people are better off than their grandparents—even their parents—were. Yet expectations continue to rise and the regime is always chasing them. Hu Jintao once told us that he needed to produce ten million jobs every year just to keep up with migration from rural areas to the cities.

The second source of strength is the population's aversion to chaos. The Chinese people have strong memories of the horrors of the Cultural Revolution.

One evening I was invited to dinner in Beijing by a former foreign minister who had been my colleague when I was in government. Somehow the conversation turned from geopolitics to personal stories. I talked about growing up in Birmingham and the changes I had witnessed in America. He talked about the Cultural Revolution.

"I was just about to go to college," he told me. "And because I was good at languages and China needed that, I was allowed to go ahead. Every night the Red Guards would come to the dorms and make us recite slogans. We just did it and they left," he continued. "But sometimes they would take someone away just to prove that they could. We would never see that person again."

My friend went on to explain that his sisters were older and thus suspect in the eyes of the regime. They were not allowed to finish college. Instead, they were made to work in factories in order to become truly proletarian in spirit. "They were better students than I was," he told me. "And now they still work in factories because they were never able to finish their education."

He concluded his story by explaining that his language skills had allowed him to be assigned to duties in Africa, where China was beginning to build a diplomatic presence. There he waited out the Cultural Revolution until it was safe to return to the Foreign Ministry.

Another colleague told a different but equally compelling story. He knew that I was a student of Russia and he asked for my views—"Do you prefer Dostoyevsky or Tolstoy? Have you read *War and Peace* in Russian?"

I answered Dostoyevsky and yes. Then I asked him, "What prompted your interest in Russian literature?"

"Well," he said, "I had a lot of time in the countryside during the Cultural Revolution. Russia was our friend." He let the last word hang in the air. "It was okay to study the language and the literature." I thought to myself that it was a clever way to get through that great national trauma.

Many Chinese suffered greater indignities than these men—and many lost everything, including parents and siblings who were killed. As one Chinese friend said to me, "We value order because we do not need another national nervous breakdown."

The Chinese people value stability—especially those who came of age during the Cultural Revolution or who saw the Tiananmen Square protests crushed—and many seem willing to forgo individual liberties to sustain it. Still, there are pressures on this neat division between politics and the rest of life. The first strains result from the regime's desire to unleash market forces in the economy. China's successful economic model was built on being the low-cost provider of labor in the international system. That attracted manufacturing capital from around the world and helped create an export juggernaut. But now Chinese incomes are increasing rapidly—another case of the government chasing rising expectations. Indeed, when there has been labor unrest the response has been quick, decisive, and often to raise wages. So manufacturing costs are higher, driving production into Southeast Asia.

Government investment was the other engine for growth—infrastructure development and the creation of new cities to accommodate the largest movement of people from rural to urban areas in history, at least 250 million so far. Now too many regional airports and highways are chronically underutilized. Rapid construction of housing is finally outpacing demand. Several provinces that borrowed heavily to finance these booms are in debt and together with state-owned enterprises (SOEs) have unhealthy balance sheets. A potential Chinese bubble has become a source of concern for the regime and for the international economy.

The top-down model of economic growth has run out of steam. A new engine will have to rest in large part on freeing market forces. But that means ceding control to multiple actors—and that has been very uncomfortable for the regime. The economic reforms announced at the last Party Plenum have been carried out in fits and starts. Reforms that can be imposed from the center—pension and health care reform, and better environmental stewardship, for example—are moving ahead. However, the government is fearful of rapidly closing inefficient SOEs because people will be put out of work. The brief experiment with encouraging ordinary people to invest in the stock market produced a serious crisis. Markets can go up, but they can go down too. The regime seemed determined to vitiate this law with intervention, only making the situation worse. People still protest outside the offices of China's version of the Securities and Exchange Commission.

The new model also depends on getting people to spend and the development of a service sector. Older citizens have largely been cared for by their extended families. Labor mobility has broken this pattern as children venture out to the cities, leaving their elders behind. In the old model, people hoarded their savings and were reluctant to consume. Now the government wants them to spend, but they won't do so without reliable savings for retirement—a pension.

The man charged with building a pension system for over a billion people told me that they are looking at all possible models. "We like the Chilean one," he said. "You mean the private pension fund where workers contribute and then the money is invested?" I asked. He nodded. Despite the stock market crash of 2015, Chinese authorities introduced reforms that required public workers to pay into the system for the first time. Many people, including almost all government workers, are now funding their own pensions, at least in part. That begins to change the relationship of the citizens to their leaders, lessening dependence on the government and emphasizing individual responsibility.

Pressures are growing too to rein in the arbitrary power of the state. The absence of sound courts and a culture of rule of law is retarding the development of the private sector. The problem is evident in the lack of protections for people's assets. Citizens watch as developers and local party leaders expropriate their land. With no legal means of recourse, they riot. China experiences roughly 180,000 protests every year, according to a professor at Tsinghua University.[6] In 2011, residents in the fishing village of Wukan demonstrated how the lack of a reliable legal system has implications for social stability. Protests over corrupt land seizures escalated into an all-out rebellion as villagers barricaded roads and kicked out local police and party officials. Order was eventually restored in a deal that allowed villagers to vote for new local leaders, in what might have been China's freest ever local election. But the experience was a searing one for the authorities. Chinese officials now readily admit that they need a reliable court system that can command trust. Could an independent judiciary be next?

The country also faces growing social inequality—the rich are getting richer while upward mobility is slowing for the poor. This has led the leadership to crack down on ostentatious wealth, particularly among children of the party's elite.

One young man made unwanted headlines when he crashed his black Ferrari after a night out in Beijing. His father was a high-ranking official. Party members have since been told to stay out of fancy restaurants and dress humbly. The "Red Nobility" has become a problem in a narrative of socialist equality.

Try as the government might to curb the wealthy, though, people find ways to spend their money and gain advantage. On a recent trip, I noticed a group of kids leaving their middle school. They were wearing running gear with a prominently displayed swoosh.

"Is that a sports team?" I asked my guide.

"No, that is what they like to wear to school. You have to have money to get your kids into that school."

Incredulous, I said, "But all schools are public." He didn't answer.

The regime's record thus far of coping with change is pretty good. But the demands are proliferating and accelerating. A few men have to find answers to myriad challenges. If you are going to be omnipotent, you had better be omniscient too.

When an authoritarian makes a good decision, he can deliver on it quickly. But when he makes a bad decision, he still delivers on it, but with little or no feedback until it is too late. Chinese leaders have made some bad decisions.

China has a horrible demographic problem stemming in part from a bad decision delivered effectively. In the hope of slowing population growth, families were allowed to have only one child. There was no population explosion. But the law of unintended consequences has kicked in. China now has an aging population and one that is skewed toward men. It turns out that families, particularly rural families, who were going to have one child wanted a boy. Many girls disappeared. Now there are reportedly as many as thirty million Chinese men without mates. The regime reversed the one-child policy in 2015, but the damage has already been done.

Similarly, the rapid industrialization of the country has had its own negative effects. Chinese cities are experiencing a pollution nightmare. It is quite literally impossible on some days to see the skyline. During a recent trip, one of my dinner guests rode his bicycle to the restaurant—wearing a gas mask. The regime has tried a variety of schemes. The most widely ridiculed is one that issues license plates with a number that designates your "driving days." People are supposed to use their cars only every other day. "Don't they know that people just buy two license plates?" a friend told me.

At first the regime tried to deny the problem, or at least to downplay it. The government issued a pollution index each day. Unfortunately, people had access to a smartphone app that measured the particulates in the air. The U.S. embassy was also displaying the real numbers on a very large screen. Eventually, the regime gave in and started to provide more realistic numbers, and it is now pushing effectively for greener policies.

This episode reveals a bigger problem for the Communist Party: The population increasingly has access to independent information. Authoritarians need to control the narrative, and that is getting hard to do. While the Chinese government works harder than any other to censor the Internet, many say that people find a way around the walls. Dissidents have not been able to use social media to organize or to mobilize on a large scale:

The government has managed to squash that kind of activity. But when there is a crisis—for instance, with tainted baby milk formula in 2008—people turn to the Web for the true story. In other words, the party may be able to stifle some of the effects of proliferating sources of information. It is devoting enormous resources to doing so, by hiring over a million people to censor the Internet. One wonders if it will ever be enough.

In short, the Chinese government faces some unpalatable choices. For any authoritarian regime, even a successful one, the question is whether, when, and how to take steps toward political reform. In advance of the 18th Party Plenum in 2012, there was great expectation that Beijing might do just that. The selection of Xi Jinping, a man with an impeccable pedigree (his father was one of Mao's lieutenants on the Long March), raised hopes that he might be China's Gorbachev. But unlike the Soviet leader, Xi would have economic prosperity as a shield against collapse. Perhaps China could find a soft landing.

The story thus far is largely in the opposite direction. Xi has amassed more power than any Chinese leader in recent memory. In the past, executive authority was divided between a strong premier with responsibility for the economy and the president, who handled everything else. Zhu Rongji and Jiang Zemin exemplified the division of labor. It allowed the prime minister space to pursue economic policy with the protection of the president, who managed the politics.

Xi Jinping has broken that model. He now heads all of the important functions of the state, from foreign policy and internal security to economic regulation and governance reform. While he seems to have absolute authority to run the country, he is likely to get total blame if he fails. Some say that this explains the most controversial of his policies—the anticorruption drive.

Believing that the "leading role of the Communist Party" is at stake, Xi has instituted a major purge of its ranks. The anticorruption campaign was initially popular—a belief in the need for it was widely shared.

Wang Qishan, a man whom I had known when in government, was tapped to lead the effort. He received me in 2015 when I was in Beijing. We shared a few old memories and talked about the general course of reform in the country. Wang was the same affable man I had come to know, until he turned to his current work. His face stiffened and he grew quite stern. "The party has to be beyond reproach if it is to maintain a leading role," he said. "There are eighty-seven million members and they must all be completely clean." He explained that he had created investigatory committees to go out to even the smallest party units and look for corruption. I remember thinking, *And you will find it, because it is everywhere.*

Later that night I met with some businesspeople. They talked about the effects of the campaign. "People who once signed a deal to spend $100 million won't spend $1 million," one person said. "Everything is grinding to a halt because everyone is scared. A lot of people are being executed." One man then told a story that is making the rounds in Beijing. It is of a famous general who had taken to playing golf on his own little nine-hole course. The land had probably been acquired by questionable means. "But he wasn't really hurting anyone. He was turned in by some local official, tried, and executed. They buried him under his favorite golf hole as a message to everyone," my guest said, shaking his head.

The atmosphere of fear among party members has led some to wonder if the anticorruption campaign has gone too far and to suggest that it is time to say, "Just don't be corrupt from here on." The party cannot tolerate constant uncertainty, they say. And there is a sense that the program has taken an arbitrary turn—no one knows who is next or what the charges will be.

While anticorruption measures are a step in the right direction in theory, other changes in China are more concerning. The independent space between politics and the rest of life appears to be shrinking. Xi has placed a new emphasis on strengthening cultural and national values—even if it means imposing them. In the face of so much upheaval, he is clearly searching for a unifying narrative. The Chinese nationalist impulse is one, and it is leading to an emphasis on China's military might and rightful place in the world. China is increasingly assertive in the Asia-Pacific region, laying claim to disputed territory and militarizing the South China Sea. This has alarmed its neighbors and caused them to bind closer to the United States for protection. Tensions in the Asia-Pacific are very high indeed.

The desire for recognition predates Xi, of course. The Beijing Olympics were a chance to showcase China, starting with a nationalist opening ceremony that sent a few chills up the spines of those who watched. Two thousand and eight perfectly synchronized drummers rising from the turf seemed to capture the mood.

But Xi has relied on not just a nationalist narrative but

an avowedly communist one. The government demands that schoolchildren once again study Mao and his Little Red Book. He has tried to reinstitute "patriotic" activities, even insisting that the ballet reflect socialist values. His crackdown on the media has led at least one editor of a prominent newspaper to quit rather than face the pressure of political controls.

The picture of China today is an odd mix of a thoroughly modern international power, craving respect but increasingly insecure about its future. At least some of that insecurity seems to stem from a lack of trust in its people's intentions. Therefore, the regime is determined to control their actions and make their intentions irrelevant. In a country of 1.4 billion people, that is a tall task.

In 2014, I spoke at the prestigious Tsinghua University in Beijing. A Chinese friend refers to the university as Stanford and Harvard all wrapped into one. I decided to speak to the students as if they were at Stanford. This wouldn't be a lecture about U.S.-China relations but about them—the students— and their ambitions and the power of education.

The question-and-answer session was a surprise to me. "What do I do if my parents don't like my major?" "I am an engineer, why should I bother with literature?" "I am a Uighur [a Muslim minority] and everyone treats my people as if we are terrorists. We are just poor. How can I help?"

They are thinking and they refuse to be programmed, I thought. *They question their parents and university officials. Can questioning the government really be that far behind?* The task for China's leaders is to preserve their system and still make room for a creative, innovative, and increasingly prosperous people. They may not take China along a democratic path, but the road that they are on could relatively soon run out of room.

⁓

In this regard, there is always a temptation to contrast the world's largest democracy, India, with its huge authoritarian neighbor, China. In India, the question of whether citizens would have a voice in how their country is run was answered with independence in 1947. Still, governing the huge country has been exceedingly difficult. Ask most CEOs about China and they talk about growth and huge markets. Ask about India and you will get a glazed look—and a lecture about bureaucracy and corruption.

Leaders are insecure in authoritarian states because they have no reliable way to judge the temperature and intentions of their people. Democratic systems have shock absorbers and plenty of feedback. Today the speed and volume of information flowing from citizens to their governments and back again is unprecedented. But democratic institutions react relatively slowly. They are protected from tyranny because leaders are constrained. Those very constraints, though, make it hard to get things done quickly.

To be fair, India has grown rapidly too and is home to some of the finest companies in the world. Mumbai, Hyderabad, and Bangalore rival almost any international technology center. But the slums of Calcutta are on par with the worst circumstances in the least-developed corners of the earth. Upon taking office as prime minister in 2014, Narendra Modi launched major plans to unravel crippling regulations and improve the atmosphere for business. He also launched a bathroom initiative, providing sanitary stations for poor Indians so that they would not relieve themselves on the street.

The Indian story is filled with contrasts of that kind. But for all of its challenges, India is a functioning democracy. When independence came in 1947, the country already had an institutional blueprint left to it by the British. There was a large and well-trained civil service; the new army was diverse, constrained by constitutional checks and thoroughly under civilian control; and leaders subjected themselves to popular vote. The country was fortunate to have an inspirational founding father in Mahatma Gandhi, and a competent and long-lived first leader in Jawaharlal Nehru, who ruled from 1947 to 1964. It seemed set to take off and be successful.

And to a certain extent it did. India has had sixteen national elections since independence and all of them have resulted in the peaceful transfer of power. It is remarkable that a country with well over a billion people who don't worship the same god manage to do this without much upheaval at all. India has the second-largest Muslim population in the world and yet has experienced very little trouble with Islamic radicalism. The exception to that rule is the terrorism that emanates from Pakistan. Indeed, one could argue that the conflict with Islamabad has held the country back, diverting resources to a conflict that has resulted in three all-out wars (in 1947, 1965, and 1971) and innumerable near misses.

A new prime minister always brings new hope of an Indian revival—a great country that can finally reach its potential.

The skepticism eventually sets in as impatience grows with the inability to deal with a suffocating bureaucracy and corruption.

But it is interesting to contrast democracy's approach to those issues with that of authoritarians. We have seen that even in the United States it took almost a hundred years to root out widespread corruption. Eventually, Teddy Roosevelt was elected on a platform of doing exactly that, and in time the problem was resolved. The press played a role, and civil society too, in supporting the changes and establishing rules of the game and punishments for violating them.

India is now engaged in an effort to finally deal with endemic corruption. Unlike in China, the drive was spurred from the bottom up, not the top down. Activist "Anna" Hazare, seeking to bring attention to the problem, went on a hunger strike in April 2011. At first the government tried to ignore him, but persistent press attention made that impossible, leading to investigations and more press coverage. The issue would become the central one of the 2014 election campaign. Narendra Modi, then chief minister (similar to a governor) of Gujarat, was elected after withering criticism of the Congress Party and Prime Minister Manmohan Singh. Clean governance and effective governance were, he argued, inextricably linked.

The private sector has played a role in the anticorruption drive too. Nandan Nilekani, a cofounder of Infosys, had an idea to improve government services and reduce corruption. He and his engineers built a sophisticated biometric identification system for the central government so that citizens would have a national ID.

I visited the Aadhaar project in New Delhi in 2013. The

brightly lit building housed engineers working intently in cubicles that surrounded a clean room. It looked just like any Silicon Valley company, sophisticated and organized. Our conversation with Nilekani was really inspiring. He clearly thought his project had a higher cause—removing the middleman, the bureaucrat, who handed out pension checks, food subsidies, and other benefits "for a fee." His eyes sparkled as he spoke of a world in which a farmer in rural India used a biometric ID to receive a benefit directly—securely and quickly. The program had the backing of the Singh government and has now convinced Prime Minister Modi of its worth as well. It is likely to be a real bipartisan achievement. India's Supreme Court has ruled that Indians cannot be forced to have an ID—that too is how democracies work. But so far more than a billion people have voluntarily signed up.[7]

It took the United States more than a hundred years to root out most corruption, but it did. There is no guarantee that India will succeed, but it has a good foundation for doing so. Officials can be held accountable publicly and transparently. That should give the effort a pretty good chance. Recent events in South Korea have followed a similar script, as citizens, the press, and the legislature have insisted on accountability at the highest levels for allegations of corruption.

By contrast, the anticorruption drive in China is all top-down. It is secretive and the Communist Party leadership is accuser, judge, jury, and executioner. That is roiling the country because the rules are not clear. And no one knows when the party purge might turn into something larger, a vendetta or a political campaign that engulfs the broader population.

Democracies are not efficient, but they may ultimately be more effective and resilient. They depend on transparency and a complex web of institutions, public and private, to keep authorities in check. Most of all, they depend on the willingness of citizens to engage those institutions and use them to demand the best of those who govern them. India has the infrastructure of democracy in place. Whatever the challenges ahead, that is a good place to start.

Chapter 9

WHAT DEMOCRACY MUST DELIVER

As my car barreled through the streets of Monrovia, I gazed out the window at the happy crowds lining the streets. It was about six in the morning and I was on my way from the airport to our ambassador's house. There I was planning to meet up with First Lady Laura Bush and together we would attend the inauguration of Liberia's first democratically elected president in thirty years. Ellen Johnson Sirleaf would also become Africa's first female head of state.

The mood was celebratory and the people jubilant. But the hard road ahead of the Liberians and their new leaders was evident—literally—at every turn. The streets were full of potholes, despite the efforts that had been made to repair roads quickly in order to receive international guests. The buildings were marked with bullet holes, fresh paint failing to mask the testament to the violence that had racked the country for decades. The water was not drinkable. And insect-borne disease, particularly malaria, was a constant threat. When I lay down to rest for a few moments before going to the ceremony, I did so encased in a mosquito net.

Liberia had no effective security forces; a population that was largely poorly educated, if not illiterate; a minimally functioning health care system; an unreliable power grid that constantly shut down even in the capital; and an economy that was limping along, principally on rubber-harvesting contracts that benefited the corrupt ministers who had negotiated them. This new democracy was a governance nightmare.

Few countries face as many challenges simultaneously as Liberia did. Founded as an American colony to receive freed slaves, it became independent in 1847 with a black American as its president.

For one hundred years, Liberia was considered one of the jewels of Africa, relatively stable and with an educated elite. A series of presidents ruled the country with an iron fist and considerable self-enrichment—but nothing that was really outside the norm for the continent as a whole.

The elites prospered, and at a time when black Americans were faring poorly in the United States, Liberians saw themselves as superior to all other Africans and their descendants. They had, after all, never been slaves. My aunt Theresa Love, a Victorian scholar, was invited to teach at the University of Monrovia in 1960. She told us of being invited on a cruise with President William Tubman and his family. "What shall we speak today?" one person asked. "Why, we shall have to speak English. Theresa doesn't speak French."

Tubman, a member of the True Whig Party, did try to improve relations between the African American inhabitants and the indigenous people. In general, the latter were looked down upon, discriminated against, and relegated to poverty and despair. But he tolerated no opposition—his soldiers gunning down a political rival, S. David Coleman, and his son in 1955 for challenging the president. That same year, he amended the constitution to allow him more than two terms. With every region a battleground in the competition between the United States and the Soviet Union, Liberian disregard for the rule of law and democracy was easily tolerated in Washington. Ironically, Voice of America—broadcasting to people trapped in communist tyranny—located one of its communication facilities in Liberia. When Tubman died after twenty-seven years as president, he was succeeded by his vice president of nineteen years, William Tolbert.

But Tolbert found ruling the country more difficult than his predecessor had. Years of pent-up frustration with inequality were taking their toll. By 1980, opposition leaders were becoming more vocal and Tolbert's response more authoritarian. The government began arresting members of the rival Progressive People's Party on charges of treason, claiming that they had been planning violent acts against the government.

The final verdict didn't come from the political opposition, however. It came from within the army. President Tolbert was assassinated in a military coup and thirteen other cabinet members were executed. Sergeant Samuel Doe assured the United States and the Liberian people that his regime would govern democratically. Constitutional reforms were initiated, and for a brief time the government appeared to be liberalizing the country's politics. That direction didn't last.

Doe, now running for president, began to harass his opposition, charging that Ellen Johnson Sirleaf—the most visible member of it—had given a speech "detrimental to the peace and stability of the country." He threatened to put her on trial for sedition. Johnson Sirleaf fled the country for the United States. Doe was elected under a cloud of irregularity—though the United States recognized him as the president of Liberia.

Doe could not govern Liberia either, as warlords took up arms in various parts of the country and challenged the government. One of them was Charles Taylor, who after seven years of civil war emerged as the most successful of the strongmen. He was elected president in 1997 but could not subdue the violent militias of other warlords. Civil war broke out again in April 1999, more brutally than before. Accord after accord failed to hold, though African and international diplomats tried to end the war.

Taylor had no incentive to do so. He and his war machine benefited from the diamond trade as the Liberians smuggled the precious stones from African mines to wealthy merchants in South Africa and Europe. This would lead the world to try to do something about "blood diamonds." And Taylor would present civilized nations with another outrage: His forces were often child soldiers, some as young as nine years old.

It was the *New York Times* front-page photograph of one of these boys that finally led the United States to say enough. I took the picture into the Oval Office with me that morning of June 28, 2003. President Bush had already seen the haunting image: A boy, no more than twelve years old, glared at the camera with an AK-47 in one hand and a teddy bear backpack around his shoulders.

When President Bush visited Africa a week later, he vowed publicly to do something to end Liberia's civil war. In a Rose Garden press conference with Kofi Annan, the UN secretary-general, he said that he would use American military forces if necessary. That certainly unsettled the Pentagon—and initially the generals said it would take two divisions to oust Charles Taylor.

In the end it took two hundred marines to secure the airport and the seaports while Nigerian-led UN peacekeeping forces entered the country. In August 2003, Taylor was escorted out by a delegation of African heads of state, John Kufuor of Ghana and Olusegun Obasanjo of Nigeria among them. This was a successful—and extremely limited—use of military force to achieve change.

Twenty-three years earlier, a military coup had sparked decades of civil war and misrule. Now a transitional government of experts and technocrats was to govern the country for two years under UN auspices. That led to Johnson Sirleaf's election and the beginning of the governance challenge ahead.

Where Do You Start?

The Liberian case is instructive because all of the problems of governance that new (or refounded) democracies face were on display. When we think of democratic transitions, we tend to have in mind the creation of political institutions—constitutions, parliaments, a judiciary, and the executive. We are concerned about protecting private space for civil society and the press. This is clearly, as we have seen in the cases above, a crucial challenge—to get the balance right between these parts of the political system and the government and the people.

Fifty-nine countries are, according to Freedom House, "partly free." They are, in the parlance used in this book, much like quasi-democratic states. They have passed the first test—people are free to elect their leaders and change them peacefully. In most cases, the press is free and civil society is allowed to function. But the institutions are weak and governance problems are manifold. This is the work of democracy promotion—to help them govern better but also democratically. Elections buy time, but the population is impatient. Any state must have the machinery to deliver essential goods and services. Sometimes it is as basic as potable water or reliable electricity.

One thing is clear: Many countries cannot provide for their people without international help. The more dire the situation, the greater the need for international assistance. But foreign assistance cannot and should not replace the national government in the provision of goods. It has to seek simultaneously to improve the lives of people and strengthen indigenous mechanisms for doing so.

The Foreign Assistance Trap

For many years, critics of foreign assistance focused on waste. During the Cold War, as we have seen with Liberia, the superpower rivalry led to strategic assistance. The goal was to induce loyalty from leaders in developing countries, no matter how corrupt they were.

My master's thesis at Notre Dame sought to understand the U.S. and Soviet motivations for granting aid to developing countries in the period from 1961 to 1973. I tested several variables: the type of political system; geographic importance; existing historical ties. The most potent explanation was competition with the other superpower. If the Soviet Union granted aid to one country, the United States was likely to grant aid to a neighbor. Clearly, the Peace Corps and USAID had larger development goals, but they were often eclipsed by the imperative to counterbalance the other side.

Not surprisingly, foreign assistance earned a reputation for waste—the proverbial money down a rathole. Many leaders in developing countries, particularly in Africa, flaunted their wealth while their people endured subsistence living. With the collapse of the Soviet Union, the argument for strategic assistance—a euphemism for funding loyalty in the Cold War—weakened, though there were other reasons for it, particularly in the Middle East. The Camp David Accords, for instance, produced a formula for aid to Israel and Egypt as long as they kept their commitments to peace. The latter has been a source of controversy as the government in Cairo has repeatedly failed to reform.

Over the last twenty years or so, however, donors have become more demanding about the uses of foreign assistance, insisting on accountability from governments. Transparency initiatives are now commonplace, helping donors to get a handle on the levels of corruption in developing countries. More than at any other time, foreign assistance is going largely to the purposes for which it was intended.

Yet there is still a question as to its effectiveness. Poverty rates have come down. Progress has been made on the Millennium Development Goals, a United Nations initiative begun in 2000 to create global partnerships for eradicating poverty, improving women's health and gender equality, reducing disease and child mortality, globalizing primary education, and promoting environmental sustainability. Over its fifteen-year timeline, the program has reached important milestones such as cutting the number of individuals living in extreme poverty and cases of infant mortality by half.

That said, there is also a sense that progress has been slow and that too many countries, some with significant resources, will forever be wards of the international system, unable to provide for their own people. There is a kind of foreign assistance trap. If someone else—in this case the international community—is responsible for delivering goods and services, the domestic machinery will never get stronger and more capable. It is important to feed people, but better if indigenous agriculture can do so. The health care and educational systems have to become capable of doing their jobs. And it would be empowering for legislators to pass bills—democratically—that dealt with a country's social ills. It is fine to have international NGOs provide services—they are often desperately needed. But at some point the government and local NGOs have to take responsibility for the welfare of the people.

We have seen repeatedly that people expect a lot of leaders when they elect them. They want life to get better and hold their government accountable if it doesn't. This fact is the cause of a good deal of the instability in new democracies. Governments rise and fall with dizzying speed because they cannot live up to expectations. When the American Founders talked about guaranteeing not just life and liberty but the "pursuit of happiness," they identified an important challenge of democracy.

Aid Through Them, Not Around Them

Elected leaders in developing countries have to show that they can provide for their people—and they need to show that they are indeed the ones doing the providing. They need a way to escape the foreign assistance trap. This issue has received greater attention in recent years from donor countries. National and international donor agencies have been moving away from traditional approaches to foreign aid based on unconditional grants and other initiatives that circumvent local institutional participation. For instance, the U.S. Agency for International Development (USAID) has recently mandated greater engagement with aid-recipient countries in order to promote increased responsibility and accountability within the development process. Across the Atlantic, the Organization for Security and Co-operation in Europe (OSCE) has delivered technical assistance to participating states in key governance-related areas such as policing, border management, elections, and others. Increasing attention has also been ascribed by international organizations like the UN to the substantial impact of diaspora communities, which often contribute to economic and institutional development in their countries of origin.

But one of the signature programs launched by the Bush

administration and sustained and extended by President Obama was designed specifically to strengthen democratic governance while delivering economic benefits to the population. The two were inextricably linked in the conception of the Millennium Challenge Corporation (MCC), which was announced in 2002 by President Bush and approved by Congress in 2004. The MCC is an independent U.S. government agency that identifies qualifying countries around the world and awards them significant sums of conditional aid in agreements called compacts. It uses independent and measurable indicators in three broad policy categories: Ruling Justly, Investing in People, and Encouraging Economic Freedom. "Control of corruption" is a key element of the Ruling Justly indicator, and since its inception, the MCC has made significant strides to spur policy reforms in its compact countries. By empowering recipient countries to take the initiative and submit their own proposals for foreign assistance, the MCC has been viewed as taking a more effective approach toward fostering economic and institutional development. This process of inducing countries to initiate policy reform to become eligible for aid has led to a demonstrable impact in the fight against poverty, bureaucratic efficiency, and infrastructure development—even in countries that have not yet won a contract.

The MCC compacts are often highly targeted. For example, Malawi received $350 million to improve hydropower generation. A significant portion of the grant was for technical assistance to improve the operational and financial management of ESCOM, the public electricity utility. The country of Georgia was granted $140 million to improve the quality of education in STEM (science, technology, engineering, and mathematics). Supported by San Diego State University, bachelor's degree programs were launched at Ilia State University, Tbilisi State University, and the Georgian Technical University. El Salvador received $461 million for an integrated set of investments in logistical infrastructure, education, and regulatory reform in order to spark private-sector-led growth. The project was managed by FOMILENIO II, a government entity with responsibility for overseeing the compact.

The road to developing the compact is also intended to be an exercise in governing. Before the MCC will even consider a request from a qualified country, the government must lead a process engaging all stakeholders. So in Jordan, with a project intended to increase the supply of water to households and businesses, farmers, business leaders, and local government officials were convened numerous times to develop the ask. Jordanian officials told us that it was a real exercise in grassroots democracy, complete with the frustrations of gaining consensus on what would be included—and what would not—in the compact request.

And sometimes the process leads to significant changes in law. I was secretary of state in 2007 when Lesotho signed a $363 million compact to encourage small business development and improvements in public health. In 2013, I shared the stage with the woman responsible for implementing Lesotho's compact at an MCC anniversary event. Sophia Mohapi had been widowed with four children at the age of thirty-three. Now she had successfully overseen a multimillion-dollar project and had even secured an additional $100 million in funding from the Lesotho government to ensure the project's sustainability. I was honored to present her with the MCC Country Commitment Award for her accomplishments. After the ceremony, Sophia came over and thanked me for the MCC. It had brought very concrete change to Lesotho, she said. When the MCC learned that married women could not hold title to a business or land in their own name in her country, the government was forced to change the law.

The MCC is not, of course, a panacea for problems of governance. Several compact recipients have been suspended for backsliding on the indicators—Madagascar and Mali lost their assistance because of military coups. The Sandinistas' efforts to rig local elections in Nicaragua caused the MCC to suspend its compact in 2008. Despite appeals by some local officials, the country's national leadership refused to meet the basics of democratic governance, and the MCC terminated its contract the following year.

There is little doubt that this approach—large assistance packages for programs developed by the government in coordination with stakeholders—is having an effect. It will take a long time to know how much the MCC is strengthening democratic governance, but the early returns are good. The MCC effect appears to be real.[1]

In February 2007, I attended a development event with Ellen Johnson Sirleaf in Washington. "How is it going?" I asked her. "We need to be an MCC country," she answered. Liberia by no means met the criteria at that time, but before we left office, it was granted threshold status so that it could make the necessary reforms. The country was finally awarded a compact in 2015 to help deal with the unreliable power supply that had stranded President Bush in an elevator in Sirleaf's office when he visited in 2008.

I went to Liberia in the summer of 2013 with a congressional delegation and Bono, who was one of the first to endorse the MCC. That day we visited a brand-new health care clinic, the JKF Medical Center in Monrovia, which had just received a grant from the Liberian government. The young director, Dr. Wvannie Mae Scott-McDonald, had been trained in the United States and returned to Liberia after the civil war ended. He was another example of the important work that people from the diaspora do in their countries of origin. The lab was clean and efficient and modern. The progress was so inspiring. *Maybe they are finally out of the woods*, I thought.

One year later, the Ebola crisis hit Liberia. The incipient health care system was quickly overwhelmed, and again, massive foreign assistance was needed to help the country cope. I called Johnson Sirleaf just to see how she was doing. The president was upbeat—particularly given the circumstances. She recalled all the United States had done and all that it was doing to help her through the latest crisis. A year after that, the World Health Organization certified Liberia as "Ebola-free." The country had survived another brush with catastrophe.

Governing is hard in the most advanced democracies. When the institutions for delivery—the civil service, the educational system, the health care system—are underdeveloped, it is especially hard. Building the infrastructure of democracy—finding the right balance within the government and between the government and its people—takes time. If, in the meantime, leaders are successful in providing for the population, they may have the time that they need.

So it has been with Johnson Sirleaf, whom Liberians reelected to a second term in 2012. Even as she has strengthened Liberia's institutions, she has never lost sight of the need to deliver for her people. In her second inaugural address she declared that her country had earned its "rightful place as a beacon of democracy," while acknowledging the many challenges that remain. "The cleavages that led to decades of war still run deep. But so too does the longing for reconciliation," she said. "True reconciliation means a process of national healing. It means learning the lessons of the past to perfect our democracy. But above all it means economic justice for our citizens and the spread of progress to all our people." And she meant it.

Chapter 10

"DEMOCRACY IS THE WORST...EXCEPT FOR ALL THE OTHERS"

The famous Churchill quote holds true today. And people, no matter how poor or how isolated, seem to know it. Afrobarometer is a research organization that measures attitudes on the African continent, including in some of the world's poorest nations. For more than a decade, it has repeatedly shown a deep public understanding of the tenets of democracy and an unmistakable preference to live in freedom.

Still, it is clear that democracy is challenged—everywhere. Young democracies struggle to meet even the most basic needs of their people. Mature democracies strain to govern effectively in today's world of instant information and immediate judgment. And in both, people, whether having lived in freedom for centuries or for just a few years, express dissatisfaction with their leaders and a lack of faith in their institutions. Therein lies the genius in Churchill's words, though. Democracy is imperfect at the beginning and will remain so. But men and women still crave it: It alone affords human beings the dignity that comes when those who would govern them have to ask for their consent. There is simply no alternative.

Even with all of its flaws, democracy is thus a necessary and worthwhile enterprise. It is a hard slog full of contradictions and compromises on the way—hopefully to something better. Its successes and failures must be addressed over history's long arc, not with reference to today's headlines.

I saw this firsthand in meeting with the leaders of Bosnia-Herzegovina in 2005. The country emerged out of the breakup of Yugoslavia and the violent conflict that ensued. When the war ended, the country was split into three ethnoreligious groups that did not trust each other and didn't really want to live together. The answer: three presidents, one for each group.

"Never address one of them without addressing the other two—and never ever speak to them collectively. They must each be called out individually," I was told. I remember thinking the whole thing a bit ridiculous, but it works—sort of. The country limps along and still does not have a unified parliament. Constitutional reform is badly needed, but for now the people just live with this unnatural and complex governing formula. The lesson is that in extreme circumstances you work with what you have, cobbling together imperfect compromises so that the country and its people can live to fight another day.

Indeed, learning to embrace the imperfect is a common theme in the stories that we have examined. Constructing democracy is messy. Of course, decent societies must make steady progress on issues of corruption and violence and inequality. Democratic governments and their people must struggle to overcome them with energy and determination. But it is useful to think of the process of building democracy as climbing steep stairs—move forward, stop on a landing if you must, consolidate, and move forward again. To stress an earlier point, democratic transitions are neither immediate successes nor immediate failures. They are constant works in progress.

Lesson One: Work with What Is There

Democratic institutions are not created in a vacuum. At the outset we identified four institutional landscapes: totalitarian collapse that leaves an institutional void; totalitarian decay that leaves institutional antecedents; authoritarian regimes and the struggle for meaningful political space; and quasi-democratic regimes with fragile and vulnerable institutions. All bring particular challenges, but our cases show that the legacy of existing arrangements must be taken into account.

The most difficult situations come from the collapse of totalitarian regimes. Since these cults of personality infuse every aspect of life—*totalitario*, in Mussolini's immortal word— the landscape is barren.

But even in these cases, it is worthwhile to take stock of what is there, rather than start anew. We have seen that America's failure to understand the institutional landscape in Iraq cost time in stabilizing the country. The Sunnis, in particular, did have institutions—the tribes, the army—but they were undervalued after Saddam's fall. A different strategy might have at least put a floor under the collapsing country and diminished the violence. But it would not have been a panacea. The immediate postwar history of Afghanistan is illustrative in this regard.

Leading up to the war and in its immediate aftermath, the United States and its allies made a deliberate effort to build on the basis of existing institutions. The war itself was fought by the militias of warlords from the north and the south of the country. America's footprint was light—principally airpower and special forces. There are iconic photographs of twenty-first-century American fighters supporting men on donkeys—yes, on donkeys.

The NSC meeting had become quite raucous that day. It was about two weeks after the 9/11 attacks and our military and intelligence forces were still not ready to launch the invasion against the Taliban. The president was getting anxious, worried that al-Qaeda might launch another attack from their sanctuary in Afghanistan. "Why aren't we ready?" he said with a distinct edge of frustration. George Tenet took the floor. "The Northern Alliance [the mainly Tajik and Uzbek militia opposed to the Taliban] says that the Russians haven't provided the equipment they promised," he said. The president turned to me: "Go right now and call Sergei Ivanov [the Russian defense minister] and see why they haven't done what they said they would do."

I left the meeting immediately and managed to get Sergei on the phone. "I know, Condi," he said. "But it isn't easy to find donkeys."

"Donkeys," I repeated.

"Yes. That's how they move in the high mountains," he replied.

In time, the men on donkeys won the war—with our help—against the Taliban, and al-Qaeda was driven out of the country. The leaders of those militias became the first leaders of their country. Hamid Karzai and his men had taken the south. Abdul Rashid Dostum, Ismail Khan, and other members of the Northern Alliance had taken the north and the west. Within three years Karzai would be president. Khan would become the powerful governor of Herat province. And Dostum would visit me as deputy defense minister in the White House.

The stout man walked into my office, clearly uncomfortable in his coat and tie. *I'll bet he's never worn a suit*, I thought to myself. Dostum tried his best to play his role, outlining the needs of the National Army of Afghanistan and describing the training of his forces. But like the other warlords, he was a peculiar pillar on which to build a democratic future for Afghanistan. The country would suffer, and does to this day, from conflict among these men and others like them—as well as their profiteering from the drug trade. They are part of the central government but guard their territorial independence jealously. And though large numbers of the militia fighters were demobilized, some remain violent.

Nonetheless, Afghanistan has held five nationwide elections since 2003.[1] The National Army can hold the large cities, but the Taliban, using sanctuary in Pakistan, is more than capable of terrorism and violence. Fifteen years after the war, the country is not stable—but it is freer.

The Afghan Constitution of 2004 guarantees the rights

of women to education and employment. They still face hardship and discrimination, but it is a far cry from the dark days of Taliban rule. There were about a million students in Afghan schools in 2001, and all were male. Today there are more than 8.4 million students—and almost 40 percent are female. By law, women make up 26 percent of the lower house of parliament, a higher level of female representation than in the U.S. Congress. The Afghan Constitution promises to uphold both sharia law and individual liberties—a compromise to get the country through its immediate challenges. It remains poised between modern democratic practices and ancient social customs like honor killings. In 2009, the government finally outlawed violence against women, including rape. Now women can take offenders to court—and sometimes they win.

A mullah who raped a ten-year-old girl in a mosque was sentenced to twenty years in prison in 2014. A young woman won a suit against her family in 2013 after it tried to force her into prostitution. On the other hand, some rulings have been rightly perceived as setbacks to women's rights, notably the light punishments for those involved in the mob killing of a young woman in 2015.

In other words, weak democratic structures being built on top of traditional ones has made progress difficult—particularly given the security situation exacerbated by the porous and remote Pakistani border. Still, Afghanistan is no longer a country in which women are, as a matter of government policy, beaten and executed for immodesty. The lunacy of the Taliban's reign is over. When asked why they executed people in a football stadium built with UN money, a Taliban spokesman replied forthrightly, "We need another stadium so we can hold games there. This one we need for executions." Afghanistan is better off, but its path since 2001 is a warning that there are downsides to building on existing institutions, even if it is necessary to do so.

In places, though, where the institutional infrastructure is richer, nurturing them makes very good sense. Poland shows that working with existing institutions—even if they are temporarily underground—improves the possibility of a successful transition when the moment comes. Solidarity was nurtured and became stronger during martial law. This was a concerted effort of the United States, the AFL-CIO, and the Catholic Church. As a result, Lech Wałęsa and his colleagues were ready to take the country forward in 1989. This gives hope that these "green shoots" can be identified and sustained even before the opening arrives. Tunisia's educated women, active labor unions, and civil society groups gave the country a good starting point.

Colombia had a rich landscape—a relatively free press, a functioning parliament, and a pattern of competitive, if dangerous, elections. Uribe was able to reinvigorate these institutions. Kenya had a brief experiment with multiparty elections that was aborted by Kenyatta and then Moi. It did have a parliament that would produce important opposition figures as the country democratized. The Kenyan people slowly rebuilt these nascent, dormant institutions. Kenya is a relatively rare case where a strong and vibrant civil society developed even under authoritarian rule. This provided a good foundation for democratic progress later on.

Russia's transition would ultimately fail, even though it had a decent institutional infrastructure, largely due to the reforms of Gorbachev and Yeltsin. In this case, though, they were not nurtured—they were largely overrun. In fact, there was a kind of disregard by the international community for what was there—swept away by rapid privatization and "shock therapy." And Russians ignored their own institutions too. Therein lies the second lesson.

Lesson Two: First Presidents Matter

Finding a balance of power between institutions of government is the single most important key to a successful transition. And the crucial element of that balance is to limit the power of the executive. The presidency must be embedded in a network of constraints—an independent judiciary, a capable legislature, and, in some cases, an empowered prime minister. All young democracies struggle with this aspect of institutional design. It is hard to do, because strong personalities will emerge and the people will desire immediate results. A single figure—the president—can emerge as a symbol of stability in troubled times. Parliaments or prime ministers can be seen as just obstacles to get around.

Russia and Ukraine had—on paper—balance between the parliament, the prime minister, and the president. But it didn't hold under pressure. In fact, Boris Yeltsin destroyed the equilibrium with his attack on the parliament in 1993 and an impatient temperament that led him to rule by decree. First presidents set the tone.

I remember meeting Nelson Mandela for the first time. He came to visit President Bush in the Oval Office. Mandela had been critical of the war in Iraq, and the president was searching for a way to get the meeting off on a good foot. "Mr. President, talk to him about AIDS relief," I suggested. "That is something you have in common."

When the two men sat down, the president decided to take a different approach. "Why didn't you run for another term?" he asked Mandela. The South African's face was lined but beneficent—there was a dignified aura about him. But the president's question caused him to break up laughing. "I wanted my African brothers to know that it is all right to leave office," he said. At that moment I thought of George Washington and his refusal to even think about becoming America's king. *First presidents matter*, I thought. *The South Africans, like the Americans, are really lucky.*

Lech Wałęsa, Poland's first president, stepped down after one term—replaced by an ex-communist, Aleksander Kwasniewski, whose democratic instincts proved to be strong. The Poles were lucky too. And though it took awhile, successive Kenyan presidents have since stepped down when rejected by the voters, and constitutional reforms have given the prime minister real power. Ellen Johnson Sirleaf has proved to be an indefatigable champion of democracy for the Liberian people.

The Russians have not been so fortunate. Boris Yeltsin had enormous credibility and authority after the collapse of the Soviet Union. But he did not use it to create a strong presidency within a balanced government. The other institutions— the parliament, the judiciary—were no match for this bull in a china shop. He ruled by decree and even took the army into the streets against them. The presidency was just too strong and unchecked: That was a problem under Yeltsin that became the death knell for freedom when Vladimir Putin inherited the mantle. The executive has to be constrained to limit human beings—those with good intentions and those with bad ones.

Lesson Three: *Wei-ji*

The Chinese characters for "crisis" describe well one of the key lessons in building democracy. It is said that *wei* means "danger" and *ji* means "opportunity." There is both danger and opportunity in a crisis. And young democracies are bound to have plenty of crises; each is a chance to strengthen the institutional infrastructure of the country. But the catch is this— leaders have to be willing to actually use the institutions to solve problems. Colombia's "democratic security" under Álvaro Uribe is a very good example of exactly this. The decades of civil war had effectively turned Colombia into a failed state. Its institutions were compromised—the judiciary, the army; and the police were ineffective and viewed as corrupt and complicit in the violence. The government did not own a monopoly on force—paramilitaries and the FARC could outgun them in large parts of the country. Defeating the insurgency and ending the civil war were accomplished simultaneously by rebuilding those institutions.

In this regard, the rebuilding of the judiciary's credibility was especially important. Citizens have to know that justice is blind and that all will be subject to the rule of law. The Constitutional Court also showed its mettle when it stood up to Uribe, telling him that he could not run for a third term.

Poland's institutions are being tested today in the struggle for control of the courts. The experience of Uribe shows why it is so important to protect an independent judiciary.

A Subset: Electoral Crises

Kenya provides a similar lesson from a different perspective. The contested election of 2007 led to widespread violence and a rejection of the results by large parts of the population. The Kenyans ended up with a power-sharing arrangement largely negotiated by outsiders. But they learned from that experience and improved the institutional infrastructure through constitutional reforms. The next election was also essentially 50-50, but this time the candidates put their faith in the Electoral Commission, the loser accepted the outcome, and the country moved on. There is no guarantee that every contested election will be resolved in this way, but having done it once, Kenyans have a good chance of doing it again.

The fact is that institutions can exist on paper, but they have no power until people come to put faith in them. No one really knows how strong an institution is until it is tested. Passing a crucible test and surviving can lead to a virtuous cycle—as institutions prove themselves, people are likely to use them again and again. That is how they become worth more than the paper they are written on.

Lesson Four: Politics Must Connect to the People

Institutions are intended to minimize the impact of individual whims on a country's course. But as we have seen, there can be a tendency for leaders to engage mostly in personal tugs-of-war. In Ukraine, the politics of personality made it difficult to get anything done, particularly after the Orange Revolution. The state of affairs was dispiriting for the population. People began to see their leaders as all about personal power all of the time.

If citizens lose interest in the politics of the country, the democratic system is compromised. That leads to another lesson: Politics in a democracy must connect to the interests and concerns of the people.

This is especially true for political parties. I met recently with a member of the Georgian parliament and an American who is helping with the elections there. The conversation turned to the problem of political parties that seem to have no real platform for governing—at least not one that addresses the questions on the minds of voters. It immediately reminded me of the problem with liberal political parties in Ukraine and Russia. The platforms rarely speak to the widows in the rust belt cities of the Russian periphery who have lost pensions or the worker whose factory has closed.

The problem is exacerbated by the fact that many liberal parties do not reach outside of the large cities. On the other hand, United Russia (Putin's party) has tentacles in every region. One of the strengths of Islamist parties like Hezbollah in Lebanon has been its outreach to the poor and the rural. Tunisia's success thus far makes the point clearly. The broad base of the labor unions and their appeal to ordinary voters—not unlike Solidarity in Poland—have helped to temper the actions of the Islamists.

If democracy is to work, people need a way to aggregate their interests and present them to those who would govern. And those who would govern have to represent those interests.

Civil society groups do this in part, but they are usually issue-limited—human rights, judicial reform, environmental stewardship, or women's empowerment. A more direct relationship between ideas to address people's daily lives and their politicians' policies needs to emerge. One would think that in the age of smartphones and the Internet this would not be such a difficult task. It has been.

Technology has been a mixed blessing for the spread of democracy. On the one hand, it has helped people to mobilize to bring down the old—in Egypt, Russia, and Ukraine. In Kenya and Colombia, it allowed people to share information about what was going on and to protest when they disagreed. But there are few examples of technology actually strengthening the institutions themselves. Ukraine has experimented with "e-government" in an effort to root out corruption and improve efficiency. India's biometric identification system has similar goals. A number of governments, such as Estonia, use the Internet as a forum for democracy, posting budgets for citizen comment.

These examples notwithstanding, the track record thus far

is not very promising. Technology has been far more successful at tearing down the old than building up the new.

Political parties do need to represent people's interests. But we have seen the dangers of the seemingly irresistible pull of sectarian parties. Many of Kenya's troubles stem from the tribal basis of its parties. And it is a reminder too that even in an ethnically divided country, the balance between devolution and central authority can be a challenge. In Kenya, federalism appears to have reinforced tribalism. In Russia, the regions became too independent under Yeltsin and served to weaken the state. Now Vladimir Putin has reversed course—and federalism is no check on the central government. Decentralization can bring government closer to the people, but in some circumstances it brings its own challenges. Federalism is healthy in most circumstances, but not all. This last point should remind outsiders who want to help to attend to local conditions in institutional design. No one size fits all.

Lesson Five: It All Takes Time

The most important lesson, though, is the need for patience. The messiness, the fits and starts, the imperfections are all a part of the process—they were for the United States, and they will be for every country that sets out on the road to democracy. It took Great Britain 240 years, from the Revolution of 1688 until 1928, to grant universal suffrage. And along the way multiple rebellions and a civil war almost allowed absolutists to triumph.

No country has had an easy path to democracy. It is well to remember again what Madison wrote in the *Federalist Papers*: "I never expect to see a perfect work from imperfect man." And to remember too that no matter how imperfect democracy is, it remains the only system that fully accords with the "non-negotiable demands of human dignity."[2]

Epilogue

THEY WILL LOOK TO AMERICA

Was it worth it?" A student in my American foreign policy class asked the question reluctantly but clearly. He meant the wars in Afghanistan and Iraq, and it is a question for which there is no facile answer. There was so much sacrifice of blood and treasure. We overthrew vicious and dangerous dictators who threatened our security. The world is better off without the regimes of the Taliban and Saddam Hussein. After the security threat was gone, we made a choice to stand for freedom in those countries and in the Middle East more broadly. It has been a struggle and there is as yet no satisfying end in sight.

The trials and tribulations of Iraq, Afghanistan, and Libya have made us impatient with people who want the liberties we enjoy. We have come to associate democratization with violence and instability. Military power is not a good way to create a democratic opening. I have never believed that and never will. But that does not mean that America can step back in promoting democratic change by other means. One of my regrets about Iraq and Afghanistan is that that message has been obscured.

Democratic institutions are the best hope for humankind—including for the Middle East. Stability born of tyranny is a false stability. It is an unequal bargain in which someone oppresses someone else. When people have no way to change their rulers peacefully, revolution may be the only available course. Reform is better, and everything that we can do to encourage and insist upon change is worth doing.

There is both a moral and a practical case for democracy promotion. In the long arc of history, we know that democracies don't fight each other. The "democratic peace" is observable. No one today is sorry that the United States helped to build a democratic Germany and Japan after World War II. Both had been aggressors against their neighbors and there was no guarantee that they would not be again. Neither country had sustained experience with democracy, and it required time for institutions to take root. But we stood alongside them, and now they help to form the foundation for international peace and prosperity.

No one today doubts that the spread of democracy through most of Latin America, Africa, and Asia and the emergence of free countries in Eastern Europe have been good for the world. In 2016, Freedom House ranked 145 out of 195 countries as "free" or "partly free." That is a reason for celebration even if there have been setbacks and reversals along the way.

It is good news that so many countries respect their people and give them a voice in their affairs. The even better news is that they are largely peaceful—Japan doesn't attack its neighbors, preferring to engage in international organizations. Tokyo is one of the world's largest foreign aid donors today. Brazil does not harbor terrorists; Ghana does not employ child soldiers; South Korea does not engage in state-sponsored human trafficking. These democratic states and others believe in and support an international system based on the rule of law.

The United States has a real interest, then, in seeing their numbers grow. Democracy promotion has been successful and is cost-effective. If you ask the general public how much money we spend on foreign assistance, you will get wildly inflated estimates. A recent poll found that the average respondent thought it was about 26 percent of the federal budget.[1] In fact, it is less than 1 percent (or a total of about $35 billion per year). Of that, roughly half goes to improving governance and supporting those fighting for liberty.

Our efforts are buttressed by effective and efficient organizations like the National Endowment for Democracy, created in 1983 by President Ronald Reagan. The NED consists of four centers that provide bipartisan expertise to democracy advocates around the world. The American Center for International Labor Solidarity engages with workers' movements, such as those that played a pivotal role in Poland and Tunisia. The Center for International Private Enterprise works with business communities, which often serve as a counterbalance to governments in autocratic and even democratizing countries. The National Democratic Institute and the International Republican Institute represent our two major political parties in working with citizens around the world to provide training on how to organize parties and run campaigns. And we have a host of additional non-governmental organizations that pitch in to monitor elections and educate human rights advocates, parliamentarians, journalists, and others who defend freedom in their countries. These efforts help to sustain advocates for religious and political freedom in countries still ruled by tyrants.

If democracy is in recession across the world, we need to make every effort to reinvigorate it. I suspect, though, that the dire warnings about its prospects stem in part from dashed expectations that democracy's march would be linear—a straight line toward progress. Instead, there have been ups and downs.

Still, the overall trajectory is worth celebrating. Just a few decades ago, Eastern Europe was trapped behind the Iron Curtain, and freedom seemed a distant prospect. A dominant form of government in Latin America was the military junta. There were few multiparty systems in sub-Saharan Africa. And virtually no one—not scholars nor the leaders and people of the region—talked about democracy in the Middle East.

So while Russia, Turkey, and Egypt discourage us, Chile, Liberia, and Tunisia should inspire us. And we can acknowledge that for every jailed dissident in China or Iran, there is someone else willing to speak out, no matter the cost.

Giving voice to the voiceless is a moral cause for a country—America—that is based on an idea: that human freedom is the source of human dignity and progress. That cannot be true for *us* and not for *them*.

"America, Be What You Claim to Be"

In the late 1940s, Judge J. Waties Waring wrote a stinging dissent in a voting rights case in South Carolina. He was troubled by the implications for justice at home, but also for America's moral standing in the world. "When this country is taking the lead in maintaining the democratic process and attempting to show the world that American government and the American way of life is the fairest and best that has yet been suggested, it is time for us to take stock of our internal affairs," he said.

Today, taking stock of our internal affairs reveals some ugly truths. Americans are experiencing a kind of crisis of confidence about our own democracy—who we are and what we value.

"We the people" is not an exclusive concept. It is not a religious, a national, or an ethnic designation. It is, in reality, based on an idea: equality under the law and equality of opportunity. Americans and their ancestors have come from every corner of the globe and enriched their new country with their energy and determination. And Americans do not see themselves as prisoners of the class into which they were born. They are united by a creed—a belief. I have often summed it up in this way: It does not matter where you came from; it matters where you are going.

Americans have remarkable institutions to help them achieve that dream. The history of the United States is in some sense a story of a long democratic transition to make "We the people" as inclusive as possible. Citizens have petitioned the government and appealed to the Constitution to be included—female, black, gay... It is a remarkable story of democratic stability born of an openness to change.

But today that essential role of institutions—to channel the need for change—is under stress. There is declining faith in our political institutions.[2] Some see them as unjust. Others see them as rigged. For others still, they are just irrelevant. And governance challenges just keep piling up—from stalled social mobility, to the tragic state of education for the poor, particularly minority kids, to the worst tensions in race relations in several decades. Troubling trends and questions hang over the future of American democracy.

Yet, as America struggles to be what it says it is, we have an important story to tell—one not of perfection but of the constant need for renewal. I have been reminded of that truth many times in my life.

As a graduate student in Moscow in 1979, I was approached on the street by a middle-aged woman. "Where are you from?" she asked.

"I am American," I said.

"But black people have internal passports and can't leave America," she said with absolute certainty.

"No," I countered, "that would be South Africa."

The woman sniffed, obviously sure that she was right and I was probably African, not American. I wanted to defend my country and the progress we had made, but she wouldn't have gotten the point. I just let it go.

Years later, sitting in our first meeting with Prime Minister Tony Blair, I was heartened by something he said: "I look at the two of you and I ask whether this could happen in Great Britain. And I say, not just yet." He was referring to the African American secretary of state, Colin Powell, and the African American national security adviser, Condi Rice, sitting on either side of the president of the United States.

Blair was not the only one to notice. President Lula da Silva of Brazil talked to me about America's journey. "I wanted to be sure to have Afro-Brazilians in my cabinet," he said. Upon taking office, he named four to his cabinet, as well as the first to the Supreme Court. When Lula appointed Edson Santos as his minister for promoting racial equality in 2008, he asked me to meet with him and to sign an accord on racial harmony. These were times when America's own democratic journey sent a positive message.

And then there was that day standing on the stage of the elegant, rose- and cream-colored Franklin Room of the Department of State. It was January 28, 2005. My uncle Alto—the one whom I had peppered with questions about the importance of the vote in Alabama—stood next to me, as did my aunts Mattie and Gee. I could feel the presence of my parents, Angelena and John—long gone to the Lord, but it seemed hovering right beside me. My other ancestors were there too—those who had lived as not quite free men and women in the Deep South and those who had died as slaves.

And there was Ben Franklin looking down on us from the magnificent portrait painted by David Martin in 1767. *What would old Ben think of this?* I thought silently as President Bush made remarks. Then Ruth Bader Ginsburg—a Jewish woman and Supreme Court justice—asked me to raise my hand. "I do solemnly swear to protect and defend the Constitution of the United States against all enemies foreign and domestic...So help me God."

The United States has been a north star for those seeking liberty not because it is perfect, but because it was born imperfect and is still struggling with imperfection. That has always been the best argument for America's example—and America's engagement. We are living proof that the work of democracy is never done. For those who are just starting—stumbling, and starting again—that is reassuring and inspiring. And it is a reason to be a voice for them as they struggle in their freedom—just as we do—to chart a better future.

2016

Democracy's story is ever evolving. There are always new challenges, new responses, and new possibilities—good and bad. So it can be said of 2016 and the rise of populism, nativism, and a tinge of isolationism. A revolt against political and economic elites, their institutions, and their globalizing and sometimes moralizing views has upended the status quo and left all to wonder, *What comes next?*

It is no surprise that this earthquake is shaking young democracies like Poland. But it is stunning that it has jolted the most mature of them—the United Kingdom, the United States, and much of Europe. In 2016, voters in the UK narrowly rejected continued participation in the European Union. Proponents of "Brexit" railed against economic red tape imposed by unelected EU bureaucrats and called for regaining control over their country's borders. Brussels, they believed, had become disconnected from their aspirations and their fears.

In the United States, a new president was elected with absolutely no experience in government of any kind—the first in the country's history. He has made clear what he thinks of America's political elites whatever their ideological stripe. They have ceased, he believes, to represent the American people—their aspirations and their fears.

Similar concerns have spread throughout the European bloc—including to France and Germany—where the far left and the far right seem to have made a common cause of battling the establishment.

Some write darkly that these trends constitute a threat to democracy—if not the end of it as we know it.[1] That seems alarmist and premature. Indeed, democracy is built for disruption with its institutions, its checks and balances, and its shock absorber—the ability of people to change their circumstances peacefully. People are exercising that right—at the ballot box, in the courts, and some in the streets.

More troubling, though, is whether the turn to nationalism and nativism will threaten the global order—the balance of power that favors freedom. Here we might ask whether history is repeating itself. Or, as Mark Twain said, whether it is at least about to rhyme.

The statesmen who inherited the broken postwar world of 1945 built a system that trusted free markets and free trade to create an international economy that would grow. They were chastened by the memory of the 1930s when beggar-thy-neighbor trading policies, protectionism, and conflict over resources led to the Great Depression and World War II. This time, they insisted that the international economy would not be a zero-sum game. Countries would find comparative advantage, trade freely, and all would benefit. For the most part, they succeeded, restoring the economies of both the victors and the vanquished—and spreading prosperity to hundreds of millions of people across the globe.

They believed too that democratic governments in Germany and Japan would never make war again. The western part of Germany was encased in the European Union so that it could be powerful but not dangerous. There it waited for the time when the collapse of communism allowed the unification of all its territory as a stable democracy. Japan too would become a constitutional monarchy—prosperous and free and no threat to its neighbors. And free markets and free peoples would all be protected by American military power. This time, America would not withdraw and leave the world to its own devices. The United States would make a remarkable pledge to Europe: "An attack upon one is an attack upon all." In commitments to Japan and eventually South Korea, the United States would become Asia's shield against aggression.

Democracy has gained adherents in the context of this global order—though admittedly in fits and starts. Can it continue to do so if America and others withdraw from the responsibilities of the system they created? What will happen to those who still seek liberty in a world told to go its own way? What becomes of those still living in tyranny if we cease to tell others that democracy is a superior form of government and that its tenets are universal?

We cannot possibly know the answer to those questions, but we do know that the Four Horseman of the Apocalypse—

populism, nativism, protectionism, and isolationism—served neither democracy nor peace very well the last time around.

We can take solace in the fact that democratic institutions are stronger this time. Germany and Japan do not cast a shadow of aggression—they are stabilizing forces for good. But the same cannot be said about Russia and perhaps China—authoritarian states that seem determined to disrupt the global order—if less violently than those who came before.

The victory for democracy is that those who longed for change have done so through it, not around it. But if the lessons of 2016 are to be learned, both insurgents and those who wish to defend the global order will be required to step back and accept some very hard truths.

The standard-bearers for those who voted to shake up the system need to find the humility to know and accept democracy's paradox: Its genius is in its openness to change, but its stability comes through institutions that embody constraint and reject absolute power. They will find that it is easier to tear down democratic institutions than to build them and work through them. And they must now deliver real prosperity for those who trusted them—not just assign blame to foreigners and immigrants who "take their jobs."

On the other hand, those who would defend the status quo—the postwar global order—need to admit that there are those who have not shared in its prosperity and are troubled by its rejection of more traditional values. In this regard, the trend toward dividing people into ever-smaller groups, each with its own particular grievance and narrative, comes at the expense of the unifying identity that all democracies need. This is especially true in the

United States, where "we the people" has no ethnic, national, or religious basis. We reinforce those divisions at our peril.

Global leaders also need to accept that there is a growing gap between those who are comfortable breaking down borders and barriers between peoples—and those who find it dizzying and even threatening.

In my classes at the Graduate School of Business at Stanford, I often encounter a student with roughly the following profile: He was born in—let's say—Brazil; then went to school in—let's say—London. This hypothetical student's first job was in—shall we say—Shanghai. And after graduate school—in Palo Alto—my student will go to work in Dubai.

But many people never live very far from where they were born. It is not surprising that their experiences, aspirations, and fears are not the same. Increasingly, neither are their possibilities for a productive life.

America's Founding Fathers understood that liberty was the necessary condition for citizens to find fulfillment. It is not, however, sufficient. Human beings have to have the opportunity to develop their potential through education. A country that fails to provide all its people with equal access to education will most assuredly be a place of hardened inequality. In that regard, no foreign power can do more harm to us than we can do to ourselves.

The Founders' prescription can be achieved—the right to life, liberty, *and* the pursuit of happiness. But that achievement involves taking a hard look at the realities facing so many Americans and making a commitment to address their fate. With that would come the confidence, as a nation, to insist that we are better off when we work to make this true not just for us—but for all humankind.

Acknowledgments

The seeds for this project, which were planted in my youth, came from my experiences growing up in Birmingham, Alabama, and the examples set by my forebears. To a remarkable degree, my parents and relatives—and even my ancestors before them—continued to believe in the Constitution despite the long odds stacked against them. Their faith in the promise of democratic institutions shaped my own views, which are reflected in these pages, and in my life's work. My thanks, first and foremost, go to them.

I could not have completed this book without the help and support of the Hoover Institution and Stanford University. My special thanks go to Roberta and Steven Denning, whose professorship I hold at the Stanford Graduate School of Business; Hoover director Tom Gilligan and his longtime predecessor, John Raisian; and my dear friends and supporters Tom and Barbara Stephenson, whose chair I hold at Hoover. There is no better place to teach and do research than Stanford University.

Many people at Stanford and elsewhere—friends, experts, and former colleagues—took time out of their busy schedules to assist me with this book. I owe a significant debt of gratitude to Nancy Biffar, Niall Ferguson, Mary Meeker, and Janine

Zacharia, who were generous enough to review the entire manuscript. Their feedback was tremendously helpful.

Others agreed to provide insights on different sections or chapters, including Carolina Barco, Jendayi Frazer, Steve Hadley, Steve Krasner, Anja Manuel, and David Welch, all of whom participated in the extraordinary events described in this book. Other participants in these events helped by answering questions or sitting for interviews, including Bob Gates, Alberto Gonzales, Jim Jeffrey, Zalmay Khalilizad, David Kramer, Barry Lowenkron, Dina Powell, Connie Rice, Jack Straw, Shirin Tahir-Kheli, and former Colombian president Álvaro Uribe. Several colleagues at Stanford were kind enough to read parts of the manuscript or answer questions as well, including Randy Bean, Chip Blacker, Kate Casey, Larry Diamond, Lazar Fleishman, Francis Fukuyama, Ayaan Hirsi Ali, David Holloway, David Kennedy, Mike McFaul, Abbas Milani, Sarah Shirazyan, and Amy Zegart. I greatly admire all of you and appreciate your willingness to lend a hand.

While writing this book I have relied on the support of many talented and dedicated people. Charles Nicas, my research director at Stanford, has been my partner in this process at every step of the way. In recent years we have watched as the story of democracy has continued to unfold, from the aftermath of the Arab uprisings, to Russia's aggression against Ukraine, to the U.S. presidential election of 2016. Throughout these events, and at every stage of the writing process, I have relied on Charles to keep me well updated and informed. He has been a sounding board for me and his advice and counsel has been immeasurably important.

One of the best parts of being at Stanford is working alongside some of the best students, and we would have been hard pressed to put together a better group than our research team for this book. Many of our research assistants were students in my classes; others started as interns in my office. All of them worked diligently to produce high-quality research while juggling course work and extracurricular activities, including in some cases Division I athletics. Our full-time research assistants, who worked with us in the summer months, included Patrick Cirenza, Jack Hennessy, Robert Kupstas, Matthew Levy, Geo Saba, Zach Sorenson, Elliot Stoller, and Aditya Todi. Our part-time research assistants, who worked with us during the school year, included Brendan Austin, Joseph Begovich, Matthew Colford, Conner Crane, Natalie Davies, Matthew Decker, Deirdre Hegarty, Jessica Renier, Katie Rovelstad, Kona Shen, Wayne Taylor, Molly Welch, and Meredith Wheeler.

I am very fortunate to have the support of a devoted staff, who have assisted me in writing this book in a variety of ways, not least of which was finding time on my schedule for me to write. Special thanks go to my extraordinary chief of staff, Georgia Godfrey, who has provided insight, advice, and friendship throughout this process. I want to thank too the steadfast members of my wonderful team—my event director, Shannon York (and her predecessor Elizabeth Sadler); and my office manager, Jules Thompson (and her predecessor Caroline Beswick), who always found ways to juggle my many commitments so that I could prioritize the writing of this book. I am grateful too for my longtime assistant Marilyn Stanley—for her tireless work on my behalf. Wayne Kabak of WSK Management, always a source of sage advice and an insightful reader, helped immensely in the production of this book and in finding the perfect home for it.

And last but not least, there are my partners at Twelve, who have been instrumental in bringing this book to fruition. Sean Desmond, my exceptional editor, helped me think through many thorny issues while trying to speak to multiple audiences. Thanks, Sean, for making this a better book than I ever could have produced without you. He and others at Twelve, including Carolyn Kurek and Rachel Kambury, have worked hard to strengthen this book in both substance and form.

To all of you—many thanks for your guidance, friendship, and patience.

Notes

Introduction: Is Democracy in Retreat?

1. Larry Diamond, "Facing Up to the Democratic Recession," *Journal of Democracy* 26, no. 1 (January 2015): 141–155.

2. A long line of distinguished scholars has emphasized the role of institutions in political and economic development, even as they have differed on some of the details of how those processes work. This book's conception of democracy—and various types of non-democratic regimes, as detailed later in the introduction—builds off this foundation. By using Douglass North's definition of institutions as "rules of the game" that "structure incentives," the book acknowledges the role of institutions as mechanisms for bargaining. It also recognizes their relation to state capacity, echoing the work of Samuel Huntington and Francis Fukuyama, who have focused on how institutions help bring order—without which political or economic development is not possible. The book's typology also places considerable weight on the institutional space afforded to various actors and the degree to which they are able to contest political issues. In that sense it is similar to the work of Douglass North, John Joseph Wallis, and Barry R. Weingast, who contrasted "open access" and "limited access" societies; and Daron Acemoglu and James A. Robinson, who similarly wrote of "inclusive" and "extractive" institutions. These concepts generally map onto the meanings of "democracy" and "non-democracy" as used in this book.

3. Douglass C. North, *Institutions, Institutional Change and Economic Performance* (Cambridge: Cambridge University Press, 1990), 3.

4. This phrase was popularized by Juan J. Linz and Alfred Stepan in "Toward Consolidated Democracies," *Journal of Democracy* 7, no. 2

(April 1996): 12–33. They credit Giuseppe di Palma with coining the phrase.

Chapter 1: The American Experience

1. For more on the Constitutional Convention of 1787, see Catherine Drinker Bowen, *Miracle at Philadelphia: The Story of the Constitutional Convention, May to September 1787* (Boston: Little, Brown, 1966); Richard Beeman, *Plain, Honest Men: The Making of the American Constitution* (New York: Random House, 2010); David O. Stewart, *The Summer of 1787: The Men Who Invented the Constitution* (New York: Simon & Schuster, 2007); Jack N. Rakove, *Original Meanings: Politics and Ideas in the Making of the Constitution* (New York: Alfred A. Knopf, 1996); Christopher Collier, *Decision in Philadelphia: The Constitutional Convention of 1787* (New York: Ballantine, 1986). For a broader but very rich account of the founding period and the republic's first years, see Joseph J. Ellis's *Founding Brothers: The Revolutionary Generation* (New York: Alfred A. Knopf, 2000).

2. The "Fourth Estate" usually refers to an entity outside the traditional power structure of a society—in this case, a free press. The original "three estates" of the ancien régime in prerevolutionary France were the nobility, clergy, and commoners. According to Thomas Carlyle, Edmund Burke coined the term when observing a parliamentary debate in 1787. Wrote Carlyle, "Burke said there were Three Estates in Parliament; but, in the Reporters' Gallery yonder, there sat a Fourth Estate more important far than they all."

3. David M. Kennedy, "The American Presidency: A Brief History," lecture at Stanford University, fall 2016.

4. The Posse Comitatus Act of 1878 was passed to prevent federal troops from ever again serving a domestic law enforcement purpose. The one exception stemmed from the Insurrection Act of 1807, which allowed the president to deploy federal troops within the United States in the event of an "insurrection, or obstruction to the laws." After Hurricane Katrina, the Insurrection Act was amended in 2006 to allow the president to deploy federal troops to restore order in the wake of a natural disaster, terrorist attack, or other public emergency. That amendment would have hastened the federal response to Hurricane Katrina had it been in place when the storm struck, but it also raised complaints from governors and states' rights activists, and it was repealed in 2008.

5. Samuel E. Finer raised this question in his classic on civil-military relations, *The Man on Horseback: The Role of the Military in Politics* (London: Pall Mall, 1962), 5. As he put it, "Instead of asking why the military engage in politics, we ought surely ask why they ever do otherwise. For at first sight the political advantages of the military *vis-à-vis* other and civilian groupings are overwhelming. The military possess vastly superior organization. And they possess *arms*" (italics in original).

6. Between 1786 and 1787, former Continental army captain Daniel Shays led a group of four thousand rebels in a series of uprisings over high tax rates, including an attempt to capture a U.S. armory. Although the rebellion was eventually quelled, it spurred economic reforms and, more important, shaped debates about the scope of the new U.S. government by highlighting the weakness of a limited national government like the one put in place by the Articles of Confederation.

7. One of Madison's mentors at Princeton, Dr. John Witherspoon, once argued that religion benefits from the spread of political liberty: "Knowledge of God and his truths have from the beginning...been confined to those parts of the earth where some degree of liberty and political justice were to be seen....Knowledge of divine truth...has been spread by liberty," he said. (Garrett Ward Sheldon, *The Political Philosophy of James Madison* [Baltimore: Johns Hopkins University Press, 2001], 28, which cites Jeffery Hays Morrison, "John Witherspoon and 'The Public Interest of Religion,'" *Journal of Church and State* 41 [Summer 1999]: 597.)

8. U.S. Bureau of Economic Analysis, "Value Added by Industry as a Percentage of Gross Domestic Product," 2015, http://www.bea.gov/iTable/ iTableHtml.cfm?reqid=51&step=51&isuri=1&5114=a&5102=5. This same fact can be demonstrated by comparing government spending as a percentage of GDP. According to 2015 data from the World Bank, government spending as a percentage of GDP in the United States (14.4 percent) was considerably lower than in a variety of other countries, including France (23.9); Canada (21.2); Japan (20.4); Brazil (20.2); and the United Kingdom (19.4). See: World Bank, "General Government Final Consumption Expenditure (% of GDP)," 2016, http://data.worldbank.org/indicator/ NE.CON.GOVT.ZS.

9. Olivier Zunz, *Philanthropy in America: A History* (Princeton, NJ: Princeton University Press, 2012), 8.

10. Ken Stern, "Why the Rich Don't Give to Charity," *Atlantic*, April 2013.

11. Arthur C. Brooks, "A Nation of Givers," *American*, American Enterprise Institute, March/April 2008, https://www.aei.org/publication/a-nation -of-givers/.

12. Alexis de Tocqueville, *Democracy in America*, vol. 1, ch. 14.

13. The Alien and Sedition Acts were actually four pieces of legislation, and only one of them, the Sedition Act, targeted speech. The act prohibited "writing, printing, uttering or publishing any false, scandalous and malicious writing or writings against the government." The law had a built-in sunset provision and was allowed to expire in 1801. The other three acts were related to the treatment and naturalization of non-American citizens within the United States.

14. As my colleague Francis Fukuyama notes, despite the progress under Teddy Roosevelt, "the end of the patronage system at a federal level did not arrive until the middle of the twentieth century." *Political Order and Political Decay: From the Industrial Revolution to the Globalization of Democracy* (New York: Macmillan, 2014), 160.

15. *Dred Scott v. John F. A. Sandford* (1857), opinion of Chief Justice Taney, Supreme Court of the United States, available at http://memory.loc.gov/ cgi-bin/query/r?ammem/llst:@field(DOCID+@lit(llst022div3))).

16. Frederick Douglass, "The Dred Scott Decision," speech before the American Anti-Slavery Society, May 14, 1857, available at https://www.lib .rochester.edu/index.cfm?PAGE=4399.

17. The KKK was refounded in the early twentieth century and had a strong following in the Midwest.

18. Today, there are more than a hundred historically black colleges operating across the country, granting undergraduate and graduate degrees to thousands of students of all races.

19. One judge from Alabama exemplifies the notion of judicial independence. Judge Frank M. Johnson, appointed to the federal judiciary by President Eisenhower in 1955, played a central role in helping to overturn Jim Crow–era laws in Alabama, even as it came at a high cost to himself in the form of harassment and ostracism from his segregationist neighbors. On the bench, he interpreted the law as he saw it, repeatedly ruling in favor of equal rights by applying the same principles upheld by the Supreme Court in *Brown v. Board of Education*, not just to schools, but to all areas of public life.

20. For further explanation of Native American history, consider the following books: Francis Paul Prucha, *The Great Father: The United States Gov-*

ernment and the American Indians (Lincoln: University of Nebraska Press, 1986); Dee Brown, *Bury My Heart at Wounded Knee: An Indian History of the American West* (New York: Picador, 2007; originally published in 1970); and Stephen Pevar, *The Rights of Indians and Tribes* (New York: Oxford University Press, 2012; originally published in 1983).

21. There were actually two matters before the Court, one involving undergraduate admissions at the University of Michigan (which were ultimately deemed unconstitutional), and one involving admissions to the University of Michigan Law School (which were not).

Chapter 2: Russia and the Weight of History

1. Josef Stalin, *On the Opposition, 1921–1927* (Peking: Foreign Language Press, 1974).

2. For example, the Strategic Defense Initiative (SDI) was a satellite-based missile defense system designed to protect America from nuclear attack. While SDI never became fully operational, its real impact was on the Soviets' thinking. It raised the stakes in the arms race and convinced many in the Soviet military that maintaining technological parity with the United States was either impossible or not worth the cost. For more on these issues, see two articles from earlier in my career: "The Party, the Military, and Decision Authority in the Soviet Union," *World Politics* 40, no. 1 (October 1987): 55–81; and "The Military-Technical Revolution and the General Staff in the Soviet Union," in Herbert Goodman, *Science and Technology in the Soviet Union* (Stanford Conference Report on Soviet Technology, 1984).

3. John Arch Getty, *Origins of the Great Purges: The Soviet Communist Party Reconsidered, 1933–1938* (Cambridge: Cambridge University Press, 1985), 8.

4. First performed in front of Tsar Nicholas I in 1836, this five-act satirical comedy takes place in a provincial town outside Saint Petersburg. A government copying clerk named Ivan Khlestakov is mistaken by the town officials for the anxiously anticipated inspector general. Upon realizing their mistake, Khlestakov accepts bribes from the officials in exchange for promising to leave the town's corruption unreported. Despite its harsh satire of the Russian civil service, the play was received well by Tsar Nicholas I, who insisted that it be produced in the Imperial Theater. The story was popularized in modern times by a film starring Danny Kaye.

5. Michael McFaul, *Russia's Unfinished Revolution: Political Change from Gorbachev to Putin* (Ithaca, NY: Cornell University Press, 2001), 65.

6. Ibid.

7. Steven Rosefielde, *Russia in the 21st Century: The Prodigal Superpower* (Cambridge: Cambridge University Press, 2005), 41.

8. "Four Power Rights and Responsibilities" refers to the post–World War II agreement between the United States, the United Kingdom, France, and the Soviet Union on the status of East and West Germany and the divided city of Berlin.

9. Michael McFaul, borrowing from the language of the French Revolution, has helpfully spoken of three Russian "republics" during this period, of which the Gorbachev reforms were the first, connecting analytically the changes in reforms of the final years of the Soviet Union to the early years of Russia's independence. In reality, that connection was broken—severed by the chaotic events surrounding the birth of a new Russia.

10. Branko Milanovic, "Income, Inequality, and Poverty During the Transition from Planned to Market Economy" (World Bank, February 1998), 12.

11. Ibid., 9.

12. Ibid., 68.

13. Matthew Johnston, "The Russian Economy Since the Collapse of the Soviet Union," Investopedia, January 21, 2016, http://www.investopedia.com/articles/investing/012116/russian-economy-collapse-soviet-union.asp.

14. These figures represent the numbers of deaths by assault. World Health Organization Mortality Database, http://www.who.int/healthinfo/mortality_data/en/.

15. These federal interventions, which included removing governors and disbanding legislatures, could be initiated two ways. The president could act in concert with the Duma and the courts, or he could act on his own if he had the support of the general prosecutor's office.

16. For those unfamiliar with these events, Putin's Russia has a history of supporting separatist groups in neighboring countries, particularly former members of the Soviet Union. In Georgia, to Russia's south, Russian support for the breakaway regions of Abkhazia and South Ossetia led to conflict in August 2008. Georgian officials played a role in provoking the violence, but the small country was clearly outmatched in the intense fighting that followed. A peace deal formally ended the conflict

after several days, but diplomatic relations between Georgia and Russia were severed, tensions remain high, and the Georgian government seems further away from ever reclaiming its breakaway regions. A similar story has unfolded in Ukraine. In February 2014, antigovernment protests forced the pro-Russian president to flee, and Russia responded by authorizing a stealth invasion of Ukraine's Crimean Peninsula. It formally annexed Crimea shortly thereafter, in what is perhaps the greatest affront to the law-based international order in Europe since World War II. Russian-backed separatists have since expanded the conflict to several provinces of eastern Ukraine, which remain deadlocked and in turmoil, with no solution in sight.

Chapter 3: *Martial Law and the Origins of Polish Democracy*

1. "Zycie Warszawy Scores Solidarity Declarations," Zycie Warszawy, December 2, 1981, Foreign Broadcast Information Service, Daily Report, Eastern Europe, FBIS-EEU-81-235, December 8, 1981, p. G10, infoweb .newsbank.com/iw-search/we/HistArchive/?p_product=FBISX&p _theme=fbis&p_nbid=U68N52XQMTQ4NTE5ODIwOC4zMTk xNTc6MToxNDoxNzEuNjYuMjA4LjEzNA&p_action=doc&p_doc ref=v2:11C33B0D5F860D98@FBISX-1256BBA5C44C47E0@ 2444947-1256BBAF0A60D088-1256BBAF2A5EF838.

2. There were several other parties as well—indeed, there were twenty-nine in 1991. Some catered to specific industries (such as the newly re-formed Polish Peasant Party); others were regionally targeted (such as the Movement for Silesian Autonomy); while others focused on specific issues (such as the Women Alliance Against Hardship). The political field consolidated in the following years, and in 2011 only five parties made it into parliament.

3. Such was the case with Croatia in 2005, when its accession talks were postponed over concerns about Croatian authorities' willingness to pursue fugitives accused of war crimes. The Croats had to take concrete steps to put those concerns to rest, and by the end of the year they had apprehended the top fugitive. But even so, when the talks finally began, Croatia still had other issues to address, ranging from judicial reforms to anti-corruption measures, before it was to be admitted as a member.

4. Democratic peace theory holds that democratic states do not go to war with other democratic states. The concept was first formulated by Immanuel Kant, who argued in a 1795 essay that "perpetual peace" could

be achieved once every state had a republican constitution, because "if the consent of the citizens is required in order to decide that war should be declared...they would be very cautious in commencing such a poor game, decreeing for themselves all the calamities of war." By the second half of the twentieth century, democracy had taken hold in enough countries to test Kant's theory, which became the subject of substantial academic research. Of all the theories in international relations, few if any have more empirical support. For more, see Michael Brown, Sean Lynn-Jones, and Steven Miller, *Debating the Democratic Peace* (Cambridge: MIT Press, 1996).

5. Anna Grzymala-Busse, "Why Would Poland Make Its Already Strict Abortion Law Draconian?," *Washington Post*, April 18, 2016, https://www.washingtonpost.com/news/monkey-cage/wp/2016/04/18/why-would-poland-make-its-already-strict-abortion-law-draconian. Additionally, see her book *Nations Under God: How Churches Use Moral Authority to Influence Policy* (Princeton, NJ: Princeton University Press, 2015).

Chapter 4: Ukraine: "A Made-Up Country"?

1. As quoted in Svetlana Alexievich, *Voices from Chernobyl: The Oral History of a Nuclear Disaster*, trans. Keith Gessen (New York: Picador, 2006), 32.

2. Paul R. Magocsi, *A History of Ukraine: The Land and Its Peoples* (Toronto: University of Toronto Press, 2010), 722.

3. Organization for Security and Cooperation in Europe, "Widespread Campaign Irregularities Observed in Ukrainian Presidential Election," November 1, 2004, www.osce.org/odihr/elections/56894.

Chapter 5: Kenya: "Save Our Beloved Country"

1. Charles Hornsby, *Kenya: A History Since Independence* (London: I. B. Tauris, 2012), 30.

2. Ibid., 47–48.

3. Ibid., 60.

4. This was the topic of Jendayi's doctoral dissertation. She argued that the Kenyan police and other non-military armed forces created prior to independence (1952–60) formed the basis of a counterweight to the military and granted civilian leaders experience in security affairs that promoted stable civil-military relations and civilian control over the military after independence in 1963. See Jendayi Elizabeth Frazer, "Sustaining Civilian

Control: Armed Counterweights in Regime Stability in Africa" (PhD diss., Stanford University, March 1994).

5. Hornsby, *History Since Independence*, 96.

6. "Kenya: GDP Per Capita (Current US$)" (World Bank, 2016), http://data.worldbank.org/indicator/NY.GDP.PCAP.CD?locations=KE &view=chart.

7. The "Washington consensus" refers to a set of ten free-market economic policy reforms widely advocated by Washington-based agencies (such as the International Monetary Fund, the World Bank, and the U.S. Treasury Department) in promoting economic expansion and trade liberalization in developing nations. The original tenets were outlined in the late 1980s and attempted to describe changing global norms for development policy.

8. Jane Perlez, "U.S. Forgives Portion of Kenya's Loan Debt," *New York Times*, January 10, 1990, www.nytimes.com/1990/01/10/business/us-for gives-portion-of-kenya-s-loan-debt.html.

9. Hornsby, *History Since Independence*, 472.

10. "Five More Reported Killed in Kenya Unrest," Associated Press, July 10, 1990, www.nytimes.com/1990/07/10/world/5-more-reported-killed-in-kenya -unrest.html.

11. Jane Perlez, "Rising Political Discontent in Kenya Is Tarnishing Its Progressive Image," *New York Times*, July 29, 1990, www.nytimes.com/1990/ 07/29/world/rising-political-discontent-in-kenya-is-tarnishing-its-pro gressive-image.html?pagewanted=all.

12. Hornsby, *History Since Independence*, 481.

13. Jane Perlez, "Stung by Protest Over Crackdown, Kenya Calls U.S. Envoy a Racist," *New York Times*, November 19, 1991, www.nytimes.com/ 1991/11/19/world/stung-by-protest-over-crackdown-kenya-calls-us -envoy-a-racist.html.

14. Hornsby, *History Since Independence*, 486–87.

15. Jane Perlez, "Kenya, a Land That Thrived, Is Now Caught Up in Fear of Ethnic Civil War," *New York Times*, May 3, 1992, http://www.nytimes .com/1992/05/03/world/kenya-a-land-that-thrived-is-now-caught -up-in-fear-of-ethnic-civil-war.html.

16. James C. McKinley Jr., "Sworn for 5th Term, Kenya's President Vows to Fight Corruption and Poverty," *New York Times*, January 7, 1998, www.ny

times.com/1998/01/06/world/sworn-for-5th-term-kenya-s-president -vows-to-fight-corruption-and-poverty.html.

17. Marc Lacey, "Kenya Joyful as Moi Yields Power to New Leader," *New York Times*, December 31, 2002, www.nytimes.com/2002/12/31/world/ kenya-joyful-as-moi-yields-power-to-new-leader.html.

18. Marc Lacey, "Kenya's Judiciary Thrown into Disarray by Inquiry," *New York Times*, October 23, 2003, www.nytimes.com/2003/10/23/interna tional/africa/kenyas-judiciary-thrown-into-disarray-by-inquiry.html.

19. Marc Lacey, "Debate on Kenya's Future: Serious Talk and Fruit Tossing," *New York Times*, October 16, 2005, http://www.nytimes.com/2005/10/ 16/world/africa/debate-on-kenyas-future-serious-talk-and-fruit-tossing .html.

20. Marc Lacey, "Debate on Kenya's Future: Serious Talk and Fruit Tossing," *New York Times*, October 16, 2005, www.nytimes.com/2005/10/16/ world/africa/debate-on-kenyas-future-serious-talk-and-fruit-tossing.html.

21. Marc Lacey, "Kenya Government Opponents Reject Protest Ban," *New York Times*, November 29, 2005, www.nytimes.com/2005/11/29/world/ africa/kenya-government-opponents-reject-protest-ban.html.

22. Jeffrey Gettleman, "Turmoil Grows in Kenya, with More Than 100 Dead," *New York Times*, December 31, 2007, http://www.nytimes.com/2007/ 12/31/world/africa/31cnd-kenya.html.

23. Jeffrey Gettleman, "Kenya Crisis Worsens as Opposition Cools to Talk," *New York Times*, January 9, 2008, www.nytimes.com/2008/01/09/world/ africa/09kenya.html.

24. "Kenyan Leaders in Call for Peace," BBC News, April 24, 2008, news.bbc .co.uk/2/hi/africa/7364273.stm.

25. Jeffrey Gettleman, "Kenyan Court Upholds Election of Candidate Facing Charges in The Hague," *New York Times*, March 30, 2013, www.nytimes .com/2013/03/31/world/africa/in-tense-kenya-court-upholds-election -results.html.

26. "Kenya: President Kenyatta's Inauguration Speech," April 9, 2013, allafrica .com/stories/201304091200.html.

Chapter 6: Colombia: The Era of Democratic Security

1. Rojas's flight was the result of strong civilian opposition and intricate and difficult negotiation between the leaders of the Liberal Party, Alberto Lleras Camargo, and the Conservative leader, Laureano Gómez, who

worked out the Agreement of Benidorm, which was signed on July 24, 1956, and was followed in March 1957 by the Declaration of Sitges. It defined the rules of the Frente Nacional ("National Front"), which sought to outline a structure that would allow the country to be ruled peacefully again. It was agreed that the parties would take alternate periods in the presidency during four terms: first Liberal, then Conservative, then Liberal, and then Conservative (although this arrangement ultimately continued longer). Half of the cabinet had to be Liberal and half Conservative. Half of the governors had to be Liberal and half Conservative. The parties worked to oust Rojas and set up a temporary junta while elections took place. The junta respected the terms.

2. Declaration of Sitges, July 20, 1957, http://college.cengage.com/history/world/keen/latin_america/8e/assets/students/sources/pdfs/119declaration_sitges.pdf.

3. Natalia Springer, "Colombia: Internal Displacement—Policies and Problems," United Nations High Commissioner for Refugees, Status Determination and Protection Information Section, June 2006, 1, www.refworld.org/pdfid/44bf463a4.pdf.

4. Juan Forero, "Administration Shifts Focus on Colombia Aid," *New York Times*, February 6, 2002, http://www.nytimes.com/2002/02/06/world/administration-shifts-focus-on-colombia-aid.html.

5. "Reaction of Sen. Patrick Leahy to the White House Budget for Fiscal Year 2003 (Including Budget Highlights)," press release, Office of Senator Patrick Leahy, February 4, 2002, http://lobby.la.psu.edu/_107th/123_Farm_Bill/Congressional_Statements/Senate/S_Leahy_020402.htm.

6. Harvey F. Kline, *Historical Dictionary of Colombia* (Lanham, MD: Scarecrow Press, 2012), 515.

7. Álvaro Uribe, Interview with Charles Nicas, May 23, 2016.

8. All the figures in this paragraph come from the World Bank and are measured in 2013 dollars.

9. Claudia Palacios, "Colombians Debate Third Term for President," CNN, December 4, 2008, http://www.cnn.com/2008/WORLD/americas/12/04/colombia.president.

10. Andre Viollaz, "UN to Monitor End of Colombia-FARC Conflict," *Agence France-Presse*, January 26, 2016, https://www.yahoo.com/news/un-monitor-end-colombia-rebel-conflict-resolution-214246221.html?ref=gs.

Chapter 7: The Middle East: Can Democracy Exist in a Cauldron?

1. "Lebanon," *CIA World Factbook*, https://www.cia.gov/library/publications/the-world-factbook/geos/le.html.

2. This data point comes from the 2016 edition of an annual survey conducted by Burson-Marsteller. For more, see the Arab Youth Survey 2016, www.arabyouthsurvey.com.

3. To write the report, the United Nations Development Program commissioned an independent team of experts from the Arab world. Nader Fergany, an Egyptian economist, served as the lead author of the report, and he worked with a collection of other Arab scholars, including: M. Abido, A. A. Ali, N. Ali, M. M. Al-Imam, M. Al-Khalidi, F. Al-Allaghi, M. K. Al-Sayed, M. Badawi, G. Corm, M. Dewidar, I. Elbadawi, A. El-Bayoumi, O. El-Kholy, F. ElZanaty, M. Amin Faris, Salim Jahan, T. Kanaan, A. Mahjoub, S. Morsy, N. Mosa'ad, M. A. Nassar, S. Ben Nefissa, H. Rashad, M. Gawad Redha, F. Sarkis, M. Za'alouk, A. Zahlan and H. Zurayk.

4. "How the Arabs Compare: Arab Human Development Report 2002," *Middle East Quarterly* 9, no. 4 (Fall 2002): 59–67, http://www.meforum.org/513/how-the-arabs-compare.

5. Condoleezza Rice, *No Higher Honor: A Memoir of My Time in Washington* (New York: Crown, 2011), 166ff.

6. "Iraq's Continuing Program for Weapons of Mass Destruction," *U.S. National Intelligence Estimate*, October 2002; Rice, *No Higher Honor*, 166–71.

7. Thomas Wagner, "Iraq Vice-President's Sister Gunned Down," Associated Press, April 27, 2006.

8. The PRT model was initially developed in Afghanistan in 2002, with the same goal of improving local governance, and it was adapted to Iraq in 2005.

9. Haider Ala Hamoudi, "Post-War Iraq: Slow and Steady Progress," *Jurist*, December 13, 2011, www.jurist.org/forum/2011/12/haider-hamoudi-iraq-withdrawal.php.

10. Bob Gates, interview with Bret Baier, "Fox News Reporting: Rising Threats, Shrinking Military," Fox News, May 10, 2016, video.foxnews.com/v/4887449378001.

11. Dr. Tahani Alsandook, Government of Iraq Ministry of Higher Education, presentation at the NAFSA 2016 Annual Conference, June 1, 2016, https://www.nafsa.org/_/File/_/iem_spotlight_aug16_iraqihighered.pdf.

12. Hafez Ghanem, "The Role of Micro and Small Enterprises in Egypt's Economic Transition," Brookings Institution, 2013, 5, https://www.brookings.edu/wp-content/uploads/2016/06/01-egypt-economic-transition-ghanem.pdf.

13. Paolo Verme et al., *Inside Inequality in the Arab Republic of Egypt: Facts and Perceptions Across People, Time, and Space* (World Bank, 2014), 47, http://www.worldbank.org/content/dam/Worldbank/egypt-inequality-book.pdf.

14. Michael Slackman, "In Egypt, Mixed Views of Politics with a Field of Choices," *New York Times*, September 4, 2005, http://www.nytimes.com/2005/09/04/world/africa/in-egypt-mixed-views-of-politics-with-a-field-of-choices.html.

15. Condoleezza Rice, "Remarks with Egyptian Foreign Minister Ahmed Ali Aboul Gheit After Meeting," State Department, February 21, 2006, https://2001-2009.state.gov/secretary/rm/2006/61811.htm.

16. *Middle East Monitor*, as quoted in "British Foreign Policy and the 'Arab Spring,'" UK House of Commons Foreign Affairs Committee, 2012, 17, http://www.publications.parliament.uk/pa/cm201213/cmselect/cmfaff/80/80.pdf.

17. Sharan Grewal, "Why Tunisia Didn't Follow Egypt's Path," *Washington Post*, February 4, 2015, https://www.washingtonpost.com/blogs/monkey-cage/wp/2015/02/04/why-egypt-didnt-follow-tunisias-path.

18. Marina Ottaway, "Egypt and Tunisia: Democratic Transitions and the Problem of Power," Woodrow Wilson Center, April 18, 2014, https://www.wilsoncenter.org/article/egypt-and-tunisia-democratic-transitions-and-the-problem-power.

19. Sarah Drury, "Education: The Key to Women's Empowerment in Saudi Arabia?," Middle East Institute, July 30, 2015, http://www.mei.edu/content/article/education-key-women%E2%80%99s-empowerment-saudi-arabia.

20. Jonathan Chew, "Women Are Taking Over Saudi Arabia's Workforce," *Fortune*, August 10, 2015, http://fortune.com/2015/08/10/women-saudi-arabia/.

21. In the Spanish case, King Juan Carlos helped usher in democratic rule after the death of longtime dictator Francisco Franco in 1975. The king assumed power in the aftermath of Franco's death and worked with rival groups from across the spectrum to facilitate free elections in 1977 and a

new constitution in 1978. Spain's success in transitioning from dictatorship to democracy without civil war or violence was unprecedented at the time.

22. The disarmament and demobilization process is a standard part of peacebuilding efforts and has been undertaken in a variety of contexts as a prerequisite to electoral participation, including in Afghanistan, Northern Ireland, and Colombia.

23. For more, see Madeleine K. Albright and Stephen J. Hadley, *Middle East Strategy Task Force: Final Report of the Co-Chairs* (Atlantic Council, November 2016), http://www.atlanticcouncil.org/images/publications/MEST _Final_Report_web_1130.pdf.

24. *West Bank and Gaza: Towards Economic Sustainability of a Future Palestinian State: Promoting Private Sector–Led Growth* (World Bank, April 2012), 39, http://siteresources.worldbank.org/INTWESTBANKGAZA/ Resources/GrowthStudyEngcorrected.pdf.

25. Jacob J. Lew, "Remarks of Secretary Jacob J. Lew at the Washington Institute for Near East Policy 30th Anniversary Gala," April 29, 2015, https:// www.treasury.gov/press-center/press-releases/Pages/jl0040.aspx.

Chapter 8: Are Authoritarians So Bad?

1. "Afghanistan's Election: Taliban? What Taliban?" *Economist*, October 14, 2004, www.economist.com/node/3291641.

2. "Afghanistan Goes to Polls," Associated Press, October 10, 2004, www .thehindu.com/2004/10/10/stories/2004101004500100.htm.

3. Ahmed Rashid, *Descent into Chaos: The US and the Disaster in Pakistan, Afghanistan, and Central Asia* (New York: Penguin Books, 2009), 260.

4. Ibid.

5. John F. Burns, "For a Battered Populace, a Day of Civic Passion," *New York Times*, January 31, 2005, www.nytimes.com/2005/01/31/world/middle east/for-a-battered-populace-a-day-of-civic-passion.html.

6. This figure from Chinese scholar Sun Liping, whose most recent data is from 2010, appears in a recent book by my Stanford colleague Anja Manuel: *This Brave New World: India, China, and the United States* (New York: Simon & Schuster, 2016), 191.

7. Manuel, *This Brave New World*.

Chapter 9: What Democracy Must Deliver

1. Bradley C. Parks and Zachary J. Rice, "Measuring the Policy Influence of the Millennium Challenge Corporation: A Survey-Based Approach,"

Institute of Theory and Practice of International Relations: The College of William and Mary, February 2013, http://www.wm.edu/offices/itpir/_documents/reform-incentives-report-mcc.pdf.

Chapter 10: "Democracy Is the Worst...Except for All the Others"

1. While Afghanistan has done a good job of keeping to its schedule of regular elections, the parliamentary elections due in 2016 became a source of dispute, as sought-after electoral reforms failed to pass and the election was delayed.
2. George W. Bush, The National Security Strategy for the United States of America, September 2002, https://www.state.gov/documents/organization/63562.pdf.

Epilogue: They Will Look to America

1. Bianca DiJulio, Jamie Firth, and Mollyann Brodie, "Data Note: Americans' Views on the U.S. Role in Global Health," Henry J. Kaiser Family Foundation, January 23, 2015, http://kff.org/global-health-policy/poll-finding/data-note-americans-views-on-the-u-s-role-in-global-health/.
2. "Americans' Confidence in Institutions Stays Low," Gallup, June 13, 2016, www.gallup.com/poll/192581/americans-confidence-institutions-stays-low.aspx; "Public Trust in Government: 1958–2015," Pew Research Center, November 23, 2015, http://www.people-press.org/2015/11/23/public-trust-in-government-1958-2015/.

2016

1. Fareed Zakaria, "America's Democracy Has Become Illiberal," *Washington Post*, December 29, 2016, https://www.washingtonpost.com/opinions/america-is-becoming-a-land-of-less-liberty/2016/12/29/2a91744c-ce09-11e6-a747-d03044780a02_story.html?utm_term=.7bcd039036ed.

Bibliography

Beeman, Richard. *Plain, Honest Men: The Making of the American Constitution*. New York: Random House, 2010.

Bowen, Catherine Drinker. *Miracle at Philadelphia: The Story of the Constitutional Convention, May to September 1787*. Boston: Little, Brown, 1966.

Brown, Dee. *Bury My Heart at Wounded Knee: An Indian History of the American West*. New York: Picador, 2007; originally published in 1970.

Brown, Michael, Sean Lynn-Jones, and Steven Miller. *Debating the Democratic Peace*. Cambridge: MIT Press, 1996.

Bushnell, David. *The Making of Modern Colombia: A Nation in Spite of Itself*. Berkeley: University of California Press, 1993.

Collier, Christopher. *Decision in Philadelphia: The Constitutional Convention of 1787*. New York: Ballantine, 1986.

de Tocqueville, Alexis. *Democracy in America*. Translated and edited by Harvey C. Mansfield and Delba Winthrop. Chicago: University of Chicago Press, 2002.

Diamond, Larry. "Facing Up to the Democratic Recession." *Journal of Democracy* 26, no. 1 (January 2015): 141–55.

Ellis, Joseph J. *Founding Brothers: The Revolutionary Generation*. New York: Alfred A. Knopf, 2000.

Finer, Samuel E. *The Man on Horseback: The Role of the Military in Politics*. London: Pall Mall, 1962.

Fukuyama, Francis. *Political Order and Political Decay: From the Industrial Revolution to the Globalization of Democracy*. New York: Macmillan, 2014.

Getty, John Arch. *Origins of the Great Purges: The Soviet Communist Party Reconsidered, 1933–1938.* Cambridge: Cambridge University Press, 1985.

Hornsby, Charles. *Kenya: A History Since Independence.* London: I. B. Tauris, 2012.

Kline, Harvey F. *Historical Dictionary of Colombia.* Lanham, MD: Scarecrow Press, 2012.

Linz, Juan J., and Alfred Stepan. "Toward Consolidated Democracies," *Journal of Democracy* 7, no. 2 (April 1996): 12–33.

McFaul, Michael. *Russia's Unfinished Revolution: Political Change from Gorbachev to Putin.* Ithaca, NY: Cornell University Press, 2001.

Magocsi, Paul R. *A History of Ukraine: The Land and Its Peoples.* Toronto: University of Toronto Press, 2010.

Manuel, Anja. *This Brave New World: India, China, and the United States.* New York: Simon & Schuster, 2016.

North, Douglass C. *Institutions, Institutional Change and Economic Performance.* Cambridge: Cambridge University Press, 1990.

Pevar, Stephen. *The Rights of Indians and Tribes.* New York: Oxford University Press, 2012; originally published in 1983.

Prucha, Francis Paul. *The Great Father: The United States Government and the American Indians.* Lincoln: University of Nebraska Press, 1986.

Rakove, Jack N. *Original Meanings: Politics and Ideas in the Making of the Constitution.* New York: Alfred A. Knopf, 1996.

Rashid, Ahmed. *Descent into Chaos: The US and the Disaster in Pakistan, Afghanistan, and Central Asia.* New York: Penguin Books, 2009.

Rosefielde, Steven. *Russia in the 21st Century: The Prodigal Superpower.* Cambridge: Cambridge University Press, 2005.

Sheldon, Garrett Ward. *The Political Philosophy of James Madison.* Baltimore: Johns Hopkins University Press, 2001.

Stalin, Josef. *On the Opposition, 1921–1927.* Peking: Foreign Language Press, 1974.

Stewart, David O. *The Summer of 1787: The Men Who Invented the Constitution.* New York: Simon & Schuster, 2007.

Zunz, Olivier. *Philanthropy in America: A History.* Princeton, NJ: Princeton University Press, 2012.

Index

Abbas, Mahmoud, 368–70, 374
Abdullah of Saudi Arabia, 357–60, 374
Abkhazia, 118, 189, 454n
Abortion, 162–63
Abramovich, Roman, 94
Abromavičius, Aivarus, 197
Abu Ghraib prison, 297
Accountability and Justice Act of 2008 (Iraq), 321
Adams, John, 48
Adams, John Quincy, 51
Adenauer, Konrad, 277
Advocacy groups, 44–45
"Affirmative access," 64
Affirmative action, 62–67
Afghanistan, 14, 419–22
    lack of "tradition" of democracy in, 25
    presidential elections of 2004, 381
    Soviet Union in, 85
AFL-CIO, 136–37, 422
African Union (AU), 224–25
Afrobarometer, 416
Agriculture, 145, 149–50, 157, 213, 238, 409
AIDS, 225–26, 424
Air pollution, 392
Al-Abadi, Haider, 327
Alabama National Guard, 38–39
Al-Askari mosque bombing, 305, 311
Alien and Sedition Acts, 48, 452n

Allawi, Iyad, 284–85, 294, 301, 325–26
"All men are created equal," 27–28
Al-Qaeda, 102, 337, 363
    in Afghanistan, 419–20
    in Iraq, 275, 296, 311, 313, 319, 320–21, 326
American Civil War, 52–53
American colonies, 28–29, 40–41
American experience, 25–67
    the Constitution, 26, 27, 30–34
    Declaration of Independence, 27–29
    role of civil society, 44–46
    role of military, 35–39
    role of religion, 39–43
    second democratic opening, 50–56
    spirit of constitutionalism, 47–49
    using the Constitution to propel democratic change, 56–67
American Indians, 61
American Revolution, 29–30, 36
American University (Cairo), 334–35
Amistad, 51
Anbar Province, 294–95, 299, 304, 311, 313, 319–21
Andropov, Yuri, 75
Annan, Kofi, 224, 226–27, 228, 230–31, 233, 406
Arab Human Development Report, 272–73, 356, 362, 460n
Arab monarchies, 355–66. See also specific countries

Arab Spring, 2–3, 6, 269, 271, 331
Arafat, Yasser, 369
Articles of Confederation, 29–30
Assad, Bashar al-, 270, 334
Atlantic Council, 371
Authoritarian regimes, 17–18, 21,
    331, 397
  Kenya, 204, 208, 209
  in Middle East, 268–69, 273
  Russia, 106, 110, 111, 114, 120,
    123, 124
Ayalon, Danny, 298
Azarov, Mykola, 192

Ba'ath Party (Iraq), 279–80, 289,
    293–94, 321
Bahrain, 268, 270, 355, 372–73
Baker, James, 147–48, 281
Balcerowicz, Leszek, 144, 151
Baloha, Viktor, 178–79
Baltimore, George Calvert, 1st Baron, 41
Barcelona Summer Olympics (1992), 98
Barco, Carolina, 236–37, 247
Barzani, Masoud, 282–84, 328–29
Basayev, Shamil, 102
Beijing Summer Olympics (2008), 395
Belarus, 89, 97, 172, 193
Ben Ali, Zine al-Abidine, 330–31, 347,
    352–53, 354
Berezovsky, Boris, 94, 107
Berlin, 25–26
Berlin Wall, 17, 138
Beslan school siege, 105
Betancourt, İngrid, 244, 254–55
Bhutto, Benazir, 223
Biden, Joe, 326
Bierut, Bolesław, 129
Bin Laden, Osama, 337
Blacker, Chip, 176
Black Panther Party, 57–58
Black Sea Fleet, 173–74
Blackwill, Robert, 2, 146

Blair, Tony, 301, 304, 306
Bolívar, Simón, 237
Bolivarian Revolution, 259–60
Borusewicz, Bogdan, 130
Boskin, Michael, 86, 147
Bosnia-Herzegovina, 417
Bouazizi, Mohammed, 347, 352, 354
Brady, Nicholas, 147
Brazil, 96, 260
Bremer, L. Paul "Jerry," 281–82,
    291–301
Brezhnev, Leonid, 74–75, 132, 143, 170
British East Africa Protectorate, 204–5
Broader Middle East and North Africa
    Initiative, 372–73
Brown v. Board of Education, 38, 452n
Bush, George H. W.
  Gulf War and, 276, 282, 291, 295
  Poland and, 1–2, 138–42, 145, 147,
    148–49, 158
  Soviet Union and, 81–82, 86
  Ukraine and, 170
Bush, George W.
  African Americans in
    administration, 66
  Arab Human Development Report
    and, 272–73
  Colombia and, 242–44, 246–48,
    250, 257–59
  Egypt and, 339
  Hurricane Katrina and, 35, 39
  Iraq and, 290–91, 300–301, 310,
    316–17, 320–21
  Kenya and, 202–3
  Lebanon and, 333
  Liberia and, 405–6
  Millennium Challenge and, 410–11
  Nairobi and, 225–26
  NATO expansion and, 114, 116–17
  Poland and, 126–27, 152
  race and college admissions, 63–64
  Russia and, 70

on "soft bigotry of low expectations,"
67
Ukraine and, 182–83, 188, 194
Bush, Laura, 402

Calhoun, John C., 48–49, 171
Cambodia, 384
Camp David Accords, 408
Capitalism
in China, 385–86
in Soviet Union, 76–77, 86, 90–91
Carmichael, Stokely, 57
Carter, Jimmy, 132, 137
Casey, George, 315–16
Casper, Gerhard, 63
Castaño, Fabio Vásquez, 239
Castro, Fidel, 239–40
Cathedral of Christ the Savior
(Moscow), 97
Catherine the Great, 173
Ceaușescu, Nicolae, 2, 194–95
Chalabi, Ahmad, 284–85, 293–94
Charles I of England, 41
Charter 77, 15
Chávez, Hugo, 22, 254, 259–60
Chechnya, 102, 104, 105, 107
Cheney, Liz, 368
Chernenko, Konstantin, 75
Chernobyl disaster, 166, 170
Chiarelli, Pete, 316
Chile, 258, 389
China, 22, 383, 384–97, 425
Chinese bubble, 388–89
Chirac, Jacques, 333–34
Christianity, 43
Chubais, Anatoly, 93, 121
Churchill, Winston, 70, 416
CIA (Central Intelligence Agency),
137–38, 280
Citizens Coalition for Constitutional
Change (Kenya), 214–15
Civic Forum, 212

Civic Platform, 161, 163
Civil-military relations, 35–36, 37
Civil Rights Act of 1964, 56, 60, 62
Civil rights movement, 50, 58–67
Civil Service Commission, 49
Civil society, 21, 406–7, 428
American experience, 31, 44–46
in Kenya, 211
myth of "democratic culture" and,
11, 12
totalitarian regimes and, 16
Clay, Henry, 49
Clinton, Bill, 62
Coalition Provisional Authority
(CPA), 281–82, 292–93,
299–300
Cohen, Jared, 377
Cold War, 2, 14–15, 74–75, 84–87,
126, 407
Coleman, S. David, 404
College admissions and race, 63–65,
453n
Colombia, 236–65, 422
election of 2002, 245, 250, 256–57
election of 2010, 262–64
making and remaking Plan
Colombia, 241–49
National Front regime, 238–39
paramilitaries' role in, 251–55
post–National Front years, 239–41
question of justice, 255–57
The Republic, 237–38
Uribe's presidency, 245–57, 261–63,
425–26
Colonial America, 28–29, 40–41
Colonization of Africa, 204–5
Commission on Security and
Cooperation in Europe (CSCE),
372–73
Committee on Civil Rights, 60
Commonwealth of Independent
States, 17, 88, 172–73

Communist Party of Poland, 131–34, 138–40, 142–43

Communist Party of the Soviet Union (CPSU), 15–17, 74–75, 77, 79, 80–83

Compromise of 1877, 54–55

Confederate States of America, 52–53

Congress of People's Deputies (Russia), 80–81

Conquest, Robert, 77

Constitution
of Afghanistan, 420–21
of Colombia, 261–62
of Iraq, 302–4
of Kenya, 213, 218–20, 232–33
of Soviet Union, 80–81, 83, 101
of Ukraine, 176
of Ukrainian Soviet Socialist Republic, 169–70
of the U.S., 26, 27, 30–34, 37, 42–43, 47

Constitutional Tribunal (Poland), 161

Continental Congress, 29, 30

Cooper, Helene, 346

Corruption
American experience, 49
in China, 394–95, 400
in India, 399–400
in Kenya, 208, 209, 216, 217, 234–35
in Poland, 155
in Russia, 94–95, 113–14
in Ukraine, 197–98

Crimea, 118, 172–74, 195, 196, 455n

Crocker, Ryan, 316

Crusaders in the Courts (Greenberg), 59–60

Cuba, 18, 22

Cuban Revolution, 239

"Cults of personality," 13–14, 331, 418

Cultural Revolution, 386–88

Cyril, Saint, 167

Czechoslovakia, 15, 132, 156, 195, 212

Czech Republic, 93, 114, 156–57

Davis, Jefferson, 52–53

Declaration of Independence, 27–29

"Deep state," 336

Democracies
in 1800, 7
in 1900, 9
in 2000, *11*

Democracy
challenges to, 416–18
myth of "democratic culture," 10–12
retreat of, 5–24
role of external actors, 20–22
scaffolding of, 8–9

Democratic institutions, 418–19, 422, 427
defined, 8, 449n
four types of, 13–20
role of, 8–9, 12–13, 31–32

Democratic peace theory, 158, 277–78, 455–56n

Democratic Union (Russia), 80

Deng Xiaoping, 385–86

Diamond, Larry, 6

Doe, Samuel, 404–5

Dole, Bob, 145

Dostum, Abdul Rashid, 420

Douglass, Frederick, 51–52

Dred Scott v. Sandford, 51–52

Drug trade, in Colombia, 236, 239–40, 241–45, 251–52

Dubai, 268

Dubçek, Alexander, 132

Du Bois, W. E. B., 55

Durov, Pavel, 110

Eastern Europe, map, *165*

Ebola virus, 414

Ecuador, 237, 254

Education
American experience, 38, 45
myth of "democratic culture" and, 10
Education reform, in Middle East,
356–62
Egypt, 330–52, 372
Camp David Accords, 408
Morsi's presidency, 348–50
Mubarak regime, 334–40
parliamentary elections of 2005,
344–45
presidential elections of 2005, 340–45
secularism in, 364–65
Egyptian Revolution of 2011, 203,
347–49
ElBaradei, Mohamed, 348
Elections, 5, 6. *See also specific country
elections*
in quasi-democratic regimes, 19–20
Electoral Commission of Kenya
(ECK), 215, 221–23
ELN (National Liberation Army), 239,
243–44
El Salvador, 412
Emancipation Proclamation, 26–27
Ennahda Party (Tunisia), 352–53
"Enumerated powers," 33–34
Escobar, Pablo, 236
Establishment Clause, 42
Ethiopia, 223
Euromaidan, 191–94
European Union (EU)
Germany and, 277
Poland and, 149, 152, 156, 157,
159–60, 161, 163
Ukraine and, 187–88, 190, 191, 196
European wars of religion, 41
Executive power
American experience, 32–33, 34,
37, 47
importance of presidency, 423–25
in Soviet Union, 80–82

Fallujah, 296, 382
FARC (Revolutionary Armed Forces
of Colombia), 239–45, 247, 248,
251, 252–55, 262, 263–65, 425
Fatah Party, 368–70
Fatherland Party (Ukraine), 186–87,
190
Fatima, Sheikha, 357
Fayyad, Salam, 374–75
Federalism, 429
American experience, 31, 33–34, 47
in Iraq, 303, 320
in Kenya, 207, 235, 429
in Russia, 97, 104–5, 429
Federalist Papers, 30, 430
Feltman, Jeffrey, 369
Fergany, Nader, 272, 460*n*
Fifteenth Amendment, 53, 59
First Amendment, 41, 42, 48
Fischer, Bobby, 85
Fitzwater, Marlin, 140
Ford Foundation, 214–15
Foreign aid, 21, 410–15
Foreign assistance trap, 407–10
"Forty acres and a mule," 53
Forum for the Restoration of
Democracy (FORD), 212–14
Fourteenth Amendment, 50, 53, 59,
60, 62
"Fourth Estate," 32, 450*n*
Frankfurter, Felix, 59
Franks, Tommy, 279
Frazer, Jendayi, 202–3, 221–22, 228,
229, 456–57*n*
Freedmen's Bureau, 53, 54–55
Freedom House, 21, 327, 407
Freedom of religion, 39–43, 328
Freedom of speech, 44, 48, 452*n*
Freedom of the press, 19, 32, 48, 80,
81, 406–7. *See also* Press
Free Exercise Clause, 42
French Revolution, 23

Front for Change (Ukraine), 190–91
Fyodor I of Russia, 71

G8 (Group of Eight), 86, 339
Gaidar, Yegor, 93
Gandhi, Mahatma, 398
García Romero, Álvaro, 256
Garner, Jay, 279–81, 294–95
Gates, Robert "Bob," 146–47, 315–16, 317, 325
Gazeta Wyborcza, 151
Gdańsk Agreement, 130–31
GDP (gross domestic product)
    Colombia, 259
    Kenya, 208
    Poland, 129
    Russia/Soviet Union, 85, 92
Gearan, Anne, 346
George III of England, 28, 32
Georgia, 115–17, 118, 124, 189–90, 332, 411–12, 427, 454–55n
Geremek, Bronisław, 151
Germany, 25–26, 86–87, 277–78.
    See also Nazi Germany
Gheit, Aboul, 336–37
Gierek, Edward, 131
Githongo, John, 219
Glasnost, 15, 77–78, 170
Godunov, Boris, 71–72
Gogol, Nikolai, 78
Gómez, Laureano, 237–38, 458–59n
Gonzales, Alberto, 65
Gorbachev, Mikhail, 1, 15–16, 74–77, 128, 139, 143–44, 170, 171–72
    lifting of the Iron Curtain, 84–88
    political and economic reforms, 75–77, 78–84, 86–87
Gorky Park (Moscow), 97
Graham, Henry V., 39
Gran Colombia, 237
Granda, Rodrigo, 253–54
Great Purge (Soviet Union), 77–78

Greenberg, Jack, 59–60
Green Revolution, 376–77
Gromyko, Andrei, 131
Grutter v. Bollinger, 63–64
Gulf Cooperation Council, 287
Gulf War, 276, 282, 291, 295
Gunderson, Brian, 362
Gusinsky, Vladimir Aleksandrovich, 107

Hadley, Stephen "Steve," 290, 314–15, 342–43, 363
Hakim, Abdul Aziz al-, 285.287, 307, 308, 324
Hamas, 365, 367, 368–70, 374
Hamilton, Alexander, 29, 32–33, 34, 36
Hamoudi, Haider Ala, 323
Hariri, Rafik, 333, 334
Hashemi, Tariq al-, 288–89, 302, 308, 326
Hayes, Rutherford B., 54
Hazare, Kisan Baburao "Anna," 399
Head, Julia, 27
Helal, Gemal, 358
Helsinki Accords, 16–17
Henry, Patrick, 33
Herbst, John, 182
Hezbollah, 267, 333, 367, 370–71, 428
Hitler, Adolf, 168–69, 195, 277
Holloway, David, 93–94
Honecker, Erich, 15
Hong Kong, 6
Hood, James, 38–39
Houphouët-Boigny, Félix, 204
Howard University, 54
Hu Jintao, 386
Hungarian Revolution, 169
Hungary, 21, 161
    NATO expansion, 114, 156–57
    as quasi-democratic regime, 20
Hurricane Katrina, 35, 39, 450n

Hussein, Saddam, 5–6, 13, 270, 274–76, 278, 279, 280, 284, 288, 291, 296, 307
Hyland, Jason P., 312

IMF (International Monetary Fund), 146–47, 177, 208–9, 218
India, 21, 365–66, 397–400
Indian Citizenship Act of 1924, 61
Indian Ocean tsunami of 2004, 223
Indonesia, 366
Infosys, 399–400
Infrastructure, 112, 282, 299, 388
Institutions. *See* Democratic institutions
Interest groups, 44–45
International Criminal Court (ICC), 233
International Tchaikovsky Competition, 85
Internet, 18, 20–21, 428
  in China, 392–93
  in Iraq, 327
  in Russia, 108–10
Iran, 269, 270–71, 286, 329, 376–79
  exchange program, 377–78
  Green Revolution, 376–77
Iranian Revolution, 362–63
Iran nuclear deal framework, 379
Iraq, 273–330. *See also* Iraq occupation; Iraq war
  constitutional ratification in, 302–4
  democratic institutions in, 269, 366–67, 418–19
  elections of 2005, 304, 332–33, 346
  elections of 2010, 325–26
  ethnic and religious tribes of, 270–71, 278–79, 282–90, 294–97, 301–3, 307–10, 313
  formation of al-Maliki government, 305–9
  governance issues in, 321–23

Gulf War, 276, 282, 291, 295
  lack of "tradition" of democracy in, 25
  legislative elections of 2005, 301–2, 382
  presidential referendum of 2002, 5–6
  as quasi-democratic regime, 19
  totalitarian collapse, 14
  transfer of sovereignty, 297–301
  troop surge of 2007, 315–21
  U.S. policy and democracy, 275–77
Iraqi Governing Council (IGC), 281–82, 283, 299–300, 301
Iraqi Interim Authority (IIA), 279–80
Iraq occupation, 278–97
  Bremer and ORHA, 279–81, 291–301
  disaffected Sunnis, 288–90
  disbanding of army, 291–94
  transfer of sovereignty, 297–301
  unforced errors, 290–94
Iraq war, 152, 273–74
Islam. *See also* Shia Muslims; Sunni Muslims
  democracy and, 362–66
  history of, 285–86
Islamic State (ISIS), 326, 328–30, 355
Israel
  Camp David Accords, 408
  Lebanon War, 267
  Palestinian-Israeli issue, 373–76
  Palestinian legislative elections of 2006, 368–70
Ivan III of Russia, 71
Ivan IV of Russia (the Terrible), 71
Ivanov, Sergei, 109, 119, 123, 419–20
Izvestiya, 80, 143–44

Jaafari, Ibrahim al-, 302, 305–7
Jackson, Andrew, 48–49
Jalal, Masooda, 381

Japan, 79, 277–78
Jaresko, Natalie, 196
Jaruzelski, Wojciech, 132, 133, 134,
    141, 142, 143
Jefferson, Thomas, 36–37, 48, 50
Jiang Zemin, 393
Jim Crow laws, 55–56, 61, 452n
John Paul II, Pope, 136–37, 138, 150
Johnson, Andrew, 53
Johnson, Lyndon, 61–62, 315
Johnson, Ross, 132
Johnson Sirleaf, Ellen, 402, 405, 406,
    413–15, 424
Jones, Dick, 369
Jordan, 268, 287, 361, 412
Jubeir, Adel al-, 358
Judicial Watch, 45
Judiciary
    American experience, 34, 47, 59
    in China, 390
    in Colombia, 249, 255, 425–26
    in Kenya, 217
    in Poland, 160–61
    in quasi-democratic regimes, 19–20
    in Russia, 110, 125
    in Ukraine, 197–98

Kacyziński, Jarosław, 160
Kalenjin tribe, 206, 206, 213
Kalugin, Nikolai, 166
Kania, Stanislaw, 131
Karua, Martha, 227–28
Karzai, Hamid, 420
Katyn massacre, 128
Kazakhstan, 174, 193
Kefaya (Egypt), 339, 347–48
Kennedy, David, 33, 34
Kennedy, John F., 42, 258
Kenya, 202–35, 422
    economic reforms, 208–10
    elections and crisis of 2007, 220–33,
        426

elections of 2002, 202–4, 215–16
elections of 2013, 233–34
end of multiparty rule, 207–16
federalism in, 207, 235, 429
foreign assistance to, 208–9
Kenyatta tenure, 204–8
Moi regime, 202–4, 208–16
road to democracy, 204–7
tribal basis of, 206, 206–7, 210–11,
    215, 234–35
Kenya African National Union
    (KANU), 205–6, 207
Kenya African Union (KAU), 204
Kenya Colony, 204–5
Kenyan African Democratic Union
    (KADU), 205–6, 207
Kenyatta, Jomo, 204–8
Kenyatta, Uhuru, 203–4, 216, 229,
    233–34
Kerensky, Alexander, 88–89
Kessler, Glenn, 345–46
KGB, 70, 88, 103, 105, 114
Khalilzad, Zalmay, 294–95, 305–8,
    316
Khamenei, Ali, 286, 378–79
Khan, Ismail, 420
Khodorkovsky, Mikhail, 94, 95
Kholmanskikh, Igor, 113
Khrushchev, Nikita, 84, 118, 169, 173
Kibaki, Mwai, 203–4, 214, 215,
    216–33
Kikuyu tribe, 206, 206–7, 213, 214,
    215, 223, 294
King, Martin Luther, Jr., 55, 57, 58
King Abdullah University of Science
    and Technology, 359
King Fahd University, 358
Kirkland, Lane, 135–36, 137
Kirkuk, 323, 328–29
Kiszczak, Czesław, 141
Kivuitu, Samuel, 222–23
Klitschko, Vitali, 192–93

Komsomol, 15
Korbel, Josef, 144–45
Kosgei, Sally, 229
Kotova, Svetlana, 110–11
Kraus, Marty, 189
Kravchuk, Leonid, 171, 175
Kuchma, Leonid, 175–82
Kufuor, John, 224, 406
Ku Klux Klan, 53–54
Kurdish Workers' Party (PKK), 282
Kurdistan Democratic Party (KDP),
    282–84
Kurds (Kurdistan), 270, 275, 278–79,
    281–84, 295, 301–4, 312, 322,
    323, 328, 329
Kuria, Gibson Kamau, 211
Kuwait, 361–62
Kwasniewski, Aleksander, 152–53,
    154–55, 424

Labor
    in China, 388, 389
    in Egypt, 353–54
    in Poland, 129–31
    in Soviet Union, 77, 91
    in Tunisia, 353–54
Laos, 384
La Violencia, 237–38
Law and Justice Party (Poland),
    160–61, 162–63
Leahy, Patrick, 244–45
Lebanon, 267, 268, 270, 271, 333–34,
    370–71, 427–28
Lebanon War, 226, 267–68
Lee, Richard Henry, 36
Lee, Robert E., 52–53
Lee Kuan Yu, 383
Lee Myung-Bak, 383–84
Legislative power, 33, 34, 47
Lenin, Vladimir, 72–73
Lenin Shipyard, 130–31
Lesotho, 412–13

Liberia, 18, 50, 402–6, 413–15
Libya, 14, 268
Ligachev, Yegor, 82–83
Lincoln, Abraham, 52, 53
Livni, Tsipi, 267
Louis XIV of France, 6
Love, Theresa, 403
Luhya tribe, 206, 215
Lula da Silva, Luiz Inácio, 260
Lumumba, Patrice, 204
Lutsenko, Yuriy, 187, 191
Luzhkov, Yuri, 97

McGlathery, Dave, 38–39
McMaster, H. R., 316
McNair, Denise, 55–56
Madagascar, 413
Madame Zhou, 384–85
Madison, James, 30, 36, 41–42, 50, 430
Mahdi, Adel Abdul, 285, 302, 307, 308
Malawi, 411
Malcolm X, 56–57
Mali, 413
Maliki, Nouri al-, 307–9, 318–21, 323,
    325, 326–27
Malone, Vivian, 38–39
Mancuso, Salvatore, 256–57
Mandela, Nelson, 101–2, 424
Manning, David, 279
Mao Zedong, 384, 385, 393, 396
March 14 Alliance, 334, 346
Margold, Nathan, 59
Marshall, Thurgood, 55, 59
Marshall Plan, 90
Marulanda, Manuel, 254–55
Marx, Karl, 2
Maryland Toleration Act of 1649, 41
Mashhadani, Mahmoud al-, 289, 302
Masri, Abu Ayyub al-, 311
Matiba, Kenneth, 210–11, 214
Mau Mau Uprising, 204–5
Mazowiecki, Tadeusz, 143, 144, 151

Medellín, Colombia, 236–37, 251, 260–61

Media. *See* Press

Medvedev, Dmitry, 105, 109, 120–21

Membership Action Plan (MAP), 115–17, 188–90

Merkel, Angela, 116, 195

Merlano, Jairo, 256

Methodius, Saint, 167

Michnik, Adam, 151

Middle East, 267–379. *See also specific countries*
map, 266
modern boundaries of, 270
problem of elections in, 367–73

Miliband, David, 222, 223–24

Military
American experience, 35–39
in Colombia, 249–50, 255
in quasi-democratic regimes, 20
in Russia, 93–94

Military Academy, U.S. (West Point), 36–37

Militias, 20, 37–38, 135, 249, 308, 313, 370

Millennium Challenge Corporation (MCC), 411–13

Miller, David D., 203

Miodowicz, Alfred, 150–51

Mitchell, Andrea, 346

Mitchell, George, 145

Modi, Narendra, 397–98, 399

Mohammad Bin Salman Al Saud, 363–64

Mohapi, Sophia, 412–13

Moi, Daniel arap, 202–4, 206, 208–16

Molotov-Ribbentrop Pact, 168

Morehouse College, 54

Morocco, 361, 371

Morris, Erik, 256

Morsi, Mohamed, 348–50

Moscow theater hostage crisis, 102

Mozah, Sheikha, 356–57

Mubarak, Gemal, 338–39

Mubarak, Hosni, 331–32, 334–40, 348–49
presidential elections of 2005, 340–45

Mubarak, Suzanne, 343

Mulford Act, 58

Muqtada al-Sadr, 287, 299, 313

Muslim Brotherhood, 337–38, 343, 344, 346, 348–51, 365, 367, 370

Mussolini, Benito, 13, 384, 418

Mussorgsky, Modest, 72

Musyoka, Kalonzo, 221, 224

Myers, Dick, 290

NAACP (National Association for the Advancement of Colored People), 56, 58–60

Nairobi, 225–26

Najaf, 284, 286

Nasrallah, Hassan, 371

National Agency for the Prevention of Corruption (Ukraine), 197–98

National anthem of Russia, 98

National Anti-Corruption Bureau (Ukraine), 197–98

National Archives, U.S., 26–27

National Army of Colombia, 252–53

National Constitutional Conference (Kenya), 218–19

National Democratic Party (NDP; Kenya), 211–12

National Endowment for Democracy (NED), 21, 110, 138

National Front (Colombia), 238–39, 458–59n

National Guard, U.S., 37–39

National Media Council (Poland), 162

National Reserve, U.S., 38

National Salvation Front (Russia), 99

NATO (North Atlantic Treaty
    Organization), 114–17, 277
  Poland and, 114, 126–27, 152,
    156–58
  purpose of, 158
  Ukraine and, 114–17, 188–90
NATO-Russia Council, 115, 116
Navalny, Alexei, 109
Nazi Germany, 13, 128–29, 168–69,
    277
Negroponte, John, 316
Nehru, Jawaharlal, 398
Nemtsov, Boris, 103
New York Times, 213, 220, 223, 244,
    340, 346, 405
Ngilu, Charity, 215
NGOs (non-governmental
    organizations), 21, 44–45,
    110–11, 409
Nicaragua, 259–60, 413
Nilekani, Nandan, 399–400
Nineveh, 304
Nixon, Richard, 62
Nkrumah, Kwame, 204
Nobel Peace Prize, 135, 353, 354–55
Noguera, Jorge, 256
Norilsk Nickel, 94
Norte de Santander Department, 251
North, Douglass, 8, 449n
North Korea, 14, 111
Nour, Ayman, 338–45, 347–48
Novaya Gazeta, 107–8
Nowak, Jan, 144–45
Nullification Crisis, 48–49
Nuser, Ernest, 178–79
Nyerere, Julius, 204

Obama, Barack, 120, 162, 195, 232,
    261, 325–26, 377, 411
Obasanjo, Olusegun, 406
O'Connor, Sandra Day, 65
Odierno, Ray, 316, 318

Odinga, Oginga, 207, 211–12, 214, 215
Odinga, Raila, 215, 220–26, 228–34
Office of Minority Business Enterprise,
    62
Office of Reconstruction and
    Humanitarian Assistance
    (ORHA), 279–81, 291–94,
    297–98
Old Arbat, Moscow, 78, 92
Oligarchs, Russian, 94–95, 113–14
Olszewski, Jan, 155
O'Neill, Paul, 274
Operation Provide Comfort, 279,
    294–95
Operation Sovereignty, 239
Orange Revolution, 183–85, 187, 200,
    427
Orbán, Viktor, 161
Organization for Security and
    Co-operation in Europe (OSCE),
    190, 193, 410
Organized crime, in Russia, 91, 95–96
Ottoman Empire, 269–70

Pace, Pete, 314–15
Pakistan, 223, 398
Palestinian-Israeli issue, 373–76
Palestinian legislative elections of
    2006, 368–70
Panama, 237
Party of Regions (Ukraine), 179, 185,
    186–87, 190–91, 193
Pastrana, Andrés, 241, 243–45
Patronage, 19, 49
Peace Corps, 408
Pensions, 389–90
Pensions (pension system)
  in Russia, 92, 97, 112
  in Ukraine, 185, 198
PEPFAR (President's Emergency Plan
    For AIDS Relief), 225–26
Perdomo, Fernando Araújo, 253

Perestroika, 15, 75–77
Perez, Anna, 279
Perry, William, 93–94
Persian Empire, 269
Peshmerga, 282–83, 303, 328
Peter the Great, 68
Petraeus, David, 315–16, 317
Philadelphia Plan, 62
Philanthropy, 45–46
Plan Colombia, 241–49, 257–58
Poland, 1–2, 15, 90, 126–64
    civil society groups in, 21
    democracy's challenges, 159–64
    democratic institutions in, 422, 426
    failing economy and labor unrest,
        129–31
    history of democracy in, 127–44
    importance of presidency, 424
    imposition of martial law, 131,
        133–34, 135, 137
    NATO expansion, 114, 126–27,
        152, 156–58
    political parties in, 153–56
    Solidarity and, 132–44, 150–51
    U.S. assistance to, 144–49
    U.S. special relationship with,
        152–53
Polish American Enterprise Fund,
    148–49
Polish Beer Lovers' Party, 153–54
Polish Constitutional Court crisis of
    2015, 160–61
Polish Round Table Talks, 139–41,
    154
Political parties, 427–28, 429
Politkovskaya, Anna, 107
Politkovskaya, Ilya, 107
Populism, 12, 24, 102, 160, 217–18
Poroshenko, Petro, 196–98, 199
Posse comitatus, 35–36
Posse Comitatus Act of 1878, 35, 450*n*
Potanin, Vladimir, 94

Powell, Colin, 26, 66, 182
    Colombia and, 245, 250
    Iraq and, 272, 273–74, 290–93
    Kenya and, 202, 216, 219
Pravda, 80
Presidency. *See* Executive power
Press, 406–7, 450*n*
    in Colombia, 249
    in Iraq, 327–28
    in Kenya, 211, 212
    in Poland, 151, 162
    in Russia, 80, 81, 106–9
Privatization, 92–95, 175
Property rights, 29, 41, 303
Provincial Reconstruction Teams
    (PRTs), 312, 318
Puritans, 40–41
Purple Finger Revolution, 332–33, 346
"Pursuit of happiness," 44, 410
Putin, Vladimir, 2, 18, 22, 70, 95, 98,
    103–14, 116–25, 173, 179, 200,
    425, 429

Qaddafi, Muammar, 330
Qatar, 356–57
Quasi-democratic regimes, 18–20,
    327, 329, 407
Quds Force, 319, 379
Qutb, Sayyid, 337

Race and college admissions, 63–65,
    453*n*
Racism, 26, 55–58, 66–67
Radio Free Europe, 144
Rakowski, Mieczysław, 144
Rand Corporation, 132
Ranneberger, Michael, 227
Rashid, Ahmed, 381
Reagan, Ronald, 62, 74, 136, 138
Reconstruction Era, 53–55
Regents of the University of California v.
    Bakke, 64–65

Reign of Terror, 23
Religion, in American experience, 39–43
Religious beliefs and individual liberty, 362–64, 365
Revenge killings, 225, 288, 308, 309–10
Reyes, Raúl, 254
Rogozin, Dmitry, 115
Rojas Pinilla, Gustavo, 238, 458–59n
Romania, 2, 15, 194–95
Romanov dynasty, 72
Roosevelt, Theodore, 49, 399
Rose Revolution, 332
Rosnano, 121
Rubia, Charles, 210–11
Rumsfeld, Donald, 272, 276, 281, 297, 307–8, 315–16, 317
Rurik dynasty, 70–71
Russia, 68–125, 422–23. *See also* Soviet Union
  as authoritarian regime, 18
  birth of new state, 88–92
  closing of democratic opening, 103–14
  economic collapse, 91–92
  elections of 1993, 98–101
  elections of 1996, 102–3
  erosion of state capacity and authority, 95–98
  failed democratic transitions, 73–74
  federalism in, 97, 104–5, 429
  importance of presidency, 423–25
  NATO expansion and, 114–17
  Poland and, 127–28
  privatization programs, 92–95
  separatist groups, 102–3, 454–55n
  Ukraine and, 22, 114–18, 166–70, 173–74, 181, 183–84, 191–92, 195–96, 200
Russian Commonwealth, 17, 88, 172–73

Russian financial crisis of 1998, 92, 177
Russian Orthodox Church, 71, 124, 125, 167
Russian Revolution, 72–73, 79–80, 89
Ruto, William, 233
Rutskoi, Alexander, 100
Rwandan genocide, 226, 230
Rywin affair, 155

Saakashvili, Mikheil, 118
Sachs, Jeffrey, 146
Sadat, Anwar, 334, 335
Saint Basil's Cathedral (Moscow), 71
Saint Petersburg, Russia, 68–70
Saleh, Fadila, 382
Santos, Juan Manuel, 263–65
Saud bin Faisal bin Abdulaziz Al Saud, 358
Saudi Arabia, 22, 270–71, 357–60, 362–64, 372
Scott-McDonald, Wvannie Mae, 414
Scowcroft, Brent, 138, 148, 149
Secularism, 364–65
Segregation, 26, 38–39, 50–56
"Separate but equal," 55
Separation of powers, 22, 31–34, 47, 402, 423
September 11 attacks, 275–76, 358, 419
Sevastopol Port, 174
Sevodnya, 107
Sharon, Ariel, 374
Shays' Rebellion of 1786, 36, 451n
Shcherbytskyi, Volodymyr, 171
Shia Muslims, 270–71, 278–79, 284–87, 301–2, 304, 305, 307–10, 322, 326, 329
"Shock therapy," 91–92
Shultz, George, 62
Siberia, 77–78
Sibneft, 94

Sidiqi, Moqadasa, 381
Siege of Leningrad, 69
Sikorski, Radek, 164, 189–90
Silicon Valley, 120–21
Singapore, 383
Singh, Manmohan, 399, 400
Siniora, Fouad, 334
Sisi, Abdel Fattah el-, 350–51
Sistani, Ali al-, 278–79, 286, 300, 304
Sixteenth Street Baptist Church
    bombing, 55–56
Skolkovo, 121
Slavery, 26–27, 49, 50–53, 385
Slovakia, 156
Smuta (Time of Troubles), 71–72
Sobchak, Anatoly, 68–69
Sochi Winter Olympics (2014), 118
Social inequality, 61, 390–91
Socialism, 84–85
Social media, 20–21. See also Internet
    in China, 392–93
    in Russia, 108–10
"Soft bigotry of low expectations," 67
Solidarity (Poland), 1–2, 126, 132–44,
    145, 149, 150–51, 153, 422
Solzhenitsyn, Alexander, 78
Somalia, 223
South Africa, 101–2, 424
South Carolina Nullification Crisis,
    48–49
South Korea, 383–84
South Ossetia, 118, 189–90, 454–55n
Soviet Union, 74–88. See also Russia
    collapse of, 13, 14–17, 68–69, 70,
        73, 74, 86–88, 106–7
    Helsinki Accords, 16–17
    lifting the Iron Curtain, 84–88
    Poland and, 128–29, 131, 132,
        134–36, 139, 143–44
    political and economic reforms,
        75–77, 78–84
    presidential system, 80–82

referendum of 1991, 83–84
    republics of, 83–84, 89
    Russian Revolution, 72–73, 89
    Ukraine and, 168–72
Space Race, 84–85
Spanish-American War, 37
Spassky, Boris, 85
Spasso House (Moscow), 108
Stalin, Josef, 77–78, 79–80, 136,
    168–69
Stand in the Schoolhouse Door, 38–39
Stanford University, 63, 65, 66–67,
    384–85
Status of Forces Agreement (SOFA),
    325–26
Stillman College, 57
Straw, Jack, 306
Student Non-Violent Coordinating
    Committee (SNCC), 57
Suleiman, Omar, 342–43, 348
Summit of the Americas (2001), 254
"Sundowning," 335
Sunni Muslims, 270–71, 278–79, 286,
    287–90, 302–3, 305, 307–10,
    312, 322, 323, 326, 418–19
Sununu, John, 82
Syria, 269, 271, 326, 333–34, 372–73

Tahrir Square protests of 2011, 2–3,
    347, 354
Taiwan, 21
Tajikistan, 332
Talabani, Jalal, 282–83, 302, 308, 321,
    324
Taliban, 419–22
Tarasyuk, Borys, 186, 196–97
Tawadros II, Pope, 350
Taylor, Charles, 405–6
Taylor, John, 147, 310–11
Tbilisi, April 9 tragedy, 16
Tbilisi State University, 412
"Tear down this wall!", 138

Tenet, George, 280, 419–20
Thermidor, 23
Thirteenth Amendment, 59
Tiananmen Square protests, 386, 388
Tocqueville, Alexis de, 47, 50, 61
Tolbert, William, 404
To Secure These Rights (1947 report), 60
Totalitarian regimes, 13–17, 331, 418
    collapse of, 13–14
    gradual decay of, 14–17
Totalitario, 13, 384, 385, 418
Transitional Administrative Law
    (TAL), 297–99, 303
Truman, Harry, 60, 136
Tsinghua University, 390, 396
Tubman, William, 403–4
Tulip Revolution, 332
Tunisia, 18, 330–32, 352–55, 366–67,
    422, 428
Tunisian Revolution, 347, 352, 354
Turbay, Jorge Eduardo Gechém, 244
Turkey, 20, 269, 364–65
Tutwiler, Margaret, 280–81
Tymoshenko, Yulia, 178, 184–88,
    190–91, 194, 200

Ukraine, 115–18, 166–201
    democratic institutions in, 427, 428
    democratic opening in, 170–72
    Euromaidan, 191–94
    importance of presidency in, 423–24
    independence for, 174–79
    NATO and, 114–17, 188–90
    Orange Revolution, 183–85, 187,
        200
    parliamentary elections of 2012,
        190–91
    political crisis of 2007, 185–88
    presidential election of 2004,
        179–82
    Putin on "made-up country,"
        117–18, 167

Yushchenko era, 179–85
Ukrainian People's Movement for
    Restructuring, 170–71
Ukrainian revolution of 2014, 193–95
United Arab Emirates (UAE), 269,
    271, 357, 360–61, 371
United Nations Millennium
    Development Goals, 409
United Self-Defenders of Colombia
    (AUC), 240–41, 243–44, 250–51
Universal Declaration of Human
    Rights, 5–6
University of Alabama, 38–39, 61
University of Michigan, 63–64, 453*n*
Uribe, Álvaro, 245–57, 259, 261–63,
    425
U.S.-Colombian Free Trade
    Agreement, 260–61
U.S.-Egyptian Free Trade Agreement,
    345
USAID (U.S. Agency for
    International Development), 110,
    408, 410

Van Cliburn, Harvey Lavan, 85
Venezuela, 22, 384
Vietnam War, 57, 315
Visegrad Group, 157
Vision 2030 (Saudi Arabia), 363–64
Vkontakte, 109–10
Voice of America, 404
Vopros, 73
Voting rights, 6–7, 380–84
Voting Rights Act of 1965, 60
Vremya, 106

Wahhabism, 363
Walentynowicz, Anna, 130
Wałęsa, Lech, 1–2, 130, 133, 134, 135,
    139–43, 150–51, 154, 422
Wallace, George, 38–39, 380
Walles, Jake, 369

Wamalwa, Michael, *206*, 215
Wang Qishan, 394
Warsaw, 1, 128–29
Warsaw Pact, 87, 127, 129, 132, 143
Washington, George, 29, 36, 79, 101, 424
"Washington consensus," 208–9, 457*n*
Washington Post, 65, 299, 313, 345, 368
Watts riots, 57–58
Wei-ji, 425–26
Weinstein, Allen, 26–27
Williams, Roger, 40
Wilson, James, 32–33
Winter Palace (Saint Petersburg), 69–70
WMDs (weapons of mass destruction), 275–76
Women's empowerment, 356–62, 421
Women's suffrage, 61
Workers' Defense Committee (Poland), 136–37
World Bank, 177, 208–9
World War I, 270
World War II, 60, 73, 128–29, 168–69, 204–5

Xi Jinping, 393–96

Yakovlev, Alexander, 85
Yandex, 121
Yanukovych, Viktor, 178, 179–82, 185, 186–88, 190–95, 197
Yatsenyuk, Arseniy, 198–99, 200
Yavlinsky, Grigory, 101
Yeltsin, Boris, 16, 70, 83–84, 87–93, 97–104, 156, 171–72, 423, 424–25
Yemen, 271, 355, 375
Youssef, Bassem, 349–50
Yugoslavia, 2, 417
Yukos, 94
Yushchenko, Viktor, 177–86, 188, 189, 197

Zacharia, Janine, 346
Zagladin, Vadim, 87
Zarqawi, Abu Musab al-, 296, 311
Zastoi, 14, 75
Zawahiri, Ayman al-, 337
Zebari, Hoshyar, 287
Zhirinovsky, Vladimir, 167
Zhu Rongji, 393
Zimbabwe, 384
ZOMO, 135

About the Author

Condoleezza Rice is the Denning Professor in Global Business and the Economy at the Stanford Graduate School of Business and a professor of political science at Stanford University. From January 2005 to 2009, Rice served as the sixty-sixth secretary of state of the United States, the second woman and the first African American woman to hold the post. Rice also served as President George W. Bush's assistant to the president for national security affairs (national security adviser) from January 2001 to 2005, the first woman to hold the position. Born in Birmingham, Alabama, Rice earned her bachelor's degree in political science, cum laude and Phi Beta Kappa, from the University of Denver; her master's from the University of Notre Dame; and her PhD from the Graduate School of International Studies at the University of Denver. Rice is a Fellow of the American Academy of Arts and Sciences and has been awarded eleven honorary doctorates. She currently resides in Stanford, California.

Mission Statement

Twelve strives to publish singular books, by authors who have unique perspectives and compelling authority. Books that explain our culture; that illuminate, inspire, provoke, and entertain. Our mission is to provide a consummate publishing experience for our authors, one truly devoted to thoughtful partnership and cutting-edge promotional sophistication that reaches as many readers as possible. For readers, we aim to spark that rare reading experience—one that opens doors, transports, and possibly changes their outlook on our ever-changing world.